LOVE DOES NOT SEEK ITS OWN

T&T Clark Enquiries in Theological Ethics

Series editors
Brian Brock
Susan F. Parsons

LOVE DOES NOT SEEK ITS OWN

Augustine, Economic Division, and the Formation of a Common Life

Jonathan D. Ryan

LONDON • NEW YORK • OXFORD • NEW DELHI • SYDNEY

T&T CLARK
Bloomsbury Publishing Plc
50 Bedford Square, London, WC1B 3DP, UK
1385 Broadway, New York, NY 10018, USA
29 Earlsfort Terrace, Dublin 2, Ireland

BLOOMSBURY, T&T CLARK and the T&T Clark logo are
trademarks of Bloomsbury Publishing Plc

First published in Great Britain 2021
Paperback edition published 2023

Copyright © Jonathan D. Ryan, 2021

Jonathan D. Ryan has asserted his right under the Copyright, Designs and
Patents Act, 1988, to be identified as Author of this work.

For legal purposes the Acknowledgments on p. viii constitute
an extension of this copyright page.

Cover design: Terry Woodley

All rights reserved. No part of this publication may be reproduced or transmitted
in any form or by any means, electronic or mechanical, including photocopying,
recording, or any information storage or retrieval system, without prior
permission in writing from the publishers.

Bloomsbury Publishing Plc does not have any control over, or responsibility for,
any third-party websites referred to or in this book. All internet addresses given
in this book were correct at the time of going to press. The author and publisher
regret any inconvenience caused if addresses have changed or sites have
ceased to exist, but can accept no responsibility for any such changes.

A catalogue record for this book is available from the British Library.

Names: Ryan, Jonathan D., author.
Title: Love does not seek its own : Augustine, economic division,
and the formation of a common life / Jonathan D. Ryan.
Description: London, UK ; New York, NY : T&T Clark, 2021. |
Revision of author's thesis (doctoral)–University of Otago, 2018. | Includes
bibliographical references and index. |
Identifiers: LCCN 2020045364 (print) | LCCN 2020045365 (ebook) |
ISBN 9780567694553 (hardback) | ISBN 9780567699695 (paperback) |
ISBN 9780567694560 (pdf) | ISBN 9780567694577 (epub)
Subjects: LCSH: Augustine, of Hippo, Saint, 354–430. Sermons. | Income distribution–
Religious aspects–Christianity. | Neighborliness–Religious aspects–Christianity. |
God (Christianity)–Worship and love. | Pastoral theology. | Christian life. |
Church–Foundation. | Church and social problems. | Church and the world.
Classification: LCC BR65.A85 R93 2021 (print) |
LCC BR65.A85 (ebook) | DDC 261/.1–dc23
LC record available at https://lccn.loc.gov/2020045364
LC ebook record available at https://lccn.loc.gov/2020045365

ISBN:	HB:	978-0-5676-9455-3
	PB:	978-0-5676-9969-5
	ePDF:	978-0-5676-9456-0
	ePUB:	978-0-5676-9457-7

Typeset by Integra Software Services Pvt. Ltd.

To find out more about our authors and books visit www.bloomsbury.com
and sign up for our newsletters.

Scripture quotations marked "NRSV" are from New Revised Standard Version Bible,
copyright © 1989 National Council of the Churches of Christ in the United States of America.
Used by permission. All rights reserved worldwide.

To Julie

CONTENTS

Acknowledgments	viii
Abbreviations	ix
INTRODUCTION	1
Chapter 1 THE CALL TO LOVE GOD AND NEIGHBOR	31
Chapter 2 DIVISION AND UNITY OF HEART	61
Chapter 3 AVARICE AND THE COMMON GOOD	87
Chapter 4 ENVY AND THE QUESTION OF NEED	117
Chapter 5 PRIDE AND THE COMMON LIFE	147
Chapter 6 SHEPHERDING THE COMMUNITY	175
Chapter 7 OBSERVING THIS INSTRUCTION WITH LOVE	201
CONCLUSION	227
Bibliography	244
Index	251

ACKNOWLEDGMENTS

The opportunity to research and write this book has been a remarkable gift. There are more people to thank than I can possibly note here, but I do wish to acknowledge some in particular:

Firstly, I am thankful for the church communities that have supported, encouraged, and inspired me over the years, most recently Highgate Presbyterian Church, and The Seedling (both in Dunedin).

This book is a revised version of my doctoral thesis, and I am grateful to the University of Otago for providing the support and resources that enabled my research, including a doctoral scholarship. The support of staff and students in the Department of Theology and Religion during my studies was very much appreciated, and I am very thankful for the support of Professor Murray Rae, whose encouragement and advice I have valued throughout my work.

I wish to make particular mention of my PhD supervisors, Revd Associate Professor Christopher Holmes and Dr. André Muller, whose support has been a gift to me. For their wisdom and insight, their patience and reassurance, and their belief in the value of this project, I am deeply grateful. They served me wonderfully as supervisors, and continued to assist me in preparing this book. I feel very fortunate to have benefited from their scholarly insight and thoughtful care.

To Professor Brian Brock and Dr. Susan Parsons (series editors), and the supportive team at T&T Clark/Bloomsbury, I extend my sincere thanks for including this book in the "Enquiries in Theological Ethics" series, and for the valuable guidance and assistance they have provided in preparing this book for publication.

I note my gratitude to the friends and family (too many to name) that have accompanied me on this journey, offering timely words of encouragement and expressions of practical support. For the support of the Ryan and Van Rij families, I am especially thankful, and I particularly acknowledge the support of my parents, Maxine and David. Finally, I wish to record here my heartfelt gratitude to my wife, Julie, and children, Daniel and Luca, for allowing me to undertake this academic project, generously and patiently gifting me the time it has required, constantly encouraging me in my work, and throughout it all, sustaining me with their love.

Extracts from Augustine *Sermons, The Monastic Rules, Homilies on the First Epistle of John, Instructing Beginners in Faith, On Genesis, Teaching Christianity, The Augustine Catechism, The City of God, The Trinity* are used with permission from New City Press.

ABBREVIATIONS

The following abbreviations for Augustine's works are used throughout this book.[1] All quotations from these works are from the translations listed here, except where otherwise noted.

Catech.	*Instructing Beginners in Faith* (*De catechizandis rudibus*)	Augustine. *Instructing Beginners in Faith*. Translated by Raymond Canning. Edited by Boniface Ramsey. The Augustine Series. Hyde Park, NY: New City Press, 2006.
Civ.	*The City of God* (*De civitate Dei*)	Augustine. *The City of God*. Translated by William Babcock. Edited by Boniface Ramsey. 2 vols. Vol. 6–7 of *The Works of Saint Augustine, Part 1: Books*. Hyde Park, NY: New City Press, 2012–13.
Conf.	*Confessions* (*Confessiones*)	Augustine. *Confessions*. Translated by Henry Chadwick. Oxford World's Classics. Oxford: Oxford University Press, 1991.
Doctr. chr.	*Teaching Christianity* (*De doctrina christiana*)	Augustine. *Teaching Christianity*. Translated by Edmund Hill. Edited by John E. Rotelle. Vol. 11 of *The Works of Saint Augustine, Part 1: Books*. Hyde Park, NY: New City Press, 1996.
Enarrat. Ps.	*Enarrations on the Psalms* (*Enarrationes in Psalmos*)	
Enchir.	*Enchiridion on Faith, Hope, and Charity* (*Enchiridion de fide, spe, et caritate*)	Augustine. *The Augustine Catechism: The Enchiridion on Faith Hope and Charity*. Translated by Bruce Harbert. Edited by Boniface Ramsey. The Augustine Series. Hyde Park, NY: New City Press, 1999.

1. I have generally used the abbreviations for Augustine's works provided by Patrick H. Alexander et al., eds., *The SBL Handbook of Style: For Ancient Near Eastern, Biblical, and Early Christian Studies* (Peabody, MA: Hendrickson, 1999), 242–4, drawing also from the abbreviations provided in Allan D. Fitzgerald, ed., *Augustine through the Ages: An Encyclopedia* (Grand Rapids, MI: Eerdmans, 1999), xxxv–xlii, with some adaption where necessary. I have also drawn from these two sources for titles of Augustine's works, though I have mainly used the English title featured in the English translation noted.

Gen. litt.	*The Literal Meaning of Genesis* (*De Genesi ad litteram*)	Augustine. *On Genesis*. Translated by Edmund Hill. Edited by John E. Rotelle. Vol. 13 of *The Works of Saint Augustine, Part 1: Books*. Hyde Park, NY: New City Press, 2002.
Op. mon.	*The Work of Monks* (*De opere monachorum*)	Augustine. "The Work of Monks." Translated by Mary Sarah Muldowney. In *Saint Augustine: Treatises on Various Subjects*, edited by Roy J. Deferrari, 321–94. Washington, DC: Catholic University of America Press, 1952.
Reg. 2	*Regulations for a Monastery*[2] (*Ordo monasterii*)	Augustine. *The Monastic Rules*. Translated by Agatha Mary and Gerald Bonner. Edited by Boniface Ramsey. The Augustine Series. Hyde Park, NY: New City Press, 2004.
Reg. 3	*Rule* (*Praeceptum*)	Augustine. *The Monastic Rules*. Translated by Agatha Mary and Gerald Bonner. Edited by Boniface Ramsey. The Augustine Series. Hyde Park, NY: New City Press, 2004.
Serm.	*Sermons*[3] (*Sermones*)	Augustine. *Sermons*. Translated by Edmund Hill. Edited by John E. Rotelle. 11 vols. Vol. 1–11 of *The Works of Saint Augustine, Part 3: Sermons*. Hyde Park, NY: New City Press, 1990–7.

2. In his translation of the monastic rules, George Lawless translates "*Ordo monasterii*" as "Regulations for a Monastery," and "*Praeceptum*" as "Rule": George Lawless, *Augustine of Hippo and His Monastic Rule* (Oxford: Clarendon Press, 1987), 74–5, 80–1. I have used these English titles in this book.

3. Regarding the numbering of the *Sermons*, I have used the system provided in Edmund Hill's *The Works of Saint Augustine* translation of the *Sermons* (see the "table" outlined in: *Sermons (1-19) on the Old Testament*, trans. Edmund Hill, ed. John E. Rotelle, vol. 1, *The Works of Saint Augustine, Part 3: Sermons* (Brooklyn, NY: New City Press, 1990), 138–63). See also P.-P. Verbraken, *Études critiques sur les Sermons authentiques de Saint Augustin*, Instrumenta Patristica 12 (Steenbrugis: In Abbatia S. Petri, 1976). The more recently discovered sermons in Volume 11 of this collection feature additional "Mainz" and "Dolbeau" numbering (for details of this numbering, see *Sermons Discovered since 1990*, trans. Edmund Hill, ed. John E. Rotelle, vol. 11, *The Works of Saint Augustine, Part 3: Sermons* (Hyde Park, NY: New City Press, 1997), 21–2). In the case of these sermons, I note these additional numbers in parentheses, e.g., *Serm.* 90A(D11/M40) refers to *Sermon* 90A (Dolbeau 11/Mainz 40). As some of the sermons collected in Volume 11 are expanded versions of sermons featured in earlier volumes, this additional designation indicates when I am referring to the more recent version.

Tract. ep. Jo.	*Homilies on the First Epistle of John* (*In epistulam Johannis ad Parthos tractatus*)	Augustine. *Homilies on the First Epistle of John.* Translated by Boniface Ramsey. Edited by Daniel E. Doyle and Thomas Martin. Vol. 14 of *The Works of Saint Augustine, Part 3: Homilies.* Hyde Park, NY: New City Press, 2008.
Tract. Ev. Jo.	*Homilies on the Gospel of John* (*In Evangelium Johannis tractatus*)	
Trin.	*The Trinity* (*De Trinitate*)	Augustine. *The Trinity.* Translated by Edmund Hill. Edited by John E. Rotelle. 2nd ed. Vol. 5 of *The Works of Saint Augustine, Part 1: Books.* Hyde Park, NY: New City Press, 2015.

The following abbreviations for sources containing Latin texts of Augustine's works are used throughout this book:

GL	Lawless, George. *Augustine of Hippo and His Monastic Rule.* Oxford: Clarendon Press, 1987.
JO 1	Augustine. *Confessions.* Edited by James J. O'Donnell. Vol. 1, *Introduction and Text.* Oxford: Clarendon, 1992.
MA 1	Augustine. *Sermones Post Maurinos Reperti.* Edited by Germani Morin. Vol. 1 of *Miscellanea Agostiniana.* Rome: Typis Polyglottis Vaticanis, 1930.
PL	*Patrologia latina.* Edited by J.-P. Migne. 217 vols. Paris, 1844–64.
RA	*Recherches Augustiniennes et Patristiques* (see bibliography for details of specific volumes consulted).
RBén	*Revue Bénédictine* (see bibliography for details of specific volumes consulted).

For quotations of biblical passages, I have generally tried to quote the text that Augustine provides (in the English translations of Augustine's works that I use, these biblical quotations are typically italicized, and when quoting from these works, I have generally retained these italics). Additional quotations from the New Revised Standard Version are marked "NRSV."

INTRODUCTION

> For when it is written of *love* that it *does not seek its own* (1 Cor 13:5), it means that it puts the common good before its own and not personal advantage before the common good. Thus the more you are concerned about the common good rather than your own, the more progress you will know that you have made.
>
> —*Reg. 3: 5.2.*

Economic inequality is a pressing issue in our time. Although in one sense it is a concern that has spanned human history, economic inequality has taken on new proportion in recent decades; for example, Max Rashbrooke reports that "New Zealand now has the widest income gaps since detailed records began in the early 1980s."[1] He also notes that "from the mid-1980s to the mid-2000s, the gap between the rich and the rest has widened faster in New Zealand than in any other developed country."[2] While this gap is typically measured in financial terms, the economic division I consider in this book is the relational divide between rich and poor. I write not as a sociologist or economist or political theorist, but as a theologian, and more specifically, as an ordained Presbyterian minister in New Zealand. In this setting, I am mindful of the diverse and inspiring ways in which Christians are seeking to respond to issues of economic inequality. However, though often subtle, this relational divide is pervasive, and can be observed not only in our neighborhoods and cities, but also in church life. Some churches are predominantly attended by poorer members, others mainly by the wealthy. But even where people gather to worship from a range of economic backgrounds, we often gravitate toward those of similar economic status, rather than those whose circumstances differ to our own. And although the church may seek to span the gap through acts of service or generosity, these actions can sometimes reinforce the divide between rich and poor, rather than overcome it. The questions that prompt this book reflect these concerns: What does it mean to be the church amidst an economically divided society? And how does God seek to form such a church?

---

1. Max Rashbrooke, "Why Inequality Matters," in *Inequality: A New Zealand Crisis*, ed. Max Rashbrooke (Wellington: Bridget Williams Books, 2013), 1.
2. Rashbrooke, "Why Inequality Matters," 1.

Why Augustine?

With these questions in view, I turn in this book to Augustine, Bishop of Hippo.[3] It can be hard to recognize how prevailing societal assumptions shape our thinking about economic inequality, material resources, and the Christian life itself, so listening to another voice from the Christian tradition can be helpful, enabling us to consider our contemporary situation in a different light. Reflecting on the value of seeking direction from earlier Christian voices, Ellen T. Charry observes that "the turn back to the tradition suggests that we moderns need the older authors' understandings of human psychology, of how knowing and loving God function in people's lives. We also need their views of their pastoral responsibility, as well as their insights into God's strategies for human flourishing."[4] While we may not share their views, Charry adds, "unless we listen to them, we have no check on the prejudices and limitations of our own time and place."[5]

In recent decades, many theologians have demonstrated the relevance of Augustine's thought to contemporary political and economic concerns.[6] Significant thought has been given to questions of (what might be described as) the "meta-relationships" between the church, the state, and wider society, often in conversation with Augustine's more overtly political work, *The City of God*. Thus, Augustine's value as a conversation partner for political, economic, and ecclesial questions at a "macro" level is already well established. I do not engage directly with this theological discussion in this book. Rather, I seek to enrich it by turning to Augustine's preaching and monastic instruction, and illustrating what Augustine teaches us at the "micro" level of daily life in the Christian community. For scholars have given much less attention to these themes in Augustine's pastoral writing, and to the question of how Augustine himself—as priest, bishop, and founder of

---

3. For biographical details on Augustine's life, see especially Serge Lancel, *Saint Augustine*, trans. Antonia Nevill (London: SCM Press, 2002). Other biographical studies that I have found helpful for this book include Gerald Bonner, *St Augustine of Hippo: Life and Controversies*, 3rd ed. (Norwich: Canterbury Press, 2002); Peter Brown, *Augustine of Hippo: A Biography*, new ed. (Berkeley: University of California Press, 2000); F. van der Meer, *Augustine the Bishop: The Life and Work of a Father of the Church*, trans. Brian Battershaw and G.R. Lamb (London: Sheed and Ward, 1961). Note also the recently published biography, Robin Lane Fox, *Augustine: Conversions to Confessions* (New York: Basic Books, 2015).

4. Ellen T. Charry, *By the Renewing of Your Minds: The Pastoral Function of Christian Doctrine* (New York: Oxford University Press, 1997), 17.

5. Charry, *By the Renewing of Your Minds*, 17.

6. See, for example, R. A. Markus, *Saeculum: History and Society in the Theology of St Augustine* (Cambridge: Cambridge University Press, 1970); William T. Cavanaugh, *Theopolitical Imagination* (London: T&T Clark, 2002); Eric Gregory, *Politics and the Order of Love: An Augustinian Ethic of Democratic Citizenship* (Chicago, IL: University of Chicago Press, 2008); Rowan Williams, *On Augustine* (London: Bloomsbury, 2016), 107–29.

a monastic community—guided the communities in his care amidst their own contexts of economic inequality. As Thomas F. Martin observes, "Augustine's monasticism offers the potential for a rich and often overlooked resource for better understanding his political thinking in practice."[7] I think the same can also be said for Augustine's *Sermons*, the texts that I primarily focus on in this book, in conversation with his monastic instruction.

Indeed, even in more specialist Augustine scholarship, Augustine's *Sermons* and monastic texts have received considerably less scrutiny until relatively recently.[8] There is now a reasonable body of work on Augustine's monastic vision, but the outworking of this vision in his instruction to the wider church community invites further exploration. In recent decades, there has been new interest in Augustine's homiletical texts.[9] However, often scholars have approached these texts from a historical and/or textual perspective, rather than with a view to their relevance to the church in our contemporary setting.

Thus, alongside existing engagements with Augustine in theological ethics, and studies of his homiletic and monastic texts in their historical setting, there is more work to be done. Specifically, with regard to the questions of the church's identity and formation amidst economic inequality that concern this book, there remains a need for scholarship that examines Augustine's own pastoral instruction, identifying his teaching and practice on these matters, and then illustrates the pertinence of these pastoral insights to the contemporary church. In this book, I aim to respond to this need.

Of course, many of the economic challenges that the contemporary church faces are different to those that Augustine's congregation faced. It is not my purpose here to provide detailed analysis of contemporary economic issues. Rather, this study

---

7. Thomas F. Martin, "Augustine and the Politics of Monasticism," in *Augustine and Politics*, ed. John Doody, Kevin L. Hughes, and Kim Paffenroth, *Augustine in Conversation: Tradition and Innovation* (Lanham, MD: Lexington, 2005), 167.

8. For example, in the epilogue that concludes the new edition of his classic biography, Brown acknowledges that he had previously not given "sufficient attention" to Augustine's "sermons and letters," and had missed "the more muted, background tones of his day-to-day life as a bishop." Brown, *Augustine of Hippo*, 446.

9. See, for example, Peter T. Sanlon, *Augustine's Theology of Preaching* (Minneapolis, MN: Fortress, 2014); Joseph Clair, *Discerning the Good in the Letters and Sermons of Augustine* (Oxford: Oxford University Press, 2016); Ronald R. Boyd-MacMillan, "The Transforming Sermon: A Study of the Preaching of St. Augustine, with Special Reference to the *Sermones ad Populum*, and the Transformation Theory of James Loder" (PhD thesis, University of Aberdeen, 2009). François Dolbeau's recent discovery of a number of previously unknown sermons has provided new texts that have not been considered by previous generations of scholarship (for details of these sermons, see François Dolbeau, introduction to *Sermons Discovered since 1990*, trans. Edmund Hill, ed. John E. Rotelle, vol. 11, *The Works of Saint Augustine, Part 3: Sermons* (Hyde Park, NY: New City Press, 1997), 13–19). I discuss a number of these sermons in this book.

highlights the smaller-scale, everyday challenges and opportunities that emerge when those of varied economic backgrounds are drawn together, and the pastoral wisdom needed for such situations. Through my discussion of Augustine's pastoral instruction, I seek to illustrate the valuable insight that his teaching continues to offer to the church today, as we wrestle with the economic divisions of our own time. I hope that this study will complement existing work on Augustine in theological ethics, and enrich it by identifying aspects of Augustine's contribution that merit further consideration.

For the pastoral and ecclesial questions that prompt this book, Augustine is an ideal interlocutor. Because his ministry responsibilities included oversight of a monastic community and a diverse range of congregations, conversation with Augustine invites us to consider different forms of "common life" among Christians, and the challenges of economic division in these varied settings.[10] Moreover, the body of Augustine's monastic and homiletic texts that remains today offers us ample insight into his pastoral instruction of these communities (see below for details of these texts, and of Augustine's pastoral responsibilities). As noted, Augustine's *Sermons* have received much less attention than his more well-known texts (*Confessions*, *The City of God*, etc.), but they are especially apt for this project. As homiletical texts, they are not a statement to society, nor do they offer a political or economic program. Rather, in the *Sermons*, Augustine has the formation of particular gathered communities of Christians in view, whom he seeks to nurture in the Christian life. As he explains to the congregation on one occasion, "I, here, am playing the part of the sower, you are God's field; don't let the seed be wasted, let it come to a good harvest."[11]

Contemporary readers may also find Augustine a constructive conversation partner because he is located at a moment in history when Christians were wrestling with questions of identity not dissimilar to those noted above. In the centuries that preceded Augustine, Christians had increasingly adopted the way of life of their Roman context, resulting in a loss of Christian distinctiveness by the middle of the fourth century, as R. A. Markus observes.[12] However, this shift troubled many Christians, and prompted some to adopt ascetic forms of Christianity that set them apart from popular society.[13] In this changing context, Markus explains, the underlying question in the "debates" of this period was "what is it to be a Christian?"[14]

---

10. I have drawn the expression "common life" from the *Rule* (*Reg. 3*: 1.7), and have generally used this instead of the word "community," which is often overused in our contemporary context.

11. *Serm.* 53A.1.

12. R. A. Markus, *The End of Ancient Christianity* (Cambridge: Cambridge University Press, 1990), 27.

13. Markus, *End of Ancient Christianity*, 34–8.

14. Markus, *End of Ancient Christianity*, 19. See also p. 31.

Included in this question were concerns about the place of material wealth in the Christian life.[15] As will be noted, Augustine offers valuable insight on issues of wealth and poverty, but as Boniface Ramsey observes, his views are consistent with the "moderate" Christian teaching of earlier centuries.[16] Similarly, Augustine offers a critique of the injustice and inequalities of Roman society,[17] yet he is not a political revolutionary, and works within the constraints of the social and political institutions of his time.[18] For the concerns of this book, however, the value of Augustine's contribution is not found in isolated statements on wealth or poverty, but rather in the way he locates such questions in a broader vision of the Christian life. As the contemporary church struggles with questions of economic division, Augustine's teaching can help us situate these questions rightly.

Notably, as I demonstrate in this book, Augustine considers issues of poverty and wealth within the context of our relationship to God and to our neighbor. Whereas we might attribute the widening divide between rich and poor to economic policy, his teaching highlights the need to consider this economic division in light of the breach of our relationship with God and neighbor. When we consider economic inequality in such terms, we are reminded that its causes are not wholly external to ourselves (such as economic paradigms or political institutions); more fundamentally, such division arises from internal dispositions of the heart (such as greed, envy, and pride) to which we are all subject. Consequently, to become a community that no longer conforms to the divisive patterns of economic inequality—to become the church—requires nothing less than the reformation of our hearts, renewing us in loving relationship with God and neighbor.

Furthermore, Augustine can help us think through these issues not only theologically, but also pastorally. Through his *Sermons* and monastic writing, Augustine displays admirable pastoral insight and wisdom, as he nurtures the diverse communities in his care. This aspect of Augustine's contribution is of particular interest to me, and in the conclusion to this book, I consider what those in pastoral ministry today might learn from Augustine's teaching and example about the formation of a common life.

---

15. As documented extensively in Peter Brown, *Through the Eye of a Needle: Wealth, the Fall of Rome, and the Making of Christianity in the West, 350–550 AD* (Princeton, NJ: Princeton University Press, 2012).

16. Boniface Ramsey, "Wealth," in *Augustine through the Ages*, ed. Allan D. Fitzgerald (Grand Rapids, MI: Eerdmans, 1999), 876.

17. E.g. *Civ.* 2.20.

18. Markus observes that, given his church context and responsibilities, Augustine was inevitably "an 'establishment' figure." Markus, *Saeculum: History and Society in the Theology of St Augustine*, 154. However, he later clarifies: "Augustine was certainly no critic of the 'establishment'; but his theology is a critique of 'establishment' theology" (p. 155).

Augustine and His Audience

In this book I focus on theological themes in Augustine's pastoral instruction, rather than historical or socioeconomic analysis. However, to understand Augustine's pastoral teaching, it is important to understand the setting in which he offered it (particularly in Hippo Regius), which in many respects is different to our own.[19] Thus, to set the scene, I offer here a broad-brush sketch of this context.

In the *Sermons*, Augustine does not offer extensive descriptions of socioeconomic context, but his comments are suggestive of economic differences in the wider community. He speaks of "the rich" lying in "beds chased in silver," while "the poor" are "bedded on the ground."[20] On another occasion he contrasts the "special, expensive foods" of wealthy listeners with the "cheap food" of "the poor."[21] In his preaching, Augustine does not attribute such inequalities to political policy or economic systems in the manner that we moderns tend to do. Peter Brown observes that "to the ancients, how individuals acted mattered far more than did the structures within which they acted."[22] Additionally, Augustine's theological convictions mean that he cannot wholly ascribe economic

---

19. For a survey of Augustine's life and thought with particular reference to his social context see especially Carol Harrison, *Augustine: Christian Truth and Fractured Humanity* (Oxford: Oxford University Press, 2000). For accounts of the economic context in which Augustine ministered, see Brown, *Through the Eye of a Needle*; Richard Finn, *Almsgiving in the Later Roman Empire: Christian Promotion and Practice (313–450)* (Oxford: Oxford University Press, 2006); Claude Lepelley, "Facing Wealth and Poverty: Defining Augustine's Social Doctrine," *Augustinian Studies* 38, no. 1 (2007): 1–17. Gillian Clark provides an overview of the relationship of Christianity to wider Roman society in this period: Gillian Clark, *Christianity and Roman Society* (Cambridge: Cambridge University Press, 2004). Note also Clark's description of the different approaches taken by historians in their writing on Late Antiquity (pp. 9–15).

20. *Serm.* 177.7.

21. *Serm.* 61.12.

22. Brown, *Through the Eye of a Needle*, 56. Even as he attends to "political" questions in *The City of God*, Augustine's approach is distinctive, for as Williams observes, "the *De civitate* is not at all a work of political theory in the usual sense, but sketches for a theological anthropology and a corporate spirituality." Williams, *On Augustine*, 111. Markus describes Augustine's tendency toward "a kind of atomistic personalism," examining "a society" in "its constituent, personal atoms," rather than reducing it to "a collective entity capable of simple moral assessment." Markus, *Saeculum: History and Society in the Theology of St Augustine*, 149–50. Regarding Markus's description, see Williams, *On Augustine*, 111.

circumstances to human agency in a way that is outside of God's providential activity.²³

However, a number of aspects of Late Antique society contributed to these economic inequalities. Describing Augustine's North African context, Carol Harrison explains that "most of the land was in the hands of the owners of large private estates which were cultivated by, or let to, tenants known as *coloni*."²⁴ The Roman economy in Late Antiquity was primarily based around the harvest, and could fluctuate significantly.²⁵ The poor were particularly vulnerable in such an economy, as Brown notes: "In the eyes of contemporaries, the primary cause of social stratification was the crushing imbalance in exposure to the risk of harvest shocks between the rich (who were cushioned against such shocks) and the poor farmers, whose sole resources lay dangerously open to the weather."²⁶ This situation meant that the Roman tax system also disadvantaged the poor, for as Gerald Bonner explains, "it made no provision for the ravages of pestilence or the effects of a bad harvest."²⁷ In addition to tax, farmers also had to pay rent to landowners, leaving farmers "with under one-third of the harvest on which they had labored."²⁸ Corrupt conduct in the collection of tax and rent further compounded the injustice of these demands, as Claude Lepelley details.²⁹ In the *Sermons*, Augustine frequently addresses issues of fraudulent, profit-seeking activity.³⁰ Another issue he acknowledges is the arrival of refugees in North Africa; Augustine urges the congregation to respond compassionately to their needs.³¹ Unlike many modern societies, the governing authorities provided little by way of a welfare safety net, for as Bonner explains, "public relief—except for the corn doles of the two capitals, Rome and Constantinople, which were an exception—was unknown in the

---

23. Ramsey, "Wealth," 880. Ramsey juxtaposes Augustine's view with that of "Pelagian" teaching, which considers economic inequalities to result from "wickedness alone"; Ramsey observes that "this argument effectively removes wealth from the ambit of divine providence" (p. 880). He later comments: "Augustine is an accepter of things as they are, in the conviction that God's hand is present, albeit invisibly, in all the details of human existence, including its inequities" (p. 880). In this book, I do not engage with these broader questions of Augustine's understanding of God's providence in relation to economic inequality, but see Chapter 4 for discussion of Augustine's instruction to those who envy the prosperity of others. See also *Serm.* 15.A.2, 6, 9; 50.3, 5; 311.12–13.
24. Harrison, *Christian Truth and Fractured Humanity*, 117.
25. Brown, *Through the Eye of a Needle*, 11–12.
26. Brown, *Through the Eye of a Needle*, 13. See Chapter 3 for further discussion.
27. Bonner, *St Augustine of Hippo*, 17. See pp. 16–17 for a description of this tax system.
28. Brown, *Through the Eye of a Needle*, 13.
29. Lepelley, "Facing Wealth and Poverty," 5–7. For Augustine's attempt to address these "injustices" see Lancel, *Saint Augustine*, 260–1.
30. E.g., *Serm.* 32.14–21.
31. *Serm.* 81.9. Lancel notes the arrival of refugees following the "capture of Rome" in 410. Lancel, *Saint Augustine*, 391–2. See also Van der Meer, *Augustine the Bishop*, 157–8.

Roman Empire."[32] Yet in this historical setting, economic resources were not the only determining factor of one's livelihood. Brown notes other critical distinctions, such as the division "between facelessness and 'honors,'"[33] or "between citizens and non-citizens."[34] Accordingly, Brown observes that "it is hard to judge social distances in the later empire"; as he indicates, those whose material circumstances were not significantly different might nonetheless be divided by such differences in social status.[35]

Augustine's own location within this social and economic context is complex.[36] In the *Confessions*, Augustine explains that his father Patrick (Patricius) "was a citizen of Thagaste with very modest resources."[37] Many years later in a sermon, Augustine describes himself as "a poor man, born of poor parents."[38] Regarding these two statements, Serge Lancel writes: "Speaking of his father's situation, and thus his own, Augustine hesitated between two adjectives, 'modest', and 'poor'. Poverty is always relative, unless the threshold is defined. Patricius must have been slightly above that threshold, for he would have ceased to be of curial rank had he fallen below it; but the threshold was sometimes fairly low."[39] Despite their limited means, Augustine's parents ensured that he received a formal education, in the hope that he would achieve secular success.[40] Augustine showed much talent, and his initial career trajectory was very promising, due in no small part to the patronage that was essential for advancement.[41] He was appointed to teaching positions in Rome, then Milan, and it appeared that even

---

32. Bonner, *St Augustine of Hippo*, 125–6. Furthermore, as Brown indicates, this "dole" was restricted to Roman citizens. Brown, *Through the Eye of a Needle*, 69. Many other factors contributed to poverty in Late Antiquity; for a more comprehensive summary, see Finn, *Almsgiving in the Later Roman Empire*, 18–26.

33. Brown, *Through the Eye of a Needle*, 4. In this context, Brown's comment about "honors" refers to appointment as "town councillor," and the recognition and status connected with this role (p. 4).

34. Brown, *Through the Eye of a Needle*, 68. As Brown illustrates, the support of a wealthy patron was another essential factor for those hoping to advance (pp. 148–57).

35. Brown, *Through the Eye of a Needle*, 6.

36. Brown, *Through the Eye of a Needle*, 150.

37. *Conf.* 2.3.5.

38. *Serm.* 356.13.

39. Lancel, *Saint Augustine*, 6. For description of this "curial" position and associated responsibilities, see p. 6. See also Brown, *Through the Eye of a Needle*, 151–2.

40. *Conf.* 1.9.14; 2.3.8. Harrison explains that education in this Roman context had a "social" purpose, seeking "to create, foster, and protect a governing élite." Harrison, *Christian Truth and Fractured Humanity*, 47. Thus she notes: "It was Patrick's social ambition for his son, rather than purely intellectual interests, which motivated him to ensure that, despite financial difficulties, Augustine received the best education available" (pp. 47–8).

41. *Conf.* 4.16.28–31; Brown, *Augustine of Hippo*, 54–61; Brown, *Through the Eye of a Needle*, 153–4.

"the governorship of a minor province" was within reach.[42] However, while in Milan, Augustine's life changed direction; as he later confesses to God, "with mounting frequency by voices of many kinds you put pressure on me, so that from far off I heard and was converted and called upon you as you were calling to me."[43] Among these "voices," the testimony of Antony's ascetic life (and of other "servants" who had similarly adopted a monastic life) played an important role.[44] George Lawless describes "the monastic ideal as exemplified by Antony" as "the central theme of Augustine's conversion."[45] Augustine relinquished his secular ambitions, instead retiring with friends to Cassiciacum for a period of contemplative retreat.[46] The following Easter (387), Augustine was baptized in Milan.[47] He then returned to his North African hometown of Thagaste, where he and his companions sought a life in God's "service."[48] Augustine had no aspiration to become a bishop, as his somewhat comic narration to the Hippo congregation indicates:

> So much, though, did I dread the episcopate, that since I had already begun to acquire a reputation of some weight among the servants of God, I wouldn't go near a place where I knew there was no bishop. I avoided this job, and I did everything I could to assure my salvation in a lowly position, and not to incur the grave risks of a high one. But, as I said, a servant ought not to oppose his Lord. I came to this city to see a friend, whom I thought I could gain for God, to join us in the monastery. It seemed safe enough, because the place had a bishop. I was caught, I was made a priest, and by this grade I eventually came to the episcopate.[49]

In Hippo, Augustine was ordained as priest in 391, and later consecrated bishop in 395.[50] Despite his new ecclesial responsibilities, Augustine maintained his monastic commitment. He lived simply, sharing goods in common with other members of the monastic community, and declining expensive gifts that his

---

42. *Conf.* 5.8.14; 5.13.23; 6.11.19.
43. *Conf.* 13.1.1.
44. *Conf.* 8.6.14–8.8.19.
45. George Lawless, *Augustine of Hippo and His Monastic Rule* (Oxford: Clarendon Press, 1987), 43. See also pp. 9–13.
46. *Conf.* 8.12.30; 9.4.7. See Chapter 6 for further discussion and references regarding Augustine's community life in Cassiciacum and Thagaste, and the subsequent transition to life as priest and bishop.
47. *Conf.* 9.6.14. Date noted by Henry Chadwick in *Confessions*, trans. Henry Chadwick, Oxford World's Classics (Oxford: Oxford University Press, 1991), 159n11, 164n19.
48. *Conf.* 9.8.17; Possidius, *The Life of Saint Augustine*, trans. Michele Pellegrino and Matthew O'Connell, ed. John E. Rotelle, The Augustinian Series (Villanova, PA: Augustinian Press, 1988), 3.1.
49. *Serm.* 355.2.
50. Bonner, *St Augustine of Hippo*, 111–12, 121.

episcopal role might attract.[51] The title of bishop carried some status (see Chapter 6 for discussion). However, the degree of influence that bishops exercised in wider society was limited; Augustine often tried to intercede with authorities on behalf of those in need, but was not always successful.[52]

As a bishop, Augustine preached in a variety of settings in North Africa, as he visited the churches in his care. Many of his homilies collected in the *Sermons* were delivered in Hippo, where Augustine was bishop. Hippo was an important North African port, connected with Rome and the wider world.[53] Located in a significant food production region, Hippo had a degree of economic prosperity,[54] yet it was also home to those in poverty.[55] Augustine's responsibilities took him to the "swarming trade-centre" of Carthage, where he frequently preached,[56] and he also delivered sermons in rural locations on his travels.[57]

Among the various church buildings located in Hippo during Augustine's ministry, Lancel identifies "the basilica of Peace" (also known as the "Major basilica") as "the principal place of worship for Hippo's Catholic community."[58] F. van der Meer suggests that this church building was "sober and modest."[59] As the congregation stood for the service, there was no seating, and a simple "wooden altar" featured at the front.[60] Behind the altar was a raised apse

---

51. *Serm.* 356.13; Possidius, *Life of Saint Augustine*, 22.1–5, 23.1, 25.1.

52. Lancel, *Saint Augustine*, 259–70.

53. Brown, *Augustine of Hippo*, 183–5. For descriptions of Hippo see also Lancel, *Saint Augustine*, 147–50; Van der Meer, *Augustine the Bishop*, 16–20.

54. Brown, *Augustine of Hippo*, 185.

55. Lepelley, "Facing Wealth and Poverty," 4. Brown notes the seasonal nature of poverty in cities like Hippo, and also comments that poverty was even greater "in the hill country south of Hippo." Brown, *Through the Eye of a Needle*, 342.

56. Van der Meer, *Augustine the Bishop*, 13. See also Lancel's description of Carthage: Lancel, *Saint Augustine*, 23–5.

57. Gillian Clark, "Pastoral Care: Town and Country in Late-Antique Preaching," in *Urban Centers and Rural Contexts in Late Antiquity*, ed. Thomas S. Burns and John W. Eadie (East Lansing: Michigan State University Press, 2001), 268–9; Michele Pellegrino, general introduction to *Sermons (1–19) on the Old Testament*, trans. Edmund Hill, ed. John E. Rotelle, vol. 1, *The Works of Saint Augustine, Part 3: Sermons* (Brooklyn, NY: New City Press, 1990), 22–3. For many of the *Sermons* the location is unknown. In this book I regularly refer to "the congregation," or "Augustine's listeners" to acknowledge that Augustine is preaching in the context of the gathered Christian community. It is not practical to note details of context for every sermon discussed, but I include details about the specific congregational settings when particularly pertinent.

58. Lancel, *Saint Augustine*, 239. For Lancel's account of this basilica (along with the older "Leontian basilica"), see pp. 238–44.

59. Van der Meer, *Augustine the Bishop*, 22. Van der Meer estimates that, as listeners in the church would be standing, "as many as two thousand may sometimes have been gathered there" (p. 22–3).

60. Van der Meer, *Augustine the Bishop*, 22–3. See also *Serm.* 355.2.

where the "bishop's *cathedra*" was located, with seating for priests alongside.[61] Regarding the frequency of Augustine's preaching, William Harmless provides helpful summary: "In Hippo both Eucharist and Vespers were held daily, or almost daily. Augustine may not always have preached at both, but he did so sometimes. Outside of Easter he preached at least four times a week; during Lent, daily; during Easter week, twice a day."[62] Within the liturgy, the sermon followed the Scripture readings and a sung psalm.[63] Regarding the use of a lectionary to determine readings, Michele Pellegrino notes that "in Augustine's time this process of organization had begun, especially for the principal seasons; on ordinary days, however, the celebrant chose the readings."[64] Augustine preached in an improvised style, without written notes or manuscript; for the text of the *Sermons*, therefore, we can be grateful for the efforts of stenographers who faithfully recorded his words as he preached.[65] Yet as Pellegrino observes, "'improvisation' certainly did not mean 'unpreparedness.'"[66] He explains that Augustine's life of prayer, reflection on Scripture, and pastoral engagement with the community would have informed his preaching,[67] while Éric Rebillard notes Augustine's prayerful reflection on the Scripture readings in advance of the service.[68] As is evident in the texts themselves, the length of Augustine's sermons varied considerably; Van der Meer estimates that they could range from "ten minutes" to "two hours."[69] However, his preaching was far from tedious; discussing one of Augustine's sermons, Ronald R. Boyd-MacMillan remarks, "he is pure theatre in his rhetorical invention, bringing the people along with him in

---

61. Van der Meer, *Augustine the Bishop*, 21, 23. Augustine's narrative in Book 22 of *The City of God* also provides some indication of the church layout (*Civ.* 22.8). See also Brown, *Augustine of Hippo*, 248. For description of Augustine's simple attire as preacher, see Van der Meer, *Augustine the Bishop*, 25.

62. William Harmless, *Augustine and the Catechumenate*, rev. ed. (Collegeville, MN: Liturgical Press, 2014), 187. See also Éric Rebillard, "Sermones," in *Augustine through the Ages*, ed. Allan D. Fitzgerald (Grand Rapids, MI: Eerdmans, 1999), 790; Van der Meer, *Augustine the Bishop*, 172–3.

63. Rebillard, "*Sermones*," 773. Harrison explains that Augustine used the "Old Latin" version of Scripture, "an early third-century Latin translation of the New Testament and the LXX characterized by its extremely literal, none too careful translation." Harrison, *Christian Truth and Fractured Humanity*, 48–9.

64. Pellegrino, general introduction to *Sermons (1–19)*, 26. (Note that Pellegrino's statement is located within his summary of the work of G.C. Willis on this topic.)

65. Rebillard, "*Sermones*," 790. For the role of these stenographers in recording Augustine's *Sermons*, see also Pellegrino, general introduction to *Sermons (1–19)*, 16–18; Harmless, *Augustine and the Catechumenate*, 191–2.

66. Pellegrino, general introduction to *Sermons (1–19)*, 17.

67. Pellegrino, general introduction to *Sermons (1–19)*, 17.

68. Rebillard, "*Sermones*," 790.

69. Van der Meer, *Augustine the Bishop*, 174.

affectionate repartee."[70] Following the sermon, the catechumens were dismissed, with "the faithful" remaining to celebrate the Eucharist.[71]

From the *Sermons* themselves it is hard to determine conclusively the make-up of the congregations that Augustine addresses.[72] However, comments in the *Sermons* suggest a colorful gathering. Some listeners follow his preaching so eagerly that they call out, anticipating his words in advance.[73] In other instances, however, he draws attention to those who come to church "to enjoy some family gossip," or those who are impatient for the service to finish so that they can get home for "their dinners."[74] The congregation included women and men (though they stood in separate locations during the service), and children and

---

70. Boyd-MacMillan, "The Transforming Sermon," 69. Boyd-MacMillan's narration of Augustine's sermons bring this dramatic quality to life: see, for example, pp. 60–9, 158–73.

71. Van der Meer, *Augustine the Bishop*, 397; Harmless, *Augustine and the Catechumenate*, 224. Van der Meer provides a richly illustrative account of a worship service in Augustine's setting: Van der Meer, *Augustine the Bishop*, 388–402.

72. Van der Meer, *Augustine the Bishop*, 129. This is partly because of the nature of these texts: Augustine's comments describing the congregation are often brief and occasional; and as Rebillard notes, later editors may have removed specific details about "the circumstances of preaching." Rebillard, "*Sermones*," 791. It is also often hard to determine where Augustine is preaching, and thus which congregation is being described. In addition to these textual factors, modern scholars have raised additional interpretive questions. For example, regarding depictions of poverty in Christian preaching, Geoffrey D. Dunn notes the challenge of "determining the extent to which these constructed scenes are a rhetorical *topos* or contain specific factual evidence." Geoffrey D. Dunn, "Poverty as a Social Issue in Augustine's Homilies," in *Studia Patristica 49*, ed. J. Baun et al. (Leuven: Peeters, 2010), 176. Clark explains that some scholars have contested the view that Christian preaching was accessible to all, instead arguing that it reflected the existing norms of classical culture and rhetoric. Clark, "Pastoral Care," 265–6. If this was the case, Clark observes, preaching "was the educated elite talking to the social elite in the language of books" (p. 266). Clark particularly notes the influential argument of Ramsey MacMullen in this regard (pp. 271–2). (See Ramsay MacMullen, "The Preacher's Audience (AD 350–400)," *The Journal of Theological Studies* 40, no. 2 (1989): 503–11.) Throughout her essay Clark questions these assumptions, and notes in her conclusion that "both texts and archaeology provide some evidence for preachers trying to reach out beyond the urban elite" Clark, "Pastoral Care," 280. See also Sanlon's assessment of MacMullen's portrayal: Sanlon, *Augustine's Theology of Preaching*, 14–15.

73. *Serm.* 76.6, and see Edmund Hill's explanatory note: *Sermons (51–94) on the New Testament*, trans. Edmund Hill, ed. John E. Rotelle, vol. 3, *The Works of Saint Augustine, Part 3: Sermons* (Brooklyn, NY: New City Press, 1991), 316n4.

74. *Serm.* 32.2; 264.1. See also descriptions in Van der Meer, *Augustine the Bishop*, 169–72.

youth.⁷⁵ Augustine's comments also suggest varied levels of education among his listeners, including the "highly educated and learned," and others "who have not been schooled in what they call the liberal arts."⁷⁶ Although educated listeners may well have appreciated Augustine's skill as a trained rhetor, Augustine nonetheless strives to include and affirm uneducated listeners, and to communicate at a level that all can understand.⁷⁷

The diversity in Augustine's audience included differences in socioeconomic background. Harrison describes the Hippo congregation as "a microcosm of society as a whole."⁷⁸ She explains that "the vast majority were poor, largely illiterate, and engaged in work upon the land," with others coming from "what we might call the urban middle-classes," and a smaller amount from "the nobility."⁷⁹ In the *Sermons*, descriptive portrayals of the wealth or poverty of these listeners are

---

75. Van der Meer, *Augustine the Bishop*, 22, 389. As Hill notes, Augustine's language in the *Sermons* is not very inclusive, and he tends to employ masculine terms when addressing the congregation (e.g., "*fratres*," though Hill notes that he often translates this as "brothers and sisters"). Hill, translator's note, in *Sermons (1–19)*, 165. However, Augustine does sometimes specifically address or acknowledge women in the congregation (e.g., *Serm.* 359B(D2/M5).3). Both Clark and Finn discuss the presence of women in congregations in this period: Clark, "Pastoral Care," 272–3; Finn, *Almsgiving in the Later Roman Empire*, 139–42.

76. *Serm.* 133.4. According to Van der Meer, the unschooled in Augustine's congregation would have made up "the majority of his audience." Van der Meer, *Augustine the Bishop*, 132. Harrison indicates that Augustine "was sensitive to the distance which education and culture, or the lack of it, could impose between Christians," and the need to engage listeners "at their different levels." Harrison, *Christian Truth and Fractured Humanity*, 24. See Chapters 5 and 6 for further discussion of these themes. For discussion of literacy and education in this context, see Clark, *Christianity and Roman Society*, 78–89.

77. Van der Meer, *Augustine the Bishop*, 258. In *Teaching Christianity*, Augustine insists that preachers "should make every effort to be understood," and that language that the "uneducated" can understand should be preferred (*Doctr. chr.* 4.10.25; 4.10.24). See also Lancel, *Saint Augustine*, 462. Clark considers whether uneducated listeners would be able to understand the sermons of educated preachers. Clark, "Pastoral Care," 278. While observing that the attempts of "an educated speaker" to speak in a "simple" style may be unsuccessful, Clark nonetheless highlights the sincere attempts of preachers (including Augustine) to communicate their message to all, commenting that "the sermons we have often show the preacher making a real effort to be understood" (pp. 278–9). See also discussion of this issue in Clark, *Christianity and Roman Society*, 85–9; Finn, *Almsgiving in the Later Roman Empire*, 139–44. Finn identifies a number of aspects of Augustine's preaching that "strongly suggest that most in the congregation could follow him" (p. 144).

78. Harrison, *Christian Truth and Fractured Humanity*, 127.

79. Harrison, *Christian Truth and Fractured Humanity*, 127.

infrequent.[80] However, the nature of Augustine's teaching in the *Sermons* presumes socioeconomic diversity within the congregation. Augustine acknowledges that the wealthy are included in the Christian community,[81] and a number of his sermons address concerns especially pertinent to the prosperous.[82] On occasion, Augustine appears to turn to wealthier members directly: "So let me remind our rich people of what the apostle reminded us all," he says in *Sermon* 14.[83] However, Augustine's comments on other occasions suggest that the rich would be a small minority in the congregation. For example, in *Sermon* 85 (delivered in Hippo), as Augustine addresses the congregation about renunciation of wealth, he notes that "most of you are poor [*pauperes*]," but insists that "the rich [*divites*] should listen too, if there are any here, that is."[84]

What does Augustine mean when he says to the congregation that "most of you are poor"?[85] Again, this is not easy to determine. Discussing this period, Richard Finn notes that "the poor did not form a single, distinct, social group or class."[86] He explains that "the Graeco-Roman world distinguished between *paupertas*, poverty as relatively straitened circumstances (though relative to what varied widely); *egestas*, poverty as material deprivation; and *mendicitas*, the absolute destitution of the person forced to beg."[87] Augustine draws on these terms in the *Sermons*, but does not employ them in a way that yields clear socioeconomic groupings.[88] "In vain do we look through Augustine's homilies for the kind of evidence that would distinguish categories of poor," Geoffrey D. Dunn states.[89] This is particularly apparent with Augustine's use of the word "*pauper*," a word that, as Finn explains, "can stretch from the relative poverty of a smallholder … to the near-total

---

80. Finn notes a similar "absence" in the *Enarrations on the Psalms*: Richard Finn, "Portraying the Poor: Descriptions of Poverty in Christian Texts from the Late Roman Empire," in *Poverty in the Roman World*, ed. Margaret Atkins and Robin Osborne (Cambridge: Cambridge University Press, 2006), 132.

81. E.g., *Serm.* 36.5. For description of "the rich" in Augustine's context, see Brown, *Through the Eye of a Needle*, 345–8; Lepelley, "Facing Wealth and Poverty," 3–4.

82. E.g., *Serm.* 177.6; 107A.2; 85.4–5.

83. *Serm.* 14.6. See also *Serm.* 61.9.

84. *Serm.* 85.2, 3 (*PL* 38:521). Location provided by Hill, *Sermons (51–94)*, 395n1. See also *Serm.* 14.1. Discussing the makeup of Augustine's congregation, Pellegrino states that "the majority were poor." Pellegrino, general introduction to *Sermons (1–19)*, 85.

85. *Serm.* 85.2.

86. Finn, *Almsgiving in the Later Roman Empire*, 19.

87. Finn, *Almsgiving in the Later Roman Empire*, 19.

88. E.g., "A helping hand must be given to the needy [*egentibus*]" (*Serm.* 359A.11 (*RBén* 49:265)); "The beggar [*mendicus*] stands at the rich man's door" (*Serm.* 56.9 (*PL* 38:381)); see quotation above from *Sermon* 85 for *pauper*. For Augustine's employment of these terms, see Finn, "Portraying the Poor," 133–8.

89. Dunn, "Poverty as a Social Issue," 178. Though note Dunn's discussion (in a later article) of terms for the poor that Augustine uses: Geoffrey D. Dunn, "Augustine's Homily on Almsgiving," *Journal of Early Christian History* 3, no. 1 (2013): 10.

destitution of the beggar."⁹⁰ Brown makes a distinction between "the destitute" and a second "category of poor persons," a diverse collection of people "ranging from prosperous artisans and shopkeepers to day laborers."⁹¹ It was this second group, Brown suggests, that "spoke of themselves as *pauperes*."⁹² He explains: "They did so much as average Americans tend to say that they are 'middle class.' For them, the word *pauper* did not automatically conjure up the image of a 'pauper'—of a beggar and a homeless person in need of food, clothes, and shelter. Rather, it conjured up a contrast. One was poor over against others who were not poor."⁹³ Brown is concerned to avoid a "polarized image of the late Roman city," where society is conceived in opposing categories of "the rich" and "the poor."⁹⁴ This is a helpful corrective for modern readers. As Brown's account indicates, the reality was likely a more varied social spectrum, which included a sizeable "middle class."⁹⁵

However, while Brown distinguishes "the outright poor" from "the *pauperes* to whom Augustine preached in Hippo and Carthage," Augustine's use of *pauperes* in the *Sermons* often appears to refer to the poorest members of society.⁹⁶ In *Sermon* 41, for example, he urges, "don't disdain and ignore the poor [*pauperes*], who have nowhere to go home to, have nowhere to take shelter."⁹⁷ "There are poor people [*pauperes*] who don't have any money, can scarcely find enough to eat every day, are so in need of other people's assistance, of their pity, that they are not even ashamed to beg," Augustine observes elsewhere.⁹⁸ Certainly, on other occasions Augustine's use of *pauperes* reflects the broad and diverse group that Brown describes (see above),⁹⁹ but when Augustine speaks of the *pauperes*, he often has those who lack the basic needs of food and shelter in mind. Finn describes well Augustine's subtle use of this term: "Augustine's common practice in the *Enarrationes* is in fact to describe recipients of alms in terms combining *pauper* with a further expression of general need or want, a combination which may

---

90. Finn, "Portraying the Poor," 135. Finn observes that Augustine typically offers "little or no further specification" when he uses "*pauperes*" (p. 135).

91. Brown, *Through the Eye of a Needle*, 342-3.

92. Brown, *Through the Eye of a Needle*, 343.

93. Brown, *Through the Eye of a Needle*, 343.

94. Brown, *Through the Eye of a Needle*, 343. See also p. 78 of this work, and additionally Peter Brown, *Poverty and Leadership in the Later Roman Empire* (Hanover: University Press of New England, 2002), 45-8.

95. Brown, *Through the Eye of a Needle*, 343. For this "middle class," see also pp. 36-9, 81 of this work, and additionally Brown, *Poverty and Leadership in the Later Roman Empire*, 49-55.

96. Brown, *Through the Eye of a Needle*, 342-3. See also p. 347.

97. *Serm.* 41.6 (*PL* 38:251). Lepelley writes of Augustine that "to the poor, he was available in a special way," and later notes his "daily, constant and concrete care of the poor and oppressed people." Lepelley, "Facing Wealth and Poverty," 2, 16. See also Brown, *Through the Eye of a Needle*, 342.

98. *Serm.* 14.1 (*PL* 38:112).

99. E.g., *Serm.* 123.5.

suggest beneficiaries low down the social strata, but which remains ambiguous about just how far down."[100] Moreover, by using these more general descriptors, Augustine enables a wider group of listeners to identify with them.[101] For in his preaching, Augustine seeks to help all listeners hear the word of God, from the richest to the poorest, and everyone in between.[102]

Another "audience" that I consider in this book is the monastic communities under Augustine's care, who also benefited from his pastoral instruction. Following his arrival and unexpected ordination in Hippo, Augustine established a monastery, as he recounts in *Sermon* 355:

> I brought nothing with me; I came to this Church with only the clothes I was wearing at the time. And because what I was planning was to be in a monastery with the brothers, Father Valerius of blessed memory, having learned of my purpose and desire, gave me that plot where the monastery now is. I began to gather together brothers of good will, my companions in poverty, having nothing just like me, and imitating me. Just as I had sold my slender poor man's property and distributed the proceeds to the poor, those who wished to stay with me did the same, so that we might live on what we had in common.[103]

The "plot" that Valerius provided for the monastery was likely located "within the perimeter enclosing the basilica and its annexes."[104] This location itself is significant: Augustine's conception of monastic life could be lived in the city; it did not require withdrawal to the wilderness.[105] Another distinctive aspect of Augustine's monastic vision is his emphasis on community. Discussing the development of early monasticism, Adolar Zumkeller observes that "Augustine shifted the notion of community to the center of monastic life."[106] Members

---

100. Finn, "Portraying the Poor," 135. In his monograph, Finn cautions against assuming that poorer listeners are absent because the preacher does not appear to mention them. Finn, *Almsgiving in the Later Roman Empire*, 141.

101. On the homiletical benefits of using these non-specific descriptors, see Clark, "Pastoral Care," 273; Dunn, "Poverty as a Social Issue," 177-9; Dunn, "Augustine's Homily on Almsgiving," 6-7; Finn, "Portraying the Poor," 133-40. See also Chapter 3 for further discussion and references.

102. E.g., *Serm.* 177.7.

103. *Serm.* 355.2.

104. Lancel, *Saint Augustine*, 235. For a description of this "garden monastery," see Adolar Zumkeller, *Augustine's Ideal of the Religious Life*, trans. Edmund Colledge (New York: Fordham University Press, 1986), 35-40. For an estimated number of members, see Brown, *Through the Eye of a Needle*, 175.

105. Markus, *End of Ancient Christianity*, 160-2; George Lawless, foreword to *The Monastic Rules*, trans. Agatha Mary and Gerald Bonner, ed. Boniface Ramsey, The Augustine Series (Hyde Park, NY: New City Press, 2004), 12.

106. Zumkeller, *Augustine's Ideal of the Religious Life*, 430. For the distinctiveness of this emphasis, see also Markus, *End of Ancient Christianity*, 77-81, 158, 162-4.

of the monastery came from different tiers of society, as Zumkeller explains: "The majority came from the lower classes: Augustine writes of slaves and freedmen, peasants, and manual laborers. Yet there were also men from wealthy and distinguished families, and even senators and substantial landowners."[107] A notable feature of the *Rule* is that it anticipates these differences, and provides guidance for how those who had previously been considered "rich" or "poor" could find a common life together.[108] Thus, Brown states that the *Rule* "was written as a Zen for the handling of social difference."[109] The example of the early Christian community in Acts 4 provided an important inspiration: the *Rule* instructed members to live in unity, with "*one soul and one heart* (Acts 4:32)," and this unity was to be expressed through their sharing of "*everything in common* (Acts 4:32)."[110]

After his appointment as bishop, Augustine realized that he would need to adapt his own monastic lifestyle to accommodate the demands of hospitality associated with his new episcopal role.[111] Accordingly, Augustine explains in *Sermon* 355, "I wanted to have a monastery of clergy in this bishops' residence."[112] The clergy who lived with Augustine in this second community often subsequently went to serve in other churches.[113] In this respect, this monastic community had a wider influence beyond Hippo.[114] Regrettably there is much less information available about the monastic community that Augustine established for women, even regarding its date and location.[115] However, it is thought that it was located in Hippo, and that for a time, "one of Augustine's widowed sisters" served as the

---

107. Zumkeller, *Augustine's Ideal of the Religious Life*, 37. In *Sermon* 356, Augustine discusses specific members of the clerical monastery who have come from diverse economic situations (*Serm.* 356.3–10). Martin explains that this aspect of Augustine's monastic community was particularly distinctive in this social context, with its strong "sense of caste." Martin, "Augustine and the Politics of Monasticism," 174.

108. E.g., *Reg*. 3: 1.5–7; 3.3–5.

109. Brown, *Through the Eye of a Needle*, 176. Brown suggests that these concerns may have prompted the composition of the *Rule* (p. 173).

110. *Reg*. 3: 1.2; 1.3.

111. *Serm.* 355.2. For these episcopal responsibilities, see Lawless, *Augustine of Hippo and His Monastic Rule*, 62.

112. *Serm.* 355.2. For a description of this clerical monastery, see Zumkeller, *Augustine's Ideal of the Religious Life*, 40–5. Lawless notes a "lack of evidence" regarding whether this community followed "a monastic code," but proposes "that Acts 4: 32–5 constituted, in effect, its basic rule of life." Lawless, *Augustine of Hippo and His Monastic Rule*, 160. In this book, I typically refer to "the monastic community" in general terms, and have not sought to delineate between the two.

113. Possidius, *Life of Saint Augustine*, 11.1–2.

114. Possidius, *Life of Saint Augustine*, 11.3; Zumkeller, *Augustine's Ideal of the Religious Life*, 83–4.

115. Lancel, *Saint Augustine*, 235.

"superior."[116] Zumkeller observes that "the Augustinian houses of nuns were on the same economic and spiritual footing as the communities of brothers."[117] This is certainly reflected in the female version of the *Rule* that exists, which is nearly identical to the male version.[118] Lawless identifies here one of the "distinctive features" of the *Rule*: "The bishop of Hippo ... stands alone in the history of early western monasticism as one whose legislative text does duty equally well for both men and women."[119]

The members of the monastic communities gathered in the church each day for a Eucharistic service, alongside others from the wider church community.[120] They also attended the larger weekly church services, and so can be considered part of the audience that Augustine addresses in the *Sermons*.[121] As I suggest at various points in this book, their presence in the church community provided a positive example of Christian devotion and unity. "We are always before your eyes," Augustine acknowledges to the wider congregation.[122] And yet Augustine urges monastics to "show equal honor and respect" toward other "members of Christ."[123] Brown observes that in Augustine's context there was a tendency to revere some as "especially chosen by God," and he notes Augustine's efforts to counter this

---

116. Zumkeller, *Augustine's Ideal of the Religious Life*, 45–6. See pp. 45–6 for a description of this monastic community for women.

117. Zumkeller, *Augustine's Ideal of the Religious Life*, 45.

118. Lawless provides details of the "feminine" version of the *Rule*, noting that although in the past many scholars have held this to be the original version, subsequent scholarship has confirmed that the "masculine" version was composed first. Lawless, *Augustine of Hippo and His Monastic Rule*, 135–48. I use the original (male) version of the *Rule* throughout this book. I regret, however, that along with Augustine's use of male terms in the *Sermons*, quotations from these texts lend a rather unbalanced "male" emphasis to discussion.

119. Lawless, *Augustine of Hippo and His Monastic Rule*, 147–8.

120. Zumkeller, *Augustine's Ideal of the Religious Life*, 49–51.

121. For example, Augustine refers to the clergy who live with him in the monastery in *Serm.* 356.14. See also references to those who have made a monastic commitment in *Serm.* 73A.3; 96.9–10; 132.3; 205.1–2 (for the latter, see Hill's comment: *Sermons (184–229Z) on the Liturgical Seasons*, trans. Edmund Hill, ed. John E. Rotelle, vol. 6, *The Works of Saint Augustine, Part 3: Sermons* (Hyde Park, NY: New City Press, 1993), 100n3). Additionally, a small number of texts in the *Sermons* appear to specifically address those who have undertaken a monastic commitment, e.g., *Serm.* 350A (see Hill's comments about the audience: *Sermons (341–400) on Liturgical Seasons*, trans. Edmund Hill, ed. John E. Rotelle, vol. 10, *The Works of Saint Augustine, Part 3: Sermons* (Hyde Park, NY: New City Press, 1995), 113n1) and *Serm.* 354 (again, see Hill's note: *Sermons (341–400)*, 162n1). For the attendance of monks at Sunday worship services, see also Gerald Bonner, commentary to *Monastic Rules*, 70.

122. *Serm.* 356.12. On the "visibility" of the monastic community and its wider influence see Martin, "Augustine and the Politics of Monasticism," 168–70, 183–4. See also Chapter 3 for further discussion.

123. *Serm.* 354.4.

stratified picture.¹²⁴ Augustine observes that those undertaking a monastic life could be consumed by pride, while "ordinary" Christians might model humility.¹²⁵ The "enemy" has "sown weeds" (Mt. 13:24–30) among "monks" and "laypeople" alike.¹²⁶ All are burdened by sin, all need God's grace, and Christ has made all members of his body.¹²⁷

The Formation of a Common Life

Although I seek to be sensitive to these details of historical context, my focus is on theological aspects of Augustine's pastoral instruction, identifying how his teaching helps us understand the church's formation and identity amidst the economic divisions of our own time. In this book I argue that the movement away from private self-interest, and toward common love of God and neighbor, is fundamental to the church's formation and identity amidst contemporary contexts of economic inequality.¹²⁸ In particular, I advance our understanding

---

124. Brown, *Augustine of Hippo*, 508–9. Besides monastic communities, Harrison notes other forms of asceticism in this context: Harrison, *Christian Truth and Fractured Humanity*, 171–4, 185. See also L. J. van der Lof, "The Threefold Meaning of Servi Dei in the Writings of Saint Augustine," *Augustinian Studies* 12 (1981): 50–4; Zumkeller, *Augustine's Ideal of the Religious Life*, 86–9.

125. *Serm.* 354.4, 9.

126. *Serm.* 73A.3.

127. *Serm.* 77A.1; 114.4; 354.4; Markus, *End of Ancient Christianity*, 64–5, 159.

128. I am indebted to the work of Markus for alerting me to these themes of "privacy" and "community" in Augustine's thought, and thus providing me with the language of "private" and "common" that I employ throughout this book. Markus, *End of Ancient Christianity*. See especially pp. 50–5, 77–81, and also R. A. Markus, "De Ciuitate Dei: Pride and the Common Good," in *Collectanea Augustiniana: Augustine: "Second Founder of the Faith,"* ed. Joseph C. Schnaubelt and Frederick Van Fleteren (New York: Peter Lang, 1990), 245–59. Describing the new understanding of sin that Augustine arrived at around the time of writing the *Confessions*, Markus writes: "Sin is seen as a withdrawal into a 'privacy' which is a deprivation. By it all community is fatally ruptured: man's community with God, community with his fellow-men, with his own self." Markus, *End of Ancient Christianity*, 51. See especially Chapter 1, where I offer further discussion and references to additional literature. I am further indebted to Markus for helping me appreciate Augustine's vision of the monastery and church in light of this understanding of sin: Markus, *End of Ancient Christianity*, 63–83, 157–79. He writes: "The most insidious form of pride, the root of all sin, was 'privacy', self-enclosure. The 'private' was the opposite of 'shared', 'common', 'public'; and the Heavenly City was the community in which full sharing would be had" (p. 78). Thus, "the two poles of social living were, at one extreme, to be enclosed in an isolated self, and, at the other, to live in full community with God and one's fellows" (p. 79). The monastic community "had a privileged relation to the community of the Heavenly City," Markus notes, later adding that it offered a glimpse of "the Church's calling to be the perfect community," "a privileged anticipation of the Church's eschatological realisation" (pp. 79–80).

of the centrality of this theme in Augustine's monastic rules and *Sermons* (texts often overlooked in contemporary theological discussion), by noting how in both contexts this formational movement shapes his pastoral instruction on matters pertinent to economic inequality, such as wealth, poverty, and attitudes toward rich and poor.[129]

Augustine's monastic instruction (principally the *Rule*) plays an important role in this book.[130] For the *Rule* offers a glimpse of Augustine's conception of a common life, where members were no longer divided from one another as rich and poor, but rather united in love, and able to share with one another, so that none experienced need.[131] Amidst the economic inequalities of our own time, this vision of economic division overcome, and a common life shared, is very compelling.

As noted, Augustine's monastic instruction was intended for a small group of people within the wider church: communities of single women or men who had committed themselves to the monastic way of life. However, I show that his vision of a common life, most clearly outlined in his instruction to the monastic community, is also reflected in his preaching to the wider Christian community. The teaching Augustine offers in the *Rule* is not restricted to this document alone; of the *Rule*, Lawless notes that "every thought expressed therein finds expression elsewhere in his myriad writings."[132] Naturally, the details of Augustine's instruction differ in the

---

129. I should note that, though central, this theme is not always overt or obvious. Discussing one of Augustine's guidelines for catechetical teaching in *Instructing Beginners in Faith* (*Catech.* 6.10), Harmless explains: "The theme of love was to undergird whatever one said, but subtly, without being overly conspicuous." Harmless, *Augustine and the Catechumenate*, 156–7. I think that the turn from private self-interest, toward common love of God and neighbor, is woven with similar subtlety through Augustine's monastic rules and *Sermons*. In singling out this theme, I acknowledge that Augustine's understanding of Christian formation includes other dimensions not necessarily encompassed by this theme.

130. For details of Augustine's *Rule* and other monastic texts see especially Lawless, *Augustine of Hippo and His Monastic Rule*. Regarding the *Rule* (*Praeceptum*), Lawless surveys debates of authorship, date, and audience (pp. 121–54), and concludes that it was composed by Augustine (p. 135), probably around the year 397 (p. 153). Lawless states elsewhere his opinion that the *Rule* was written for the members of "the garden monastery at Hippo." Lawless, foreword to *Monastic Rules*, 11. The details of the *Regulations for a Monastery* (*Ordo monasterii*) are more complex, as Lawless's survey of scholarship indicates: Lawless, *Augustine of Hippo and His Monastic Rule*, 167–71. Lawless acknowledges that the author of this document "remains anonymous" (p. 171), but he appears to favor Augustine as the most likely author (pp. 169, 171). See also discussion of these monastic documents in Bonner, commentary to *Monastic Rules*, 23–45; Zumkeller, *Augustine's Ideal of the Religious Life*, 283–7. In this book, I primarily draw on the *Rule* (though I discuss the opening precept of the *Regulations for a Monastery* in Chapter 1).

131. *Reg. 3*: 1.2–3.

132. George Lawless, "The Rule of Saint Augustine as a Mirror of Perfection," *Angelicum* 58 (1981): 474.

Sermons, where he is typically addressing a broader range of listeners, including those with family or employment responsibilities. The monastic life was not accessible to all, and not all aspects of his monastic instruction are relevant to ordinary Christians. And yet, Augustine does not promote two separate forms of Christian life. Regarding Augustine's reworking of the monastic ideal, Markus writes: "The quest of perfection could not be allowed to be the monopoly of one group of Christians. The Christian community could not be allowed to be divided by a double standard, one for the ordinary Christian, another for an ascetic elite … : there is a single final end all must strive to attain, and a single Christian morality all must follow."[133] The same vision informs Augustine's monastic instruction and his preaching. All are called toward the same goal, and although listeners may be at markedly different stages of the journey, they walk the same formational road.

The phrase "love does not seek its own," featured in the title of this book, is drawn from one of the precepts in the *Rule*, where Augustine in turn draws these words from 1 Corinthians 13:5.[134] I have foregrounded this particular rule, because it succinctly describes the formational movement that concerns this book:[135]

> So, then, no one should work at anything for himself. All your work should be shared together with greater care and more ready eagerness than if you were doing things for yourself alone. For when it is written of *love* that it *does not seek its own* (1 Cor 13:5), it means that it puts the common good before its own and not personal advantage before the common good. Thus the more you are concerned about the common good rather than your own, the more progress

---

133. Markus, *End of Ancient Christianity*, 77. See also Lawless, *Augustine of Hippo and His Monastic Rule*, 59.

134. Reg. 3: 5.2. "*Caritas enim, de qua scriptum est quod 'non quaerat quae sua sunt'* … " (GL:94). Note that the phrase "love does not seek its own" that I have used in the title and throughout the book is drawn from the translation provided by Agatha Mary and Gerald Bonner (as quoted below). Other English translations render this phrase slightly differently. For the influence of Paul's Corinthian letters on Augustine's *Rule* see Andrea Gerlin, "Community and Ascesis: Paul's Directives to the Corinthians Interpreted in the Rule of Augustine," in *Collectanea Augustiniana: Augustine: "Second Founder of the Faith,"* ed. Joseph C. Schnaubelt and Frederick Van Fleteren (New York: Peter Lang, 1990), 303–13.

135. I am indebted to Zumkeller for first drawing my attention to the formational significance of this precept: Zumkeller, *Augustine's Ideal of the Religious Life*. Of the phrase from 1 Corinthians 13:5, Zumkeller writes that Augustine viewed these words as "a statement of the essential characteristic of Christian spiritual love" (p. 154). Regarding the precept's subsequent instruction about concern for the "common good," Zumkeller explains that Augustine "understood this statement to be a basic rule for daily living in the monastery which could free its individual members from narrow self-seeking and fill them with the love of Christ" (p. 154). Martin indicates that for Augustine these words of 1 Corinthians 13:5 are not only "a foundational monastic text," but also "the hallmark of true Christian dedication." Martin, "Augustine and the Politics of Monasticism," 179.

you will know that you have made. And thus the love that abides for ever will reign in all matters of passing necessity.[136]

I will illustrate the importance of this statement during the course of this book. However, I offer here a few preliminary observations to outline the programmatic significance of this rule. (1) The first two sentences (in this English translation) locate this instruction within the practical work of the monastery. Like the rest of the *Rule*, this directive is not simply concerned with interior piety; rather it addresses everyday challenges of living alongside others, and the temptation of self-interest within the context of one's labor. This practical emphasis is also reflected in the precepts that immediately precede and follow this one, which attend to the distribution of clothes, and the receiving of gifts.[137] (2) The third sentence expresses the central thread of this book: that the love that God gifts to us is a love that "*does not seek its own*," but rather calls us away from self-interest and pursuit of personal gain.[138] In practical terms, Augustine instructs, this love is demonstrated when concern for the "common good" takes priority over our own interests.[139] In its plainest sense, this is another form of the instruction to love our neighbor—to seek the well-being of all in the community.[140] And yet, for Augustine, this is

---

136. *Reg. 3:* 5.2. Lawless notes how Augustine weaves together classical and biblical concepts in this precept: "An amalgam of Stoic political–ethical philosophy from Cicero is melded with 1 Cor 13: 5; 12: 31 and also Acts 4: 35 to monitor the interaction between the common good (*commune*) and the individual good (*proprium*) as a cardinal principle in Augustine's understanding of community life." Lawless, foreword to *Monastic Rules*, 13. On Augustine's use of these classical concepts in the *Rule* see also Raymond Canning, "Common Good," in *Augustine through the Ages*, ed. Allan D. Fitzgerald (Grand Rapids, MI: Eerdmans, 1999), 220; Harrison, *Christian Truth and Fractured Humanity*, 183. Canning also notes Luc Verheijen's analysis of these concepts in Augustine's work: Canning, "Common Good," 221. For Verheijen's study, see "La charité ne cherche pas ses propres intérêts," in Luc Verheijen, *Nouvelle approche de la Règle de Saint Augustin*, vol. 2 (Louvain: Institut Historique Augustinien, 1988), 220–89. Martin clarifies that for Augustine "'*sua quaerentes*' functions virtually interchangeably with the notion of '*propria*' or '*privatus*.'" Martin, "Augustine and the Politics of Monasticism," 180. For further discussion of these concepts in Augustine's teaching, and additional references, see esp. Chapter 1.
137. *Reg. 3:* 5.1, 3.
138. *Reg. 3:* 5.2.
139. *Reg. 3:* 5.2. For Augustine's understanding of the "common good," see Brown, *Through the Eye of a Needle*, 177–83; Raymond Canning, "St. Augustine's Vocabulary of the Common Good and the Place of Love for Neighbour," in *Studia Patristica 33*, ed. Elizabeth A. Livingstone (Leuven: Peeters, 1997), 48–54; Canning, "Common Good," 219–22. See also discussion and references in Chapter 3.
140. See T. J. van Bavel, commentary to *The Rule of Saint Augustine: Masculine and Feminine Versions*, trans. Raymond Canning, Introduction and commentary by T. J. van Bavel (London: Darton, Longman and Todd, 1984), 91.

also a call to love God, who (as the following chapters explain) alone is the good that can be enjoyed in common, and by whom we can love others in common.[141] (3) In the fourth sentence, Augustine casts this instruction in a formational light. The love that he has just described is not something we experience, whole and complete, at the outset of the Christian life. Rather we make "progress" in this love throughout the course of our life, and our increasing regard for the "common good" becomes an indicator of this love's formation within us.[142] Augustine "saw in an individual's concern for the community ... a clear sign and a reliable measure of his spiritual progress," Zumkeller observes.[143] I am approaching the *Sermons* with this formational dynamic in view: asking how Augustine seeks to nurture the formation of love for God and neighbor amongst his listeners; considering what he believes to hinder or help this love; and noting the signs he identifies of this love's flourishing. (4) The final sentence provides the essential theological basis for the preceding sentences. The goal of this formational process is that God's love might "reign in all matters of passing necessity" within the community.[144] For Augustine, such "matters" pertain to this temporal life, where need and want is experienced, including the economic hardship to which the poorest amongst us are subject.[145] Amidst the neediness of this life, our hope is to see God's love reign, rather than our own self-interested desires. However, the critical insight is that this transformative love comes as the gift of God. The common life that Augustine calls members of the monastic community toward does not result simply from striving to get along together. Rather, it arises from God's gift of love.

In these four respects, this precept from the *Rule* concisely expresses the formational process that I outline in this book, in which God's love begins to reshape our lives, drawing us away from preoccupation with our private concerns, and outward toward love of God and neighbor. However, other aspects of Augustine's monastic instruction enable this formational movement to be considered in greater detail. Firstly, this instruction identifies specific areas in the life of a community where this transformation is likely to be needed, such as our envious preoccupation with the resources of others, or our tendency to elevate ourselves above others.[146] These aspects of Augustine's instruction indicate that he was well acquainted with the practical challenges of encouraging a common life amongst those of different backgrounds; as Lawless observes, Augustine's monastic instruction reflects not the "musings of an armchair theologian," but rather the

---

141. *Serm.* 47.30; John Burnaby, *Amor Dei: A Study of the Religion of St. Augustine* (Eugene, OR: Wipf and Stock, 2007), 127.
142. *Reg. 3*: 5.2.
143. Zumkeller, *Augustine's Ideal of the Religious Life*, 154. See also Agatha Mary, *The Rule of Saint Augustine: An Essay in Understanding* (Villanova, PA: Augustinian Press, 1992), 224.
144. *Reg. 3*: 5.2.
145. See Chapter 4 for discussion.
146. *Reg. 3*: 3.3–5; 1.6–7.

work of "a seasoned practitioner."[147] Arguably the greater challenge for Augustine, however, was shepherding the wider Christian community in this direction, where there was even greater disparity of circumstance and commitment. And yet, as I demonstrate in this book, in the *Sermons*, Augustine's overall goal remains the same, calling his listeners away from a life of self-interest, and toward love of God and neighbor. Furthermore, many of the specific issues that Augustine addresses in his monastic instruction in relation to this theme, he also raises with the wider church community: generally in a different manner to reflect their different context, but often with striking correspondences.[148]

Secondly, Augustine's monastic instruction provides a glimpse of the common life that God forms among us, as we are renewed in love for God and neighbor. All work toward "the common good"; resources are shared "according to need"; each member is valued, regardless of previous social distinctions; and love for God is recognized as the source of Christian unity.[149] Markus explains that in its life of "concord and singlemindedness, with all property shared," the monastic community Augustine envisaged was "a microcosm of the City of God"; it thus reflected the "eschatological vocation of the whole Church."[150] Understandably, in the *Sermons*, Augustine does not expect members of the wider congregation to share their life together in the same fashion as the monastery. However, as I demonstrate in the following chapters, a movement toward a greater commonality of life can be observed, as members of the congregation learn to look beyond social differences, to recognize the new life they share in Christ, to share resources with one another, and to celebrate God's unifying work among them. Thus I use the expression "common life" in this more expansive sense, referring both to the unified life that we share in Christ and to the practical outworking of this unity in the varied contexts of our everyday life.

The Monastic Rules and the Sermons

The thematic resonances between Augustine's monastic instruction and the *Sermons* are not surprising; as noted, the relationship between Augustine's monastic community and the wider church was a close one, with Augustine exercising pastoral leadership in both contexts. However, I do not attempt to provide a historical account of this relationship, nor to argue a "text-critical" case for the influence of the *Rule* upon the *Sermons*. Rather, I am interested in the way in which Augustine's monastic instruction sheds light upon the *Sermons*, drawing

---

147. Lawless, *Augustine of Hippo and His Monastic Rule*, 160.
148. Noting the "ordinariness of the problems" anticipated in the *Rule*, Mary observes that "few of them are unique to monastic situations." Mary, *The Rule of Saint Augustine*, 42.
149. *Reg. 3*: 5.2; 1.3; 1.7; 1.2.
150. Markus, *End of Ancient Christianity*, 78, 79–80.

our attention to pastoral themes and emphases that might otherwise go unnoticed. In this respect, exploring the *Sermons* in conversation with the *Rule* is an exercise in intertextuality, reading one set of texts through another, in the hope that we might hear with greater clarity the voice that speaks in both.

In practical terms, this approach also aids the interpretation of the *Sermons*, which number over 560, and (in their recent English translation) are spread across eleven volumes.[151] The *Sermons* span the whole of Augustine's pastoral ministry, covering a breadth of biblical texts and liturgical occasions, and were delivered in numerous congregational settings.[152] The size and diverse nature of the *Sermons* leave them open to multiple interpretations, depending on which particular sermons are deemed to be significant, and representative of the whole.[153]

Reading the *Sermons* alongside the *Rule*, therefore, is my attempt to read Augustine with Augustine; to interpret this broad and eclectic collection of sermons in light of the concise and deliberate instruction of *Rule*.[154] Through my reading of the *Sermons* alongside the *Rule*, I also hope to offer a constructive contribution to existing scholarship. In particular, I think there is a closer correspondence between Augustine's monastic instruction, and his preaching to the wider congregation

---

151. For details of the number of sermons in this collection, see Pellegrino, general introduction to *Sermons (1–19)*, 15–16; Dolbeau, introduction to *Sermons Discovered since 1990*, 13.

152. Rebillard describes the *Sermons* (also referred to as "*Sermones ad populum*") as "all the discourses preached by Augustine and not included in a continuous commentary of a book of the Bible." Rebillard, "Sermones," 773. Thus, the *Sermons* do not include Augustine's *Enarrations on the Psalms*, *Homilies on the First Epistle of John*, or *Homilies on the Gospel of John*. Although I discuss the *Homilies on the First Epistle of John* on occasion in this book, I have not engaged with these other two collections.

153. Furthermore, as Hubertus R. Drobner outlines in his article, it is difficult to establish exact dates for the *Sermons*: Hubertus R. Drobner, "The Chronology of St. Augustine's *Sermones ad Populum*," *Augustinian Studies* 31, no. 2 (2000): 211–18. Where I have noted dates for sermons, they are generally those provided by Hill in his notes accompanying each sermon, unless otherwise indicated. See also the summary table of dates for the *Sermons* provided in: *Sermons (1–19)*, 138–63.

154. As earlier noted, the *Rule* was likely composed in 397, and so I acknowledge that reading the *Sermons* alongside this document may give greater emphasis to the ideas important to Augustine at that point in his ministry (though note that Lancel suggests that the years 396–7 featured "the richest results, in both the pastoral field and his development of fundamental texts": Lancel, *Saint Augustine*, 187). Interestingly, whereas I am interested in reading these texts together with a view to interpreting the *Sermons*, Lawless commends a similar approach for interpreting the *Rule*. Lawless, "Mirror of Perfection," 470. Noting that "it is a dense document," he writes that "one is obliged, therefore, to read Augustine on Augustine for a fuller understanding of this particular text" (p. 470).

than has often been acknowledged.[155] I illustrate that by considering these two forms of pastoral instruction together, we can see Augustine's teaching on the identity and formation of the wider church in new light.

I have structured the following chapters around seven instructions (or sets of instructions) from the *Rule* (and in Chapter 1, from the *Regulations for a Monastery*). Although this selection is in no way representative of Augustine's monastic instruction as a whole, I have chosen these particular precepts (or excerpts of precepts) because they are especially relevant to the questions of economic division that concern this book. These monastic precepts feature as an epigraph at the beginning of each chapter. Taking the theme indicated by the introductory monastic rule, each chapter explores this theme in Augustine's pastoral direction in the *Sermons*, illustrating how it contributes to the formation of love for God and neighbor among the wider congregation. Although the chapters draw broadly from the corpus of the *Sermons*, each chapter foregrounds one sermon in particular, in order to illustrate how Augustine approaches the theme in question on a particular occasion.

In examining Augustine's pastoral instruction, my concern is a contemporary one, as I consider how Augustine might instruct the church in our time. In so doing, I operate with the theological and homiletical assumption that the God who spoke through Augustine's preaching some sixteen hundred years ago continues to speak through this preaching today.[156] Such an assumption would not be foreign to Augustine. In the *Sermons*, he often acknowledges a similar historical divide, noting that his congregation cannot encounter Christ face-to-face, in the manner that the first disciples enjoyed many centuries earlier. However, Augustine insists in Sermon 301A (as he prepares to reflect on a gospel passage), "just because we didn't yet exist then, that's no reason why we should suppose it wasn't said to us."[157] When Christ speaks in the gospels, he continues to address his followers

---

155. Note that some scholars have suggested that Augustine's *Rule* offers a valuable sketch of Christian community that is relevant to the church as a whole: Charles W. Brockwell, Jr., "Augustine's Ideal of Monastic Community: A Paradigm for His Doctrine of the Church," *Augustinian Studies* 8 (1977): 91–109; Lawless, "Mirror of Perfection," 460–74; Martin, "Augustine and the Politics of Monasticism," 165–86. However, these three articles mainly focus on the *Rule*, articulating the nature of Augustine's vision outlined therein, rather than exploring how Augustine expressed these themes in his wider pastoral instruction (the focus of my work). Note also that while homilies that specifically discuss monastic life (e.g., *Serm.* 354–6) have already received much attention in relation to Augustine's monasticism, my focus is on sermons that have the life of the wider congregation in view (the majority of the *Sermons*).

156. Drawing on the work of Hans-Georg Gadamer, who questioned the view of "an unbridgeable distance between original author and contemporary interpreter," Charry indicates the validity of reading texts from the Christian tradition with a view to "furthering effective Christian practice." Charry, *By the Renewing of Your Minds*, 16–17.

157. *Serm.* 301A.1.

directly. "He speaks even now, when the gospel is chanted," Augustine reminds the congregation.[158] Certainly, as creatures, we are constrained by time and place, and thus we must be mindful of the historical and cultural particularities that shape Augustine's world, and our own. But "where, though, is God not, or when is God ever absent?" Augustine enquires.[159] Because God is not subject to the limitations of history, God is no less present to a congregation in fourth- or fifth-century North Africa (or in twenty-first-century New Zealand) than in first-century Galilee.

As a preacher, Augustine's role is to help the congregation hear the voice of God that addresses them through Scripture. The task of preaching cannot be conceived apart from this voice, as Augustine reminds listeners at the beginning of *Sermon* 48: "We heard the readings of the divine utterances while they were being recited. That is the material that has been given me to talk about. That's what I have to get wise to, that's from what I have to sow what wisdom I have gotten."[160] The call to preach is not an invitation to air one's own ideas; rather the preacher is called to pass on what they themselves receive from God.[161] Augustine preaches in the hope that the eternal wisdom of God (and not his own limited human wisdom) might be heard through him.

For the voice of God to be heard, it is not only the preacher who is dependent upon God, but also the listeners. Thus Augustine completes these introductory comments with the prayer: "May he make good in your minds whatever I have done less well, because even what I do manage to convey to your ears is not worth anything, is it, unless he does the whole work in your minds."[162] The words of the preacher will only bear fruit if God is at work within the listeners. As Augustine explains in his *Homilies on the First Epistle of John*, if we are to learn, we must be taught "within" by Christ through the Holy Spirit: "He who teaches, then, is the inner teacher: Christ teaches; his inbreathing teaches. Where his inbreathing and his anointing don't exist, words sound without to no avail."[163]

Reading Augustine's *Sermons* with a concern for the contemporary church is entirely in keeping with Augustine's own homiletical understanding. He instructs his listeners that when the Scriptures are faithfully preached, Christ (the head) is addressing his body, the church: "The head is teaching his members, the tongue talking to his feet."[164] The ministry of preaching is a primary means by which

---

158. *Serm.* 301A.1; see also *Conf.* 11.8.10.
159. *Serm.* 301A.1.
160. *Serm.* 48.1. Harmless captures well the role of Scripture in Augustine's preaching: "His sermons teem with biblical quotations, biblical allusions, biblical images. Augustine did more than comment on the Bible: he *spoke* Bible, making its words his words." Harmless, *Augustine and the Catechumenate*, 210.
161. See Chapter 6 for further discussion of this view of the preaching task.
162. *Serm.* 48.1.
163. *Tract. ep. Jo.* 3.13. For Augustine's concept of Christ as the "inner teacher," see Burnaby, *Amor Dei*, 153–6; Sanlon, *Augustine's Theology of Preaching*, 59–62, 74–5.
164. *Serm.* 399.15.

Christ cares for his body, the church. And the church, as Augustine conceives it, is not an entity limited to a particular time or place, because Christ has drawn the church into himself as his body.[165] When Augustine preaches, Christ is teaching his body, including those today who are also members of his body. Of course, the circumstances of Augustine's listeners—historical, social, political—are markedly different from our own, and these differences of context should not be overlooked. Not all of Augustine's comments are relevant or helpful for our contemporary context. Furthermore, we must be wary of reading anachronistically, as if Augustine thinks just as we do. Even our ideas of economic inequality/equality reflect a certain modern way of thinking, and as will become apparent, as a premodern, Augustine approaches these questions quite differently. However, rather than assessing his teaching according to our modern criteria, I seek to illustrate how his teaching challenges our modern assumptions, questioning, for example, the idea that we know how to love our neighbor, or that economic equality is an end in itself. This too, can be part of the lesson we can learn through Augustine's *Sermons*, as we consider how Christ continues to teach his body through them.

Outline

Writing on Augustine is a daunting undertaking, given the breadth of his own writing, and the seemingly endless expanse of contemporary Augustine scholarship. While I hope to offer a useful and distinctive contribution to existing scholarship, I am also mindful of Augustine's prayerful acknowledgment that "your truth does not belong to me nor to anyone else, but to us all whom you call to share it as a public possession."[166] I am enormously grateful to the many scholars whose work has helped me to recognize, with them, the truth of God to which Augustine bears witness.

It will be clear to the reader that this book is broad in scope. The "big picture" nature of this project means that I cannot engage every aspect in detail. Practically speaking, I have worked with English translations of a limited selection of Augustine's writings, drawing on the original Latin text only when necessary.[167] Similarly, while mindful of the significant contributions to Augustine scholarship in other languages, I have only engaged with English-language secondary literature.

Tracing the influence of classical philosophy on Augustine's thought is also beyond the scope of this study. This is, of course, a topic worthy of investigation, and aspects of Augustine's teaching discussed in the following pages may invite such comparison. Nonetheless, this book focuses on the conversation between Augustine's monastic and homiletic texts, and their relevance to the contemporary

---

165. *Serm.* 341(D22/M55).19.
166. *Conf.* 12.25.34.
167. I am especially grateful to Hill for his remarkable work of translating the vast collection of *Sermons*.

church, and I have not attempted to also address the conversation between Augustine and his classical interlocutors. At various points in the book, however, I have noted relevant scholarship on such matters, which I hope will assist those interested in this question.[168]

As earlier noted, the chapters of this book are each introduced with a precept (or precepts) from Augustine's monastic instruction, and explore this theme in Augustine's *Sermons*. In Chapter 1, I introduce Augustine's teaching on love of God and neighbor, outline the formational movement that I explore throughout this book (from private self-interest toward common love of God and neighbor), and show how this relates to issues of economic division. In Chapter 2, I reflect further on the division that inevitably results from our self-interested departure from God, and the work of the Triune God to restore us to unity with God and one another. In Chapters 3, 4, and 5, I consider the theological dynamics of avarice, envy, and pride (attributes that Augustine closely associates with the self-interest of sin). I illustrate how his teaching on these issues relates to his teaching on wealth and poverty, and how on these occasions he again encourages a formational movement toward love of God and neighbor. In Chapter 6, I consider this formational movement in relation to Augustine's teaching on pastoral ministry, which is also susceptible to self-interest. In Chapter 7, I consider the question of how the Christian community should understand its spiritual progress, and the danger Augustine identifies of claiming this progress as the fruit of our own endeavor. Finally, in the Conclusion, after recapitulating the formational movement discussed in this book, I reflect on what the contemporary church (and particularly those in pastoral ministry) can learn from Augustine regarding the nurture and formation of a common life amidst economic division.

---

168. As a general guide to Augustine's thought in its classical context, a work that I have found especially helpful is Harrison, *Christian Truth and Fractured Humanity*. See also Brown, *Through the Eye of a Needle*, 177–83; Burnaby, *Amor Dei*; Clair, *Discerning the Good*; Lancel, *Saint Augustine*.

Chapter 1

THE CALL TO LOVE GOD AND NEIGHBOR

Before all else, dearest brothers, let God be loved and then your neighbor, because these are the chief commandments which have been given us.

—*Reg. 2:* 1

When Augustine invites his congregation to consider Christ's call to love God and to love neighbor (Mt. 22:34–40) in *Sermon* 90A(D11/M40), he is not simply asking them to ponder a theological theme. Rather, he hopes that they themselves might hear Christ addressing them with these commands. Drawing his listeners into this gospel scene, he invites them to stand in the place of the enquiring lawyer and voice his question, so that they might hear Christ's words in reply: "So let us make our own the desire of the man who asked him what the great commandment was in the law.... Let us, though, ask the question as believers, in order as questioners to find the truth; let us too say, 'Lord, *which is the great commandment in the law?*' (Mt 22:36)."[1] In his commandment to love God and neighbor, Christ responds to our questions about what it means to live rightly before God.

Amidst the economic divisions of the present day, we too are in need of such guidance. For while few would dispute that the church should be concerned about economic inequality, many questions arise about how the church should respond. What is the particular role that the church is called to play? How does the narrative of faith shape our response to others in need? Is the worshiping and devotional life of the Christian community relevant to such matters, and if so, how? With such concerns in view, this chapter considers the role of love for God and neighbor in Augustine's instruction to the Christian community. These two loves are foregrounded at the beginning of Augustine's monastic instruction, orienting the community toward that which is of greatest importance.[2] In this chapter I demonstrate that the call to love God and neighbor similarly shapes Augustine's direction to the wider church community. And yet, in doing so, my purpose is not

---

1. *Serm.* 90A(D11/M40).1.
2. *Reg. 2:* 1.

to analyze a theme or principle,[3] but rather, by drawing on Augustine's pastoral instruction, to illustrate how Christ's commandment addresses our contemporary questions about how to live rightly in an age of economic inequality.

Love of God and neighbor is a regular theme in Augustine's preaching, although he does not always quote Matthew 22:37–40 (or parallel texts) directly. Of particular interest for this chapter is *Sermon* 90A(D11/M40), which Augustine preached in 397, possibly in Carthage.[4] In this sermon, Augustine attends to the nature of our love for our neighbor, helping his listeners to appreciate that in order to love our neighbor rightly, we must learn to love God. Exploring Augustine's instruction in *Sermon* 90A(D11/M40) provides a basic frame for this chapter, in which I also consider a variety of other sermons and relevant works.

Reading and Living with Love

What does it mean to be the church, in contexts of ever-increasing division between rich and poor? Grappling with this question, we may begin by turning to Scripture for guidance. But which Scriptures should guide us? Are we to protest against those who "trample on the poor" (Amos 5:11, NRSV)? Should we be working for change as "God's servants" (Rom. 13:6, NRSV) amidst governmental institutions? Should we focus on proclaiming "good news to the poor" (Lk. 4:18, NRSV) or on confronting the rich (e.g., 1 Tim. 6:17–19)? Those seeking to be faithful to the calling of God's people cannot help but be overwhelmed by these requirements. However, in *Sermon* 90A(D11/M40), Augustine invites listeners to

---

3. Regarding scholarship that explores love of God and neighbor in Augustine, particular mention must be made of Canning's survey, both for its comprehensive scope and for the compelling case Canning makes for the unity of these two commands in Augustine's thought: Raymond Canning, *The Unity of Love for God and Neighbour in St. Augustine* (Heverlee-Leuven: Augustinian Historical Institute, 1993).

4. *Sermon* 90A(D11/M40) is included amongst the sermons collected together in *Sermons Discovered since 1990*. The Latin text of this sermon is found in Augustine, *Vingt-six Sermons au Peuple d'Afrique*, ed. François Dolbeau, 2nd ed., vol. 147, Collection des Études Augustiniennes—Série Antiquité (Paris: Institut d'Études Augustiniennes, 2009), 59–67. Given its recent discovery, *Sermon* 90A(D11/M40) has received less scrutiny than Augustine's other sermons on this theme. However, Anthony Dupont provides a helpful technical analysis of this sermon (with a particular interest in dating): Anthony Dupont, "*Sermo* 90A (Dolbeau 11, Mainz 40). Self-Love as the Beginning of Love for Neighbour and God," *Augustiniana* 57 (2007): 31–48. Hill notes that Lambot locates this sermon in Carthage, July 397: *Sermons Discovered since 1990*, 85n1. Dupont does not comment on the sermon's location, but concurs that 397 is its likely date: Dupont, "Sermo 90A," 31-3, 45-8. Lancel notes that in 397 Augustine had a busy season of preaching in Carthage, and describes *Sermon* 90A(D11/M40) as "one of the finest sermons of the summer of 397." Lancel, *Saint Augustine*, 194–8.

approach Christ with the question, "Lord, *which is the great commandment in the law?*" (Mt. 22:36), and to hear his response: "*You shall love*, he says, *the Lord your God with your whole heart and with your whole soul and with your whole mind. This is the first and great commandment. But the second,* he says, *is like this one: you shall love your neighbor as yourself. On these two commandments depend the whole law, and the prophets*" (vv. 37–40).[5]

In his response, Christ interprets the Scriptures, and Augustine understands this to be a demonstration of Christ's kindness toward his followers. "The law," Augustine explains, is "like an endless forest, sprouting commandments on every page."[6] However, Christ, who "is full of mercy," has "enclosed the length and breadth of the law in a short precept."[7] Although not all have time or ability to read the entire Scriptures, Christ has made the message of the Scriptures accessible to all in this succinct instruction.[8] For Augustine, Christ's call to love God and neighbor is the lens through which the rest of Scripture must be read. Those being received into the catechumenate are taught to interpret Scripture in this way: in *Instructing Beginners in Faith*, Augustine advises that when a part of Scripture does not appear to direct us toward love of God and neighbor, it should be interpreted "in a figurative sense," and even then, should be understood "in terms of its relationship to that twofold love."[9] And in *Teaching Christianity* (*De Doctrina Christiana*), Augustine commends this interpretive approach to aspiring preachers.[10]

Christ's instruction enables us to attend to that which is of greatest importance in the Christian life. The expansiveness of Scripture, with all its instruction and demands, might appear overwhelming to the average Christian, resulting in indecisiveness or idleness. By elevating the call to love God and neighbor, however, Christ spurs us into action, as Augustine explains in *Sermon* 90A(D11/M40): "Mercy has put a stop to laziness; don't think any more about how long it will take you to learn them [the commandments], but rather about how to carry out what you have learned in a trice."[11] By interpreting Scripture in this way, Christ's purpose is not simply to enable us to read rightly, but to live rightly.

Indeed, Christ's call to love God and neighbor guides much of Augustine's instruction about the Christian life. This is reflected at the very beginning of the *Regulations for a Monastery*, where Augustine emphasizes the primacy of these two

---

5. *Serm.* 90A(D11/M40).1, 3.
6. *Serm.* 90A(D11/M40).2.
7. *Serm.* 90A(D11/M40).2. See also *Serm.* 9.7; 399.2–3.
8. *Serm.* 399.2. *Sermon* 399 shares a number of similarities with *Sermon* 90A(D11/M40). Van Bavel provides a commentary on *Sermon* 399: T. J. van Bavel, "Augustine on Christian Teaching and Life," *Augustinian Heritage* 37, no. 1 (1991): 89–112.
9. *Catech.* 26.50. For Augustine's "figurative" reading, see Harmless, *Augustine and the Catechumenate*, 213–14.
10. E.g., *Doctr. chr.* 1.35.39–1.36.40. For a brief comparison of Augustine's approach to love for God and neighbor in *Sermon* 90A(D11/M40) and in Book One of *Teaching Christianity* see Dupont, "Sermo 90A," 47–8.
11. *Serm.* 90A(D11/M40).2.

loves for the monastic community: "Before all else, dearest brothers, let God be loved and then your neighbor, because these are the chief commandments which have been given us."[12] Amidst the many other monastic guidelines Augustine provides, love of God and neighbor remains the fundamental and ultimate task of the Christian community. All other monastic precepts must be directed toward this end. Furthermore, the call to love God and neighbor must be emphasized at the outset, because without this love, the monastic rules will be pursued in vain. As Augustine instructs the wider congregation, "without this twin love, the law cannot be fulfilled."[13] A unified community that shares its resources with the needy is praiseworthy, yet unless it is motivated by and directed toward the love of God and neighbor, it cannot attain to that which is truly good.

As this chapter demonstrates, Christ's call to love God and neighbor also plays a broader interpretive function for Augustine, shaping his theological perspective as a whole.[14] When discussing the sickness of humanity in *Sermon* 278, he describes the call to love God and neighbor as two "prescriptions" that Christ, the doctor, has provided for the healing of "two sorts of sins: by one you sin against God, by the other against human beings."[15] Just as Augustine seeks to read Scripture in light of Christ's call to love God and neighbor, he also reads our human situation in this light. Sin has this dual orientation: in our turn toward self-interest, we have alienated ourselves from God and neighbor. Thus, when Augustine addresses the Christian community about issues of wealth and poverty, he is not simply concerned with the reallocation of resources, but more fundamentally about the restoration of these relationships, prescribing Christ's call to love God and neighbor as the necessary remedy.

Beginning with the Neighbor

Do the commandments to love God and to love neighbor compete with one another? Augustine poses this question to the congregation in *Sermon* 90A(D11/

---

12. *Reg. 2*: 1. Although as noted in the Introduction, the authorship of the *Regulations for a Monastery* has not been confirmed, this opening precept (*Reg.* 2: 1) is certainly consistent with Augustine's thought, as Zumkeller observes: "One cannot, in fact, formulate better the essence of Augustine's monastic legislation than by this, the Gospel's chief command." Zumkeller, *Augustine's Ideal of the Religious Life*, 260.

13. *Serm.* 125.10.

14. Harrison notes the "eudaemonistic" backdrop of Augustine's ethical thought (a philosophical approach concerned with "the nature of happiness"). Harrison, *Christian Truth and Fractured Humanity*, 79. However, Christ's command to love God and neighbor presented a fundamental challenge to the singular goal of eudaemonism, prompting both tensions and transformations in Augustine's use of this framework, as Oliver O'Donovan thoroughly documents in: Oliver O'Donovan, *The Problem of Self-Love in St. Augustine* (New Haven, CT: Yale University Press, 1980).

15. *Serm.* 278.6.

M40). "When you hear, *Love God with whole heart, whole soul, whole mind*, there seems to be no room for love of neighbor," Augustine observes.[16] Conversely, the congregation has also heard Paul instruct that "*Whoever loves neighbor has fulfilled the law* (Rom 13:8)"; and yet in his comprehensive call to love of neighbor (vv. 9–10), Paul makes no mention of love of God.[17] How is it possible, then, to faithfully obey both commandments? Does our love for God diminish the love with which we might love our neighbor? Does loving our neighbor inhibit us from fully devoting ourselves to God?[18] This tension can be observed as the contemporary church considers its calling amidst economic inequality. For some, the church's task is primarily an ethical one: we must love our neighbor more, and not waste time and resources on worship or theological contemplation. For others, it is these doxological tasks that are fundamental, and we must not allow social or political concerns to distract us from loving God. For Augustine, however, both views—and the dichotomy they presume—are problematic, as this chapter will illustrate.

But where does one who wants to respond to Christ's instruction to love God and neighbor begin? Contemplating the call to love God is a daunting task, Augustine acknowledges.[19] The question of love of neighbor, however, is more accessible to our human experience—"we've all got neighbors," Augustine notes—and so he proposes to begin there.[20]

Augustine does not understand "neighbor" in a literal or restrictive sense. For example, on one occasion, Augustine explains that "every human being" is our neighbor, even our enemy, for "we all derive from the first two parents" (Adam and Eve).[21] Because of this shared ancestry, the call to love our neighbor directs us toward the needs of all human beings.[22] Even when Augustine uses the familial term "brother," as in his *Homilies on the First Epistle of John*, he emphasizes the broad scope of this love: "You should love all people, even your enemies, not because they are your brothers but so that they may become your brothers."[23] Thus, for Augustine, the term "neighbor" (or "sister" or "brother") is not defined by our existing (and fragmented) pattern of social relationships; we cannot limit our love of neighbor, for example, to those already proximate to us. Rather, for Augustine to love the neighbor is to love every person, because every person has the potential to become our neighbor.

Loving our neighbor does not detract from our love for God; rather, Augustine notes in *Sermon* 90A(D11/M40), it is the necessary starting point. This observation

---

16. *Serm.* 90A(D11/M40).4.
17. *Serm.* 90A(D11/M40).4.
18. Dupont observes that this "apparent problem" that Augustine poses lends "a strong dynamism" to this sermon: Dupont, "Sermo 90A," 36.
19. *Serm.* 90A(D11/M40).5.
20. *Serm.* 90A(D11/M40).5.
21. *Serm.* 149.18.
22. Although, in *Teaching Christianity*, Augustine does observe that proximity often plays a role in discerning which neighbor to love (*Doctr. chr.* 1.28.29).
23. *Tract. ep. Jo.* 10.7. See also *Tract. ep. Jo.* 1.9; 8.10.

arises from 1 John 4:20: "*if you do not love the brother whom you can see, how will you be able to love the God whom you cannot see?*"[24] Although learning to love the unseen God may seem a difficult task, the neighbor whom we can see before us provides an occasion for the exercise of love to begin. In the neighbor, we learn to love, and in learning to love, to love God.[25] Thus in 1 John 4:20 Augustine finds "a rule to follow: let us start from our neighbor, in order to arrive at God."[26]

But what does it mean to *love* our neighbor?[27] Here, Augustine begins to unravel our assumptions. We might equate love of neighbor with a general concern for humanity, for example, or a sort of basic human social bond. "What's so great about that?" Augustine provocatively asks and notes the "mutual love" that creatures ordinarily share.[28] A general respect and affinity for other human beings, though not to be belittled, is not the sort of love that Augustine believes Christ is calling us toward.

Nor can love of neighbor be equated with familial affection; again, Augustine observes, this is not especially noteworthy, for even "tigers love their cubs."[29] But Augustine probes this answer further: "how can you prove that you love your son?" he asks his imaginary interlocutor.[30] The answer Augustine anticipates is that this parent was setting aside "an inheritance" for their child.[31] Is love for one's child evidenced by accumulating wealth on their behalf? Can this be regarded as love of neighbor? Again, Augustine finds this explanation wanting, and proceeds to consider this question in greater depth.[32]

We Cannot Be Trusted with Our Neighbor

Returning again to Christ's words, Augustine finds further guidance: "This is the rule: *You shall love your neighbor as yourself*" (Mt. 22:39).[33] Whether you truly love

---

24. *Serm.* 90A(D11/M40).5.
25. *Serm.* 90A(D11/M40).12; *Tract. ep. Jo.* 9.10. See discussion below.
26. *Serm.* 90A(D11/M40).5.
27. O'Donovan discusses the different words Augustine uses for love ("*dilectio*," "*caritas*," "*amor*"). O'Donovan, *Problem of Self-Love*, 10–11. Although "different strands" may be observed in Augustine's understanding of love, O'Donovan explains that "such distinctions cannot be made simply on the basis of vocabulary alone" (p. 10). O'Donovan notes different "nuances" in Augustine's use of these words, but he suggests that "considerations of style rather than of theological content are predominant" (p. 11). See also *Civ.* 14.7.
28. *Serm.* 90A(D11/M40).6.
29. *Serm.* 90A(D11/M40).6.
30. *Serm.* 90A(D11/M40).6.
31. *Serm.* 90A(D11/M40).6.
32. *Serm.* 90A(D11/M40).6. Canning discusses Augustine's contrast between love for family and "Christian love" (with reference to *Tract. Ev. Jo.* 65.1). Canning, *Unity of Love for God and Neighbour*, 177–8.
33. *Serm.* 90A(D11/M40).7.

your neighbor depends on whether you truly love yourself; "the whole question turns on this point," Augustine insists.[34] Thus we must consider the nature of our love for self.[35] Yet this self-examination is not a departure from the needs of others; rather, we must engage this question for the sake of our neighbor. Indeed, Augustine reminds his listeners in *Sermon* 399, because we are to consider all people neighbors, we must take this question all the more seriously: "How important it is to examine whether you love yourself, since so many neighbors are to be entrusted to you, for you to love them as yourself."[36] To truly love the neighbors placed in our care, the question of our love for self is critical.

For as Augustine proceeds to reveal in *Sermon* 90A(D11/M40), although we might think we know what it means to love our self, we may again be mistaken. His listeners, he anticipates, would claim to love themselves, saying: "When I'm hungry I feed my body, because I love myself. I don't want to be worn out with toil, because I love myself. I don't want to be trapped in poverty, because I love myself."[37] However, when love of self is conceived in this manner, we are not loving ourselves, but hating ourselves, Augustine claims, quoting the psalmist: "*For whoever loves iniquity hates his own soul* (Ps 11:5)."[38]

In what sense can these seemingly innocuous conceptions of self-love (ensuring material well-being, avoiding hardship, etc.) be considered iniquitous? For Augustine such formulations of self-love are problematic because they are not oriented toward God. In his earlier contrast with the love displayed by animals, Augustine notes that unlike animals (over which humankind has "power" (Gen. 1:26-28)), God has made humanity "according to his image."[39] "Notice what you have under you," he instructs, "and by what love of his image you yourself have been very differently conformed to the creator."[40] In what way have human beings, as bearers of God's image, been "differently conformed to the creator"? Augustine does not elaborate here. However, he provides a clear statement in his *Homilies on*

---

34. *Serm.* 90A(D11/M40).7.

35. Love of self takes a variety of forms in Augustine's thought. Burnaby provides a threefold classification that is widely recognized: Burnaby, *Amor Dei*, 117-26. The first form of self-love Burnaby describes is "natural and morally neutral," and is characterized by "self-preservation" (p. 118). The second, "morally wrong" form is likened to "self-assertion," a rejection of God in favor of self (pp. 118-21). The third form is "morally right," and occurs when the self loves God, thus loving oneself truly (pp. 118, 121-6). While approving Burnaby's classification, O'Donovan goes on to identify "four aspects of love" in the work of Augustine (each aspect relating to Burnaby's three forms in different ways), allowing him to examine the nuances of self-love in greater detail: O'Donovan, *Problem of Self-Love*, 18-36. This reveals the complexity of self-love in Augustine's thought, leading O'Donovan to conclude that "it is not in itself a finished, self-conscious theological artifact" (p. 138).

36. *Serm.* 399.4.

37. *Serm.* 90A(D11/M40).7.

38. *Serm.* 90A(D11/M40).7. See also *Trin.* 14.14.18.

39. *Serm.* 90A(D11/M40).6.

40. *Serm.* 90A(D11/M40).6.

the First Epistle of John: "But where has he [man] been made to the image of God? In his understanding, in his mind, in the inner man, in that which understands the truth, distinguishes righteousness and unrighteousness, knows by whom he was made, and is able to understand his creator and to praise his creator."[41] "Mind is image of God in its capacity to remember, understand, and love God," Stephen J. Duffy explains.[42] However, as Augustine explains in *Sermon* 90, this image of God within us is "defaced" and "worn down" by "earthly desires."[43] Hence the "*iniquity*" of the expressions of self-love that Augustine cites in *Sermon* 90A(D11/M40).[44] For his imagined interlocutor, self-love is a matter of securing food, labor, wealth, and health.[45] All these things are good, and part of God's good creation.[46] However, when our attention becomes fixed upon them, rather than upon God, we no longer live in the manner for which God created us. Our love becomes "disordered," oriented toward our self and lesser goods, rather than toward God, who is our true good.[47] The self-love of the interlocutor shows no regard for God

---

41. *Tract. ep. Jo.* 8.6.

42. Stephen J. Duffy, "Anthropology," in *Augustine through the Ages*, ed. Allan D. Fitzgerald (Grand Rapids, MI: Eerdmans, 1999), 28. Williams explains that "the image of God in us is not a structure of correspondence between our minds and God's mind; it is the mind completely caught up in contemplating God—aware of itself before God, opening its intelligence to God…, directed in love towards God." Williams, *On Augustine*, 136. This image and its "renewal" within us is an important theme in *The Trinity* (e.g., *Trin.* 14.17.23); see discussion in Khaled Anatolios, *Retrieving Nicaea: The Development and Meaning of Trinitarian Doctrine* (Grand Rapids, MI: Baker Academic, 2011), 258–62, 267–70, 278; Charry, *By the Renewing of Your Minds*, 144–7; Williams, *On Augustine*, 131–40, 173–5; Zumkeller, *Augustine's Ideal of the Religious Life*, 172–4.

43. *Serm.* 90.10.

44. *Serm.* 90A(D11/M40).7.

45. *Serm.* 90A(D11/M40).7.

46. Augustine does not see material goods as themselves evil: see, for example, *Serm.* 50.6–7. See also Chapter 3 for further discussion.

47. Augustine does not specifically employ the language of "ordered" or "disordered" love in *Sermon* 90A(D11/M40). However, he expresses this concept clearly in *Sermon* 21, where he urges listeners to order their love for created goods toward God: "God made you as something good under him, and he made something lower on the scale, under you as well. You are under one, you are over another. Don't give up the higher good and bow yourself down to the lower good…. How is it that you sin, after all, but by treating the things you have received for your use in a disordered way, or out of turn?" (*Serm.* 21.3). See also *Doctr. chr.* 1.26.27–27.28; *Civ.* 15.22. Harrison provides a summary of the development of this theme in Augustine's thought: Harrison, *Christian Truth and Fractured Humanity*, 97–100. O'Donovan's description of the "four aspects of love" in the work of Augustine provides helpful insight into the different (and developing) ways in which Augustine employs the concept of ordered love: O'Donovan, *Problem of Self-Love*, 18–36. In relation to a disordered love of self, see also pp. 60–7. For Augustine's understanding of the ordered nature of reality, see further discussion in Chapter 5, and also D. J. MacQueen, "Contemptus Dei: St

or neighbor; rather, it is defined as the self preserving the self, the self providing for the self, the self protecting the self: "When I'm hungry I feed my body, because I love myself."[48] For Augustine, this is not true self-love, but rather self-deception. For attempting to love oneself apart from God is a ruinous endeavor, as he later explains: "If you lower your love down from there [God] to yourself, you won't be in him, but in yourself; so that's when you will perish, because you will be in a place of perishing."[49]

This iniquitous love also has consequences for our neighbor, as Augustine indicates in *Sermon* 90A(D11/M40). God is the good that is common to all, "the good which belongs in its entirety to each and every one, however many more come to possess it."[50] By contrast, material goods, by their very nature, are subject to diminishment. Thus, Augustine believes that the riches that the wealthy accrue come at the expense of others; "you can't have gold unless someone else loses it," he states in another sermon.[51] When we try to secure material goods for ourselves, we deny these goods to others. Therefore, the interlocutor's disordered love for these lesser goods makes them party to an economy of iniquity: "If you want to thrive on another person's misfortunes, if you want things to go badly with someone else so that they may go well with you … you are loving iniquity, hating your own soul."[52] Iniquity begets iniquity. A misdirected form of self-love is not only injurious to oneself; it also inflicts harm on others.

If this is the nature of our self-love, then we are unable to truly love our neighbor. Indeed, attempting to love our neighbor as our self in *this* sense results in a fundamental contradiction, for if they attain the material prosperity we desire,

---

Augustine on the Disorder of Pride in Society, and Its Remedies," *Recherches Augustiniennes et Patristiques* 9 (1973): 230–7; N. Joseph Torchia, "The *Commune/Proprium* Distinction in St. Augustine's Early Moral Theology," in *Studia Patristica 22*, ed. Elizabeth A. Livingstone (Leuven: Peeters, 1989), 356–63. Clair observes that whereas scholars sometimes present Augustine's teaching on "properly ordered love" in a "mechanical" fashion, "this rendition of how Augustine treats the moral life turns out to be oversimplified and misguided when viewed through his letters and sermons." Clair, *Discerning the Good*, 1.

48. *Serm.* 90A(D11/M40).7.
49. *Serm.* 90A(D11/M40).9. Duffy explains for Augustine, "all choices and acts are born of desire, appetite, and hence are rooted in love, either in the love that grace alone makes possible, *caritas*, or in sinful love, *cupiditas*." Duffy, "Anthropology," 30. Harrison notes how Augustine's view differs from our typical modern conception of the will: Harrison, *Christian Truth and Fractured Humanity*, 92. She later adds: "For Augustine the will is synonymous with love; to will is not just to rationally deliberate and choose to act, rather it is to love something and to be moved to act on the basis of that love" (pp. 94–5). Gregory observes that "the problem of political morality for an Augustinian is not so much that that we love others too little," but rather "that we love too much in the wrong ways." Gregory, *Politics and the Order of Love: An Augustinian Ethic of Democratic Citizenship*, 39.
50. *Serm.* 90A(D11/M40).8.
51. *Serm.* 32.21.
52. *Serm.* 90A(D11/M40).7.

our own material prosperity may be diminished. Augustine describes the irony of this conflicted situation brilliantly for his congregation:

> You want the person you love to have as much as you have, even if you don't want to give him half of what you have. You see, you don't want him to grow rich at your expense, you don't want his good to be to the detriment of your good. Why is this? Because you reckon gold to be a good thing, the reason you consider yourself a great guy is that you possess gold; you want him to increase, not yourself to decrease.[53]

Although Augustine's listeners might genuinely want to love their neighbor, they may find themselves hindered by their disordered love: a love that no longer has God, the common good, in view, but rather one's own private good.

Such disordered desires not only hinder us from helping our neighbor; they in fact contribute to our neighbor's demise. Even though we might see ourselves as healthy benefactors, our true state may be more dire than the destitute neighbor we hope to serve. Consumed by love for lesser goods, we will (mis)lead our neighbor in the same direction, as Augustine explains: "After all, you cannot but wish to draw the person you love to what you yourself love. And you love iniquity; that's what you are going to bring the person whom you love as yourself."[54] If we love ourselves by accruing material possessions and seeking a lavish lifestyle, the neighbor we are trying to love will inevitably be drawn toward the same vision of the good life. If this is the case, Augustine declares to his congregation, "I'm not entrusting your neighbor to you."[55] If we cannot love our self rightly, we will be a liability to our neighbor—and then, Augustine laments to his congregation, he will have not one lost person to seek out, but two.[56]

Leaving Home

Now in the midst of *Sermon* 90A(D11/M40), Augustine's underlying pastoral concern comes to the fore. Set apart from God, we are unable to truly love our self, let alone our neighbor. "If you stay in your own company, you are entrusting yourself to yourself, you're going to lose yourself, you're not a suitable person to look after yourself."[57] To illustrate this situation for the congregation, Augustine draws on the parable of the prodigal son: "Call to mind how he went off and got lost, the one that said to the father who was looking after him, *Give me the sum*

---

53. *Serm.* 90A(D11/M40).8.
54. *Serm.* 90A(D11/M40).8. See also the *Confessions*, where Augustine recalls his misleading influence on friends (*Conf.* 4.4.7; 6.12.21).
55. *Serm.* 90A(D11/M40).7.
56. *Serm.* 90A(D11/M40).7.
57. *Serm.* 90A(D11/M40).9.

that concerns me (Lk 15:12)."[58] This parable provides a rich depiction of our self-imposed alienation from God, along with the diminishment that results, and the call to return.[59] Although *Sermon* 90A(D11/M40) discusses the parable fairly briefly, other sermons that draw on the prodigal son narrative offer glimpses of these developing themes in Augustine's preaching.[60]

The parable begins with the younger son at home with his father. In *Sermon* 90A(D11/M40), Augustine offers little comment on this original location of the son, simply noting that the father "was looking after him."[61] Similarly, in *Sermon* 96, he briefly observes that the property of the son "was being kept very well for him with his father."[62] However, Augustine regularly reminds his congregation of the goodness found in God's company, an observation he underscores with reference to Psalm 73:28: "*For me, though, to cling to God is good.*"[63] This verse becomes a recurring motif in *The City of God*, and in this work, Augustine depicts the goodness of our original state in creation more fully: "In paradise, then, man lived as he wanted for as long as what he wanted was at one with God's command. He lived in the enjoyment of God, from whose goodness he himself was good. He lived without any lack, and he had it in his power to live this way forever."[64] Human life can be described here as good because it is lived in the company of God who is good, and accordingly is characterized by freedom, enjoyment, and absence of need. God is also a good that is enjoyed in common; those who enjoy God are drawn together into a "holy society both with him to whom they cling and with each other."[65] Through this communion with God comes communion with one another.[66]

However, the younger son spurns this goodness found in his father's company, and sets out on his own.[67] In Augustine's teaching, this movement depicts

---

58. *Serm.* 90A(D11/M40).10.

59. For Augustine's use of this parable, see also *Conf.* 1.18.28; 3.6.11; 4.16.30; 5.12.22; 8.3.6.

60. I focus particularly here on *Sermons* 96, 142, 179A, and 330. In locating these sermons within the broader evolution of negative self-love in Augustine's thought, I am indebted to O'Donovan's detailed commentary in O'Donovan, *Problem of Self-Love*, 93–111. However, as noted in the Introduction, it is difficult to date the *Sermons* with confidence: see Drobner, "The Chronology of St. Augustine's Sermones ad Populum," 211–18. Thus, I do not attempt to offer an account of the historical development of this theme within the *Sermons*. Note that Markus argues that this negative self-love emerges earlier in Augustine's work than O'Donovan suggests. Markus, "Pride and the Common Good," 248–51.

61. *Serm.* 90A(D11/M40).10.

62. *Serm.* 96.2.

63. *Serm.* 156.7.

64. *Civ.* 14.26. For Psalm 73:28 in *The City of God* see especially *Civ.* 10.25.

65. *Civ.* 12.9.

66. This communion is also reflected in the original harmony of relationship between Adam, Eve, and God, as described in *The City of God* (*Civ.* 14.10, 26).

67. *Serm.* 90A(D11/M40).10.

humanity's fall. William S. Babcock observes that, for Augustine, "the start of human evil" is not found "in the open and public forum of the deed," but "in the hidden and secret chamber of the will."[68] This "fall of the will," Babcock explains, takes the form of "a turn from the greater to the lesser good, from God to self," a movement that "is at once an act of self-assertion and an act of self-deprivation."[69] In this turn toward self, we distance ourselves from God; as Augustine notes of the younger son in *Sermon* 90A(D11/M40), "his preferring his own company took him a long way away from his father."[70] In other sermons, Augustine interprets this departure in light of 2 Timothy 3:2, where Paul begins a litany of sins with the statement, "*There will be people loving themselves.*"[71] Noting the principal place of self-love in this sequence, Augustine gives it greater attention in *Sermon* 330 and 179A, where he describes love of self as "the core" or "one source" of evil.[72] In *Sermon* 96, he preaches this message even more plainly: "Man's first ruin was caused by love of self."[73]

Augustine presents this negative form of self-love most dramatically in *The City of God*, where the "earthly city" is characterized by "love of self, even to the point of contempt for God."[74] John Burnaby comments that in Augustine this form of self-love, directly opposed to love of God, "is neither egoism nor egocentrism, but 'egotheism'—not selfishness but blasphemous rebellion."[75] Similarly, Oliver O'Donovan makes the valuable observation that when Augustine is talking of self-love in this sense, it is a "*comparative* evaluation"; the problem is not that the worldly city loves itself, but that it "loves itself so much that it despises God by comparison."[76] This dynamic, though less pronounced than in *The City of God*, can be observed in these sermons when Augustine alerts his listeners to the dangers of this self-love. For example, in *Sermon* 142, he explains that "pride ... had itself

---

68. William S. Babcock, "Augustine on Sin and Moral Agency," *The Journal of Religious Ethics* 16, no. 1 (1988): 42. For Augustine's understanding of sin, see also James Wetzel, "Sin," in *Augustine through the Ages*, ed. Allan D. Fitzgerald (Grand Rapids, MI: Eerdmans, 1999), 800–2.

69. Babcock, "Augustine on Sin and Moral Agency," 42.

70. *Serm.* 90A(D11/M40).10. Augustine will often clarify that, although we may depart from God, God remains ever present with us (e.g., *Conf.* 13.1.1).

71. *Serm.* 330.3.

72. *Serm.* 330.3; 179A.4.

73. *Serm.* 96.2.

74. *Civ.* 14.28.

75. Burnaby, *Amor Dei*, 121. This is the second form of self-love in Burnaby's schema (noted above).

76. O'Donovan, *Problem of Self-Love*, 64. In addition to the descriptions provided by Burnaby and O'Donovan, I have also found helpful the accounts that MacQueen and Markus provide of the dynamics of this negative self-love: MacQueen, "Contemptus Dei," 237–59; Markus, *End of Ancient Christianity*, 50–1; Markus, "Pride and the Common Good," 245–59.

made the human heart exalt itself against God and turn away from life."[77] Similarly, in *Sermon* 96, the one who "loved himself" is described as having "turned away to disregarding God's will and doing his own."[78]

When we turn away from God we become lost (Lk. 15:24, 32), because when we depart from God, we also depart from ourselves. "If you fall away from your God, you very soon fall away from yourself too, and turn your back even on yourself," Augustine notes in *Sermon* 90A(D11/M40).[79] In the prodigal son narrative, the phrase *"returning to himself"* (Lk. 15:17) alerts us to this second departure, Augustine explains: "'Returning to himself'; you can see that he had even turned his back on himself."[80] In *Sermons* 96, 179A, and 330, Augustine continues to follow the sequence of 2 Timothy 3:2 to depict this inevitable second movement. For example, in *Sermon* 179A, Augustine comments first on the opening phrase of 2 Timothy 3:2: "There you are, you've chosen to love yourself. Let's see if you even manage to remain in yourself. It's not true, you can't remain there; fallen away from God, you've also fallen away from yourself."[81] This subsequent fall is indicated by Paul's second phrase, Augustine explains: "After saying *For people will be in love with themselves,* he immediately added, *lovers of money* (2 Tm 3:2)."[82] Though at first we thought we were loving ourselves, our love is soon given over to money (or other worldly goods). And so, Augustine observes, we begin to "disintegrate with dissipation," arriving at the dissolute state of the younger son: "Just look, you've even become lost to yourself, once you have withdrawn from God. What's left for you, but to squander the inheritance of your mind, living recklessly with harlots, that is to say with lusts and various greedy desires, and to be compelled by want to feed pigs?"[83]

A State of Deprivation

Within Augustine's thought, the problem of economic inequality is best situated at this low ebb of the prodigal son narrative, which is characterized by both extravagant expenditure (Lk. 15:13), and severe want (vv. 14–16).[84] In our modern context, discussions of economic inequality tend to focus (understandably) on the immediate material dimensions of the problem. Useful as these contributions are, their field of vision is truncated. Such attempts can be likened to an attempt to

---

77. *Serm.* 142.2.
78. *Serm.* 96.2.
79. *Serm.* 90A(D11/M40).10. See also *Conf.* 5.2.2.
80. *Serm.* 90A(D11/M40).10.
81. *Serm.* 179A.4.
82. *Serm.* 179A.4.
83. *Serm.* 96.2; 179A.4.
84. Our situation differs from the paradisiacal state of Adam and Eve; Burnaby explains that "we do not begin with 'adherence to God', but in a state of separation from Him." Burnaby, *Amor Dei,* 187.

analyze the younger son's plight in verses 13–16, without paying attention to the broader narrative context. What economic system encouraged the younger son's prodigal spending, we might ask? Should he have been subject to an inheritance tax? What welfare systems were in place to protect him from famine? These are important questions, which the church is right to consider. But to focus *solely* on these questions is to assume that we ourselves are "okay," and not in need of examination.

By contrast, for Augustine, those who have departed from God are far from healthy. This vitiated state is vividly depicted in *Sermon* 142, when Augustine alerts his congregation to the consequences of our prideful departure from God. This movement is a "turn away from life," and the soul now finds itself in a "state of debility."[85] Augustine again describes this disintegration of the self in two stages:

> You see, it [the soul] had looked at itself, and been very pleased with itself, and become a lover of its own power. It has drawn away from him [the Lord], and has not remained in itself; that's why it is both driven out of itself, and excluded from itself and pushed sliding down the slippery slope into things outside itself.[86]

As he continues, Augustine indicates in a striking passage that this debilitated self is no longer capable of living justly: "So, being driven out of itself, in a manner of speaking it lost itself; and because it doesn't even know how to take a look at its own actions, it justifies its iniquities. It grows insolent and proud in self-will and self-indulgence, in positions of rank and authority and wealth, in vain and empty power."[87] The message is clear: when divided from God, we become unable to see ourselves clearly. Our behavior becomes self-serving, and disregards both God and neighbor. As this passage implies, the ramifications are far-reaching, as the self seeks to dominate others, accruing wealth and power for itself, and justifying its unjust

---

85. *Serm.* 142.2. Augustine consistently reminds his congregation that God is good and that all that God has created is good (e.g., *Serm.* 29.1). As he instructs his readers in the *Enchiridion on Faith, Hope, and Charity*, evil is not created by God, and so has no substance in itself; accordingly, evil can only exist as a corruption of something good (*Enchir.* 3.9–4.14). The evil of economic inequality, then, cannot exist in itself, but only as the contamination of something which God has created good. Understanding evil this way shapes our understanding of the response needed; for Augustine, "evil is eliminated ... by healing and rectifying the nature that had become vitiated and depraved" (*Civ.* 14.11).

86. *Serm.* 142.3. Disintegration necessarily results from this departure because, as Burnaby explains, "all things that are have being because they are from God." Burnaby, *Amor Dei*, 37. Thus Burnaby describes sin as the soul's "movement towards disintegration—a verging *ad nihilum*, an 'unmaking'" (p. 37). Commenting on the society that is not oriented toward God, MacQueen states that "such a community is ontologically unstable." MacQueen, "Contemptus Dei," 257. MacQueen later describes traits of the society marked by this instability or "disorder": see pp. 259–78. Augustine explains elsewhere that "the punishment of every disordered mind is its own disorder" (*Conf.* 1.12.19). See Babcock, "Augustine on Sin and Moral Agency," 38.

87. *Serm.* 142.3.

actions. Our turn away from God toward self is not merely a "spiritual" problem; it impairs every aspect of our existence, including the economic and political.

As earlier noted, in some sermons, following 2 Timothy 3:2, Augustine identifies perilous self-love as the cause of our ruinous circumstances; "the apostle traced all evil back to that one source," he explains.[88] However, on other occasions he makes specific reference to the dynamics of pride or avarice as he attempts to describe this self-love (see especially Chapters 5 and 3, for examples). His emphasis on pride and avarice is not arbitrary, but rather arises out of his reading of Scripture: he notes that Sirach 10:13 describes pride as *"The beginning of every sin,"* and that 1 Timothy 6:10 identifies avarice as *"the root of all evils."*[89] Augustine does not see disagreement in these two passages, as he explains in Sermon 198(D26/M62):

> That pride, though, is the first sin is stated openly somewhere else: *The beginning of every sin is pride* (Sir 10:13). And how then is *avarice the root of all evils* (1 Tm 6:10)? Because to want more than God is avarice, to want more than is enough is avarice. Only God, after all, is enough for the soul, which is why Philip says, *Show us the Father, and it is enough for us* (Jn 14:8). But what could be prouder than to forsake God through overweening self-confidence? What more avaricious than not being satisfied with God? Pride, therefore, is the same thing as avarice at the origin of sins.[90]

---

88. *Serm.* 179A.4; see also *Serm.* 96.2; 330.3.

89. *Serm.* 198(D26/M62).33. Augustine's quotation of Sirach 10:13 differs from modern translations. J. F. Procopé provides a brief account of how this phrase came to be inverted in the Latin text used by Augustine: J. F. Procopé, "*Initium omnis peccati superbia*," in *Studia Patristica 22*, ed. Elizabeth A. Livingstone (Leuven: Peeters, 1989), 315.

90. *Serm.* 198(D26/M62).33. Scholars offer various explanations of the roles of pride and avarice in Augustine's account of sin's origin. John C. Cavadini states that avarice is "a form of pride, and only as such is it the origin of sin." John C. Cavadini, "Pride," in *Augustine through the Ages*, ed. Allan D. Fitzgerald (Grand Rapids, MI: Eerdmans, 1999), 680. MacQueen writes that "avarice in a more generalized sense is indistinguishable from pride," but identifies pride as the "source." MacQueen, "Contemptus Dei," 249, 238. In a more recent article, Jesse Couenhoven presents the argument that "while Augustine probably did believe, in his earlier years, that pride is the basic sin, he changed his views during his debates with the Pelagians and advocated instead the thesis that sin, post-fall, does not take on any one form." Jesse Couenhoven, "'Not Every Wrong Is Done with Pride': Augustine's Proto-Feminist Anti-Pelagianism," *Scottish Journal of Theology* 61, no. 1 (2008): 33. Couenhoven acknowledges feminist scholars who have argued that the theological stress on pride as the "basic sin" does not take into account the experience of women (pp. 33–6). Couenhoven's article seeks to illustrate that Augustine himself developed a broader view. I note that, in Augustine's attempts to describe this fundamental departure from God, he is trying to explain something that he views as ultimately inexplicable in cause (*Civ.* 12.6–9; see Babcock, "Augustine on Sin and Moral Agency," 41–7). Thus, while for Augustine, language of pride and avarice best expresses this fundamental movement of sin, sin is not reducible to these concepts as we typically understand them. See also *Gen. litt.* 11.15.19.

The nature of our fall from God comes into clearer focus when read through the lenses of both pride and avarice. While the desire denoted by pride can be distinguished from that of avarice, what they share is the fundamental refusal of relationship with God, motivated by the mistaken belief that "more" can be found by turning toward oneself.[91]

This self-interested departure from God also marks a departure from our neighbor. Markus notes Augustine's increasing awareness of the way sinful self-interest jeopardizes human community, and identifies the significance of *The Literal Meaning of Genesis* (begun 401) in Augustine's development of this understanding.[92] "He now searched for the roots of human sin in man's liability to close in on himself," Markus writes.[93] In his account of the fall in Book 11 of this commentary, Augustine again draws on Sirach 10:13 and 1 Timothy 6:10, as he tries to describe sin's origin:

> Rightly has scripture designated pride as the beginning of all sin, saying, *The beginning of all sin is pride* (Sir 10:13). Into this text can be slotted rather neatly that other one also from the apostle: *The root of all evils is avarice* (1 Tm 6:10), if we understand avarice in a general sense as what goads people to go for anything more greedily than is right because of their superiority and a kind of love for their very own property.[94]

At this intersection of pride and avarice, Augustine locates the "ruinous self-love," which seeks its own status and private property apart from God.[95] The word "private" is very apt, Augustine notes, for it suggests "loss rather than gain in value; every privation, after all, spells diminution."[96] This movement away from God is a loss because it is a departure "from what is common [*communi*] to what is its own property [*proprium*]."[97] Markus thus comments: "Sin is seen as a

---

91. See also *Civ.* 14.13. Considering Augustine's reflections on the proud and avaricious nature of sin, MacQueen observes: "These definitions, then, confirm the fact that the 'love' or 'will' characterizing Satan and his angels is above all else a 'love of self.'" MacQueen, "Contemptus Dei," 239. In this book, following Augustine's reading of 2 Timothy 3:2, I primarily speak of "self-love" or "self-interest" to denote this fundamental dynamic of sin, rather than avarice or pride.

92. Markus, *End of Ancient Christianity*, 51. For this development, see also Markus, "Pride and the Common Good," 247–52. As noted in the Introduction, I am indebted to Markus for helping me appreciate this aspect of Augustine's thought.

93. Markus, *End of Ancient Christianity*, 51.

94. *Gen. litt.* 11.15.19.

95. *Gen. litt.* 11.15.19.

96. *Gen. litt.* 11.15.19.

97. *Gen. litt.* 11.15.19 (*PL* 34:437). See also *Civ.* 12.1; *Trin.* 12.9.14. Torchia surveys Augustine's use of "*proprium*" and "*commune*," noting the philosophical context of this contrast: Torchia, "The Commune/Proprium Distinction," 356–63. Torchia explains that "one's *proprium*, that is, that which pertains exclusively to oneself, refers to one's property,

withdrawal into a 'privacy' which is a deprivation. By it all community is fatally ruptured: man's community with God, community with his fellow-men, with his own self."[98]

In this passage Augustine again draws on 2 Timothy 3:2 to illustrate that, in the case of humankind, this "general avarice, of which pride is the source" leads to a "particular kind" of avarice, namely, love of money.[99] He explains: "Not even human beings, after all, would be lovers of money, unless they thought that the richer they were, the more superior they would be too."[100] Notably, he contrasts this disordered love with 1 Corinthians 13:4–5: "In contrast with this disease *charity does not seek her own*, that is, does not rejoice in private pre-eminence and superiority; and rightly therefore is also *not puffed up* (1 Cor 13:5.4)."[101] He then places these "two loves" in striking juxtaposition: "one social, the other private, one taking thought for the common good because of the companionship in the upper regions, the other putting even what is common at its own personal disposal because of its lordly arrogance … one of them wanting for its neighbor what it wants for itself, the other wanting to subject its neighbor to itself."[102] In *The City of God*, Augustine develops these themes into an expansive theological critique of human society.[103] Love distinguishes the two cities: "in one the love of God comes before all else and in the other love of self."[104] In the former is found "a love that rejoices in the common and immutable good and joins many hearts into one"; the latter,

---

personal possession, or private interest" (p. 358). Conversely, "the *commune*, that is, the common and public, refers to that which is experienced by all who perceive something, without any deterioration or change in the thing" (p. 358). Torchia later notes that for Augustine, "sin entails a narrowing of one's vision to a circumscribed sphere of private concerns" (p. 362). See also Brown, *Through the Eye of a Needle*, 177–83; Canning, "St. Augustine's Vocabulary of the Common Good," 48–54; Canning, "Common Good," 219–22.

98. Markus, *End of Ancient Christianity*, 51. Markus observes elsewhere that "the emphasis in his [Augustine's] later writings is on sin as isolation, the retreat of the self from community into privacy, from 'sociable' openness into self-enclosure." Markus, "Pride and the Common Good," 251. For additional reflections on this *Gen. litt.* passage see Burnaby, *Amor Dei*, 120–1; Harrison, *Christian Truth and Fractured Humanity*, 190.

99. *Gen. litt.* 11.15.19.
100. *Gen. litt.* 11.15.19.
101. *Gen. litt.* 11.15.19.
102. *Gen. litt.* 11.15.20.
103. Harrison suggests that Augustine's intention in *The City of God* was not to write "a work of political philosophy," but rather "to demonstrate the unrealizability of classical ideas of the State." Harrison, *Christian Truth and Fractured Humanity*, 220.
104. *Civ.* 14.13.

however, is characterized by pursuit of private good, and is consequently "divided against itself by lawsuits, wars and conflicts."[105]

The Call to Return

As earlier noted, apart from God, we are "lost."[106] In another sermon, Augustine suggests that, having wandered *"into a far country* (Lk 15:13)," we have contracted "amnesia," forgetting the home from whence we came.[107] However, he continues, "this amnesia is driven from our hearts by the Lord Christ, king of that country, as he comes to join us in our exile."[108] God "goes in pursuit of those who have run away," and "finds those who have got lost."[109] "God's is the only love that is utterly without self-regard," Rowan Williams comments.[110] "He seeks us, urgently, relentlessly, passionately, out of the changeless movement of a love that seeks the joy and fulfilment of everything in its createdness and limitation," Williams adds.[111] Through the call to love God and neighbor, Christ beckons us to return,[112] directing our love toward the one who is truly good: *"You shall love the Lord your God with your whole heart, with your whole soul and with your whole mind* (Mt 22:37)."[113]

---

105. *Civ.* 15.3, 4. It is not always clear in Augustine's various discussions of the fundamental dynamics of sin whether he has the fall of the angels in view, or the fall of Adam and Eve, or characteristics of ongoing human sinfulness—or indeed whether he would intend such distinctions. MacQueen explains that while there is "a general similarity" between Adam's pride and our own, pride manifests itself differently in our post-fall context; whereas Adam's sin could only be an "inordinate desire for a spiritual good," we have "lost the wisdom which Adam once enjoyed," and so our pride is borne out amidst our misguided pursuit of lesser goods. MacQueen, "Contemptus Dei," 247–8, 252. Cavadini notes of pride that "after the first sin of the devil and of Adam and Eve, it is rarely committed alone but is rather the form of all subsequent sin, obsessively reenacted in every particular sin." Cavadini, "Pride," 679. Note also Couenhoven's interpretation: Couenhoven, "Not Every Wrong Is Done with Pride," 38.
106. *Serm.* 90A(D11/M40).10.
107. *Serm.* 362.4.
108. *Serm.* 362.4. Regarding Augustine's emphasis on Christ's role in enabling us to recognize our plight and to find our way home (discussed in these next two sections), I have found the following discussions helpful: Anatolios, *Retrieving Nicaea*, 241–80; Williams, *On Augustine*, especially pp. 11–14, 141–53.
109. *Serm.* 216.11.
110. Williams, *On Augustine*, 209. n.b. This quotation and the quotation that follows from p. 209 are drawn from the sermon that concludes Williams's volume. See also pp. 72–5, 149.
111. Williams, *On Augustine*, 209.
112. *Conf.* 4.11.16; 4.12.18.
113. *Serm.* 90A(D11/M40).9. See *Catech.* 4.8; and see also *Sermon* 348 where Augustine juxtaposes love of God and neighbor with the love of "oneself in oneself" (*Serm.* 348.2).

Christ's call awakens us from our private, self-oriented existence, bringing us to our senses, and revealing the true nature of our situation.[114] In *Teaching Christianity*, Augustine locates this moment of revelation at the outset of the journey of Christian formation: "One first has to discover oneself, in the scriptures, as tied up in love of this world, that is of temporal things, and far removed from such love of God and such love of neighbor as scripture itself prescribes."[115] Christ encounters us through the preaching and reading of Scripture,[116] enabling us to see the disordered nature of our love. The unsettling realization that we have exchanged the abundance of the father's house for a desperate life among the pigs begins to sink in. It is in this moment of *"returning to himself"* (Lk. 15:17) that the younger son's turn toward home begins; this is his "first step in correcting himself."[117] Because our lost state is such that we have even fallen away from ourselves, this returning to ourselves is a necessary part of our return. "That's why such people are told, *Come back, transgressors, to the heart* (Is 46:8)," Augustine explains, "come back to yourselves, so that you may be able to come back to the one who made you."[118] Yet Augustine's emphasis on the revelatory role of Christ

---

114. "In calling us out of this condition of exile, divine revelation exposes and confirms our situation of estrangement," Anatolios writes (with reference to Book 4 of *The Trinity*). Anatolios, *Retrieving Nicaea*, 271. Regarding Augustine's discovery in the *Confessions* that "he was far from God in the *regio dissimilitudinis*" (*Conf.* 7.10.16), Lancel notes that there are "Plotinian" affinities. Lancel, *Saint Augustine*, 85. However, he identifies an important difference: "for Augustine, it is when the soul turns towards God and enters his light that it perceives the situation, becomes aware of the abyss separating it from him as an ontological difference between the created and the Creator" (p. 85; see also 488n26).

115. *Doctr. chr.* 2.7.10. This teaching is reflected in Augustine's famous conversion scene (*Conf.* 8.12.29). See also *Serm.* 154.1.

116. *Serm.* 90A(D11/M40).1; see also discussion and references in Introduction.

117. *Serm.* 90A(D11/M40).10.

118. *Serm.* 90A(D11/M40).10. See also *Conf.* 4.12.18–19. In his discussion of "interiority" in Augustine's preaching, Sanlon notes the significance Augustine gave to "the heart" ("*cor*"). Sanlon, *Augustine's Theology of Preaching*, 75–8. Regarding the themes of "interiority" and "self-knowledge" in Augustine's thought, see Anatolios, *Retrieving Nicaea*, 271–4; Phillip Cary, "Interiority," in *Augustine through the Ages*, ed. Allan D. Fitzgerald (Grand Rapids, MI: Eerdmans, 1999), 454–6; Duffy, "Anthropology," 27; Sanlon, *Augustine's Theology of Preaching*, 71–81; Williams, *On Augustine*, esp. 1–24, 155–70. Discussing *The Trinity*, Anatolios explains: "By improperly identifying itself with what it is not, the mind loses sight of its own act of self-presencing. This fate is unavoidable unless the mind attends to God according to its proper creaturely mode of being and thereby knows itself and loves itself in subordinate relation to its knowing of God and loving of God." Anatolios, *Retrieving Nicaea*, 273. This "knowledge of God," Anatolios later adds, is made possible through Christ (pp. 274–5). Responding to readings that suggest that Augustine's teaching leads to "modern" notions of the "self," Williams observes of "the self" that "this agency is not a self-subsisting reality, first recognizing itself, then moving on to see God reflected in its own luminosity: its deepest

reminds us that this self-discovery comes as an act of God's grace; as he teaches his listeners on another occasion, "you do not know how to find yourself unless the one who made you searches for you."[119]

This movement of returning to oneself is not sufficient, however. We cannot simply resolve to disengage ourselves from a culture of "dissolute living" (Lk. 15:13, NRSV), devising our own form of ethical life, for we remain in ourselves. "Don't stay in yourself," Augustine cautions, "in case you lose yourself again."[120] Instead, we must to return to God. Just as the younger son had first abandoned God in favor of self, and then self in favor of worldly goods, Augustine emphasizes two sequential movements of return: "As soon as he had returned to himself, you see, he was determined not to stay in himself, because *returning to himself, he said: I will arise and go to my father* (Lk 15:17–18)."[121] Augustine elaborates further in *Sermon* 330: "First come back to yourself from the things outside you, and then give yourself back to the one who made you."[122] Again, it is our Creator who enables this giving back of oneself, this turning toward God in love. Burnaby explains that, in Augustine's understanding, Christ's role is not only revelatory, but creative, renewing love within us: "Redemption is in the fullest sense a new creation, restoring in sinful man the love toward God which he had lost."[123]

This subsequent movement of return to God involves the relinquishment of the claim to self-interest that prompted our departure.[124] We cannot genuinely love God while maintaining our self-interested state. As Raymond Canning

---

level of self-recognition is when it sees its dependence on the strictly unconditioned and unlimited act of God's gift, and so also sees the ways in which it blocks off its own maturation by refusing dependence, love, worship." Williams, *On Augustine*, 22–3. See also pp. 132–3. Williams also clarifies that in Augustine's teaching, "our self-knowledge is in practice bound up with the common life of the believing community and its disciplines" (p. 23).

119. *Serm.* 13.3. Even on the occasions when Augustine appeals to the concept of a natural self-love in order to direct his audience toward proper love of God and self, God's intervention is nonetheless required; as O'Donovan concludes (following a comprehensive survey of these texts), "it remains the case that the man who would learn to love himself aright must sit down in the school of Christ and learn to love God." O'Donovan, *Problem of Self-Love*, 92.

120. *Serm.* 90A(D11/M40).10.

121. *Serm.* 90A(D11/M40).10.

122. *Serm.* 330.3.

123. Burnaby, *Amor Dei*, 170–1. As Anatolios observes, "the way to true knowledge of God is that provided by God himself." Anatolios, *Retrieving Nicaea*, 274.

124. O'Donovan, Canning, and Burnaby each refute the critique (expressed most notably by Anders Nygren) that Augustine's conception of love of God is inherently self-interested. For relevant discussion see O'Donovan, *Problem of Self-Love*, 137–59; Canning, *Unity of Love for God and Neighbour*, 117–54; Burnaby, *Amor Dei*, 121–6.

illustrates, Christ's command to love God wholeheartedly does not allow for this possibility.[125] Loving God does enable us to truly love our self. However, Canning observes a "paradox," in that it is "only when the subject is *ex toto* given to God— i.e. when the subject is *ex toto* directed away from his instinctually egoistic self— does he truly love himself and find preservation for himself."[126] Therefore, if God has freed us from the fetters of our worldly loves, we should not then continue to pursue private gain, as Augustine indicates in a prayerful meditation in the *Confessions*:

> You hear the groans of prisoners (Ps. 101: 21) and release us from the chains we have made for ourselves, on condition that we do not erect against you the horns (Ps. 74: 5f.) of a false liberty by avaricious desire to possess more and, at the risk of losing everything, through loving our private interest more than you, the good of all that is.[127]

God offers us liberation, but to receive this freedom we must relinquish our claim to self-interest. Williams clarifies that it is not an "abandonment of the world of material things" that is needed, but rather "the abandonment of attachment to the projects and desires of the unregenerate will."[128] We must relinquish the disordered love that has sought the created in place of the Creator.

Such a relinquishment includes a renunciation of our prideful assertion of independence from God. Christ invites us to leave behind our "individual, personal, 'private' will," Burnaby explains.[129] In *Sermon 330*, Augustine considers Christ's instruction in Matthew 16:24: "What, I ask you, is the meaning of *If anyone wishes to come after me, let him deny himself, and take up his cross, and follow me?*"[130] From a human point of view, this instruction seems counter-intuitive, Augustine concedes: "How can someone deny himself who loves himself?"[131] And yet he urges his listeners to trust in Christ's direction, for "the one who was good enough to create knows how to restore."[132] And according to the Creator's teaching, it is by denying our self that we truly love our self; for "*Whoever loves his soul*, he says, *let him lose it* (Jn 12:25)."[133] In this sermon, Augustine reads the prodigal son narrative in light of these gospel instructions, noting that having returned to himself, the younger son then denies himself as he returns to his father: "How does he deny himself? Listen. *And I will say to him, I have sinned*, he said, *against heaven and before you*. He's denying himself: *I am now not worthy*

---

125. Canning, *Unity of Love for God and Neighbour*, 139–41, 149–54.
126. Canning, *Unity of Love for God and Neighbour*, 152.
127. *Conf.* 3.8.16.
128. Williams, *On Augustine*, 143.
129. Burnaby, *Amor Dei*, 123.
130. *Serm.* 330.2.
131. *Serm.* 330.2.
132. *Serm.* 330.2.
133. *Serm.* 330.2. See also *Serm.* 117.1–2.

to be called your son (Lk 15:17–19)."[134] The younger son does not return to the father, only to reassert his original claim of autonomy. Rather, he acknowledges his earlier departure as a transgression, and realizing that he can no longer claim to be good himself, he entrusts himself into the merciful goodness of his father.

Those who love self and those who love God, O'Donovan notes, are "traveling in opposite directions."[135] We cannot journey homeward while persisting in this self-love. Thus while O'Donovan acknowledges the "evil motives and daily sin" that can still hinder a Christian's progress, he argues that "self-love, *this* self-love, is an attitude of opposition to Christ which he [the Christian] must, and can, have done with."[136] And yet, this idolatrous self-love is not easily discarded. Rather, as J. Patout Burns indicates, this temptation persists: "The Spirit dwelling in the believer does not fully supplant the inherited self-love and lust."[137] Burns explains that "God is truly loved but not with the whole heart, as the commandment and truth require; a deep-seated love of self and delight in carnal satisfactions continue to divide the person's strength."[138] The *Sermons* clearly indicate Augustine's awareness that the members of his congregation do not travel in uniform fashion.

---

134. *Serm.* 330.3.

135. O'Donovan, *Problem of Self-Love*, 97.

136. O'Donovan, *Problem of Self-Love*, 106. Here, O'Donovan makes a distinction between Augustine's teaching on this "perverse self-love," and his teaching on Philippians 2:21 and 1 Corinthians 13:5, arguing that the latter "might very well have contributed to the concept of perverse *amor sui* but did not do so" (pp. 105–6). O'Donovan argues that Augustine particularly has the "ministers of Christ" in view when using these texts (p. 106). Accordingly, O'Donovan claims, "To 'seek one's own' in this context is not to choose the radical alternative to the worship, praise, and love of God but to carry over into Christian discipleship some traces of the old Adamic spirit, some reservation about total and unconditioned self-giving" (p. 107). However, in the *Sermons*, Augustine's use of these two verses, though limited, is nonetheless more wide-ranging. Although Augustine often does have the clerical or monastic life in view (e.g., *Serm.* 46.2; 78.6), he also uses these verses when addressing the wider congregation about greed (*Serm.* 107A.1), when challenging them to love God rather than "*iniquity*" (Ps. 11:5; see *Serm.* 90.6), and in one instance, Augustine uses these verses in an account of humanity's fundamental rejection of God (*Serm.* 51.34). Note also MacQueen's statement: "Whether overt or covert, whether in the cloister or the hearth, pride can find a home anywhere—and everywhere. But regardless of the variables of place or time, this vice reduces essentially to a perverse love of self." MacQueen, "Contemptus Dei," 287. See also Harrison's comments about the ongoing challenge of self-love within the monastery: Harrison, *Christian Truth and Fractured Humanity*, 190–1. In Chapter 6 of this book, I discuss the temptation of self-love amongst pastors.

137. J. Patout Burns, "Grace," in *Augustine through the Ages*, ed. Allan D. Fitzgerald (Grand Rapids, MI: Eerdmans, 1999), 397.

138. Burns, "Grace," 397.

In *Sermon* 346B, for example, he portrays some members as "running" homeward, while others are "sluggish," and others still are "going backwards."[139] Augustine's congregation was a diverse audience, including curious onlookers, and those yet to make the commitment of baptism.[140] Augustine knows too well that many among the baptized do not model the Christian love of which he preaches, and he often cautions the newly baptized against their bad example.[141] And even among listeners whose love for God is sincere, this message remains vitally important. The alienated state of the son may no longer be their own, but it remains instructive for them to "call to mind how he went off and got lost," as a reminder of both the place from which they have come, and of the necessity of pressing onward to God.[142]

The Way

Returning home is no easy task. We travel toward God by love,[143] yet the journey is lifelong, and en route we face many obstacles and distractions.[144] But at the outset of this pilgrimage, a more fundamental problem presents itself: Where are we going? We cannot find our own way home.[145] That said, Augustine proclaims in *Sermon* 261 that "what was a long way away from you has come down right next to you through a man."[146] Christ is not only our goal, but also the way by which we travel to that goal: "By Christ as man you wend your way to Christ as God."[147] Drawing on John 1, Augustine then explains that because "*the Word was made flesh and dwelt among us*" (v. 14), we can love Christ as both neighbor and God.[148]

Across the *Sermons*, Augustine develops this theme in a variety of interrelated teachings. For example, in *Sermon* 16A Augustine notes that Christ spanned the distance between us and God "in the form of a servant."[149] To journey toward God, we must "imitate Christ" in his poverty and humility; we must "*walk as he walked* (1 Jn 2:6)."[150] In this sense, it is by revealing the path of humility that Christ becomes the way for us (see Chapter 5 for this important theme).

---

139. *Serm.* 346B.2.
140. See Introduction, and Harmless, *Augustine and the Catechumenate*, 188–9.
141. E.g., *Serm.* 223.1–2.
142. *Serm.* 90A(D11/M40).10.
143. *Doctr. chr.* 1.17.16.
144. *Serm.* 346B.2.
145. E.g., *Conf.* 10.42.67. As Burnaby notes, Augustine's insistence on this point marked an important departure from Neoplatonism, which thought that God could be reached via contemplation: Burnaby, *Amor Dei*, 70–1.
146. *Serm.* 261.7.
147. *Serm.* 261.7. For this theme, see Brian Daley, "A Humble Mediator: The Distinctive Elements in Saint Augustine's Christology," *Word and Spirit* 9 (1987): 105–8.
148. *Serm.* 261.8.
149. *Serm.* 16A.9.
150. *Serm.* 16A.10. See also *Serm.* 123.1.

In *Sermon* 123, Augustine explains: "Christ as God is the home country we are going to; Christ as man is the way we are going by."[151] Soon after, Augustine notes that Christ "is both there, seated at the right hand of the Father, and here, suffering want in his poor"—an obvious parallel to his earlier statement.[152] The inference is clear: while one day we shall meet the ascended Christ in the Father's household, on our present pilgrimage, we encounter Christ in the neighbor, and especially in the poor. Augustine then develops this point further in relation to Acts 9:4 and Matthew 25:31–46, where Christ speaks of being present in the persecuted and needy: "Fear Christ up above, recognize him down below. Have Christ up above lavishing bounty, recognize him here needing charity. Here he's poor, there he's rich. That Christ is poor for us here, he tells us himself: *I was hungry, thirsty, naked, a stranger, in prison.* And to some he said *You helped me,* to some *You didn't help me.*"[153] This is another sense in which Christ is the way for us. Although God might seem distant and beyond reach, the Word who became flesh continues to dwell among us, present in the poor and afflicted.[154] Not only is this an act of solidarity with the suffering;[155] Christ dwells among the poor for the sake of all. "Christ is poor for us."[156] By presenting himself to us in the needy neighbor, Christ provides us with a means to love him—and thus to travel toward him.

On other occasions, Augustine develops this theme further again. In *Sermon* 263A (preached for Ascension Day), Augustine again recalls Acts 9:4 and Matthew 25:35, reminding the congregation that Christ, though ascended, remains present with us: "He has already been exalted above the heavens; and yet he suffers on earth whatever hardships we experience as his members."[157] Note that here, however, Augustine emphasizes Christ's presence within the church, which is his body. As Christ's body, on our earthly pilgrimage we find hope in the ascension, for Christ our head is already present at our destination.[158] But if we want to ascend with Christ, we must be in Christ, for "*Nobody has gone up to heaven, except the one who came down from heaven, the Son of man who is in heaven* (Jn 3:13)."[159] In this statement, Christ is referring to himself, Augustine notes, but in light of "the unity by which he is our head and we his body."[160] Christ draws us into himself, in order to draw us to our destination. Thus Augustine depicts Christ calling out, "Be my

---

151. *Serm.* 123.3.
152. *Serm.* 123.3.
153. *Serm.* 123.4.
154. Commenting on Christ's ongoing presence in the needy, Canning observes that "Christ does this out of that same self-emptying love for human beings which is expressed in the Incarnation." Canning, *Unity of Love for God and Neighbour*, 361. See also pp. 416–18.
155. E.g., *Serm.* 113B.4.
156. *Serm.* 123.4.
157. *Serm.* 263A.1.
158. *Serm.* 263A.2.
159. *Serm.* 263A.2.
160. *Serm.* 263A.2.

members, if you wish to ascend into heaven."¹⁶¹ This is yet another sense in which Christ is the way for us: he incorporates us into his body, so that we might join him (our head) in heaven.¹⁶² And on our earthly pilgrimage, it is by loving Christ in his members that we travel toward him as our destination.¹⁶³

Loving Our Neighbor

If Christ is the way, then we cannot make the long journey of return alone. To love Christ, we must venture out from the isolation of self-interest, and meet him in the impoverishment of our neighbor, and in the needs of his members. For Augustine, the Christian life on pilgrimage to God is a life shared with others. Modern individualistic conceptions of faith would be foreign to Augustine, and he rebukes those who think it possible to love God independent of their neighbor.¹⁶⁴

Indeed, in the very act of loving our neighbor, we come to encounter God, Augustine explains to the congregation in *Sermon* 90A(D11/M40). Reflecting on 1 John 4:16, "*God is charity*," he instructs: "If you love, love too the very thing you love with, and you are loving God."¹⁶⁵ In Augustine's understanding, this does not reduce God to a subjective emotion or experience; to the contrary, he believes that the teaching of 1 John 4:16 is given to *prevent* us from "concocting a god for ourselves."¹⁶⁶ The reason for Augustine's confidence is that he believes genuine love to be the gift of God's very own self. T. J. van Bavel notes that the love Augustine has in view is not "an abstract idea or substance," but rather "the personal God."¹⁶⁷ This is more clearly evidenced in other sermons where Augustine discusses 1 John 4:16 in relation to the gift of the Holy Spirit, described in Romans 5:5: "*For the love of Christ has been spread out in our hearts—not our own doing though, but— through the Holy Spirit who has been given to us* (Rom 5:5). If love has been spread out in our hearts, and *God is love* (1 Jn 4:8.16), there you have a pledge, however

---

161. *Serm.* 263A.2.

162. For Augustine's theology of the *totus Christus*, see Canning, *Unity of Love for God and Neighbour*, esp. 359–68; T. J. van Bavel, "The 'Christus Totus' Idea: A Forgotten Aspect of Augustine's Spirituality," in *Studies in Patristic Christology*, ed. Thomas Finan and Vincent Twomey (Dublin: Four Courts Press, 1998), 84–94; Williams, *On Augustine*, esp. 25–32, 198–9. Canning indicates a degree of development in Augustine's use of the *totus Christus* motif in relation to love of God and neighbor: Canning, *Unity of Love for God and Neighbour*, 257–64.

163. See also *Sermon* 91 for this ecclesial participation in Christ as the way (*Serm.* 91.7), and the accompanying pastoral application to love one another (.9).

164. E.g., *Tract. ep. Jo.* 9.10–11.

165. *Serm.* 90A(D11/M40).12. See also *Trin.* 8.8.12.

166. *Serm.* 90A(D11/M40).12.

167. T. J. van Bavel, "The Double Face of Love in Augustine," *Augustinian Studies* 17 (1986): 177.

slight, that God is walking about in us."[168] When we genuinely love our neighbor, we encounter God, because it is God's very presence within us that enables this love.[169]

Thus, for Augustine, the neighbor plays an important role in our journey of Christian formation, for it is by loving our neighbor that we come to love God.[170] As Augustine proposed to his congregation earlier in *Sermon* 90A(D11/M40), "let us start from our neighbor, in order to arrive at God" (following 1 Jn 4:20).[171] At that point, Augustine expressed reservation about the congregation's ability to love their neighbor, directing them to Christ's command to love God (see above). Although Paul summarizes the law with the single command of love of neighbor (Rom. 13:8–10), Augustine notes, Christ's command to love God was necessary so that we might love our self, and thus our neighbor, rightly.[172] However, if our love is shaped by love of God, then genuine love of neighbor becomes possible: "If that is what you love ... then I will entrust your neighbor to you, because I can see where you are aiming at and wending your way to. You will lead him there, nor can you lead one whom you love as yourself anywhere else; you are now, after all, also loving yourself."[173] Oriented toward God, our love becomes rightly ordered. We are truly loving ourselves because we are seeking that which is truly good.[174] We learn how

---

168. *Serm.* 23.8. See Chapter 2 for discussion of Augustine's interpretation of Romans 5:5.

169. Augustine develops this theme further in his *Homilies on the First Epistle of John*; see esp. *Tract. ep. Jo.* 5.7; 7.4–6; 9.10. Van Bavel provides a helpful overview of this development, and responds to objectors: Van Bavel, "Double Face of Love," 172–81. See Chapters 2 and 7 for further discussion.

170. Does this mean that love of neighbor is simply a means to an end? In a survey of passages where Augustine talks of loving our neighbor in order to love God, Canning demonstrates that "love for neighbour is not a merely preparatory step on which the subject can turn his back once he has taken it." Canning, *Unity of Love for God and Neighbour*, 69. See pp. 33–78 for his survey. Three of Canning's insights are of particular relevance here: Firstly, our neighbor benefits when we orient our love for them toward God because God is a good enjoyed in common (pp. 43–5). Secondly, following Christ's example, love for neighbor should be "self-giving," not "self-seeking" (pp. 72–3). And thirdly, love of neighbor does not cease when we reach our end in God (pp. 74–8). Regarding this question, much attention has been devoted to the first book of *Teaching Christianity*, where Augustine speaks of "using" the neighbor. See Oliver O'Donovan, "*Usus* and *Fruitio* in Augustine, *De Doctrina Christiana* I," *The Journal of Theological Studies* 33, no. 2 (1982): 361–97; Canning, *Unity of Love for God and Neighbour*, 79–115; Burnaby, *Amor Dei*, 130.

171. *Serm.* 90A(D11/M40).5. Regarding the precedence of love of neighbor, Van Bavel explains: "In the practical order of action, love for our brothers and sisters comes first, for it is in everyday life that the claims of love are felt most concretely." Van Bavel, "Double Face of Love," 171.

172. *Serm.* 90A(D11/M40).12–13.

173. *Serm.* 90A(D11/M40).11.

174. *Serm.* 90A(D11/M40).8–9.

to use material goods rightly: not as ends in themselves, but as resources that can aid us on our journey toward God.[175] And consequently we can love our neighbor rightly, because our love for them is, like our love for self, directed toward God.

When Augustine urges his congregation to lead their neighbor to God (as above), his hope is that they might love their neighbor in such a way that the neighbor also comes to know and love God, who is their true good. Indeed, as Augustine's exhortation suggests, this is no longer a matter of rational decision: "You will lead him there, nor can you lead one whom you love as yourself anywhere else."[176] Augustine playfully illustrates this teaching for his listeners by pointing out a member of the congregation, and drawing attention (presumably in jest) to their fanatical interest in a particular "bullfighter."[177] Such an enthusiastic love would not only prompt this person to arise "at the crack of dawn" so they could be ready at the bullring gates when they opened, Augustine suggests; it would also lead them to rouse their neighbor at this early hour, so that the neighbor (once she or he had recovered from this uninvited awakening) might also enjoy the celebrated bullfighter together with them.[178] In contrast to the covetousness of our worldly desires, when we love God we cannot help but share this good in common.[179]

By leading our neighbor to God, we are loving them as ourselves. To do otherwise—to wish for our neighbor a construal of the good life apart from God—would be to love our neighbor less than we love ourselves. However, Augustine's exhortation to lead our neighbor to God should not be understood in a narrow, over-spiritualized sense, as if we were only truly loving our neighbor when "evangelizing" them, and not when attending to their practical needs. As this book demonstrates, Augustine clearly believes that love for neighbor demands practical expression, such as feeding the hungry, and giving to the poor.[180] However, these actions of love for the neighbor should be oriented toward God, for only then do we genuinely have the neighbor's best interests at heart. O'Donovan's comments on "*benevolentia*" (or "benevolent love") in Augustine's thought are illuminating in this regard.[181] O'Donovan describes "*benevolentia*" as "the will that something which has its existence from God should fulfill its existence for God."[182] Outlining this form of love, he makes the important insight that, in seeking this goal for our neighbor, we are not forcing our own goals upon them, but rather are

---

175. E.g., *Serm.* 177.2. For discussion of Augustine's distinction between "use" and "enjoyment" of material goods, see Chapter 4.
176. *Serm.* 90A(D11/M40).11.
177. *Serm.* 90A(D11/M40).11.
178. *Serm.* 90A(D11/M40).11.
179. *Serm.* 90A(D11/M40).8.
180. Observing that pre-400 Augustine tends to emphasize the spiritual dimension of love for neighbor, Canning indicates that "there is nevertheless an impressive body of post-400 texts which present material giving to the poor as a highly significant dimension of love for neighbour." Canning, *Unity of Love for God and Neighbour*, 179.
181. O'Donovan, *Problem of Self-Love*, 32–6.
182. O'Donovan, *Problem of Self-Love*, 33.

recognizing the purpose for which they have been created, a purpose "received from without."[183] To love our neighbor in accordance with God's purpose for them is to love them fully.[184]

As Augustine draws toward the conclusion of *Sermon* 90A(D11/M40), it becomes apparent that the problem he had posed at the beginning has been resolved during the course of the sermon.[185] Love of God and love of neighbor are not at odds with one another, for neither can be considered apart from the other.[186] Therefore, Augustine tells his congregation: "Choose whichever love you like. You choose love of neighbor; it won't be genuine unless God is also loved. You choose love of God; it won't be genuine unless neighbor is also tacitly included."[187] Augustine's comment may reflect a certain ambivalence about the sequence of love of God and neighbor, but his sermon has emphatically reminded the congregation of the centrality of these two loves. Our return to God is a lifelong journey of the heart.[188] We travel, not by performing ethical duties or adhering to a religious code, but by loving. As Augustine puts it in *Sermon* 346B: "The steps, you see, which we take along this highway are the love of God and of our neighbor."[189] This instruction remains central to the church's calling amidst present contexts of economic inequality. If, following Augustine's analysis, we understand economic inequality to be symptomatic of a more fundamental departure from God (and consequently, from neighbor), then we will recognize that political or economic

---

183. O'Donovan, *Problem of Self-Love*, 34. Regarding Augustine's focus on loving the neighbor by leading them to God, O'Donovan elaborates: "It is not that he rejects other goals which may be adopted from time to time but that this one is fundamental, for it is the only purpose that the subject can conceive for the object which he can be absolutely sure is not a willful imposition." O'Donovan, *Problem of Self-Love*, 34–5.

184. Augustine develops this teaching in social terms in Book 19 of *The City of God*. Although seeking the peace of the earthly city, the city of God "directs this earthly peace toward the heavenly peace … namely, a perfectly ordered and wholly concordant fellowship in the enjoyment of God and of each other in God" (*Civ.* 19.17). Thus, the city of God "signifies not itself but another" (*Civ.* 15.2). See Markus, *Saeculum: History and Society in the Theology of St Augustine*, 68–9. For the church as "sign," see pp. 180–6. For the work of social transformation as sign, see Rowan Williams, *The Wound of Knowledge: Christian Spirituality from the New Testament to St. John of the Cross*, 2nd, rev. ed. (Cambridge, MA: Cowley, 1990), 86.

185. *Serm.* 90A(D11/M40).4.

186. Canning thoroughly documents this unity in Canning, *Unity of Love for God and Neighbour*. See especially Chapter 6, where (drawing on the findings of earlier chapters), he makes the case for unity conclusively.

187. *Serm.* 90A(D11/M40).13.

188. Canning observes that after 412, Augustine increasingly emphasizes that love of God and (perhaps to a lesser degree) love of neighbor only find perfection eschatologically: Canning, *Unity of Love for God and Neighbour*, 19–25.

189. *Serm.* 346B.2.

solutions, while important, are not enough. A deeper response is required: a transformation of our heart.

Conclusion

In the closing sentence of *Sermon* 90A(D11/M40), Augustine exhorts his congregation: "So let us be fervent in works of mercy, and in this time of dearth of temporal goods let us love our neighbors, so that we may deserve to experience judgment with mercy."[190] Edmund Hill suggests (with reference to François Dolbeau) that this "dearth" refers to the period in the harvest cycle when food was in short supply, with "the granaries ... almost exhausted, and the new harvest not yet gathered."[191] Accordingly, the issue of scarcity of resources would likely have preoccupied many in this congregation as they gathered for worship.

It is striking that Augustine has not directly referred to these circumstances until the final words of his sermon. Instead, during this challenging season, the congregation has heard again the words of Christ calling them to love God and neighbor, reminding them what is of greatest importance. That does not mean Augustine has ignored their material concerns. Rather, Augustine has drawn the congregation into conversation with Christ, allowing Christ's words to respond to and interpret their concerns.

In our contemporary context, confronted with individuals and communities in economic need, we too need Christ's instruction to guide us. As earlier noted, the range of possible responses is seemingly endless. Should we respond at a personal level, supporting neighbors who are struggling, or should our efforts be at a political level, advocating for societal change? When we encounter someone in need, should we give directly, or are our resources better distributed when given to a food bank or social service? Faced with such choices, we can easily become overwhelmed, confused, and paralyzed.

Augustine helps us recognize that Christ's call to love God and neighbor is the necessary starting point for the Christian community, as his monastic instruction outlines.[192] This emphasis is instructive for the present-day church, where we are often quick to accept the diagnoses of economic inequality offered by secular commentators, along with their recommended remedies. Certainly there is much to be learnt from such economic and political analyses, but Augustine invites a deeper scrutiny, turning our attention to our own hearts and lives. For Christian formation, as Augustine conceives it, is firstly and finally about learning to love rightly.

---

190. *Serm.* 90A(D11/M40).14.
191. Hill, in *Sermons Discovered since 1990*, 86n22. For discussion of such harvest shortages, see Chapter 3, and Brown, *Through the Eye of a Needle*, 11–14.
192. *Reg.* 2: 1.

For contemporary readers, perhaps the full import of this teaching emerges when Augustine considers our love of neighbor. Few would deny the importance of this task, but an especially confronting aspect of Augustine's teaching in this chapter is the question of whether we know how to truly love our neighbor. In our eagerness to leap to the neighbor's aid or start a charitable project, are our actions and assumptions shaped by love of God, or by love of something else? For example, we might be obsessed with home renovation television shows, devoting our time and resources to updating our home in the latest styles. Encountering a neighbor living in more basic circumstances, an instinctive response might thus be to improve their home, contributing the stylish furnishings that they cannot afford. This response might be generous and well-intentioned, but are we truly loving our neighbor here, or projecting our own misguided desires onto their circumstances? The point here is not that such practical assistance is wrong (for it could genuinely arise out of love for God and neighbor), but rather to be alert to the nature of the love that guides our response—and, moreover, to recall the fundamental importance of nurturing our love for God, in order that we might better love our neighbor.

When, at the conclusion of *Sermon* 90A(D11/M40), Augustine finally acknowledges "this time of dearth of temporal goods," his instruction to the congregation appears understated, almost an afterthought: "let us love our neighbors."[193] And yet, his entire sermon serves to make this simple instruction possible for his congregation. Unless God is loved, the concerns of the Christian community amidst economic inequality will be misguided, and they will not be capable of loving their neighbor. And unless the neighbor is loved, the Christian community will not be able to truly love God. Indeed, they cannot be a community at all, for while the idea of God might appeal to them, they remain within themselves, lost in a distant country.

---

193. *Serm.* 90A(D11/M40).14.

Chapter 2

DIVISION AND UNITY OF HEART

> In the first place—and this is the very reason for your being gathered together in one—you should live in the *house in unity of spirit* (Ps 67:7[68:6]) and you should have *one soul and one heart* (Acts 4:32) centered on God.
>
> —*Reg.* 3: 1.2.

Why should Christians be especially concerned about the social divisions of economic inequality? And why is the formation of a common life an important part of the church's response? While Christians may meet together for Sunday worship, other expressions of community life can often be regarded as extra-curricular aspects of Christian faith, an optional extra for the committed few. Yet Augustine's teaching reveals that forging unity among believers is a central part of God's formational work in the church, as I demonstrate in this chapter.

The communal life of the early Christians, as described in Acts 4:32–35, was programmatic for Augustine's monastic community. Harrison comments that, although many previous monastics had been inspired by this text, Augustine's use of these verses is "absolutely distinctive."[1] Of particular note is the emphasis Augustine places upon the unity of the Jerusalem believers, which informs his vision of the monastic community.[2] Markus also notes this emphasis in Augustine's monasticism, explaining that "Augustine shifted much of the stress previously laid on asceticism towards the values of communal living and the virtues which foster it."[3]

In Acts 4:32–35 the narrative first describes the unity of the early Christians, and then their sharing of resources. Augustine maintains this sequence in the opening instructions of the *Rule*. He begins by stressing the priority of unity among members: "In the first place—and this is the very reason for your being gathered together in one—you should live in the *house in unity of spirit* (Ps 67:7[68:6]) and you should have *one soul and one heart* (Acts 4:32) centered on God."[4] Though once divided from each other, God has gathered the members together, uniting them in heart and soul. As a consequence, they should no longer cling possessively to

---

1. Harrison, *Christian Truth and Fractured Humanity*, 182.
2. Harrison, *Christian Truth and Fractured Humanity*, 182–3.
3. Markus, *End of Ancient Christianity*, 78.
4. *Reg.* 3: 1.2.

their resources, but rather be willing to share what they have, as Augustine outlines in the subsequent rule, which begins: "And then, you should not call *anything your own, but you should have everything in common* (Acts 4:32)."[5] In granting precedence to the call to unity, Augustine does not diminish the importance of this subsequent call to share resources. Rather, he provides this act of redistribution with its proper theological context; such sharing arises out of, and bears witness to, the unity of love that God forges among the community members.

This emphasis on unity is also reflected in Augustine's *Sermons*. As I demonstrate in subsequent chapters, Augustine frequently challenges the rich, draws attention to the needs of the poor, and calls church members to share their resources. However, in addressing these economic concerns, his more fundamental concern is the underlying division that produces them: for apart from God we become divided from one another, preoccupied with individual needs and wants.

In this chapter I consider Augustine's pastoral instruction on division and unity in the *Sermons*, with a view to questions of economic inequality. Of particular interest is *Sermon* 71 (dated 417–20), a lengthy homily in which Augustine reluctantly tackles the difficult question of blasphemy against the Holy Spirit (Mt. 12:32).[6] The confrontational nature of this gospel text, along with the backdrop of Donatist debate in which Augustine is considering these themes, gives the sermon a polemical character.[7] However, the result is a profound exploration of the unifying work of the Holy Spirit, who overcomes the divisiveness of the world, and restores us to unity with God and one another (it is primarily this aspect of *Sermon* 71 that I consider here, although I discuss Augustine's interpretation of this blasphemy later in the chapter). While on this occasion Augustine does not make explicit the implications for divisions between rich and poor, he spells this out in other sermons, which will be considered alongside *Sermon* 71. Reading these sermons together, I demonstrate how Augustine alerts his congregation to the divisiveness of the world, and draws their attention to the God who seeks to gather them together in unity.

---

5. *Reg.* 3: 1.3. Verheijen provides a definitive survey of Augustine's use of Acts 4:32–35 in Luc Verheijen, *Saint Augustine's Monasticism in the Light of Acts 4.32–35*, The Saint Augustine Lecture 1975 (Villanova University Press, 1979). He explains that Augustine uses these verses in a distinctive formulation (p. 5). Verheijen also provides a succinct summary of Augustine's developing use of this passage (pp. 79–80). Van Bavel gives a similar account of this development: T. J. van Bavel, "The Evangelical Inspiration of the Rule of St Augustine," *The Downside Review* 93, no. 311 (1975): 87.

6. The Latin text of this sermon is found in *PL* 38:445–67, with a more recent critical edition provided in P.-P. Verbraken, "Le Sermon LXXI de Saint Augustin sur le blasphème contre le Saint-Esprit," *Revue Bénédictine* 75, no. 1–2 (1965): 54–108. The date range mentioned here is that noted by Hill: *Sermons (51–94)*, 246, 270n1.

7. Modern readers may be hesitant about engaging with a sermon that has a polemical context. Regarding this concern see Michel René Barnes, "Augustine in Contemporary Trinitarian Theology," *Theological Studies* 56, no. 2 (1995): 245–50.

A Divided Heart

"It's a real problem that we are faced with, in this passage read just now from the gospel," Augustine begins in *Sermon 71*.[8] As he later confesses, until this point in his preaching ministry, he has "avoided" the troubling question of blasphemy against the Holy Spirit that this gospel text raises.[9] Yet on this occasion, Augustine explains, "I was so struck by the gospel when it was read, that I really thought God wanted you to hear something on this matter through my ministry."[10] As he prepares to tackle this question, Augustine sets the scene for his congregation. Christ has healed a man possessed by demons, prompting the accusation of the Pharisees: *"This man only casts out demons by Beelzebub the prince of demons"* (Mt. 12:24).[11] In his response, Christ states that *"Every kingdom divided against itself will be laid waste"* (Mt. 12:25), not only refuting their charge, but also alerting his listeners to the inherent divisiveness of "the devil's kingdom."[12] By contrast, it is *"by the Spirit of God"* that Christ is casting out demons (Mt. 12:28), and therefore Christ is challenging the divisive "kingdom of the devil."[13] When Augustine tackles Jesus's caution against blasphemy against the Holy Spirit later in this sermon, his interpretation will be informed by this earlier scene in the gospel passage: Christ, in the power of the Spirit, confronting the divisiveness of the world.

For Augustine, the fallen world is a *"kingdom divided against itself"* (Mt. 12:25).[14] As noted in Chapter 1, separation from God brings separation from one another, and even from ourselves. This division is manifested not only in the observable segregations of human society, but also within the hidden reaches of our hearts. For Augustine, our turn from God is a movement from singular devotion to conflicting desire.[15] When the prodigal son sets out on his own, the myriad desires of the world lure him outside of himself (see Chapter 1). "If you love yourself in yourself," Augustine cautions, "you are bound to fall away even from yourself, and go looking for many things besides yourself."[16] In turning away from God, we do not simply exchange one singular love for another; instead, a multitude of desires divide our affection. Augustine makes efforts to alert the congregation to this danger. In *Sermon 65A*, Augustine emphasizes the endless variety of worldly desires: "Improper and unworthy loves are all around us with their billing and cooing. On every side they are inveigling and holding back those who are eager to fly; visible things are almost forcing themselves on our love.... It is impossible to

---

8. *Serm.* 71.1.
9. *Serm.* 71.8.
10. *Serm.* 71.8.
11. *Serm.* 71.1.
12. *Serm.* 71.1. For the divisive nature of the devil, see also *Serm.* 198(D26/M62).42.
13. *Serm.* 71.2.
14. *Serm.* 71.1.
15. Regarding this internal division, see *Conf.* 8.9.21–10.22; 8.10.24.
16. *Serm.* 179A.4; cf. *Conf.* 2.1.1.

count the things that are suggested every day by unlawful love."[17] Here, Augustine is evocatively juxtaposing the multiplicity of worldly desires with the simplicity and unity that characterizes love for God. The world entrances us, dividing our devotion, and we can no longer pray with the psalmist's unity of heart, *"One thing have I asked of the Lord"* (Ps. 27:4).[18] Internally, our hearts are divided between the competing desires of the world. And externally, a social fragmentation takes place, as fevered pursuit of the world's many enticements divides us from one another.

Worldly desires do not only divide us by their variety, however. They are divisive in nature, part of the *"kingdom divided against itself."*[19] The world apart from Christ does not have true coherence or unity; it is marked by conflict and contention within. In *Sermon 71*, Augustine illustrates this internal divisiveness for the congregation with an eclectic list of examples, including "the spirit of avarice and the spirit of extravagance," "the spirit of Juno and the spirit of Hercules," and "the Donatist and the Maximianist."[20] In each case, Augustine notes, both parties "are divided against each other" and yet "both belong to the devil's kingdom."[21] Thus he summarizes: "All the vices and errors of mortals are contrary to one another and divided against each other, and they all belong to the devil's kingdom."[22]

In this list, Augustine's example of the division between avarice and extravagance—"the one hoarding, the other splashing money around"—is especially pertinent to this discussion, drawing our attention to the internal divisiveness of the desire for wealth.[23] Even if we devote ourselves to the pursuit of our own prosperity, this is not a unified or unifying love. Rather, this desire is populated by many contradictory impulses, such as avarice and extravagance. Augustine animates this conflict for his listeners in *Sermon 86*, when considering Jesus's instruction to the rich young man (Mt. 19:16–22): "Sometimes two opposing mistresses take possession of a person: avarice and extravagance. Avarice says, 'Save'; extravagance says, 'Spend.' Under two such mistresses, giving contradictory orders, making contradictory demands, what are you going to do?"[24] While both avarice and extravagance are forms of self-interest, and both overlook the needs of our neighbor, they nonetheless pull the lover "in opposite directions."[25] Augustine hopes that, unlike this rich man who listened "with a contrary heart," his congregation might instead be receptive to Jesus's liberating words.[26] Yet, enslaved by this divided desire, we struggle to respond to the singular call of Jesus to "follow me" (Mt. 19:21, NRSV).[27]

---

17. *Serm.* 65A.2.
18. *Serm.* 65A.3.
19. *Serm.* 71.1.
20. *Serm.* 71.4. For this division within the Donatist church arising from the excommunication of Maximianus, see Lancel, *Saint Augustine*, 280.
21. *Serm.* 71.4.
22. *Serm.* 71.4.
23. *Serm.* 71.4.
24. *Serm.* 86.6.
25. *Serm.* 86.5, 6.
26. *Serm.* 86.2, 7.
27. *Serm.* 86.5.

Divided from Our Neighbor

Our divided heart is reflected in our divided society.[28] As noted in the Introduction, Augustine provides little comment in the *Sermons* on the systemic or structural forces that divide rich and poor, in the manner that modern readers might expect. Rather, Augustine helps us recognize how love (rightly oriented) draws us together, or (wrongly oriented) divides us.[29] In Augustine's instruction on wealth and poverty in the *Sermons*, we can observe this divisive dynamic in two senses. The first, a more passive form of division, is the sense of disconnection of the rich from the needs of the poor. Preoccupied with pursuing our own private gain we become detached from the needs of others, perhaps without even realizing it. Augustine frequently draws upon the parable of the rich man and Lazarus (Lk. 16:19–31) to depict this dynamic. Although Lazarus, "the poorest of the poor," is lying right outside the rich man's gate, the rich man, "callously hardhearted," disregards him.[30] Augustine describes this negligence as an "inhumanity."[31] Sometimes he attributes this disregard for the poor to avarice or pride,[32] but in either case, this disregard reveals an underlying sense of disconnection, whereby we no longer understand ourselves to share a common identity or unity with the poor. Augustine alerts his listeners to this disconnectedness when urging them to respond to the needs of their neighbor in his *Homilies on the First Epistle of John*:

> Your brother is hungry, he is needy. Perhaps he is anxious and is being pressed by a creditor. He has nothing, you have something. He is your brother. You have been purchased together; your price is the same; both of you have been redeemed by the blood of Christ. See if you are merciful, if you have the goods of the world. Perhaps you are saying, "What does this have to do with me? Am I going to give away my money so that he won't be troubled?" If this is how your heart responds to you, the Father's love doesn't abide in you.[33]

The interlocutor's response, "What does this have to do with me?" is indicative of their disconnectedness. It no longer occurs to them that they share a common

---

28. An interesting example of the interrelatedness of these ideas in Augustine's thought is found in his developing use of Acts 4:32a: see Verheijen, *Saint Augustine's Monasticism*, 6–14. See also Kazuhiko Demura, "*Anima Una et Cor Unum*: St Augustine's Congregations and His Monastic Life," in *Prayer and Spirituality in the Early Church, Volume 4: The Spiritual Life*, ed. Wendy Mayer, Pauline Allen, and Lawrence Cross (Strathfield, NSW: St Pauls Publications, 2006), 259–60.
29. E.g., *Serm.* 359.1–2.
30. *Serm.* 178.3.
31. *Serm.* 178.3.
32. E.g. *Serm.* 36.9 (for avarice), *Serm.* 61.2, 8 (for pride). See Chapters 3 and 5 for further examples and discussion.
33. *Tract. ep. Jo.* 5.12.

identity with the poor, by virtue of their shared humanity and their unity in Christ. They have become divided from others and their needs.

Augustine also acknowledges the way in which pursuit of material goods pits us against one another, dividing us in a more active sense. Augustine addresses this concern in *Sermon 359*, where he begins by lamenting the absence of the "*concord between brothers*" that Scripture commends (Sir. 25:1).[34] "What is indeed deplorable is that such a great thing is so rare in human affairs; the thing is admired by all, actually practiced by so few," he comments.[35] This prompts Augustine to ask: "What makes it so difficult for brothers to live in concord with each other?"[36] The answer, he concludes, is "the fact that they are at odds about earth, that they want to be earth."[37] Instead of lifting our hearts to God, the common good, our desire has turned toward material goods, which leads to conflict with our sister or brother, as we seek to gain more for ourselves.[38] Thus Augustine notes of the discordant brothers: "How is it there is one womb between them, and not one spirit, if not because their souls are bent double, and each of them only has eyes for his own portion."[39] Van Bavel makes reference to this passage from *Sermon 359* in his discussion of the *Rule*, where he comments: "To have his own possessions makes a person concentrate on himself. It is, thus, a source of division, since material things are necessarily limited and often cannot be used by a number of people at the same time."[40] This conflict over material resources also results in their unjust distribution: in Augustine's illustration, one brother is "full of fatness," the other "weighed down with want."[41]

Following this reflection on division over material goods, in *Sermon 359* Augustine turns to consider the division between Catholic and Donatists.[42]

---

34. *Serm.* 359.1.
35. *Serm.* 359.1.
36. *Serm.* 359.1.
37. *Serm.* 359.1.
38. Thus in *The City of God* Augustine notes: "Since its good is not the sort of good that brings no anxieties to those who love it, the earthly city is often divided against itself by lawsuits, wars and conflicts." *Civ.* 15.4; see William Babcock, introduction to *The City of God (Books 1–10)*, trans. William Babcock, ed. Boniface Ramsey, vol. 6, *The Works of Saint Augustine, Part 1: Books* (Hyde Park, NY: New City Press, 2012), xxxii. Markus illustrates how Augustine's account of the discord of the earthly city contrasts with Eusebius's belief that God was bringing unity through the Roman Empire: Markus, *Saeculum: History and Society in the Theology of St Augustine*, 47–53.
39. *Serm.* 359.2.
40. Van Bavel, "Evangelical Inspiration of the Rule," 92–3.
41. *Serm.* 359.2.
42. For a general summary of the Donatist conflict, and Augustine's response to it, see Harrison, *Christian Truth and Fractured Humanity*, 145–57.

When preaching on division and unity, Augustine typically has this conflict in view. Many of his sermons on these themes were given at the height of this crisis, during the years leading up to and following the Carthage conference of 411.[43] The Donatist separation from the wider church concerned Augustine greatly, and clearly motivated his regular homiletical calls to unity. However, themes of division and unity in Augustine's preaching are more than anti-Donatist polemic. The emphasis on unity in the *Rule* suggests that from the outset of his episcopal ministry Augustine saw unity as fundamental to the identity and witness of the church. It is thus more helpful to think of Augustine's sermons on division and unity reflecting an underlying theological impulse in Augustine's thought that, while most apparent in his sustained engagement with the Donatists, nonetheless underpins his understanding of the Christian life as a whole. Furthermore, Augustine's call to unity amidst these ecclesial divisions should not be seen as having no import for economic divisions in the community. Brown argues that Augustine's "need to preserve the sense of unity in his flock, especially against Donatist criticism, led him to gloss over, even perhaps to collude with, the very real divisions between rich and poor."[44] However, by instructing his congregation about God's unifying work, Augustine does not ignore the inequalities between rich and poor, but rather acknowledges the only basis upon which these divisions can truly be overcome.[45]

Moreover, it is important to recall that the dispute between Catholics and Donatists did not take place in an economic vacuum. Debate over material goods was a significant cause of antagonism between Donatists and Catholics, Van der Meer notes, as legal rulings against the Donatists required them to hand over their church property to the Catholic Church.[46] To prevent their property being seized, some wealthy Donatists were inclined to join the Catholic Church, W. H. C. Frend observes.[47] Maureen A. Tilley's recent study on the role of family and finance in the Donatist conflict is especially illuminating.[48] Noting that Augustine's episcopal role required him to mediate disputes, Tilley explains that, amidst a city divided by the Donatist conflict, Augustine faced "significant pastoral challenges" in the

---

43. For details of this Carthage conference, see W. H. C. Frend, *The Donatist Church: A Movement of Protest in Roman North Africa* (Oxford: Clarendon Press, 1952), 275–89; Lancel, *Saint Augustine*, 293–300.

44. Brown, *Augustine of Hippo*, 247. See also Brown, *Through the Eye of a Needle*, 348–9.

45. Note also that in *Sermon* 359, Augustine uses the same biblical imagery (dividing an "inheritance" (Lk. 12:13–15)) to firstly address economic division, and then the ecclesial division of the Donatists (*Serm.* 359.3–4).

46. Van der Meer, *Augustine the Bishop*, 113.

47. Frend, *The Donatist Church*, 250.

48. Maureen A. Tilley, "Family and Financial Conflict in the Donatist Controversy: Augustine's Pastoral Problem," *Augustinian Studies* 43, no. 1/2 (2012): 49–64.

form of "intra-family and financial conflicts."[49] The Catholic–Donatist divide was reflected within the life of many families, and Tilley notes how imperial laws against Donatist property in the early fifth century heightened this tension and "promoted family division."[50] Surveying Augustine's response, Tilley observes that "he seemed genuinely concerned with families riven by the Donatist controversy," and provides a series of examples that demonstrate this pastoral concern.[51] Thus, even when Augustine's sermons are clearly responding to the Donatist conflict, his teaching on division and unity should not be considered solely in doctrinal or polemical terms, but rather in relation to the diverse concerns of his congregation (including their economic needs) that could lead to conflict with others.[52]

As Augustine explains in *Sermon* 71, all the disparate forms of worldly division are part of "the devil's kingdom"—and yet, Augustine reminds his listeners, because this kingdom is internally divided, it "will not remain standing."[53] The world apart from Christ does not have true coherence or unity; it is marked by conflict and contention within. Furthermore, our attempts to establish unity apart from Christ will ultimately fail. In our time, we may desire to see communities where divisions between rich and poor are overcome, and resources are shared with one another—surely a laudable goal. Systems of material redistribution or philosophical ideals may help such communities, but if they become our focus, division will inevitably

---

49. Tilley, "Family and Financial Conflict," 49–50. Regarding this episcopal responsibility, Brown explains that "Constantine had ratified the right of the bishop to act as the supreme arbiter of civil suits brought before him by the faithful." Brown, *Poverty and Leadership in the Later Roman Empire*, 67. See also Harrison, *Christian Truth and Fractured Humanity*, 123–5; R. Pierce Beaver, "Augustine of Hippo, Servus Servorum Christi," *Church History* 3, no. 3 (1934): 196–8. Van der Meer describes Augustine's patient service in this role, suggesting that "perhaps this was the most burdensome part of his office." Van der Meer, *Augustine the Bishop*, 258–61. Neil B. McLynn offers a different portrayal: Neil B. McLynn, "Administrator: Augustine in His Diocese," ed. Mark Vessey and Shelley Reid, *A Companion to Augustine* (Malden, MA: Blackwell, 2012), Wiley Online Library, 315–16.

50. Tilley, "Family and Financial Conflict," 55. Tilley provides a useful table that summarizes the legislation enacted during 405–14 against Donatists on pp. 63–4.

51. Tilley, "Family and Financial Conflict," 57, 57–62. Although Augustine had eventually given his consent to this legislation against Donatist property, Tilley explains that, as Augustine became aware of the negative impact of these laws, "he sought to ameliorate some of the effects of the laws on families" (p. 62).

52. While such economic factors in the Donatist conflict should not be overlooked, nor should they be overemphasized, as if the controversy can *only* be explained in socioeconomic terms, and without any theological context. The interpretation of some twentieth-century commentators (most notably Frend) tended in this direction, but has subsequently been corrected by later scholars. Harrison surveys this scholarship in Harrison, *Christian Truth and Fractured Humanity*, 147–9, including notes 122–5. See also Lepelley's critique of Frend's portrayal of the Donatist conflict: Lepelley, "Facing Wealth and Poverty," 7–10.

53. *Serm.* 71.4.

result, when material goods are coveted, and ideals are contested. Instead, we need to redirect our hearts toward the one who is not subject to division, and in whom alone unity is found.

The Undivided God

Unlike the one who divides us, Christ has come to gather us together (Mt. 12:30; 23:37). Contrary to the accusations of the Pharisees, Christ does not cast out our demons of division by the divisive spirit of Beelzebub, but rather by the Holy Spirit, who is not divided.[54] The undivided God overcomes our division.

In *Sermon* 71, Augustine's discussion of the unity of God begins nearly midway through the sermon, yet it provides the foundation for the sermon's main focus: the unifying work of the Holy Spirit. Here Augustine reminds the congregation that the God whom they gather to worship is three persons—Father, Son, and Holy Spirit—yet one God:

> Now you know, dearly beloved, that in that invisible and inviolable Trinity which the true faith and the Catholic Church professes and proclaims, God the Father is not the Father of the Holy Spirit but of the Son; and God the Son is not the Son of the Holy Spirit, but of the Father; and that God the Holy Spirit is not the Spirit only of the Father or only of the Son, but of both Father and Son; and finally that this Trinity, while in it the distinct properties and subsistence of each of the persons is maintained, is nonetheless one God, not three gods, because of the undivided and inseparable essence or nature of its eternity, truth and goodness.[55]

---

54. *Serm.* 71.36.

55. *Serm.* 71.18. Barnes observes that many twentieth-century theologians place Augustine's trinitarian thought in opposition to his Greek contemporaries; Augustine's emphasis on the unity of the Triune God, it is argued, results in a diminished sense of the distinctiveness of the divine persons. In response, Barnes demonstrates the problems of this view, and of the presuppositions that underlie it. Barnes, "Augustine in Contemporary Trinitarian Theology," 237–50. Joining Barnes in this critique, Lewis Ayres also notes that other scholars have dismissed Augustine's theology as "insufficiently trinitarian," which they ascribe to a perceived dependency upon "an alien 'Platonic' metaphysics": Lewis Ayres, "The Fundamental Grammar of Augustine's Trinitarian Theology," in *Augustine and His Critics: Essays in Honour of Gerald Bonner*, ed. Robert Dodaro and George Lawless (London: Routledge, 2000), 52. Ayres refutes this argument, showing that while Augustine's theology benefited from the insights of Platonic thought, his emphasis on the inseparability of God primarily reflects his commitment to the creedal confessions of the church (pp. 53–9). See also Lewis Ayres, "'Remember That You Are Catholic' (*Serm.* 52.2): Augustine on the Unity of the Triune God," *Journal of Early Christian Studies* 8, no. 1 (2000): 39–82.

While it is "the property of all three" of the Triune persons "to be equal to each other," each person also has "distinct properties": "The property of the Father is to be the author and origin of the others, the property of the Son is to be born, the property of the Holy Spirit is to be the communion of Father and Son."[56] It is this property of the Holy Spirit, as the communion of Father and Son, that particularly interests Augustine in this sermon. The Holy Spirit is shared in common by the Father and the Son, a "gift which they both possess as one."[57] This shared life of communion between the Triune persons contrasts with our fallen human relationships, where self-interest and claims of private ownership results in division.

It is God's intention, however, that we might too enjoy the gift of communion with God and with one another. For this reason, the Father and Son have sent the Holy Spirit to overcome our division, and draw us together in unity: "By what is common to them both the Father and the Son wished us to have communion both with them and among ourselves; by this gift which they both possess as one they wished to gather us together and make us one, that is to say, by the Holy Spirit who is God and the gift of God."[58] The Holy Spirit, as communion between Father and Son, restores us to communion with God and one another.

This communion is formed through love, and it is the gift of the Holy Spirit that enables this love within us. This insight is reinforced by Augustine's reading of Romans 5:5: "*charity has been poured into our hearts through the Holy Spirit which has been given to us.*"[59] Indeed, as Augustine observes on other occasions, this love is not only a gift from God; it is God's very self, loving within us: "So entirely is love or charity the gift of God that it is even called God, as the apostle John says: *Charity is God*, and whoever remains in charity remains in God, and God in him (1 Jn 4:16)."[60] The gift of unity with God and one another is not granted to us in a discrete, detached fashion; rather, it is the very presence of God, actively at work within us, that creates this unity.[61]

Christian unity, therefore, arises as the work of the unifying God among us. It is not the outcome of human enterprise; we cannot cast out our own division, nor are we able to fashion for ourselves the love that enables unity with God and one

---

56. *Serm.* 71.18.
57. *Serm.* 71.18.
58. *Serm.* 71.18. For the Holy Spirit as both "giver" and "gift," see Matthew Levering, "The Holy Spirit in the Trinitarian Communion: 'Love' and 'Gift'?," *International Journal of Systematic Theology* 16, no. 2 (2014): 136.
59. *Serm.* 71.18. As Burnaby observes, Augustine consistently interprets "the love of God" in Romans 5:5 as referring to "our love for God and not God's love for us." Burnaby, *Amor Dei*, 99. Levering provides helpful context for this interpretation: Levering, "The Holy Spirit in the Trinitarian Communion," 131n18.
60. *Serm.* 156.5.
61. For additional teaching on this theme, see *Tract. ep. Jo.* 7.4–6. See also Levering's discussion of Augustine's exegesis of 1 John 4 in *The Trinity*: Levering, "The Holy Spirit in the Trinitarian Communion," 129–31.

another. Rather, we are gathered together "by the Holy Spirit who is God and the gift of God."[62]

Making Room

"Perfect love or charity is the final, perfect gift of the Holy Spirit," Augustine teaches his listeners.[63] The journey toward this love, however, begins with the Holy Spirit's "first gift," "the forgiveness of sins."[64] In order that we might enjoy the gift of unity with God and one another, the spirit of division must be overcome, for our sin has resulted in "estrangement" from God.[65] As earlier noted, this separation from God also results in division with one another, and even within ourselves. Imprisoned by sin, we are "barred from the possession of those things that are really and truly good"—the common possession of God in whom we find communion.[66]

In the "rebirth" of baptism, we receive "the forgiveness of all past sins," which "takes place in the Holy Spirit."[67] Through this gift, we are freed "from the power of darkness"; the spirit of division is cast out.[68] It is proper that division be cast out by the Holy Spirit, Augustine explains, because of the special role of the Holy Spirit within the unity of God: "It was very fitting that the spirit who is divided against himself should be driven out by that Spirit whom Father and Son, not divided against themselves, have in common."[69] As the communion of Father and Son, the Holy Spirit enables us to enjoy communion with God and one another.

That is not to suggest, however, that the Holy Spirit works separately from the Father and the Son. Augustine is concerned to ensure his listeners do not misunderstand him here. Although Scripture often identifies a work or action with a particular person of the Trinity, Augustine teaches them that "with all these ways of speaking we still have to understand that the activities of the divine three are inseparable."[70] He later explains that "it is the Trinity that performs the works of each of the persons in the Trinity, two of them cooperating in the work of the other, harmonious action characterizing all three, inability to perform marking none of them."[71] Augustine's careful qualification of this question, and his lengthy discussion of the Triune persons in general, might appear overly labored and unnecessarily dogmatic in the context of a congregational sermon. However, Augustine's concern

---

62. *Serm.* 71.18. Note that in *Sermon* 265, Augustine discusses this enabling role of the Holy Spirit in terms of love of God and neighbor (*Serm.* 265.8-9).
63. *Serm.* 71.19.
64. *Serm.* 71.19.
65. *Serm.* 71.19.
66. *Serm.* 71.18.
67. *Serm.* 71.19.
68. *Serm.* 71.19.
69. *Serm.* 71.27. See also *Serm.* 71.19, 25.
70. *Serm.* 71.26.
71. *Serm.* 71.27.

is not abstracted from the life of the church. While the gospel text has led him to focus particularly on the Holy Spirit, he is wary of doing so in manner that would undermine the unity and inseparability of Father, Son, and Spirit—the very basis for the ecclesial unity that he is commending to his congregation.

The overcoming of sin and its divisive effects upon us is only the beginning of the Holy Spirit's transformative work. In baptism, the Holy Spirit that forgives our sin also comes and dwells within us, so that we become a "temple of the Holy Spirit."[72] The casting out of the spirit of divisiveness takes place so that we might receive the Holy Spirit, who is the agent of our unity. "The one by whom we are cleaned up through receiving his pardon, we also receive as a guest living in us to help us do justly and to grow till we become perfect in justice."[73] It is the Holy Spirit, dwelling within us, that enables the church to live in unity, and to seek the way of justice together. Thus, when instructing the monastic community to be "*united in mind and heart* (Acts 4:32)," Augustine reminds them that they are "temples" in whom God dwells.[74]

Being Formed into One

The unity brought about by the Holy Spirit takes a particular shape. We are not unified because of mutually agreed values or a common way of life, but rather because of our mutual participation in the one body of Jesus Christ.[75] Augustine gives a helpful summary of this unifying work in a Pentecost sermon, where he speaks of "the scattered members of the human race" being gathered into "one body," and "attached to their one head, Christ, and so reunited, and fused together into the unity of the holy body by the fire of love."[76]

In *Sermon 71*, Augustine makes only passing mention of the body of Christ, explaining that our unity in Christ's body is part of the Holy Spirit's work: "The companionship, you see, by which we are made into one body of the only Son of

---

72. *Serm.* 71.33. For the association of baptism and becoming temples of the Holy Spirit, see *Serm.* 398.13. Stanislaus J. Grabowski explains that the Holy Spirit's work of indwelling should not be understood apart from the Father and Son: Stanislaus J. Grabowski, "The Holy Ghost in the Mystical Body of Christ According to St. Augustine," *Theological Studies* 5 (1944): 455.

73. *Serm.* 71.33.

74. *Reg. 3:* 1.8. Note that in this precept Augustine describes the community members as "temples," rather than as together forming one "temple" (as in the earlier quotation from *Serm.* 71.33). Grabowski describes and distinguishes this "individual" and "corporate inhabitation" in Grabowski, "The Holy Ghost in the Mystical Body of Christ," 478–81. See also *Serm.* 136B.3; *Civ.* 10.3.

75. For this unity in Christ, see *Trin.* 4.7.11–4.9.12. Augustine explains the relationship between the "temple" and "body of Christ" images in *Serm.* 217.4.

76. *Serm.* 271.

God, is his special concern."[77] However, Augustine speaks about our incorporation into the body of Christ on many other occasions, most notably when he is instructing his listeners about the sacraments of baptism and Eucharist.

Through baptism, we become members of the body of Christ.[78] In Augustine's context, preparation for baptism was substantial and demanding (at least by modern standards). After an initial period of instruction as catechumens, candidates entered a more intense phase of fasting and preparation, culminating in their baptism at Easter.[79] To describe the radical new baptismal identity that results, Augustine frequently draws on the biblical imagery of new birth. Teaching the "*competentes*" the Lord's Prayer in preparation for baptism, Augustine explains that they "have already been conceived," and will soon be "brought forth from the womb of the Church" through "the font" of baptism.[80] This new birth enables us to address God as "*Our Father,*" Augustine explains.[81] This common parentage unites those who would normally be socially or economically divided. Augustine spells this out clearly when teaching the Lord's Prayer to the *competentes* on another occasion: "You see, you are going to say *Our Father who art in heaven*. You have begun to belong to a huge family. Under this Father rich and poor are brothers; under this Father master and slave are brothers; under this Father emperor and private soldier are brothers."[82] The new birth of baptism marks entry into a new family in Christ, where those from dramatically different walks of life find a common place of belonging.

However, while baptism is clearly foundational to the unity found in Christ, Augustine more frequently emphasizes this unity when teaching on the Eucharist, which he describes as "the sacrament of unity."[83] Augustine's sermons on the Eucharist to the "*infantes*" are particularly instructive in this regard.[84] In these sermons, he draws on the rich imagery of the Eucharistic meal to explain how we,

---

77. *Serm.* 71.28.
78. *Serm.* 224.1.
79. Van der Meer, *Augustine the Bishop*, 353–69. See also Harmless, *Augustine and the Catechumenate*; Robert L. Wilken, "Tutoring the Affections: Liturgy and Christian Formation in the Early Church," *Antiphon* 8, no. 3 (2003): 21–7. Many of the sermons discussed in this section arise from this formational context. For a clear outline of the place of these sermons in the process of Augustine's catechetical instruction, see especially Chapters 6 and 7 of Harmless, *Augustine and the Catechumenate*.
80. *Serm.* 56.5. Augustine describes the *competentes* as those who are "asking together" (*Serm.* 216.1). For discussion of this phase of baptismal preparation, see Harmless, *Augustine and the Catechumenate*, 291–347. As Harmless outlines, this included instruction in the creed (pp. 322–36), followed by the teaching of the Lord's Prayer (pp. 336–45).
81. *Serm.* 56.5.
82. *Serm.* 59.2.
83. *Serm.* 229A.1.
84. Augustine explains that the *infantes* are those who "have just now been born to Christ" through baptism (*Serm.* 228.1). For further description of the *infantes*, see Harmless, *Augustine and the Catechumenate*, 370–1. Harmless explains that Augustine offered "a brief catechesis on the Eucharist" to the newly baptized (p. 372). See pp. 372–81 for discussion of these sermons.

though many, are formed into one body. This imagery gathers together the whole of the catechetical formation process, and brings it into focus at the Eucharistic table. *Sermon 272*, a brief message given to the *infantes* at Pentecost, provides an illustrative example. Turning first to the bread, Augustine recalls Paul's instruction: "*One bread, one body, we being many are* (1 Cor 10:17)."[85] He explains:

> Remember that bread is not made from one grain, but from many. When you were being exorcised, it's as though you were being ground. When you were baptized it's as though you were mixed into dough. When you received the fire of the Holy Spirit, it's as though you were baked. Be what you can see, and receive what you are.[86]

The bread-making illustration helps the *infantes* appreciate how God has been at work throughout these various aspects of their formation, and the goal of unity toward which this formation has been directed. Like the elements on the table, these aspects of formation may have appeared ordinary, yet God has been working mysteriously through them, forming many into one.[87]

Turning to the Eucharistic cup in *Sermon 272*, Augustine continues on this theme:

> Just as many grains are mixed into one loaf in order to produce the visible appearance of bread, as though what holy scripture says about the faithful were happening: *They had one soul and one heart in God* (Acts 4:32); so too with the wine. Brothers and sisters, just remind yourselves what wine is made from; many grapes hang in the bunch, but the juice of the grapes is poured together in one vessel.[88]

Augustine uses the image of winemaking to illustrate the same formational process: the gathering together of many into one. It is significant that on this occasion Augustine links this Eucharistic unity with the Acts 4 community. This reminds his

---

85. *Serm.* 272.
86. *Serm.* 272. For other occasions when Augustine uses this illustration, see *Serm.* 227; 229.1; 229A.2. For this bread-making image, and also that of winemaking (discussed below), see also Harmless, *Augustine and the Catechumenate*, 376–9, 403.
87. *Serm.* 229A.1. Cavanaugh highlights the "public" significance of the Eucharist, and the challenge it presents to modern notions of the individual and property: Cavanaugh, *Theopolitical Imagination*, 46–52. "In the Eucharist the foundational distinction between mine and thine is radically effaced," he notes (p. 47). In *Being Consumed*, Cavanaugh notes the contrast between the Eucharist and patterns of consumerism: "The act of consumption of the Eucharist does not entail the appropriation of goods for private use, but rather being assimilated to a public body, the body of Christ. As Augustine reminds us, God is the food that consumes us." William T. Cavanaugh, *Being Consumed: Economics and Christian Desire* (Grand Rapids, MI: Eerdmans, 2008), 95. See pp. 53–8, 94–100.
88. *Serm.* 272.

listeners that they should not consider the revered example of these early Christians to be unattainable in their own time and place, nor should they consider this unity to be the province of a select few (such as the monastics). The same God who was at work at Pentecost, gathering together the believers and uniting them in heart and soul, continues to be at work within all members of the church community, including when we gather together to share the communion meal.[89]

By participating in the Eucharist we participate in God's unifying work amongst us. "What you receive is what you yourselves are, thanks to the grace by which you have been redeemed," Augustine explains.[90] At the Eucharistic table, we receive the gift of God's unity. Luc Verheijen expresses it well: "In the Eucharist we meet, in a sacramental way, the peace and the unity of Christ, and there, progressively, they become our peace and our unity."[91] And yet, while emphasizing God's role in the unifying work of the Eucharist, Augustine also highlights the importance of our response. He challenges the congregation to receive this sacrament—and indeed, to live their lives—in accordance with the unity it commends to them. "Be what you can see, and receive what you are," Augustine charges his listeners.[92] Conversely, when we fail to live as one, the unity of the Eucharist provides a sort of internal critique of our division. Thus Augustine observes that when the Donatists receive the Eucharist, "they receive what is a testimony against themselves; because they insist on division, while this bread is a sign of unity."[93]

The Unity of the Body

Through the gift of the Holy Spirit, "the Father and the Son wished us to have communion both with them and among ourselves."[94] Both aspects of communion are made possible through our incorporation into Christ. Firstly, by forming us into his body, Christ unites us to himself.[95] This is wholly an act of gracious

---

89. In his article, Wilken highlights the way in which liturgy "tutors the affections." Wilken, "Tutoring the Affections," 25. However, reflecting on formation within the context of liturgy, he observes: "In this setting formation is not heroic, it is brought about by the regular, repetitive and deliberate actions of people engaged in a communal task. Yet it is not their own work; it is the work of the One who is present in the Eucharist. Liturgy teaches us that formation is finally not a matter of striving but of grace" (p. 26).

90. *Serm.* 229A.1.

91. Verheijen, *Saint Augustine's Monasticism*, 94.

92. *Serm.* 272. For other exhortations, see *Serm.* 227 and *Serm.* 229.2. Augustine reminds listeners in *Sermon* 90 that a faithful Christian life is not simply a matter of receiving the sacraments, which "are common to the bad and the good" (*Serm.* 90.5). Rather, it is genuine love (1 Tim. 1:5) that distinguishes the faithful (.6).

93. *Serm.* 229.2.

94. *Serm.* 71.18.

95. Regarding the unity of the *"totus Christus,"* I have found Canning's discussion helpful: Canning, *Unity of Love for God and Neighbour*, 359–68.

generosity, for although Christ lacks nothing and is "complete" in himself, "he was prepared to be complete together with us," Augustine explains.[96] In *Sermon* 137, Augustine speaks movingly of Christ's identification with his people amidst our trials, and the compassionate love it reveals. Augustine invites the congregation to "observe the loving affection of this head of ours," and reminds them of Christ's presence in the poor and suffering.[97] Augustine then notes that when Christ addresses those who fed the hungry and clothed the naked (Mt. 25:34–40), he speaks "as though he had received it all personally himself."[98] This reveals the unity between Christ, the head, and his body. To illustrate this for his listeners, Augustine invites them to reflect on the unity of their own physical bodies:

> In a crush of people jammed in a narrow space, when someone treads on your foot, doesn't your head say, "You're treading on me"? Neither your head nor your tongue is being trodden on by anybody; it's up on top, it's perfectly safe, nothing bad has happened to it. And yet because through the binding power of love there is a unity from the head right down to the feet, the tongue didn't detach itself from that unity, but said, "You're treading on me," though nobody had touched it.[99]

In the same way, Augustine suggests, although Christ the head does not hunger, he says "*I was hungry, and you gave me to eat*" when the hungry ones in his body are fed.[100] This displays the remarkable unity between Christ (as head) and his body, a unity which is brought about by the Holy Spirit, the "binding power of love."

Secondly, we too are drawn together in love. As Canning notes, it is unity with the head that forms the basis of this unity with one another.[101] The Holy Spirit that unites Christ the head with his body also unites the members of his body, in one unifying work. Like the "human spirit" that "quickens all the parts" of the human body, the Holy Spirit enlivens and draws us together as members of Christ's body.[102] Consequently, we too experience the pain suffered by other members.[103] Therefore, for Augustine, compassion, companionship, and mutual love are not incidental to the Christian life; rather, they are vital signs of life in Christ. The "health" of the

---

96. *Serm.* 341(D22/M55).19.
97. *Serm.* 137.2.
98. *Serm.* 137.2.
99. *Serm.* 137.2.
100. *Serm.* 137.2.
101. Canning, *Unity of Love for God and Neighbour*, 362, 384. Canning emphasizes the Christological dimensions of this unity (whereas in this chapter I focus on the Holy Spirit's role in this unifying work). He writes: "The driving force of this dynamic image is the divine power of Christ's love for his body. Love will not permit the head to abandon the body. Indeed, if the body were deserted by its head, the members could not love one another. The love of *idem ipse* with his members constructs a deep foundation for unity among the members themselves" (p. 362).
102. *Serm.* 268.2.
103. *Serm.* 268.2.

body of Christ, Augustine teaches, is "the unity of its members and the framework of love."[104] Love for one another is thus the primary indicator of the work of the Holy Spirit among us.

Augustine's emphasis on the companionship brought about by the Holy Spirit is informed, in part, by the Pentecost narrative. In *Sermon* 71, he associates the Pentecost sign of "languages" with the "companionship" in the body of Christ that the Holy Spirit enables.[105] "Because it's languages that bind human societies more closely together," he explains, "so it was appropriate to signify by the languages of all nations this companionship of the children of God and members of Christ that was going to exist in all nations."[106] Accordingly, the Holy Spirit's presence continues to be indicated, Augustine teaches, "if you are held in the bond of the peace of the Church, which is spread out among all nations."[107] In the *Homilies on the First Epistle of John*, Augustine applies this teaching in more personal terms. If the presence of the Holy Spirit is no longer marked by the Pentecost sign of languages, "how does anyone know that he has received the Holy Spirit?" Augustine asks.[108] "Let one question one's heart," he instructs.[109] "If a person loves his brother, the Spirit of God is abiding in him."[110]

Unity in the body of Christ does not, in itself, mean economic uniformity (although, as subsequent chapters outline, it has economic implications). Indeed, the very fact that both rich and poor can be members of the same body is what makes this unity so extraordinary—not least in our contemporary context, where the wealthy and the destitute rarely share a common place of belonging.[111] Christ forms both into his one body. Thus Augustine can address both rich and poor as members of the body of Christ.[112] Despite their varied circumstances, their lives are now bound up with one another. This unity among members enables a new awareness of each other's needs, to the degree that the "hurt" of one member is felt by the whole body.[113] Such a bond prompts the other members to respond with genuine concern and practical care.

---

104. *Serm.* 137.1. Williams describes the "active" nature of God's love in the relationships between members of Christ's body: "The other in the Church is a place where Christ's love is active; and the love that is Christ's acting in me moves out to the love acting in the other which simultaneously moves towards me." Williams, *On Augustine*, 199.
105. *Serm.* 71.28.
106. *Serm.* 71.28.
107. *Serm.* 71.28.
108. *Tract. ep. Jo.* 6.10.
109. *Tract. ep. Jo.* 6.10.
110. *Tract. ep. Jo.* 6.10.
111. Martin contrasts the life of unity Augustine outlines in the *Rule* with the Roman vision of "*concordia*," which "was understood to be between already established orders and privileged classes: it was by no means a *concordia universalis*." Martin, "Augustine and the Politics of Monasticism," 174.
112. E.g., *Serm.* 53A.6.
113. *Serm.* 268.2.

Of course, Augustine is mindful that his listeners often fail to display such love for their sister or brother, whether through forgetful neglect or willful prejudice. Although unity comes as a gift, it nonetheless requires ongoing pastoral nurture. In *Sermon* 137, Augustine employs the imagery of sickness and health to describe this aspect of Christian formation: "Anyone who grows cold in love is sick in the body of Christ."[114] We may be present in the body of Christ, but we have lost sensation, becoming numb to the needs and concerns of other members.[115] Therefore, in his preaching, Augustine is often seeking to revive this love for others.[116] Having warned his congregation about this ailment, Augustine also encourages them not to lose hope, for "God, who has already raised our head on high, has the power to heal the sick members too."[117] Indeed, Augustine's preaching ministry can itself be understood as part of this healing: through the preaching of the word, Christ tends to his body, restoring love amongst his members.[118]

One in Heart

For Augustine, the Holy Spirit's unifying power was most profoundly displayed in the early Christian community of Acts 4. From among those who had been opposed to Christ, thousands of people had sought forgiveness and received the Holy Spirit (Acts 2:27–42), and as a consequence, "*They had one soul and one heart* (Acts 4:32)."[119]

When Augustine makes reference to the Acts 4 community in *Sermon* 71, it is clear that he does not consider their exemplary unity to be a unique occurrence in history. Rather, their example is illustrative of the ongoing work of the Holy Spirit in overcoming division. Here, Augustine instructs his congregation that, unlike the one who is "divided against himself," the Holy Spirit

> is not only not divided against himself, but also makes those whom he gathers together undivided, by forgiving them the sins that are divided against

---

114. *Serm.* 137.1.
115. Grabowski explains the importance of Augustine's conception of the "twofold inhabitation" of the Holy Spirit (individual and corporate) for understanding this aspect of this teaching. Although those in the church who are sick, lacking love for other members, may have lost the "personal indwelling" of the Holy Spirit, they still remain "attached to the living body," which the Holy Spirit animates in this corporate sense. Stanislaus J. Grabowski, "The Holy Ghost in the Mystical Body of Christ According to St. Augustine II," *Theological Studies* 6 (1945): 68–9.
116. E.g., *Tract. ep. Jo.* 5.12.
117. *Serm.* 137.1.
118. "Christ is preaching Christ, the body preaching its head, and the head looking after its body." *Serm.* 354.1.
119. *Serm.* 229G.5(6).

themselves, and by dwelling in them once they are cleansed, in order that there may be, as it says in the Acts of the Apostles, one heart and soul of the multitude of those who believed.[120]

The Holy Spirit who was once at work among the Jerusalem community is here described in present and active terms: casting out the spirit of division, dwelling within us, and drawing us together in "heart and soul."

In the *Rule*, the description of unity in Acts 4:32 is presented as foundational for the monastic community: "In the first place—and this is the very reason for your being gathered together in one—you should live in the *house in unity of spirit* (Ps 67:7[68:6]) and you should have *one soul and one heart* (Acts 4:32) centered on God."[121] Augustine's language stresses the primacy of unity: "In the first place"; "this is the very reason for your being gathered together in one."[122] This unity is further reinforced at the end of this first chapter of the *Rule*: "Therefore you should all live *united in mind and heart* (Acts 4:32) and should in one another honor God, whose temples you have become."[123] The love of members for one another, and the unity it forms, becomes a way of honoring God.

It is Augustine's idiosyncratic tendency to append the words "toward God" ("*in deum*") to the phrase "one soul and one heart" from Acts 4:32.[124] Commenting on this addition in *Sermon 77* (where Augustine quotes: "*And they had*, as it says, *one soul and one heart toward God* (Acts 4:32)"[125]), Hill notes that although these extra words did not feature in Latin bibles, they did feature in Augustine's *Rule*, and suggests "it would seem likely that they creep into his sermons from there."[126] In itself, this is significant, for (if Hill's supposition is correct) it illustrates a tangible influence of the *Rule* upon the *Sermons*. However, of greater importance is the reason why Augustine routinely chooses to make this addition. While God could implicitly be assumed as the focus of the believers' unity in Acts 4:32, Augustine appears concerned to make this explicit. For, as he sometimes concedes, a certain sort of unity can be found apart from God: "Those who watch plays together love each other, those who get drunk together in shebeens love each other, those who share a bad conscience with each other love one another."[127] A common love

---

120. *Serm.* 71.35. On Augustine's use of Acts 4:32a in this passage, see Verheijen, *Saint Augustine's Monasticism*, 14n20.
121. *Reg. 3*: 1.2.
122. Lawless notes that in this precept, Augustine emphasizes unity four times in a single sentence: Lawless, *Augustine of Hippo and His Monastic Rule*, 156–7.
123. *Reg. 3*: 1.8.
124. Verheijen, *Saint Augustine's Monasticism*, 15. Note that this phrase is rendered "centered on God" in Mary and Bonner's translation of *Reg. 3*: 1.2 (quoted above); in Canning's translation of the *Rule*, he renders this phrase "on the way to God." *Rule of Saint Augustine*, 11.
125. *Serm.* 77.4.
126. Hill, in *Sermons (51–94)*, 325n11.
127. *Serm.* 332.1.

does draw people together, whether for better (e.g., pursuing a charitable goal) or worse (e.g., nationalistic zeal), yet these fleeting objects of devotion will ultimately disappoint us; they cannot offer a true and lasting unity. Instead, Augustine urges his listeners toward the unity that comes from loving God: "Love each other all the more by being united in loving one who cannot ever displease you, the savior."[128] True unity is found when we are united in love of God.[129] Love of God enables unity because, unlike the earthly things that preoccupy us, God cannot be divided or diminished by our desire.[130] "So if brothers wish to live in concord with each other," Augustine advises in *Sermon* 359, "they should not love earth.... Let them seek possession of a property which cannot be divided, and they will always live in concord."[131]

For this reason, the liturgical instruction "*Lift up your hearts*" is no platitude for Augustine, but rather an ever-needed reminder to the worshiping community to redirect our love from earth to heaven, the members of the body looking to their head.[132] For when we are oriented toward God together, our division is overcome. To illustrate this ecclesial unity for his hearers, Augustine draws on the vivid image of Christ's tunic which, because it was "woven in one piece from the top" (Jn 19:23, NRSV), was not divided by the soldiers at his crucifixion. "What does it mean that it is woven from the top?" Augustine enquires of the congregation.[133] "The same as why we are told 'Lift up your hearts.' And thus all who have their hearts lifted up, up to the top, cannot be divided into parts, because they will belong to that tunic which cannot be divided."[134] On another occasion he explains: "That garment was

---

128. *Serm.* 332.1. Commenting on Augustine's discussion in *The Trinity* of Christ's prayer for the unity of believers (*Trin.* 4.9.12), Williams observes: "The focus is on the total unity between Son and Father, which is to be reflected among the disciples: this is to be not merely the natural unity between members of the human species but a harmonious *will*, a tending toward one and the same blissful heavenly end." Williams, *On Augustine*, 145.

129. Commenting on Augustine's use of Acts 4, Bonner observes that the community Augustine envisaged was not just "an association of monks living under a common rule," but rather "a band of brothers held together by love of God and love of each other." Bonner, commentary to *Monastic Rules*, 64. Such is Augustine's conviction that unity emerges out of our common love for God that when discussing Acts 4:34–35 it prompts him to assert that a common life came more readily to the Jewish believers because, unlike the Gentiles, "they already worshiped one God" (*Serm.* 252.3). See also *Doctr. chr.* 3.6.10; *Catech.* 23.43.

130. It is because God (unlike earthly goods) is not material, that God is not divisible. Ayres acknowledges (with reference to the *Confessions* Book Seven) that Augustine's encounter with Platonic thought helped him arrive at this insight: Ayres, "Grammar of Augustine's Trinitarian Theology," 53–4. However, as Ayres also notes, Augustine often had to remind his congregation not to conceive of God in material terms: Ayres, "'Remember That You Are Catholic,'" 58.

131. *Serm.* 359.2.
132. *Serm.* 227.
133. *Serm.* 159B(D21/M54).18.
134. *Serm.* 159B(D21/M54).18.

an advertisement for unity, that garment was a declaration of charity, it is charity itself, woven from the top."[135] Whereas our earthly longings make us easily divided, when our heart is lifted up to God, we are knit together with charity.

Augustine understands this unity found in God to be fundamental to the witness of the church in the world. Through its life lived in orientation to God, the church not only reminds a divisive world what unity looks like, but in whom such unity is to be found. In Augustine's monastic community, this distinctive witness was particularly apparent, as Markus observes: "Its existence here and now proclaimed a permanent challenge to all other forms of social existence, a question mark placed against the structures of domination inherent in the society of fallen men, an ideal Augustine held up to his lay congregations to imitate in 'building the temple of God.'"[136] The unity of the monastic community presented a tangible witness to God's ongoing work in overcoming division and restoring unity. However, as Markus's final comment suggests, Augustine does not understand this as a task for the monastery alone, but rather for the whole Christian community. Indeed, the unity of the monastics cannot be conceived apart from the unity of the church, for both expressions of unity are the work of the one Spirit. Verheijen explains: "The fraternal unity in monasteries was for him [Augustine] a small-scale presentation of *ecclesial* unity. Within the 'great Church,' to which they belonged just as the other faithful, the 'servants of God in the monastery' came together to dwell *in unum*, in order to live intensely the spirit of unity which, in principle, was that of the entire 'great Church.'"[137] The nature of monastic life allowed members to express this unity in a unique fashion, but the call to bear witness in the world through a life of unity remains the call of the whole church.

While encouraging this unity among listeners, Augustine nonetheless reminds them that its perfection remains an eschatological goal.[138] "Perfect love or charity

---

135. *Serm.* 265.7.

136. Markus, *End of Ancient Christianity*, 81. Markus highlights here the distinctiveness of a community that is "ruled by humility not power, living in concord without exploitation" (p. 81). By contrast, in Augustine's view, the political institutions of the earthly city depend on restraint and coercion in their attempts to achieve "some minimal cohesion" in society, as Markus explains in an earlier work: Markus, *Saeculum: History and Society in the Theology of St Augustine*, 95. For the changing "apologetic" function of the visible Christian community in Augustine's writing, see William J. Collinge, "Developments in Augustine's Theology of Christian Community Life after A.C. 395," *Augustinian Studies* 16 (1984): 49–63.

137. Verheijen, *Saint Augustine's Monasticism*, 65. John Paul Hoskins provides a brief survey of the relationship between this monastic and ecclesial unity in Augustine's thought: John Paul Hoskins, "*Acts* 4:32 in Augustine's Ecclesiology," in *Studia Patristica 49*, ed. J. Baun et al. (Leuven: Peeters, 2010), 73–7. See also Demura, "*Anima Una et Cor Unum*," 257–66.

138. As Markus notes, Augustine's emphasis on the church's eschatological perfection challenged the Donatist insistence on the purity of the church in this present life: Markus, *End of Ancient Christianity*, 52–3. See also Markus, *Saeculum: History and Society in the Theology of St Augustine*, 112–26, 166–8.

is the final, perfect gift of the Holy Spirit," he teaches.[139] For Augustine, unity and concord characterize the future life we will enjoy together in God's company: "All the citizens of that city, you see, will be urging each other to equal heights of praise with the most ardent charity toward one another and toward God."[140] But in this life, Verheijen observes, the unity of the Christian community is "precarious," "inchoative," and awaits perfection.[141] This is true even of the exemplary unity of the monastic community. Noting an instance in which Augustine speaks of the monastery as "the City of God," Markus explains that this must be understood in relation to the "eschatological vocation of the whole Church."[142] In this sense, he adds, the monastic community "is a privileged anticipation of the Church's eschatological realisation."[143] The unity that the Holy Spirit forms among us is thus a work in progress, awaiting a future completion. Yet even in this form, it can be a sign of hope. Martin observes that although Augustine's monastic community is "still on pilgrimage," it "nonetheless offered in the present moment promise and hope, witness and example, consolation and comfort, but also challenge and demand for embracing and giving expression to a new vision of community, one that has still only begun to unfold."[144]

The Centrality of the Church

Throughout *Sermon* 71, Augustine wrestles with Jesus's difficult teaching about blasphemy against the Holy Spirit (Mt. 12:31–32). He emphasizes that this teaching does not pertain to blasphemy in general, but to the speaking of a particular word against the Holy Spirit.[145] What, then, is this word? Augustine determines that it is our refusal of the gift of forgiveness that the Holy Spirit offers.[146] As long as we speak this word of refusal, we cannot receive the forgiveness that the Holy Spirit offers to us.

In considering the nature of the blasphemous word against the Holy Spirit in *Sermon* 71, Augustine has had to ask "Who is the Holy Spirit?" and "What is the nature of the Holy Spirit's work among us?" As discussed, it is the Holy Spirit's work in unifying the church that comes to the fore in this sermon, which leads Augustine to further conclude that we also refuse the Spirit when we set ourselves

---

139. *Serm.* 71.19.
140. *Serm.* 362.29.
141. Verheijen, *Saint Augustine's Monasticism*, 94.
142. Markus, *End of Ancient Christianity*, 79.
143. Markus, *End of Ancient Christianity*, 80. See also p. 81.
144. Martin, "Augustine and the Politics of Monasticism," 184. See also Martin's earlier comments on the "hopeful" nature of Augustine's portrayal of Christian community (p. 166).
145. *Serm.* 71.9–10.
146. *Serm.* 71.20.

apart from the church that the Spirit gathers together.[147] Therefore, he insists, "Since the forgiveness of sins can only be given in the Holy Spirit, it can be given in that Church alone which has the Holy Spirit."[148] Such a claim may appear offensive in modern times, where the common patristic belief that salvation cannot be found outside of the church ("*extra ecclesiam nulla salus*"[149]) is no longer widely held.[150] However, while this part of Augustine's sermon may rightly raise some concerns,[151] the theological significance of his association of the Holy Spirit's forgiving work with the life of the church should not be overlooked.

By way of review: the Father and the Son have sent the Holy Spirit so that we might "have communion both with them and among ourselves."[152] The Holy Spirit forgives our divisive sin, and fills us with love, uniting us with both God and one another. Communion with God and with one another is thus intrinsically linked, for it is the work of the same Spirit. Therefore, Augustine rightly understands the forgiving, renewing, uniting work of the Holy Spirit to have an ecclesial locus, for we cannot be drawn into communion with God while remaining apart from the community that the Holy Spirit gathers.[153]

---

147. *Serm.* 71.28.

148. *Serm.* 71.33. Grabowski clarifies that Augustine does not consider the Holy Spirit's work to be limited to the bounds of the church: Grabowski, "The Holy Ghost in the Mystical Body of Christ," 467.

149. Lancel attributes this expression to Cyprian: Lancel, *Saint Augustine*, 282. For the influence of Cyprian's view of the church on both Augustine and the Donatists, see Bonner, *St Augustine of Hippo*, 278-94.

150. Stanley Hauerwas observes that in modernity, many Christians have lost sight of the necessity of the church as a "political community" for salvation: "By being established, at least culturally established in liberal societies, it became more important that people *believe* rather than be incorporated into the church." Stanley Hauerwas, *After Christendom? How the Church Is to Behave If Freedom, Justice, and a Christian Nation Are Bad Ideas* (Nashville, TN: Abingdon Press, 1991), 26, 25.

151. Such concerns may be alleviated by Augustine's teaching that the "blasphemy against the Spirit" which he identifies in this sermon "cannot be detected in anybody ... as long as they are still in this life" (*Serm.* 71.21). Augustine believed that the "separation" of the "wheat" from the "weeds" (Mt. 13:24–30) would only take place eschatologically (*Serm.* 73.4). By contrast, Lancel notes that the Donatists believed that this separation had already taken place. Lancel, *Saint Augustine*, 283-4.

152. *Serm.* 71.18.

153. Burnaby comes to a similar conclusion: "Behind all the misconstruction and abuse of that principle [*Extra Ecclesiam nulla salus*] there remains the truth that neither sin or forgiveness can be comprehended in terms of a relation of 'the alone to the Alone'. The solitary soul *cannot* be 'in Christ'." Burnaby, *Amor Dei*, 177. He adds that "the love of God cannot exist apart from love of the brethren" (p. 177). (Burnaby's quotation of "the alone to the Alone" is from Plotinus.)

As the contemporary church considers how to respond to the divisiveness of economic inequality, Augustine's teaching reminds us that this unifying work has an essentially ecclesial shape. The church is not incidental to God's salvific work; rather it is the place where the Holy Spirit's gift of community is formed. Furthermore, Augustine's teaching also alerts us to the danger of establishing alternative forms of Christian community apart from the wider church, lest we find ourselves working against God's broader purposes in overcoming division and restoring unity.

Toward the conclusion of *Sermon* 71, Augustine underscores this teaching by recalling Christ's words in Matthew 12:30: "*Anyone who is not with me is against me; and anyone who does not gather with me scatters.*"[154] If Augustine's teaching on this topic appears confrontational, these words of Jesus are no less direct. To be with Jesus is to be with those he has gathered. In *Sermon* 71, Augustine has presented this message in uncompromising terms. However, that does not mean his purpose has been to condemn those outside the church. Nearing his conclusion, he reminds the congregation that God "doesn't desire the death of the wicked as much as that they should be converted and live."[155] For this reason, God gave the gift of the Holy Spirit, so that our divisive sin might be overcome.[156] Augustine's pastoral intent, then, has been to remind his listeners where this gift may be found, in the hope that all would gather with Christ, through the work of the Holy Spirit, and receive the gift of unity with God and one another.

Conclusion

Augustine's concern for unity draws our attention to a world that is "divided against itself."[157] This division is an inevitable consequence of our turn from God, the common good, to our own private interests. As is well evidenced in the economic inequality of our own time, our preoccupation with material goods distances us from the needs of others, or sets us against them. Internally, our hearts are also divided, torn by competing desires.

The life of God, by contrast, is united. As Augustine teaches, Father, Son, and Holy Spirit "enjoy entirely equal divinity and inseparable unity."[158] God desires to share this gift of unity with us, overcoming our division. Augustine explains that "by what is common to them both the Father and the Son wished us to have communion both with them and among ourselves."[159] And so, even across the

---

154. *Serm.* 71.36.
155. *Serm.* 71.37.
156. *Serm.* 71.37.
157. *Serm.* 71.1.
158. *Serm.* 71.18.
159. *Serm.* 71.18.

economic segregations of contemporary society, the Holy Spirit works among us, casting out our division, gathering us together, and restoring us in relationship with God and one another. Unlike the desire for wealth that divides, the Holy Spirit gifts us with a love that unites, drawing us toward God, and toward one another.

Accordingly, Augustine reminds us that the gift of community is not incidental to the Christian life. We cannot be reconciled to God while remaining divided from the community that God gathers. Rather, the movement from division toward a common love for God and neighbor is foundational to Christian formation.

For those in pastoral ministry, it is instructive to consider how Augustine uses key moments in the worshiping life of the congregation (e.g., baptism, Eucharist) to emphasize this aspect of Christian identity. As we prepare an individual for the sacrament of baptism, how might we help them (or in the case of infant baptism, their parents) understand this corporate aspect of faith: that baptism is not solely a personal affair, but a weaving of our self into the life of others? Our common baptism means that privileged and penniless alike now share one life in Christ, yet there is need for teaching—both for those preparing for baptism and for the whole congregation—to help us grapple with this aspect of our Christian identity. So too with the Eucharist: as we invite people to the Lord's table, what liturgical actions and instructions might narrate the bond that connects us with our neighbor in the pew, whose material circumstances may differ from our own, yet who shares the same loaf, the same cup (1 Cor. 10:16–17)? Augustine's preaching on these topics (as surveyed in this chapter) provides valuable examples for us to consider.

Just as this unity is central to our formation, so also is it central to the church's witness in a divided world. Confronted with situations of need, many churches are eager to "make a difference," and providing food and material aid will seem an obvious way to demonstrate the church's concern. And indeed, the sharing of resources is an important and necessary part of the church's response (as discussed in following chapters). However, this is not the most prophetic aspect of the church's witness, for in contemporary society many different groups and agencies work to distribute food parcels and financial assistance. By contrast, in the forming of the Christian community, as God draws together those who had once lived divided, a beautiful and distinctive picture of unity is offered to the wider world. What becomes profound here is not, for example, that the business executive has gifted money to the beneficiary, but rather that both share a common identity; they share a relationship, they spend time together, they know one another.

Thus, as churches consider their response to economic inequalities in their context, a fitting place to begin is with the unifying work that God is already doing among them, in the formation of Christian community. Where is this unity being experienced? How does our common identity in Christ shape the way we relate to one another? How does it reframe the way we see our economic differences? How might this become the basis for our response to wider needs in the community? And in all this, how can our lives and actions point toward the God who heals us of our divisiveness? We can offer such a witness when, as with Augustine's community, and the first Christians, we live with "*one soul and one heart* (Acts 4:32) centered on God,"[160] our lives pointing toward the one in whom true unity is found.

---

160. *Reg.* 3: 1.2.

Chapter 3

AVARICE AND THE COMMON GOOD

And then, you should not call *anything your own, but you should have everything in common* (Acts 4:32).
—*Reg.* 3: 1.3.

At the moment of entering the monastery those who had any property in the world should gladly choose to have it become common property.
—*Reg.* 3: 1.4.

The sharing of property was a significant feature of life in Augustine's monastic community. When Possidius discusses their way of life in his biography, it is this aspect that he emphasizes: "The most important provision was that no one in that community was to have any property of his own, but rather they were to have all things in common, with each being given what he needed."[1] The instruction to share property in common features early in the *Rule*, and in later precepts, Augustine gives specific guidance regarding the use and sharing of resources.[2] These instructions contribute to the overall formational movement of the *Rule*, where Augustine directs members to leave behind a life of self-interest, and turn toward the interests of others.[3] Where resources were once claimed for private enjoyment, they are now to be used for the benefit of all.

In our own time, this aspect of monastic life remains an inspiring example, and provides a dramatic contrast to the unequal and individualistic use of resources in contemporary Western society. Yet, while we might admire this aspect of life in Augustine's monastic community, for many (probably most) in the church, it remains an unachievable form of Christian life, whether due to family or work commitments, or other personal circumstances. This was also true for the members of the wider Christian community in Augustine's care, most of whom were unable to live the form of Christian life outlined in the *Rule*. However, when Augustine instructs the wider congregation about their use of resources, there

---

1. Possidius, *Life of Saint Augustine*, 5.1.
2. See especially *Reg.* 3: 1.3–5; 3.3–5; 4.1; 5.1–3, 8–11.
3. *Reg.* 3: 5.2.

remains significant thematic continuity with his instruction to the monastic community. Here, the same formational movement can be found, as he challenges the selfish desires of his listeners, and calls them to share what they have with others. For Augustine, this is a movement from avarice to love.

In this chapter I trace the movement from avarice toward love in Augustine's *Sermons*. Augustine preached often on wealth and poverty, and in this chapter I do not attempt to summarize all his teaching on this topic. Rather, I focus on this one thread, demonstrating how Augustine's call away from self-interest, and toward love of God and neighbor, comes to bear on the use of our resources. For whereas greed prompts us to hoard material resources for our self, love is demonstrated through our sharing of resources, and our concern for the needs of others. Augustine clearly expresses this message in *Sermon* 107A, which guides this chapter.[4] Hill suggests that this sermon was given "between 413 and 420," likely amongst a "small rural congregation" located "in the Hippo diocese or region."[5] Though I pay particular attention to *Sermon* 107A, I consider this text in dialogue with other relevant sermons, with the purpose of illustrating the pertinence of Augustine's call from avarice to love for the church today.

Attending to the Roots

In *Sermon* 107A, Augustine describes the movement from avarice to charity in arboreal terms. Christ is the planter and pruner of trees, coming among us to plant good trees that will bear good fruit, and to prune or even "uproot" those that do not (Mt. 7:17-19).[6] Two trees are particularly in view in this sermon: the bad tree of "cupidity" (or avarice), and the good tree of charity.[7] The former is unable to produce good fruit; the latter can yield no bad fruit.[8] Christ is attending to these trees, Augustine notes, through the gospel passage that has just been heard among the congregation, which "is itself a sermon that has been striking bad trees."[9] Similarly, Augustine believes that his own sermon, inasmuch as Christ speaks through it, "is an axe aimed at the root of the bad tree."[10]

---

4. The Latin text is found in C. Lambot, "Nouveaux Sermons de S. Augustin I–III 'De lectione evangelii," *Revue Bénédictine* 49 (1937): 271–8.
5. Hill in *Sermons (94A-147A) on the New Testament*, trans. Edmund Hill, ed. John E. Rotelle, vol. 4, *The Works of Saint Augustine, Part 3: Sermons* (Brooklyn, NY: New City Press, 1992), 125n1.
6. *Serm.* 107A.1.
7. *Serm.* 107A.1.
8. *Serm.* 107A.1.
9. *Serm.* 107A.1.
10. *Serm.* 107A.1.

Augustine often identifies greed (or avarice) as "*the root of all evil* (1 Tm 6:10)," and charity as "the root of all good things."[11] In our contemporary context, this emphasis on greed and charity might be dismissed as "moralizing," accustomed as we are to focusing on "practical" responses to economic inequality: food banks, welfare policy, taxation reform. However, in instructing his congregation about greed and charity, Augustine is neither ignoring the very real concerns of material wealth and poverty, nor avoiding practical response. Rather, he is attending to the underlying causes that produce economic inequality, and ensuring the necessary foundation for a healthy response. An invasive weed will remain unless its root is removed; a planted tree will not grow and bear fruit unless its roots are nourished. Commenting elsewhere on Christ's teaching on trees and their fruit in Matthew 12:33, Augustine explains: "He was speaking, you see, against the sort of people who thought they could say good things or perform good works while remaining bad themselves. This, the Lord Jesus says, is not possible, because the person has to be changed first, before the works can be changed in quality."[12] Unless we, as people, are transformed, no end of policy reform or philanthropic projects will overcome the divisions of economic inequality.

Augustine's teaching on avarice in *Sermon* 107A arises out of Luke 12:13–21, which features the account of a brother seeking the division of his inheritance, and the parable of a rich man building barns. As Augustine will capably demonstrate in this sermon, both gospel narratives strike hard against the bad tree of avarice; however, the sharpest edge of the axe is formed by the intervening instruction of Jesus, "*Beware of all greediness*" (v. 15).[13] "What's the sense of 'all' here?" Augustine enquires.[14] Guided by the surrounding passage, he explains that Jesus is cautioning against "avarice even for things which are called your own."[15] We might understand "greed" to denote our covetous desire to acquire more; not satisfied with what we have, we seek out what belongs to others. Certainly, in other sermons Augustine explores these characteristics of greedy behavior.[16] But on this occasion, Augustine understands Christ to be addressing avarice in another sense. Christ's caution against *all* greediness, illuminated by the gospel narratives that enclose it, exposes the underlying roots of greed: a disordered desire that seeks its own good, apart from God and neighbor.[17] The underlying dynamics of sin are reflected in this

---

11. *Serm.* 179A.5. See Chapter 1 for discussion of avarice as the "root" of sin. Commenting on a passage from *Sermon* 177, Brown states that "on the subject of avarice, he [Augustine] insisted that he had nothing new to say." Brown, *Through the Eye of a Needle*, 54. However, as Augustine later explains in this sermon, what distinguishes Christian teaching from that of the "poets" and "philosophers" is "that it is for God's sake that we do whatever we do" (*Serm.* 177.1–2)—a distinction which, for Augustine, is fundamental.
12. *Serm.* 72.1.
13. *Serm.* 107A.1.
14. *Serm.* 107A.2.
15. *Serm.* 107A.2.
16. E.g. *Serm.* 177; 178.
17. See Chapter 1 for discussion of this disordered love.

desire; as Augustine explains in another sermon, the avaricious soul, "hankering after something more," departs from God in order to "have something extra."[18] As a result, in contrast to the "charity that does not seek its own," this soul seeks "to enjoy something as his very own private property."[19] D. J. MacQueen describes this avarice as "a privative love that prefers the part to the whole, the transient to the eternal, and ultimately, the self to God."[20] Greed sets us apart from both God and neighbor; we cling to our goods for our own private benefit, rather than enjoying them in common with others. Our private claim to these material goods may be legally entitled and socially acceptable, yet Christ's instruction reveals this desire to be a form of avarice. Hence Augustine's observation that this message is "aimed at the root of the bad tree," for it attends to greed at this hidden, subterranean level.[21]

The self-interested nature of avarice can be further discerned by comparing it with the good tree of charity. Augustine envisages the protest of a listener: "'I,' you say, 'neither wish to lose what's mine, nor to make off with what belongs to others.'"[22] Augustine responds: "That's the excuse of a kind of greed or cupidity, not the glorious boast of love or charity. Of charity it is said, *It does not seek its own good, but that of others* (1 Cor 13:5; Phil 2:4). It doesn't seek its own convenience, it seeks the welfare of the brethren."[23] The protesting listener denies that there is anything wrong with their desire to preserve their own goods. However, when contrasted with the way of charity, the avaricious root of this desire can be identified more clearly. For love willingly foregoes the desire to preserve one's own private good, instead seeking that which will benefit others. In the *Rule*, Augustine similarly draws upon 1 Corinthians 13:5 to emphasize this outward orientation of love: "All your work should be shared together with greater care and more ready eagerness than if you were doing things for yourself alone. For when it is written of *love* that it *does not seek its own* (1 Cor 13:5), it means that it puts the common good before its own and not personal advantage before the common good."[24] The avarice that seeks its own benefit has no place in the monastery, for the members have been called to practice love, which looks to the common good of all. Augustine seeks to encourage this same orientation among the wider Christian community.[25] As

---

18. *Serm.* 51.34.
19. *Serm.* 51.34. See Chapter 1 for discussion of these dynamics of sin, including the contrast between "common" and "private." For Augustine's understanding of avarice, see also D. J. MacQueen, "St. Augustine's Concept of Property Ownership," *Recherches Augustiniennes et Patristiques* 8 (1972): 199–203.
20. MacQueen, "St. Augustine's Concept of Property Ownership," 203.
21. *Serm.* 107A.1.
22. *Serm.* 107A.1.
23. *Serm.* 107A.1.
24. *Reg. 3:* 5.2. See Introduction for further comment on this passage.
25. Note that my interpretation differs from that of Brown, who emphasizes the difference between Augustine's views on property in "normal society" (where "private property" was a necessary part of fallen human existence), and his instruction to the monastic community to share property in common: Brown, *Through the Eye of a Needle*, 180.

Christ prunes back greed amongst the congregation, Augustine hopes to see the good growth of charity take its place—and with that, the good fruit borne of this tree: a loving concern for the good of others.[26]

The Claim of Entitlement

Why is greed for things that are our own a problem? The two stories that bracket Christ's caution against greed (Lk. 12:15) illustrate this, as Augustine demonstrates in *Sermon* 107A. Augustine turns first to the story of the two brothers (Lk. 12:13–15), where a man says to Jesus, "*Lord, tell my brother to divide the inheritance with me* (Lk 12:13)."[27]

Initially, Augustine observes the reasonableness of the man's request. The man's brother, Augustine explains, has taken the entire family inheritance, rather than dividing it fairly.[28] In approaching Jesus, therefore, the man is only "seeking what was his own, not someone else's."[29] Augustine knows that his congregation will identify with the justness of the brother's claim. By inviting his listeners to sympathize with the brother, Augustine brings their own sense of entitlement into play. Clearly Augustine was well attuned to this tendency among his congregation, and in another sermon on this Lukan passage, he lists ways in which they defend entitlement to their wealth: "You've acquired it by your labor, you've acquired it justly; you are a legitimate heir … ; and you keep a tight and greedy grip on it, with a perfectly good conscience, just because you haven't come by it in a wrongful way, and you are not after someone else's property."[30] Augustine observes that his listeners have no moral qualms about closely guarding their property because they believe they can rightly claim it as their own. The man approaching Jesus shares a similar understanding, Augustine notes: "So this man thought he had a just desire, because he was looking for his own share, not coveting another person's, and apparently confident of the justice of his case, he appealed to the just judge."[31] Notably, not only is the man convinced "of the justice of his case"; he also

---

26. See also Augustine's account of our "renewal" in *The Trinity*, which includes a movement from "greed" to "charity" (*Trin.* 14.17.23).
27. *Serm.* 107A.1.
28. *Serm.* 107A.1. As a bishop, Augustine regularly had to adjudicate disputes; see Chapters 2 and 6 for further comment on this role.
29. *Serm.* 107A.1; see also *Serm.* 107.2.
30. *Serm.* 107.8.
31. *Serm.* 107A.1. In our time, this entitlement mentality is exacerbated by the individualistic character of modern culture. Cavanaugh observes that our modern understanding of the state is based upon "an assumption of the essential individuality of the human race." Cavanaugh, *Theopolitical Imagination*, 17. Closely bound up with this assumption, he explains, is the view that individuals can rightfully claim private property as their own (pp. 17–18). Thus Cavanaugh observes that "the distinction between mine and thine is … inscribed into the modern anthropology" (p. 17).

assumes that Jesus, "the just judge," shares his understanding of justice.³² And yet, Augustine observes, Jesus is unwilling to play the role envisaged for him, instead countering with a question, "*who appointed me a divider of the inheritance between you?* (Lk 12:14)."³³ To those with an entitlement mentality, this response appears outrageous. Surely the way to restore justice is to demand that the man receive his fair share?³⁴ However, the refusal of Jesus to adjudicate such an appeal calls into question this assumption.

As Augustine interprets Jesus's unexpected response, it is important to recall that Augustine is not presenting a treatise on economic justice. Rather, he is preaching to the Christian community, and his primary concern is helping his listeners hear the voice of Christ through this gospel passage. Augustine will concede elsewhere the necessity of laws within the earthly city to constrain the greedy.³⁵ However, while we may be legally entitled to claim our own goods, Jesus nonetheless calls his listeners to regard them in a different way, as Augustine's reading of this passage suggests. Surprisingly, Augustine notes, Jesus's refusal of the man's request results in gain, not loss: "He refused what he was being asked for, but what he gave is much more than what he refused."³⁶ Jesus refuses the man's request because he is not seeking what is truly good. For the claim to one's own is still a form of greed, seeking for ourselves what God made for the benefit of all. Furthermore, Augustine explains, it is not a path that yields what is truly good for all, because greed for one's own is inherently divisive. Whereas charity enables us to enjoy God's abundant provision together, the claim to our own sets us apart from our neighbor, and impoverishes us both.³⁷ "Anything divided is diminished," Augustine succinctly states.³⁸ He evocatively illustrates this principle by contemplating the situation of the two brothers:

---

32. *Serm.* 107A.1.
33. *Serm.* 107A.1.
34. Again, modern conceptions of society may intensify our incredulity at Jesus's refusal. Commenting on the modern state's "'theological' anthropology," Cavanaugh explains that "the recognition of our participation in one another through our creation in the image of God is replaced by the recognition of the other as the bearer of individual rights." Cavanaugh, *Theopolitical Imagination*, 44. Accordingly, justice is conceived of as the safeguarding of these rights (a task entrusted to the state) (p. 44).
35. MacQueen, "St. Augustine's Concept of Property Ownership," 193. MacQueen notes that Augustine does acknowledge the "right of ownership" (p. 194). However, as MacQueen goes on to illustrate, Augustine's writings reflect a very nuanced view of property ownership. Thus, MacQueen later observes that "Augustine's doctrine can not be interpreted as asserting the existence of an unlimited right to private property deriving solely and immediately from the natural law"; and that "the *ius privatum*" is therefore "relative and conditional" (p. 220). See further discussion below.
36. *Serm.* 107A.1.
37. *Serm.* 107A.1.
38. *Serm.* 107A.1.

If they had stayed amicably together in their home, as they had when their father was still alive, they would each have possessed the whole estate. For example, if they had had two country cottages, they would both have belonged to both of them, and if you had asked about either of them, they would both have said it was theirs.... But if each brother had taken one of them, the estate would be diminished, the answer would change. Then if you asked, whose is this cottage, he would answer, "Mine." Whose is that one? "My brother's." You haven't acquired one, but lost one, by dividing them.[39]

The fact that they are brothers is not lost on Augustine. In this elaboration on the gospel passage, Augustine suggests that their original state was one of familial unity, where the brothers enjoyed together the abundance of their father's household. Understood in this context, the demand for one's own share of the inheritance, like the demand of the prodigal son, is a disruption and diminishing of this abundance (Lk. 12:13; 15:12). For this reason, Jesus does not grant the brother's request. Though his claim to the inheritance may be legally entitled, it will result in the diminishment, not the fulfillment, of the good.

Building Barns

Turning to the second story in this Lukan passage (Lk. 12:16–21), Augustine explains that Jesus provides this parable "to put us on our guard against all avarice."[40] The parable gives an account of a wealthy man whose land "produced abundantly" (Lk. 12:16, NRSV). Though an abundant harvest would normally be cause for celebration, for this rich man it proved a problem; "he's put in a tight spot by plenty, not scarcity," Augustine marvels.[41] For though he was already rich, and had no need for surplus wealth, greed for one's own demanded that he retain the additional crops. Therefore, the rich man determines, "*I will pull down the old storerooms and make new and more spacious ones, and fill them. And I will say to my soul: Soul, you have many goods for a long time. Relax, eat, drink, have a good time*" (vv. 18–19).[42]

Brown's description of the harvest economy in the fourth century helps us appreciate the connotations this parable may have had for Augustine's audience. As the economy in this period was primarily based on the harvest, it was determined by the harvest calendar, and also vulnerable to significant fluctuations due to varying climate.[43] Brown notes that the poor were particularly exposed to the shortages caused by these variable conditions.[44] However, he explains, with grain values increasing during the scarcer periods of the calendar, the rich could use these same conditions to their profit: "Those who could store the surplus

---

39. *Serm.* 107A.1.
40. *Serm.* 107A.2.
41. *Serm.* 107A.2.
42. *Serm.* 107A.2.
43. Brown, *Through the Eye of a Needle*, 11–12.
44. Brown, *Through the Eye of a Needle*, 13.

of the harvest by gathering it into their granaries were the ones who could take advantage, every year, of this rise in prices. Further harvest shocks might turn the regular sale of grain into a 'killing' in times of shortage."[45] Against such a backdrop, the parable of a rich man building bigger storerooms is a disturbing symbol of the self-interest of the rich.

Augustine observes in *Sermon* 178 that, like the brother seeking his inheritance, this rich man was only claiming "his own crops," and not what belonged to another.[46] However, although this rich man may not have robbed the poor in a legal sense, Augustine believes that our accumulation of wealth comes at the expense of others.[47] In particular, Augustine draws attention to the "superfluous" nature of the rich man's wealth: until now, the harvest that filled his existing barns served him adequately, so what need has he for the surplus?[48] Those with excess wealth have more than they could possibly consume, Augustine observes; "you can see how all the rest is just lying around superfluous."[49] Augustine's concern with superfluous wealth arises out of his nuanced understanding of property ownership, to which MacQueen provides a valuable guide. In Augustine's understanding, material goods, with all of creation, belong to God (Ps. 24:1).[50] Therefore, although we can, in a certain sense, own such goods, we do so in a qualified way. As MacQueen explains, "While anyone may rightfully (*iure privato*) acquire possessions—'private property', to use the traditional pleonasm—the *ius divinum* allows no man to claim them as exclusively and unreservedly his."[51] We can rightfully make use of the goods which we legitimately need, but should not claim more than we need—that is, superfluous wealth. Indeed, as MacQueen further observes, "What the wealthy possess over and above their basic needs, i.e. those external goods which, precisely, make them rich, constitute in turn so many requirements of the destitute."[52] Augustine puts it plainly to listeners: "Your extras are someone else's necessities."[53]

45. Brown, *Through the Eye of a Needle*, 14.
46. *Serm.* 178.2.
47. E.g. *Serm.* 32.21.
48. *Serm.* 107A.2; 107.5.
49. *Serm.* 107A.2.
50. MacQueen, "St. Augustine's Concept of Property Ownership," 196, 213.
51. MacQueen, "St. Augustine's Concept of Property Ownership," 213; cf. Zumkeller, *Augustine's Ideal of the Religious Life*, 145, 151. MacQueen explains that, for Augustine, the question of our rightful ownership of property is bound up with our "just *use*" of this property: MacQueen, "St. Augustine's Concept of Property Ownership," 218. See pp. 209-18 for discussion of this theme.
52. MacQueen, "St. Augustine's Concept of Property Ownership," 213. Ramsey explains that Augustine's view of wealth contrasted with two alternative positions held by his contemporaries. Ramsey, "Wealth," 877. He notes that a prevalent view among the affluent was "that wealth existed solely for the enjoyment of its owner" (p. 877). A different view was held by ascetics (such as the Manicheans and Pelagians), who "espoused a radical rejection of wealth" (p. 877). For Pelagian teaching on wealth, see Brown, *Through the Eye of a Needle*, 308-21.
53. *Serm.* 39.6. Augustine regarded the property of the church in a similar fashion, as Bonner observes: Bonner, *St Augustine of Hippo*, 126.

Accordingly, while Jesus makes no mention of the poor in this parable, Augustine invites his listeners to consider those overlooked by the rich man in his hoarding. The concern of the rich man was "not how to be generous in distributing the surplus, but how to store it," Augustine observes in *Sermon* 107.[54] "Where, I ask you, were the poor?" he exclaims in *Sermon* 107A.[55] The option of sharing the abundance of the harvest with the needy apparently does not occur to the man. In Augustine's retelling of this parable, he sometimes suggests that the rich man consciously dismisses the needs of the poor, instead attending to his own appetite: "He was planning to sate his soul with excessive and unnecessary feasting, and proudly disregarding all those empty bellies of the poor."[56] In other sermons, Augustine implies that the rich man is so consumed with greed for his own, that he is oblivious to the poor.[57] Whether the rich man is aware of his needy neighbors or not, however, greed to preserve his own prevents him from responding to them with love.

This greed stifles charity not only for one's neighbor, but also for God. In the earlier story of the man seeking his claim of the inheritance, Augustine's account suggests that by desiring his own earthly wealth "too much," he risks withdrawing his "heart from heaven."[58] Our greedy desire to preserve our own draws us away from loving God. These two loves are also placed in opposition at the end of the parable of the rich barn builder. This man discovers that his life is about to end, and that he cannot take his wealth with him (v. 20). Like the preceding story of the two brothers, the rich man's desire to claim his own ultimately results in loss, rather than prosperity. Jesus then concludes with the challenge, "*So is everyone who hoards for himself and is not rich toward God*" (v. 21).[59] Again, this illustrates that our desire to hoard resources for ourselves prevents us devoting ourselves to God.

Taking the Axe to Avarice

Creating space for charity to grow is no easy task, for when avarice takes root, it quickly spreads and takes over our lives. Augustine also draws on other metaphors to caution the congregation against the controlling influence of avarice. In *Sermon* 107A, for example, he evokes the image of a master–slave relationship to explain what happens when we become greedy for our money:

> It means you won't be the master of your money, but its slave, and being its slave, you will follow wherever it drags you. Aren't you its slave, when you are dragged

---

54. *Serm.* 107.5.
55. *Serm.* 107A.2.
56. *Serm.* 36.9.
57. *Serm.* 32.27; 107.6.
58. *Serm.* 107A.1.
59. *Serm.* 107A.7.

along by greed for it? Doesn't love of it wake you up from your sleep? If you were the slave of a man, he would probably let you sleep sometimes. If you haven't got any money and are grasping, your very greed keeps you awake in order to get it. If you've got money, you're kept awake by fear of losing it.[60]

While the affluent in the congregation may themselves be masters, if greed has taken hold of them, in truth, they have less freedom than the slaves in their care. Other listeners may be slaves or servants, but their circumstances will not necessarily be improved by trying to gain wealth, for the working conditions are even worse for those under the charge of greed.[61]

When avarice dictates the use of our resources, we are unable to share what we have. Instead, as Augustine notes, we become anxious at the prospect of losing our wealth, and hungry to acquire more. Our focus is not on the needs of others, but on protecting and increasing what is our own. In *Sermon* 177, urging his congregation to leave greed behind, and to exercise "concern for others," Augustine again employs the master–slave imagery: "There's something you can do with gold, if you're its master, not its slave. If you're the master of gold, you can do good with it; if you're its slave, it can do evil with you."[62] Here Augustine contrasts the slavery of avarice with the freedom of charity.[63] Because charity is not obsessed with protecting its own resources, it is free to seek the interests of others; we can thus "do good" with "gold." In particular, Augustine encourages his congregation to generously share their resources with the needy through the practice of almsgiving.[64] However, such demonstrations of charity are not possible until we have been freed from the enslavement of avarice.

---

60. *Serm.* 107A.4. The enslavement Augustine describes in this passage is symptomatic of disordered love. As Torchia notes (with reference to *"lascivia"*): "By treating corporeal goods as ends in themselves, one fails to assign them their proper place and use, falling under the sway of that which one should order and govern." Torchia, "The Commune/Proprium Distinction," 362.

61. Notably, Augustine often challenges the assumption of his poorer listeners that they are exempt from biblical teaching against greed. Even if they have little resources, they may be more fiercely consumed with desire for worldly goods than the rich (e.g., *Serm.* 114B(D5/M12).11). "Though he was no respecter of wealth, it never occurred to Augustine to flatter the poor," Van der Meer comments. Van der Meer, *Augustine the Bishop*, 138. Augustine engages all listeners as moral agents, for none are immune to the disordering of their love, and all must be nurtured in love for God.

62. *Serm.* 177.3.

63. *Serm.* 177.3.

64. The question of Augustine's teaching on almsgiving is an expansive one, which cannot be considered in full here (e.g., I do not discuss here the atoning role of almsgiving). For broader surveys of Augustine's teaching on almsgiving see Boniface Ramsey, "Almsgiving in the Latin Church: The Late Fourth and Early Fifth Centuries," *Theological Studies* 43, no. 2 (1982): 226–59; Finn, *Almsgiving in the Later Roman Empire*. Finn refers to Augustine throughout his monograph, but see pp. 147–50 for details on appeals for almsgiving in Augustine's *Sermons*.

To that end, Augustine exerts much homiletical energy in trying to loosen avarice's hold. This aspect of Augustine's teaching demonstrates remarkable pastoral insight, attending to particular manifestations of avarice, as he attempts to pry open its grasp. "What is it that misleads people into the calculations of avarice?" Augustine asks in *Sermon* 177.[65] He anticipates a range of common concerns: some listeners may worry about whether they will have enough resources if they live a long life; others are saving in case of unexpected legal expenses.[66] Augustine appears well acquainted with the manifold excuses that hinder people from sharing their resources with others. In response, he tackles these manifestations of avarice from a variety of angles, often turning the very logic of avarice against itself.[67]

In *Sermon* 107A, Augustine draws attention to the folly of the rich man's greed. This man thought he was securing his future by hoarding his harvest; thus he says to himself, "*Soul, you have many goods for a long time*" (Lk. 12:19).[68] However, it turns out that the rich man is mistaken, for his life will shortly end, and he will no longer possess the wealth he has stored (v. 20). Commenting on this passage, Augustine does not negate the rich man's desire for a secure future; rather, he demonstrates that hoarding wealth is an ill-conceived way to achieve this security. Therein lies his folly, as Augustine notes: "You're a fool precisely on the point where you think you're clever. Why have you done this? In order to say to your soul, 'You have many good things for such a long time.' *This very night your soul is being demanded of you* (Lk 12:16.20). Where's that long time?"[69] Trying to gain security by hoarding earthly wealth is short-sighted, reflecting a forgetfulness of our creaturely finitude, and of our Creator.

As Augustine frequently reminds his listeners in other sermons, even in the course of this life, our material wealth is not a reliable source of security. Avarice may demand that we protect our resources in "some strong room, some walled chamber, or iron chest," Augustine satirically observes in *Sermon* 86.[70] "Put in all the security devices you like," he insists; this wealth may still be compromised by "an inside job," or someone may try to take our life in order to gain our wealth, or our wealth may be corroded by "rust and moth," even while we are protecting it from outside.[71] Amassing wealth, whether in barns or banks, is thus a misplaced source of security even in this life.

Similarly misplaced is the notion that sharing our resources with the needy results in a loss of security—another excuse that Augustine often anticipates. When dominated by avarice for one's own, the act of giving to others will inevitably be experienced as loss. Thus the rich man decided to hoard the surplus harvest in his barn, rather than distribute it among the hungry. However, in *Sermon* 107A

---

65. *Serm*. 177.5.
66. *Serm*. 177.5, 11.
67. This homiletical strategy is well demonstrated in *Serm*. 86.7–17.
68. *Serm*. 107A.2.
69. *Serm*. 107A.2.
70. *Serm*. 86.8.
71. *Serm*. 86.8.

Augustine reminds his listeners that, had he shared this surplus with his neighbors in need, he would have been giving it to Christ: "What the limited space of your storerooms wouldn't hold, your brother would accept, your Lord would accept, who said, *When you did it to one of the least of mine, you did it to me* (Mt 25:40)."[72] If we are giving to Christ when we give to the poor, the assumption that such an act results in loss is called into question: "You entrust it [your wealth] to your storeroom, and you won't lose it? You transfer it to heaven, and you will?"[73] Again, Augustine problematizes the notions of security and loss that may have hindered his listeners from responding generously to the needs of others.

Alongside the misguided ideas of security that avarice fosters, Augustine also challenges notions of entitlement among the congregation. Enquiring after the rich man's surplus, Augustine asks, "all this you've nowhere to put: who gave it to you?"[74] Some listeners may believe that, as self-made men or women, they themselves have generated their wealth, and therefore feel no obligation to share what they consider to be rightfully theirs. To the contrary, Augustine reminds them that everything they have comes as a gift from God, and therefore they too should be willing to give.[75] He puts it plainly in *Sermon* 50, when directing listeners to God's instruction in Haggai 2:8: "*Mine*, he says, *is the gold and mine is the silver*, not yours, you wealthy ones of the earth. So why do you shy away from giving what is mine to the poor, or why, when you do give from what is mine, do you think so highly of yourselves?"[76] Such teaching dramatically redefines how we understand "our" resources: the act of giving is not a diminishment of "our" property, nor a demonstration of "our" benevolence, but rather the rightful distribution of God's gifts.

Augustine strikes at avarice from yet another angle in *Sermon* 107A, contrasting our notions of earthly wealth with God's abundance. This reflects Jesus's concluding words in the parable, where he challenges listeners to be "rich toward God" (Lk. 12:21, NRSV).[77] Here Augustine playfully tries to make a "financial case" for renouncing avarice, and living generously toward God and neighbor. It is as if Augustine is attempting to enter into the minds of those dominated by avarice, appropriating avarice's calculating language of profit and loss in order to depose it from within.

For example, those fixated upon gaining and securing wealth should consider the abundance of heaven, Augustine advises. "What you have is the fruits of the earth; you haven't got eternal life, have you? What a marvelous, great estate that

---

72. *Serm.* 107A.2.
73. *Serm.* 107A.2.
74. *Serm.* 107A.2.
75. See MacQueen, "St. Augustine's Concept of Property Ownership," 213.
76. *Serm.* 50.2.
77. While we may be surprised by Augustine's use of financial metaphors, it is important to recall that he is generally following the precedent of Scripture, and indeed, of Jesus's own teaching. Thus Ramsey observes that Augustine and his contemporaries "were ultimately only translating scriptural data into more graspable terms." Ramsey, "Almsgiving in the Latin Church," 259.

is!"[78] Unlike earthly property portfolios, subject to change and loss, the "estate" of heaven is one we will enjoy "in perpetuity."[79] The wealth of heaven offers a security and abundance that cannot be found in earth. Therefore, those who object to sharing their earthly wealth with the needy should reconsider. For giving to the poor will not result in loss, Augustine explains to the congregation, but extraordinary profit. Indeed, he suggests, the returns are unbelievable, comparing it to an investment opportunity where one gives silver, and receives back the same weight in gold.[80] "You would positively hug yourself for joy, at being permitted to reap such magnificent dividends," Augustine tells his listeners.[81] We should approach opportunities to give with the same enthusiasm. In this case, however, we are not exchanging silver for gold. Rather, Augustine explains, "you give what you have to leave here anyhow, you receive what you can never lose."[82] That is, by sharing our temporal goods with others, we in turn will receive the eternal abundance of heaven.

Augustine whimsically employs financial illustrations such as these to demonstrate that, even by its own calculating logic, avarice for one's own is not profitable. The risks are great, the benefits short-lived, the yield limited. If Augustine appears to concede the desires of greed, it is in order to direct them toward God. He hints at this pastoral intention on another occasion, when he explains that "greedy cravings should not be eliminated, but changed."[83] Greed may be a misdirected form of love, but a love it remains. Augustine's intention is thus to help this misdirected love find its proper object.

However, we must be careful not to misread this aspect of Augustine's teaching.[84] When he employs such financial metaphors, he does so elaborately and evocatively, and it is tempting to interpret them as stand-alone teachings, independent of their broader homiletical and theological context. This can lead to the conclusion that Augustine encourages his listeners to seek God in a self-interested way.[85] However, when this aspect of Augustine's teaching is read in light of his broader homiletical intentions, and in the context of his overarching theological convictions, a different picture emerges.

78. *Serm.* 107A.2.
79. *Serm.* 107A.2.
80. *Serm.* 107A.2.
81. *Serm.* 107A.2.
82. *Serm.* 107A.2.
83. *Serm.* 313A.2.
84. Brown observes that "modern" readers may be apprehensive about such teaching because we are accustomed to seeing "commerce" and "religion" as occupying "distinct spheres." Brown, *Through the Eye of a Needle*, 84–5.
85. For example, see Burnaby's concern on this point: Burnaby, *Amor Dei*, 132. (Canning responds to Burnaby's critique at a number of points in his monograph; see especially his discussion of self-interest and giving: Canning, *Unity of Love for God and Neighbour*, 394–412.) Dunn also comments on Augustine's use of "self-interest" to encourage giving: Dunn, "Augustine's Homily on Almsgiving," 5–6.

Augustine uses financial metaphor primarily for the benefit of his listeners. They may not yet understand the biblical passage being discussed, or the theological insight Augustine is trying to convey, but they do understand the rules of commerce that govern their everyday existence. Augustine's creative use of illustrations from this familiar context (property holdings, investments, exchange rates) demonstrates his desire to communicate in terms that are accessible to all. This practice reflects Augustine's understanding of how God communicates to us through Scripture. Scripture often "appears to speak in a crude, materialistic way," Augustine notes elsewhere, but he explains that this is for the benefit of "carnal, materialistic people."[86] The financial images Augustine draws on ultimately fall short of the spiritual truth that he attempts to communicate by using them—yet communicate he must.

Furthermore, Augustine does not use these financial metaphors uncritically. For example, Canning demonstrates that, when inviting listeners to "loan" money to Christ in the poor, Augustine significantly reworks the features of this familiar commercial image so that it faithfully reflects the theological message he seeks to convey.[87] To employ the imagery of commerce is not necessarily to concede to its terms. Rather, as illustrated above, by utilizing the terms and concepts of commerce, Augustine is able to subvert and problematize the claims of avarice from within. The use of financial metaphor can therefore be considered part of his homiletical attempt to take the axe to avarice, in order to allow charity to grow.

Although Augustine is inviting the congregation to respond with material resources, and although he often uses financial metaphors to describe the theological significance of such giving, it is a transaction of the heart that he has in view.[88] As Chapter 1 demonstrated, the orientation of the heart is Augustine's overriding pastoral concern. If his listeners greedily desire wealth, then their heart has departed from God. "For where your treasure is, there your heart will be also" (Mt. 6:21, NRSV). As Augustine sympathetically explains in *Sermon* 86, "None of us, after all, can help thinking about our treasure, or following its fortunes on a kind of mental journey in our hearts. So if our fortunes are buried in the ground, our thoughts will drag our hearts downward."[89] As he goes on to remind the

---

86. *Serm.* 23.3. Augustine also expounds this principle in *Trin.* 1.1.2. For comment on this passage from *The Trinity*, see Anatolios, *Retrieving Nicaea*, 243.

87. Canning, *Unity of Love for God and Neighbour*, 404–7.

88. Thus, on other occasions, Augustine explains to listeners that unlike the purchase of a "valuable property" which would require their "gold or silver," to acquire "eternal life" the asking price is their very self: "Give yourself, and you've got it" (*Serm.* 127.3). Noting Augustine's use of "financial images," Sanlon writes: "The use of money in his preaching was ... not primarily transactional and rationalistic, but desirous and heart-centered. The temporal image of money opens a window on the interior desires and invites journeying listeners to reflect whether they will lust for temporal or eternal riches." Sanlon, *Augustine's Theology of Preaching*, 111. For these themes of "interiority" and "temporality" in Augustine's preaching on wealth, see pp. 99–120.

89. *Serm.* 86.1.

congregation, this disordered desire for earthly goods is at odds with the liturgical call to lift our hearts to God.[90] He elaborates further in *Sermon* 345: "*Lift up your hearts* is said, and straightaway you answer, *We have lifted them up to the Lord*. You're lying to God.... You say, *We have lifted them up to the Lord*, and in fact you have buried your heart in the earth; because *where your treasure is, there will your heart be also*."[91] Buried by greed, our heart needs to be lifted up, and redirected toward God. And if our heart is linked to our treasure, then our treasure needs to be redirected toward God. "If any of you really want to lift up your hearts, then it's up there, up there that you must deposit what you love," Augustine instructs in *Sermon* 86.[92] When our treasure is located "in a heavenly savings deposit, our hearts will be lifted upward."[93]

Augustine's detailed imagery should not be read too literally. He does not conceive of heaven as populated with bank deposit boxes and opulent estates, and he often reminds his listeners not to think of heaven in these "materialistic" terms.[94] When we overcome our greedy desires, and share resources with the poor, we are not transferring money to heaven, but our hearts. In the action of giving, our love, previously obsessed with preserving our own assets, turns upward and outward, toward God and neighbor.

The wealth of heaven, moreover, is not a resource or asset that could become an object of greedy desire. Augustine steers the congregation away from this way of thinking. In *Sermon* 107A, anticipating that his listeners might say of God, "He's going to fill my house with gold, with silver," Augustine instead responds: "Recognize and love the one who made you, and he will fill you, not with something of his, but with himself. You will possess God. You will be full of God. That is the great wealth of the soul."[95] This response, which concludes a long sequence of financial illustrations, reveals the theological substructure of his preceding comments. Whereas the rich barn builder, preoccupied with hoarding his harvest, neglected to see Christ in the poor, Augustine challenges his listeners: "Recognize and love the one who made you." Giving to the poor, in Augustine's understanding, is an expression of love toward God, who is present in our neighbor. As we turn toward God in love, God generously responds by giving his very self. Because God himself, and not an external reward, is the "wealth of the soul," it is not possible to love God in a greedy, self-seeking way.[96] As Burnaby observes, "*Deus ipse praemium*, understood as Augustine meant it to be understood, does not encourage but forbid self-centredness."[97] In another sermon, Augustine cautions

---

90. *Serm.* 86.1.
91. *Serm.* 345.5.
92. *Serm.* 86.1.
93. *Serm.* 86.1.
94. E.g. *Serm.* 177.10.
95. *Serm.* 107A.3.
96. Canning, *Unity of Love for God and Neighbour*, 63. See also discussion of this question in Chapter 1.
97. Burnaby, *Amor Dei*, 251.

the congregation against loving God for other forms of reward.[98] Instead he urges his listeners: "Love him, and love him freely, for nothing. You see, if you love him on account of something else, you aren't loving him at all."[99]

It is because, in the Incarnate Christ, God dwelt among us, and continues to be present amidst the hungry and the suffering, that we have opportunity to demonstrate love for God. This belief is critical to appreciating Augustine's teaching on almsgiving.[100] Canning explains:

> Augustine's apparently mechanical, almost business-like descriptions of the set-up of salvation find their proper place in his thought only when they are set in the context of the love by which God in "his universally extended agapè" identifies himself with each and every poor person, and by which, *in pauperibus*, God seeks and demands and accepts alms until the end of the world.[101]

As outlined in Chapter 1, while the destination of life with God might appear unattainable, Christ has become for us the way. Augustine frequently draws attention to the witness of Matthew 25:31–46 and Acts 9:4, which attest to Christ's presence in the stranger and the suffering.[102] In these neighbors, Christ meets us on our journey, and enables us to demonstrate our love for him through practical expression. Thus, in *Sermon* 107A, Augustine imaginatively addresses the rich barn builder: "The one who made you is in desperate need of things from you."[103]

---

98. *Serm.* 72(D16/M46–47).17.

99. *Serm.* 72(D16/M46–47).17.

100. Canning, *Unity of Love for God and Neighbour*, 365, 401. I am indebted to Canning's detailed treatment of this theme in this closing chapter of his monograph (pp. 331–420). Here, Canning clearly demonstrates the importance of locating Augustine's teaching on almsgiving within a Christological context (particularly that of the *totus Christus*, as revealed by Mt. 25:31–46).

101. Canning, *Unity of Love for God and Neighbour*, 401. The phrase quoted by Canning is from John Burnaby. Similarly, discussing the theme of "reward" in *Sermon* 91, Canning observes that "the stress is on faith in what *Christ* has done, is doing and will do, not on the efficacy of one's beneficence and of duty done to procure rest and riches in the vision of God." Canning, *Unity of Love for God and Neighbour*, 62–3.

102. *Sermon* 345 provides an interesting example of this teaching, for here Augustine acknowledges that some might consider it contrary to the doctrine they have received regarding Christ's ascension (*Serm.* 345.4). Drawing on Acts 9:1–4 and Matthew 25:35–40, Augustine explains that the Christ whom the congregation confesses has "ascended into heaven" is the very Christ whom they continue to encounter in the poor (.4). Note that Canning challenges Burnaby's claim that Luke 6:37–38 governs Augustine's reading of Matthew 25:31–46 (see Burnaby, *Amor Dei*, 132–4); Canning demonstrates that Augustine primarily has the *totus Christus* in view when using this Matthean text. Canning, *Unity of Love for God and Neighbour*, 344–6.

103. *Serm.* 107A.2.

As the eternal Word, Christ needs no thing, and provides us with all things; as the Word made flesh, Christ encounters us through the needs of the poor, and waits to receive things from us. Thus Augustine's invitation: "Recognize and love the one who made you."[104]

Fellow Travelers

Cautioning his congregation against avarice for their own, Augustine seeks to nurture the growth of charity. In *Sermon* 107A, he encourages his listeners to express this charity through the act of giving to the poor. As noted, Augustine identifies how almsgiving enables us to overcome our greedy desire for our own wealth, instead transferring our affection to God. However, can such acts of giving also enable love for the neighbor, nurturing common relationship between rich and poor?

Some scholars have raised questions about this aspect of Augustine's preaching. For example, Dunn states that "the promotion of almsgiving in Augustine's homilies had little to do with care for the poor, who are simply the objects through whom the rich can be saved."[105] In his survey of almsgiving in this period, Ramsey raises a related issue regarding the homiletical identification of the poor with Christ, suggesting that "in the Church in the West at this time ... we are faced with a kind of social monophysitism that failed to give due recognition to the individual nature of the poor over against Christ."[106] In the preaching of this period, Ramsey also notes a lack of detailed descriptions of the poor recipients themselves, observing that they were not often portrayed "as persons in their own right."[107]

Regarding the question of whether the particular identity of the needy recipient is erased by their homiletical identification with Christ, Canning offers helpful insight. He argues that Christ's identification with the poor (as expressed in Augustine's preaching), far from obscuring the poor, in fact draws the congregation's

---

104. *Serm.* 107A.3.
105. Dunn, "Augustine's Homily on Almsgiving," 11. (Canning notes similar objections: Canning, *Unity of Love for God and Neighbour*, 394–5, 400.) One homiletical illustration that can give this impression is Augustine's description of poor recipients of alms as "porters" (e.g., *Serm.* 107A.2). For discussion of this image, see Canning, *Unity of Love for God and Neighbour*, 396–8, 403–4; Finn, *Almsgiving in the Later Roman Empire*, 188. It is important to also note that Augustine does not typecast the poor to the role of recipients. Rather, he insists that all members of the congregation can be givers, regardless of their economic status (as will be discussed later in this chapter).
106. Ramsey, "Almsgiving in the Latin Church," 254.
107. Ramsey, "Almsgiving in the Latin Church," 253. Dunn similarly notes the absence of such descriptions of the poor in Augustine's preaching: Dunn, "Poverty as a Social Issue," 177–9.

attention to the poor, who "could so easily be overlooked."[108] Canning explains that irrespective of the "motivations" that Augustine engages in his preaching to advocate for the poor, or the "images" that Augustine employs to depict the works of charity, these "are all secondary in comparison to the fact that Christ loves the poor person as a poor person to such an extent that it is Christ himself who stands before one in the poor."[109] As a result, "the donor is always first confronted with the challenge to be oriented away from self and to go out to the poor in recognition and support."[110] Drawing the congregation's attention to Christ's presence in the poor therefore serves to benefit, and not disadvantage, those in need.

Finn considers the lack of detailed description of the poor in Augustine's *Enarrations on the Psalms*, and offers perceptive comment. He explains that, by speaking of the poor in general terms of "need," preachers were able to avoid descriptions based on "social identity," which could nurture a sense of "contempt" toward the poor.[111] "The more graphic or detailed the portrayal of the destitute in sermons the greater the risk of triggering that conventional response of contempt," Finn observes.[112] Augustine avoids these detailed descriptions, Finn argues, so that he instead can foster "the foreshortening of social distances."[113] Earlier in his essay, Finn describes this dynamic in Christian preaching: "A frame which distances the rich or better-off from the poor, or the conjunctural poor from the very poor, is replaced by one which draws them together as sharing a like plight, equally needy in different respects."[114] The lack of specific descriptions of the poor in Augustine's preaching need not, therefore, be taken to indicate his lack of concern for the poor recipients themselves, nor a disregard for their unique circumstances and concerns. Rather, Augustine's employment of general, non-specific descriptions reflects his broader goal of overcoming (and not reinforcing) the social divisions between rich and poor.

This goal is reflected later in *Sermon* 107A, where Augustine gives greater attention to the relationship between rich and poor. Here, he comments first on economic differences observable in society. "Sometimes the just suffer starvation, and see the wicked burping from indigestion," he notes, mindful of the indignation

---

108. Canning, *Unity of Love for God and Neighbour*, 402.
109. Canning, *Unity of Love for God and Neighbour*, 402.
110. Canning, *Unity of Love for God and Neighbour*, 402. See also pp. 413–20.
111. Finn, "Portraying the Poor," 133–4. In making this observation, Finn draws on the work of Evelyne Patlagean. Note also Finn's discussion of this topic in Finn, *Almsgiving in the Later Roman Empire*, 182–8. See also Naoki Kamimura, "The Emergence of Poverty and the Poor in Augustine's Early Works," in *Prayer and Spirituality in the Early Church, Volume 5: Poverty and Riches*, ed. Geoffrey D. Dunn, David Luckensmeyer, and Lawrence Cross (Strathfield, NSW: St Pauls Publications, 2009), 286–7, 293.
112. Finn, "Portraying the Poor," 136.
113. Finn, "Portraying the Poor," 140. Finn notes that this "foreshortening" can be understood as part of Augustine's efforts (in the *Enarrations on the Psalms*) "to stress our common identity as members of Christ's body under a common head" (p. 139).
114. Finn, "Portraying the Poor," 134.

that arises from such situations.[115] When the opulence of the rich visibly neighbors the destitution of the poor, our sense of injustice is heightened. How can God allow such an unjust juxtaposition? Augustine's view of God's providence often leads him to conclude that the proximity of the poor to the rich is an occasion for testing: an opportunity for the rich to exercise love,[116] or an opportunity for the poor to exercise faith, in the manner of Job.[117] While we might find the idea of God using poverty as a test morally problematic,[118] it leads Augustine to the more salutary teaching that God is at work in the coexistence of rich and poor, and is seeking to draw them together.

This teaching often arises out of the proverb, "*Rich and poor have met each other, but the Lord made them both* (Prv 22:2)."[119] It is a difficult translation, but for Augustine the statement "*Rich and poor have met*" appears to refer to the fleeting and dismissive encounters that might take place between rich and poor, such as a wealthy person hastily passing a beggar on the street. Thus, when commenting elsewhere on this verse, he notes, "this one's well dressed, that one's in rags—but only when they met each other."[120] Such an encounter is barely a meeting at all, reinforcing the distance between rich and poor rather than bridging it. However, the possibility of their meeting—the very fact of their (co)existence—points toward the second clause: "*but the Lord made them both*."[121] Augustine explains: "Where have they met each other? On some road. What is this road? It's this life."[122] Although the circumstances of rich and poor may appear dramatically different, they have both been created by God, and thus share the road of "this life" in common.

Augustine then alerts his congregation to the significance of such encounters between rich and poor on the road of life. For while his listeners might have considered a meeting of rich and poor as a one-way transaction that costs the rich and benefits the poor, Augustine recasts this encounter in a mutually beneficial light: "They both walk along the road, the one loaded, the other traveling light. But the one who's traveling light is hungry, the one who's loaded is grunting and groaning. Let the one who's loaded lighten his burden."[123] While the poor are hindered by hunger, the rich are burdened by affluence; in order for them to "both arrive" on their journey to God, each needs the assistance of the other.[124] Therefore,

---

115. *Serm.* 107A.5.
116. *Serm.* 53A.6.
117. *Serm.* 107A.5; 25A.3.
118. For Augustine's teaching on God's "testing," see *Serm.* 2.2.
119. *Serm.* 107A.5.
120. *Serm.* 53A.6.
121. *Serm.* 107A.5.
122. *Serm.* 107A.5.
123. *Serm.* 107A.5.
124. *Serm.* 107A.5. See also *Sermon 164*, where Augustine develops this image further when preaching on the text, "*Carry your burdens for each other* (Gal 6:2)" (*Serm.* 164.9). Van Bavel notes how Augustine's instruction on the "burden" of wealth developed in his teaching, with a growing emphasis on "the building up of community with one another." Van Bavel, commentary to *Rule of Saint Augustine*, 48. See also Ramsey, "Almsgiving in the Latin Church," 255–9.

rich and poor have not only met each other; they have been given to each other. If traveling the road of life alone, both poor and rich face insurmountable challenges: the one from deprivation, the other from over-satiation.¹²⁵ But God's intention is that they should travel together, and share one another's loads. When encouraging rich and poor to share one another's burdens in *Sermon* 25A, Augustine emphasizes the givenness of this relationship when he tells the "rich man" that "the poor man has been appointed your comrade in this life."¹²⁶ On other occasions, Augustine describes the rich and poor as "companions" on the journey, as they assist each other.¹²⁷ In *Sermon* 53A, Augustine locates the image of poor and rich as traveling companions within the more explicitly ecclesial context of the body of Christ:

> The head is in heaven, but he's got members on earth; let the member of Christ give to the member of Christ, let the one who has give to the one who lacks. You are a member of Christ, and you have something to give; he's a member of Christ, and he is in need in order that you may give it. You are both walking along the same road, you are companions together. The poor man's shoulders are free, you the rich man are weighed down with packages. Give away some of what you are staggering under, give some of your heavy load to the needy; in this way lighten your own burden, and your companion's lot.¹²⁸

The pastoral direction to share one another's burdens takes on additional depth in this passage when considered in the context of the body of Christ. In the first part of this passage, Augustine does not distinguish the rich and poor travelers, but rather reminds his listeners of their mutual identity as members of the body of Christ: "Let the member of Christ give to the member of Christ."¹²⁹ Such a statement recalls Augustine's statement that "when the members love each other, the body loves itself."¹³⁰ The charity that Augustine has in view is not of the rich coming to the rescue of the poor, but of rich and poor together experiencing the charity of God, giving and receiving from one another as they are drawn together as mutual participants in Christ's body, "one Christ loving himself."¹³¹

---

125. *Serm.* 164.9.
126. *Serm.* 25A.4. Similarly, in *Sermon* 39, Augustine explains that God provides for the poor through the rich (*Serm.* 39.4).
127. *Serm.* 61.12; 164.9. See discussion in Chapter 5 of the "companionship" Augustine encourages between rich and poor in the monastery (*Reg. 3:* 1.7).
128. *Serm.* 53A.6.
129. *Serm.* 53A.6. In his discussion of Augustine's teaching to the rich and poor, Brown emphasizes the continuity with existing social conventions. Brown, *Through the Eye of a Needle*, 347–52. By contrast, I have tried to highlight in Augustine's teaching the radical reworking of the identity of both rich and poor (and of their relationship) that takes place within the body of Christ.
130. *Tract. ep. Jo.* 10.3.
131. *Tract. ep. Jo.* 10.3.

Learning to Share

In order to share with others, we must be willing to relinquish the claim to our own. In the case of the monastic community, members must heed the instruction to "not call *anything your own,*" so that they might "*have everything in common* (Acts 4:32)."[132] When instructing the wider congregation in *Sermon* 107A, Augustine clarifies that he is not expecting his listeners to renounce ownership of property in the same fashion. Reflecting further on the instruction to "beware of all greediness," he comments: "You see, you are not being told not to have any property of your own, are you? Have it, but without being greedy about it."[133] And yet, while the outward expression may differ, Augustine is nonetheless directing his congregation toward a similar movement: a relinquishment of greed for one's own, in order that love may respond to the needs of others.

Acts 4:32–35 is not a primary text for addressing wealth and poverty in the *Sermons*. However, the example of this apostolic sharing of goods could be an inspiration to the congregation, as well as to the monastic community. On occasion, Augustine points to this Jerusalem community as an example of renunciation.[134] Or, when considering the conversion of Jewish believers, it is this renunciation and sharing of resources in Acts 4:32–35 that Augustine cites as evidence of "just how thoroughly and perfectly they were converted."[135] But it was not only by quoting this biblical text that Augustine kept this example before the congregation. Augustine's monastic community, located at the very heart of church life in Hippo, provided a continuing enactment of Acts 4:32–35. "At the moment of entering the monastery those who had any property in the world should gladly choose to have it become common property," Augustine instructs in the *Rule*.[136] Subsequent provisions in the *Rule* suggest that, even after such a renunciation, the temptation to claim one's own would remain: Augustine provides further guidance, to prevent members squabbling over the clothes in the common wardrobe, or claiming gifts as their own.[137] At times the monastic community may have considered themselves a very poor example of the common life modeled by the early Christians, but an example they remained.

Indeed, Augustine was well attuned to the formative influence of the example of other Christians, whether for better or for worse.[138] His awareness of the influence of the monastic community is clearly displayed in his introductory comments in *Sermon* 355:

> We live here with you, and we live here for you; and my intention and wish is that we may live with you in Christ's presence forever. I think our way of life is plain

---

132. *Reg. 3:* 1.3.
133. *Serm.* 107A.4.
134. E.g., *Serm.* 301A.4.
135. *Serm.* 77.4.
136. *Reg. 3:* 1.4.
137. *Reg. 3:* 5.1, 5.3.
138. E.g. *Serm.* 228.

for you to see; so that I too may perhaps make bold to say what the apostle said, though I can't of course be compared with him: *Be imitators of me, as I too am of Christ* (1 Cor 4:16). And that's why I don't want any of you to find an excuse for living badly.[139]

Augustine is mindful that the example of his monastic community is visible to the wider congregation.[140] In this sermon, it is particularly the community's sharing of goods in common, according to the apostolic pattern, that Augustine has in view. On this occasion, Augustine is at pains to safeguard the positive example of the monastic community, following the discovery that Januarius, a member of the community, had contradicted his commitment to "the common life" by secretly making a will.[141] While this sermon mainly attends to the fallout from Januarius's decision, it also provides Augustine with a positive opportunity to bolster the positive influence of the monastic community among the congregation, by reminding them again of their way of life:

> You all know, or almost all of you, that we live in the house which is called the bishop's house in such a way as to imitate, to the best of our ability, those holy people about whom the book of the Acts of the Apostles says, *Nobody called anything their own, but they had all things in common* (Acts 4:32). But some of you, perhaps, are not such keen examiners of the way we live that you know this in the way I would like you to know it; so let me spell out in more detail what I have just said in a few words.[142]

Augustine then recounts the story of his own relinquishment of worldly wealth and ambition, his arrival in Hippo, and the formation of the monastery.[143]

Although on this occasion Augustine invites his listeners to imitate this monastic example, it is not his expectation that they would do so in the same manner. He is mindful that most members of the congregation have responsibilities that prevent them from following the form of renunciation outlined in the *Rule*, and his pastoral instruction on wealth is sympathetic to their context.[144] This adaptability

---

139. *Serm.* 355.1.
140. Martin highlights the "visibility" of Augustine's monastery and its influence on the wider community: Martin, "Augustine and the Politics of Monasticism," 168–70. See also Markus, *End of Ancient Christianity*, 202.
141. *Serm.* 355.3. For discussion of Januarius's error and Augustine's response, see Lancel, *Saint Augustine*, 230–2; Van der Meer, *Augustine the Bishop*, 201–6.
142. *Serm.* 355.2.
143. *Serm.* 355.2.
144. As Lepelley notes, Augustine was aware that radical acts of renunciation by the wealthy could sometimes have negative consequences for those dependent on them, as in the case of Melania and Pinianus: Lepelley, "Facing Wealth and Poverty," 13–14. See also Brown's account of the renunciation of Melania and Pinianus, and its social consequences: Brown, *Through the Eye of a Needle*, 291–300.

in Augustine's teaching should not be understood as an attempt to pander to the rich by easing the call of discipleship. Rather, as Lepelley argues, it needs to be understood against the backdrop of the growing appeal of asceticism (including Pelagian teaching), whereby the Christian life, defined by renunciation and celibacy, became "the privilege of a small elite."[145] By contrast, Lepelley explains, "Augustine always asserted the possibility and the legitimacy of a secular christian way of life."[146] Moreover, as Zumkeller highlights, even within Augustine's monastic community, renunciation of material goods was directed toward a greater purpose; it was "a way to realize the consummate community of love in the monastic life."[147] As he explains, such relinquishment enabled members to devote themselves more fully to the needs of one another.[148]

While Augustine does not insist that members of the congregation renounce their property in the same fashion as the monastic community, his instruction to each reflects a common movement of the heart: the call to relinquish the greedy claim to one's own, and pursue the generous life of charity.[149] In *Sermon* 107A, having cautioned his listeners against greed for one's own, Augustine encourages them to "hold onto what you have in such a way that you provide for the needy."[150] This instruction, though not as exacting as the monastic directive to count all their resources as "common property," is given in the same spirit.[151] We are to loosen the tight grip on our own resources, so that they can be shared with those in need. When advocating this manner of holding, Augustine sometimes draws attention to 1 Corinthians 7:29–31, where Paul instructs *"those who buy"* to be *"as though they did not possess,"* and *"those who make use of this world as though they did not make use of it"* (1 Cor. 7:30, 31).[152] Augustine provides vivid illustration of this principle in *Sermon* 125, where he likens our love to "the hand of the soul," which can only hold "one thing" at a time.[153] Consequently, in order to love God, we must first release our tight grip upon the world.[154] However, he notes, this relinquishment may be expressed in different ways:

---

145. Lepelley, "Facing Wealth and Poverty," 12.
146. Lepelley, "Facing Wealth and Poverty," 12. See also the Introduction for discussion of Augustine's desire to avoid an elitist conception of monastic life.
147. Zumkeller, *Augustine's Ideal of the Religious Life*, 148.
148. Zumkeller, *Augustine's Ideal of the Religious Life*, 148.
149. In Augustine's view, the orientation of the heart is of greatest importance; as MacQueen explains of Augustine's teaching on wealth, "everything will depend upon the quality of the respective 'desires' or 'loves' by which such objects are pursued, and the final end or ultimate goal to which they are referred." MacQueen, "St. Augustine's Concept of Property Ownership," 201.
150. *Serm.* 107A.7.
151. *Reg. 3*: 1.4.
152. *Serm.* 125.7.
153. *Serm.* 125.7.
154. *Serm.* 125.7.

> Now have I said, "You shouldn't possess things, whoever you are"? If you can manage that, if perfection requires it of you, then try not possessing things. But if you can't manage it, if there are ties and obligations which prevent you, then certainly possess property, don't be possessed by it; hold it, don't be held by it; be the master, not the slave of your estate.[155]

It is notable that in this passage, Augustine allows the possibility that his listeners are being invited to renounce their wealth according to the monastic pattern,[156] while also teaching "ordinary" listeners how to adopt this spirit of renunciation in a manner appropriate to their situation.

As the avaricious love for things loses its hold upon us, we become free to love God and neighbor. Augustine describes this movement—from love of world toward God and neighbor—in various ways. For example, when Augustine preaches on Matthew 19:21, he first challenges his listeners to respond to Christ's command to "go, sell your possessions, and give the money to the poor" (Mt. 19:21, NRSV). In Augustine's view this need not require an ascetic renunciation of property; for these ordinary listeners, a faithful response to Christ's command could be expressed through interior renunciation, and the sharing of resources with the poor.[157] However, Augustine often indicates that this expression of renunciation must be followed by a movement toward God: a sequence that he observes in Christ's command in this gospel passage. "So is the person already perfect who has sold everything he has and given it to the poor?" Augustine enquires.[158] "No; you see, that's why he [the Lord] added, *and come, follow me* (Mt 19:21)."[159] In this sense, giving to our neighbor enables us to relinquish love of wealth, leading us toward greater love of God.

By contrast, when Augustine preaches on 1 Timothy 6:17-19, the movement is from the world to God, and then toward the neighbor. Here, he follows Paul's sequence of thought in verses 17-18, where the rich are cautioned against putting "*their hopes in the uncertainty of riches*," and instead directed toward the "*living God*" (v. 17).[160] However, this renouncement of wealth and return to God must be accompanied by an outward turn toward the needs of one's neighbor, as indicated by the apostle's next command: "*Let them be ready to give, let them share*" (v. 18).[161]

---

155. *Serm.* 125.7.
156. Hill indicates that the monastic life is being commended in this passage: *Sermons (94A-147A)*, 264n22.
157. For interior renunciation as a response to this command, see *Sermon* 301A.3-5. For giving to the poor as a response to this command, see *Sermon* 86.2-3. See also MacQueen's comments on Augustine's use of this biblical text: MacQueen, "St. Augustine's Concept of Property Ownership," 194.
158. *Serm.* 142.13.
159. *Serm.* 142.13.
160. *Serm.* 177.9.
161. *Serm.* 177.10. Note that Brown offers a different appraisal of Augustine's teaching on this biblical passage: Brown, *Through the Eye of a Needle*, 352.

Such acts of sharing provide visible evidence of the inner renunciation of wealth, as Augustine explains in *Sermon* 177: "You were saying, 'I do have gold, but I don't love it.'"[162] Augustine is well aware that wealthy congregants could falsely claim that they had spiritually renounced their wealth—and so he asks for proof.[163] "'How,' you say, 'shall I prove it?' From what follows: *Let them be rich in good works, always ready to give.* Be rich to this end, that you are always ready to give."[164] Thus Augustine reminds them that sharing of resources with one's neighbor is necessary evidence that love for God has supplanted our love for the world.

God Is Available to All

Having taken the axe to avarice in *Sermon* 107A, it is Augustine's hope that charity will grow in its place. At the beginning of the sermon, he instructed the congregation about the nature of charity: "*It does not seek its own good, but that of others* (1 Cor 13:5; Phil 2:4). It doesn't seek its own convenience, it seeks the welfare of the brethren."[165] In the *Rule*, Augustine elaborates on this definition: "For when it is written of *love* that it *does not seek its own* (1 Cor 13:5), it means that it puts the common good before its own and not personal advantage before the common good."[166] In attempting to nurture this love that seeks the good of others, however, Augustine has not presented his listeners with a social or economic program through which the "common good" might be realized.[167] Rather, he has encouraged them to direct their love toward God.[168] For it is by learning to love God that our greedy desire to claim things for our own is overcome.

---

162. *Serm.* 177.10.
163. *Serm.* 177.10.
164. *Serm.* 177.10. As Augustine observes elsewhere: "If the mind cannot clearly perceive whether it despises the possession of them [riches], that can be simply tested by giving them away" (*Conf.* 10.37.60).
165. *Serm.* 107A.1.
166. *Reg. 3:* 5.2. For Augustine's understanding of the "common good," see Canning, "Common Good," 219-22. See also Canning, *Unity of Love for God and Neighbour*, 232-9; Canning, "St. Augustine's Vocabulary of the Common Good," 48-54. Regarding the meaning of the common good within the particular context of Augustine's *Rule*, see Martin, "Augustine and the Politics of Monasticism," 178-81.
167. Questions regarding the role of the state in promoting the common good—whether in Augustine's thought, or in our own context—are beyond the scope of this book. However, for discussion of these issues, see William T. Cavanaugh, *Migrations of the Holy: God, State, and the Political Meaning of the Church* (Grand Rapids, MI: Eerdmans, 2011), 7-45; Markus, "Pride and the Common Good," 253-4; Williams, *On Augustine*, 107-29.
168. This does not mean that Augustine is devaluing the task of seeking the common good within society. Rather, he reminds us where this good comes from, and to direct our hearts accordingly. See *Serm.* 72(D16/M46-47).18.

In *Sermon* 355 Augustine narrates how the monastic community came to share their resources together: "Just as I had sold my slender poor man's property and distributed the proceeds to the poor, those who wished to stay with me did the same, so that we might live on what we had in common."[169] It is an impressive account of their commitment to a common life. However, Augustine then immediately adds: "But what would be our really great and profitable common estate was God himself."[170] In this subsequent statement, Augustine is not downplaying the importance of the monastic community's commitment to share resources in common. Rather, he is reminding his listeners that a common love of God is the basis of the monastic community's shared life, for God is their true common good.[171]

Unlike material goods, God cannot be claimed for our own private enjoyment.[172] Even though we might address God in personal terms, he remains accessible to all, as Augustine explains wonderfully in *Sermon* 47, when reflecting on the use of the expression "My God":

> You say it without a qualm, and you say it truly, because he is yours, and you haven't stopped him being anyone else's. After all, you don't say "My God" in the same way as you say "My horse." It's your horse, not someone else's horse.... He is the God of all people, offering himself to be enjoyed by all in common, totally in all, totally in each. After all, those who each say "My God" don't divide him up among themselves.[173]

Continuing to develop this teaching, Augustine uses the example of sound to explain how God can be enjoyed by each, yet be accessible to all.[174] Light provides a further illustration:

> And the eyes of all people possess it [light] equally, they don't divide it between them. No rich man puts up fences in it, nor by staking a prior claim to see in it does he exclude or severely limit the eyes of the poor man. Let the poor man say "My God"; let the rich man say "My God"; the first has less, the second has more—but money, not God.[175]

The examples of sound and light are only approximations.[176] However, Augustine draws on them to help the congregation appreciate how, unlike material goods,

---

169. *Serm.* 355.2.
170. *Serm.* 355.2.
171. As Augustine writes in *The City of God*: "Those who hold this good in common form a holy society both with him to whom they cling and with each other" (*Civ.* 12.9).
172. Burnaby, *Amor Dei*, 127; Canning, *Unity of Love for God and Neighbour*, 43–4.
173. *Serm.* 47.30.
174. *Serm.* 47.30.
175. *Serm.* 47.30. Torchia explains that in God "a fullness that can be universally shared" is found, and discusses Augustine's use of the "senses" to illustrate this teaching: Torchia, "The Commune/Proprium Distinction," 357–9.
176. For the limitations of such metaphors for God, see *Serm.* 120.2.

God can truly be a good common to all. The economic forces and greedy behaviors that favor the rich and deprive the poor in this case do not hold sway. Rather God is "enjoyed by all in common."[177] Moreover, this good can *only* be enjoyed in common.[178]

When our hearts are turned toward God, the common good, this love is reflected in our concern for the common good of others.[179] In the monastic community, unity found in the love of God enables members to share what they have in common.[180] Similarly, had the disputing brothers (Lk. 12:13–15) been united in love for God, rather than divided by earthly desires, they could have enjoyed their inheritance in common: "they could each have had the whole of the estate they were seeking to divide, if they had lived together in harmony," Augustine observes.[181] In *Sermon* 107A, Augustine has sought to nurture a love that is "*rich toward God*" (Lk. 12:21) and that "seeks the welfare of the brethren."[182] In particular, he has encouraged them to demonstrate this love through the practical act of giving. However, the estate of heaven is not limited to those who make radical renouncements of wealth. An astute observer of human motivation, Augustine knows that one can give impressively while lacking love, and that great love can be expressed even if one has little to share.[183] What is important in the giving and redistributing of wealth is the orientation of the heart. "God doesn't weigh up people's resources but their willingness," Augustine observes.[184] He reiterates this point at the conclusion of *Sermon* 107A, when he acknowledges that, although "poor [*pauperes*]," the members of this congregation "are building a church."[185] He encourages them in this endeavor, but reminds his listeners that, as they contribute toward this work, it is not the size of their donation, but the willingness of their heart that is significant.[186]

Therefore, while giving is an important way of expressing love for God and neighbor, that does not mean that the wealthy have privileged access to God, nor

---

177. *Serm.* 47.30.
178. As Burnaby observes: "Goodness … is only possessed at all in so far as it *is* shared." Burnaby, *Amor Dei*, 127. See also Canning, *Unity of Love for God and Neighbour*, 233–4.
179. Canning states that "for Augustine … God's being the highest and truest common good provides the conditions for an unfeigned and salutary love of neighbour." Canning, "St. Augustine's Vocabulary of the Common Good," 54.
180. *Reg.* 3: 1.2-3.
181. *Serm.* 107A.1. Notably, Augustine also employs this imagery of a shared inheritance when speaking of the common parentage we receive in baptism: see *Serm.* 260C.1.
182. *Serm.* 107A.7, 1.
183. *Tract. ep. Jo.* 6.2.
184. *Serm.* 107A.7.
185. *Serm.* 107A.9 (*RBén* 49:278). Augustine's description of his audience as "poor," alongside this mention of their church building activities, prompts Hill's suggestion (noted earlier) that this sermon is preached to "a small rural congregation." *Sermons (94A-147A)*, 125n1. For discussion of this church building project, see Brown, *Through the Eye of a Needle*, 356; Dunn, "Poverty as a Social Issue," 179.
186. *Serm.* 107A.9.

are the destitute disadvantaged. Augustine demonstrates this in the latter part of *Sermon* 107A by inviting listeners to recall the gospel account of a widow making her offering in the temple (Lk. 21:1–4).[187] In retelling the story, he notes that "the bystanders were observing the huge offerings of the rich and admiring them."[188] "Who bothered even to see that widow?" Augustine asks.[189] "Well the Lord did; he not only saw her, he saw only her and recommended her example to those who didn't see her."[190] Within the Christian community, we may give greater attention to donations of greater material worth, whether the generous bequest left by a benefactor, or the substantial tithe of an affluent member. However, Augustine reminds his listeners, Jesus sees differently. The poor among his congregation should not feel inferior because they have little material wealth to offer. In God's eyes, Augustine explains, the measure of charity is not "people's resources but their willingness."[191] He illustrates this by comparing the example of Zacchaeus with that of the widow. In contrast to the "two farthings" of the widow, Zacchaeus, a prosperous tax collector, gave half of his property to the poor (Lk. 19:8).[192] "If you compare half of Zacchaeus' goods and two farthings, there's simply no comparison. Compare the willingness of Zacchaeus and the willingness of the widow. In the first instance you will find sheer inequality, in the second absolute similarity."[193] On purely economic terms, Zacchaeus' situation is privileged, while the widow has little of material worth to offer. And yet the material poverty of her offering does not disadvantage her from participating in God's kingdom, for "what is little for the poor is much for the one who knows poor and rich alike."[194] Teaching elsewhere on Zacchaeus and the widow, Augustine states that the kingdom of God "is given equally to both rich and poor."[195] As he explains, "In that kingdom Zacchaeus will not be richer than that widow, even if here he gave much more than she did. He, after all, gave half his goods to the poor, she gave two farthings. They were ill-matched in their means, they were equals in charity."[196]

Conclusion

As the contemporary church considers issues of economic inequality, our primary interest may be in practical responses to this problem. Should we spend less on

---

187. *Serm.* 107A.7.
188. *Serm.* 107A.7. For the public nature of the offerings given in church by the rich, see Brown, *Through the Eye of a Needle*, 317–18.
189. *Serm.* 107A.7.
190. *Serm.* 107A.7.
191. *Serm.* 107A.7.
192. *Serm.* 107A.7.
193. *Serm.* 107A.8.
194. *Serm.* 107A.8.
195. *Serm.* 114B(D5/M12).11.
196. *Serm.* 114B(D5/M12).11.

our groceries, or live in more modest houses? Will it make a difference if we buy locally made or ethically sourced goods? What changes to our economic system will yield fairer outcomes? However, Augustine's *Sermons* invite us to dig deeper. As demonstrated, Augustine comments often on practical matters of money and property in his preaching. And yet, his particular pastoral concern is attending to the underlying issues. In *Sermon* 107A, he draws our attention to "the root of the bad tree": an avaricious desire to claim and secure what we consider to be rightfully ours.[197] This desire draws us into ourselves, and away from God and neighbor. Augustine's teaching invites us to look beneath the surface, questioning our own underlying assumptions and attitudes. For example, his caution against "avarice even for things which are called your own" challenges individualistic understandings of property.[198] Within the contemporary church, our "right" to private property ownership is often presumed, not questioned, from the pulpit. Thus, as we read Augustine's *Sermon* 107A, perhaps we too experience the surprise of the man in Luke 12:13–15, when Jesus refuses his request to make a ruling on the man's claim upon his own property. Augustine's teaching on "superfluous" wealth is similarly challenging.[199] It is perhaps more common for us to ask, "how much should I give to others," than to consider "how much should I retain for myself." If we do decide to give away a small percentage of our income (e.g., a tithe), we may then assume that the rest belongs to us, to use as we wish—it is not available for the neighbor. By contrast, Augustine's teaching challenges this assumption, inviting us to think carefully about what we need (and to provide for ourselves accordingly), but then to make the remainder available to the need of others. In applying this teaching in a congregational setting, it would not be helpful to be overly prescriptive; individual circumstances vary, and a practice that might be profoundly liberating for some could become paralyzingly legalistic for others. However, we would do well to consider the spirit of Augustine's teaching on this topic, and consider how it speaks to our own situation.

Augustine's *Sermons* challenge the Christian community to attend to greed at this more fundamental level. Taking the "axe" to "the root of the bad tree," Augustine employs a number of rhetorical strategies and illustrations to stem the growth of avarice.[200] Even if his imaginative use of financial metaphor seems unappealing in our context, it remains indicative of the homiletic efforts required of preachers attempting to attend to avarice's hold. Moreover, Augustine's teaching on giving to those in need provides a valuable theological framework for understanding such gifts. In our contemporary context, gifts to the needy can often be portrayed as heroic displays of philanthropy, whereby we, with admirable generosity, donate some of our resources to another. The role of the giver in this exchange is foregrounded and celebrated. We could learn a lot, therefore, from

---

197. *Serm.* 107A.1.
198. *Serm.* 107A.2.
199. *Serm.* 107A.2.
200. *Serm.* 107A.1.

Augustine's alternative portrayals of the act of sharing, where (to recall one example) the wealthy giver is cast as one struggling under a heavy "burden," in need of others who can share the weight of their surplus resources.[201] Augustine's creative descriptions of the act of giving remind us that there is more than one way to narrate such encounters. The church must be careful not to unconsciously adopt the image of the celebrated benefactor rescuing the helpless pauper that is often prevalent in wider society, instead carefully considering how our theological beliefs regarding ourselves, our resources, and our neighbor should shape our understanding of the act of sharing.

Giving to those in need indicates that, in the place of avarice, love has begun to grow: the love that "*does not seek its own good, but that of others* (1 Cor 13:5; Phil 2:4)."[202] The example of Augustine's monastic community offers us a glimpse of what a community shaped by this love might look like. No longer claiming their resources as their own, instead they shared "*everything in common* (Acts 4:32)."[203] The *Sermons* indicate how this vision can be faithfully adapted for those in the wider Christian community who are unable to participate in such a form of life. Here too, the same formational movement can be encouraged: the call to no longer cling tightly to our own resources, but rather to express our love for God and neighbor by sharing with those in need.

---

201. *Serm.* 107A.5; 53A.6.
202. *Serm.* 107A.1.
203. *Reg. 3:* 1.3.

Chapter 4

ENVY AND THE QUESTION OF NEED

If special treatment in the way of diet is given to those who are not strong as a result of their former way of life, others who are stronger because they have had a different manner of life must not be aggrieved or think it unfair. Nor should they think the former luckier in getting something that they themselves do not get. Rather, they should be thankful that they are strong enough to do what others cannot.
—*Reg. 3: 3.3.*

It is better to need less than to have more.
—*Reg. 3: 3.5.*

In his introduction to *Sermon 359A*, Augustine recalls Paul's instruction in Romans 8:24–25: "*For hope*, as the apostle says, *which is seen is not hope; for why should anyone hope for what he can see? But if*, he goes on, *we hope for what we cannot see, we wait for it with patience.*"[1] "It's about this patience that I wish to speak to your graces whatever the Lord grants me to say," Augustine continues.[2] In this sermon, Augustine encourages the congregation to live patiently, setting their hearts and minds upon this hope that is presently unseen. Meanwhile, however, the prosperity of others can be seen, and presents a significant test to the patience of believers. When his listeners observe that their neighbor has more than them, or when they glimpse the luxurious life of the wealthy, envy is a common response.

As the contemporary church grapples with challenges of economic inequality, the issue of envy needs our scrutiny.[3] In Latin, the association between envy

---

1. *Serm.* 359A.1.
2. *Serm.* 359A.2.
3. As will be discussed, when discussing envious responses to another's prosperity in the *Sermons*, Augustine often talks in terms of greed, rather than envy. In this respect, my use of the word envy in this chapter is perhaps more expansive than Augustine's. However, I have done so to delineate the focus of this chapter (the greedy/envious response that arises from seeing the prosperity of others) from the focus of Chapter 3 (greed for one's own).

(*invideo*) and seeing (*video*) is clearly apparent.[4] And in our image-obsessed, technology-fueled era, the sight of the prosperity of others is ubiquitous, whether a glimpse of a friend's house renovations on social media, or a glossy depiction of luxury on television.

While greater economic disparity might exacerbate envy, such grievances could also arise within the relative equality of Augustine's monastic community. Although they shared their resources, one member might discover that another had received more than them from the common store: perhaps a warmer cloak, or an extra portion of food.[5] Such differences might seem negligible, but they remained differences nonetheless, and as Augustine anticipates in the *Rule*, they could lead to resentment when members of the community became preoccupied with what others had, and what they did not.[6]

Envy is symptomatic of a self-seeking love that no longer has regard for God or neighbor. We become consumed with desire for lesser goods, rather than seeking satisfaction in the good that is God. And fueled by this disordered love, we regard our neighbors with rivalry, rather than affection. Accordingly, Augustine's pastoral response is to redirect the hearts of his listeners toward God. In God alone can our hearts be satisfied, and setting our sights upon God redefines our understanding of happiness, quelling our insistent need for more, and helping us to be content with what we have. Because the satisfaction found in God's company is an eschatological goal, a hope that cannot yet be seen, the Christian life is characterized by patient longing. For Augustine, however, this longing requires active demonstration in the present, including practical responses of love toward our neighbor. Augustine develops a number of these themes in *Sermon* 359A, which gives shape to this chapter, in conversation with other sermons and the monastic rules. No date has been established for this sermon, but it was given to a congregation at Tuneba.[7]

Seeing Another's Prosperity

"The haves" and "the have-nots" are common descriptors for rich and poor in popular discussions of economic inequality. Their regular use reflects the widely held assumption that one's life should be measured by what one has—or does not have. Those who have are assumed to be happier and more successful. Those who have not believe life will be improved by having more, and become envious of what they do not have.

---

4. Sophie Lunn-Rockliffe notes the association of envy with "observing and seeing" in the classical tradition. Sophie Lunn-Rockliffe, "The Diabolical Problem of Satan's First Sin: Self-Moved Pride or a Response to the Goads of Envy?," in *Studia Patristica 63*, ed. M. Vinzent (Leuven: Peeters, 2011), 131.
5. *Reg. 3*: 3.3–4; 5.1.
6. *Reg. 3*: 3.3–4; 5.1.
7. The Latin text is found in Lambot, "Nouveaux Sermons," 258–70. Hill provides details regarding dating and location: *Sermons (341–400)*, 220n1.

Augustine captures this sentiment brilliantly in his *Sermons*. In *Sermon* 302, for example, he observes: "The person at the bottom of the heap longs to climb to the top, the person at the top dreads sliding down to the bottom. The have-nots envy the haves; the haves despise the have-nots."[8] In *Sermon* 345, he perceptively describes the envious attention the poor give to the rich: "They grumble, sigh, praise them, envy them, would love to be on their level, lament that they are so much below it, and among their praises of the rich they frequently say this sort of thing: 'These are the only ones, these the only ones who really live.'"[9] Within our contemporary setting, Augustine's description remains an accurate portrayal of the seemingly contradictory responses that a glimpse of the rich produces. We adulate the rich and famous, because they portray a lifestyle that we aspire to—and yet at the same time, we enviously resent them, for they have this lifestyle, and we do not. Both responses, however, confirm our misguided belief that those who have wealth are "the only ones who really live."[10]

Augustine raises this issue with the congregation midway through *Sermon* 359A: "People who are down on their luck see others who in this world are called fortunate and said to be blessed, and they want to be like that themselves, and they imagine that when they are like that themselves, they won't any longer be in evil straits."[11] As Augustine's comment suggests, this response arises from seeing: the sight of the prosperity of others prompts us to desire what they have, and our vision of the good life is shaped accordingly. Describing Augustine's account of envy and pride, Sophie Lunn-Rockliffe notes that whereas pride is "internally generated and directed," envy is "externally directed."[12] Envy responds to the desirable circumstances of another.

The wealth of the rich could certainly be seen by members of Augustine's congregation. Brown highlights the visible character of wealth in Late Antiquity.[13] Describing the distinctive clothing and jewelry of the wealthy in this period, he comments that "rich men and women alike were expected to stand out like birds of paradise in a flock of starlings."[14] Brown also observes an accompanying "explosion of color" in the homes of the affluent.[15] Lepelley notes the "beautiful mosaics" that have been discovered in the homes of the rich from this period, and (having quoted Augustine's comments in *Sermon* 345, cited above) he explains that the "luxury" of these homes would have "roused the resentment of the poor in their time."[16] Van der Meer comes to a similar conclusion when describing the expansive rural estates surrounding Hippo, upon which poor "tenant farmers"

---

8. *Serm.* 302.2.
9. *Serm.* 345.1.
10. *Serm.* 345.1.
11. *Serm.* 359A.6.
12. Lunn-Rockliffe, "Diabolical Problem of Satan's First Sin," 124.
13. Brown, *Through the Eye of a Needle*, 27–30, 192–4.
14. Brown, *Through the Eye of a Needle*, 28.
15. Brown, *Through the Eye of a Needle*, 192–3.
16. Lepelley, "Facing Wealth and Poverty," 4.

worked.[17] "The owners, who usually lived far away, were rarely seen but were for all that the objects of envy," he notes.[18] Amidst such economic inequality, it is easy to appreciate how the leisured lifestyle of wealthy landowners might prompt envy among poor laborers on the estate, or among those passing by.

Yet Augustine's monastic instruction suggests that even when economic differences are reduced, envy can still remain. For example, the monastic community held clothing in common (as with other material goods), and garments were distributed from a "single storeroom" to each member "according to need."[19] However, Augustine is aware that, despite this austere program of sharing, disputes could still occur over clothing, such as when "someone complains that he has received something that is not as good as what he had before."[20] Other instructions in the *Rule* anticipate the resentment that could arise when one member was discovered to have something that others did not, such as a different allocation of "food, clothing, bedding or covering," or "special treatment in the way of diet."[21] In comparison to the more substantial economic differences Augustine notes in his *Sermons*, such grievances might seem petty and inconsequential; it was not a question of whether one lived in a "mansion of marble" or a "shack full of smoke,"[22] but rather whether you received one cloak or two from the common store, or were given an extra portion of food at mealtimes.[23] And yet, these are not trifling matters for Augustine. He is aware that envy among members, even over the most minute differences, could result in discord that would undo their unity.

This desire for the prosperity of another runs contrary to Christian faith. Commenting in *Sermon* 359A on those who see the "fortunate" ones, and "want to be like that themselves," Augustine cautions that "this is a twisted frame of mind, and not a Christian one, marked by greed [*cupiditate*], not by faith."[24] It should be noted that here Augustine describes this desire as "greed"; he does not use the term "envy" (*invidia*) in *Sermon* 359A, nor in the *Rule*.[25] However, for Augustine, envy and greed are closely related, as are envy and pride, as *Sermon* 399 illustrates. Here, Augustine responds to the claim of a fictive listener that "I do love my neighbor as myself."[26] The listener, however, loves money, and thus struggles to love their

---

17. Van der Meer, *Augustine the Bishop*, 26.

18. Van der Meer, *Augustine the Bishop*, 26. Lepelley also notes (with reference to Possidius) that Augustine was apprehensive about the church receiving land or large gifts, lest it prompt envy: Lepelley, "Facing Wealth and Poverty," 14. See also *Serm.* 354.2.

19. *Reg. 3*: 5.1; 1.3.

20. *Reg. 3*: 5.1.

21. *Reg. 3*: 3.4; 3.3.

22. *Serm.* 170.4.

23. *Reg. 3*: 3.3–4; 5.1.

24. *Serm.* 359A.6 (*RBén* 49:261).

25. In the *Sermons*, Augustine sometimes uses other words for envy or jealousy, such as "*aemulatur*" (e.g., *Serm.* 142.12 (*PL* 38:783)) and "*zelavi*" (e.g., *Serm.* 301.7 (*PL* 38:1384); *Serm.* 19.4 (*PL* 38:134–5)).

26. *Serm.* 399.5. See Chapter 1 for Augustine's discussion of this claim.

neighbor in the same fashion, for it would result in the diminishment of their own wealth.[27] This is the voice of avarice, Augustine suggests.[28] And yet, as he proceeds, he then cautions them against envy:

> You see, I'm afraid that in fact you are being envious. I mean, how can you be sociable and friendly in your prosperity, when someone else's prosperity racks you with envy? Aren't you afraid, when your neighbor begins to grow rich, and begins as it were to rise, and to come after you, aren't you afraid he may follow you, afraid he may pass you?[29]

Whereas avarice prevents their love of neighbor because they fear having less wealth, envy prevents love of neighbor because the listener resents the thought of the neighbor having more than them. Augustine's description suggests that this envy is as much to do with the status that accompanies wealth, as the wealth itself.

In this sermon, Augustine goes on to note that "the mother of envy is called pride."[30] In tracing envy back to pride, Augustine reminds us that a certain sort of anthropology is prerequisite for envy to exist. Augustine provides helpful explanation in *The Literal Meaning of Genesis*:

> Since pride, then, is the love of one's own superiority, while jealousy is the hatred of another's good fortune, it is easy to see which comes from which. I mean, anyone in love with his own superiority will be jealous of his peers because they are treated as his equals, and of his inferiors in case they should become his equals, and of his superiors because he is not treated as their equal. Thus it is pride that makes people jealous, not jealousy that makes them proud.[31]

Envy presumes that we have already set ourselves apart from God and our neighbor, with a proud "love of one's own superiority." Whereas in God's company, all can enjoy the good that is God without jealousy, it is apart from God that our love of lesser goods is marked by rivalry and competition.[32]

---

27. *Serm.* 399.6.
28. *Serm.* 399.6.
29. *Serm.* 399.7.
30. *Serm.* 399.7. See also *Serm.* 354.6.
31. *Gen. litt.* 11.14.18. Edmund Hill notes that he is translating *"invidia"* as "jealousy" in this section: *On Genesis*, trans. Edmund Hill, ed. John E. Rotelle, vol. 13, *The Works of Saint Augustine, Part 1: Books* (Hyde Park, NY: New City Press, 2002), 438n14. Augustine is considering the fall of the devil in this passage, and the question of the sin that prompted this fall. For envy and the devil see also *Civ.* 14.11; *Serm.* 399.7; *Tract. ep. Jo.* 5.8. For discussion of the roles of pride and/or envy in the devil's fall, see Neil Adkin, "Pride or Envy? Some Notes on the Reason the Fathers Give for the Devil's Fall," *Augustiniana* 34 (1984): 349–51; Lunn-Rockliffe, "Diabolical Problem of Satan's First Sin," 121–40.
32. *Serm.* 357.1.

Envy inhibits love. The "envious person" cannot have charity.[33] When governed by envy, we are unable to seek our neighbor's well-being, for their prosperity threatens our own. As Augustine puts it in the passage earlier quoted from *Sermon 399*: "Aren't you afraid, when your neighbor begins to grow rich, and begins as it were to rise, and to come after you, aren't you afraid he may follow you, afraid he may pass you?"[34] His comments capture well the rivalrous nature of envy. In this regard, it is helpful to recall Brown's caution against viewing the society of this period in the "binary" terms of "the rich" and "the poor."[35] He explains that such a "polarized" view can lead us to overlook "the more subtle, intermediate gradations of late Roman society."[36] Notably, in between the very wealthy and the utterly destitute existed the "*pauperes*," who "were far from a monochrome group."[37] Considered against this more nuanced backdrop, we can better appreciate the adversarial dynamics of envy. For example, while the homes of the wealthy elite may have been particularly impressive, Brown explains that villas could also be adapted for those with smaller budgets.[38] In their variety of forms, he notes, these villas "hint at the strong competitive urges of a widespread class of landowners, each of whom was anxious to stake out a claim on the landscape."[39] This suggests that even someone with enough means to purchase a villa might envy those whose villa was larger or more lavishly decorated. Accompanying this rivalry for upward mobility was the fear of decline. Brown explains: "What even the most prosperous members of the *populus* lacked was not money—it was security. They were not poor, but they always lived in fear of impoverishment.… They felt themselves on a slope that always tilted perilously toward the bottom of society."[40] The envy of another's rise was compounded by the very real prospect of one's own fall.

Envy not only inflames our desire for advancement; it can also prompt desire for our neighbor's diminishment. "What is envy," Augustine asks in *Sermon 353*, "but hatred of another's good fortune?"[41] And as he goes on to enquire, "Can you be truly envious without wishing the person ill, whose good fortune is tormenting you?"[42] At its worst, envy can lead to hostility against our neighbor, as the Cain and

---

33. *Serm.* 142.12.
34. *Serm.* 399.7.
35. Brown, *Through the Eye of a Needle*, 78. See also Brown, *Poverty and Leadership in the Later Roman Empire*, 45–8.
36. Brown, *Poverty and Leadership in the Later Roman Empire*, 47.
37. Brown, *Through the Eye of a Needle*, 343. See Introduction for discussion.
38. Brown, *Through the Eye of a Needle*, 193.
39. Brown, *Through the Eye of a Needle*, 193–4. See also pp. 21–30 for context regarding this competitive impulse in Late Antiquity.
40. Brown, *Through the Eye of a Needle*, 345. Brown argues that Augustine's sermons were typically addressed to such "members of the *populus*," in which case Augustine's teaching on envy would have been especially apt (pp. 345, 347). See, however, discussion in my Introduction regarding the social make-up of Augustine's congregation.
41. *Serm.* 353.1.
42. *Serm.* 353.1.

Abel narrative gravely illustrates (Gen. 4:1–16).[43] Reflecting on this narrative (and on 1 Jn 3:12) in another homily, Augustine puts the matter plainly: "Where envy exists, then, there can be no brotherly love."[44] If our goal is love for one another, then envy cannot be ignored.

As well as stifling love for our prosperous neighbor, envy also inhibits love of our impoverished neighbor. In *Sermon* 9, Augustine insightfully identifies this tendency among his listeners:

> Lastly why, in this matter of worldly status, are you not satisfied with being better off than many; why, instead, do you want to be rich, equal to people who are richer than you are? You don't consider how many poorer people you surpass; you want to overtake richer people.… Nobody thinks of the extreme want of countless beggars, nobody looks back at the hordes of the poor trailing behind you, but all eyes are fixed on the smattering of rich people ahead of you.[45]

Because our gaze is toward those who have more than us, those with less do not attract our attention, and we become blind to their need. This leads to the intriguing conclusion that to love our needy neighbor, we must learn not to envy our wealthier neighbor.

Augustine is also aware that the worldly prosperity of others can become an obstacle in our love of God, especially when it is the undeserving who prosper. "People are habitually upset by this," Augustine observes in *Sermon* 25A.[46] "They see evil people prevailing successfully all along the line in all their business which is admittedly earthly and temporal, but is still good. And they sigh in their miseries, and can scarcely restrain their thoughts from blaming God."[47] The prosperity of the unjust prompts protest alongside envy. Augustine notes that God anticipates such concerns in the words of the psalmist: "*Do not be jealous of evil-doers, nor envy those who work iniquity*" (Ps. 37:1).[48] "But that's precisely what you were doing, isn't it," challenges Augustine, "being jealous and envious, when you kept on saying to yourself 'Why do they flourish?'"[49] In Psalm 73:1–3, Augustine similarly notes the psalmist's experience of envy, observing that their

---

43. *Civ.* 15.5, 7.
44. *Tract. ep. Jo.* 5.8. See also Augustine's discussion of the envy of infant siblings: *Conf.* 1.7.11.
45. *Serm.* 9.19.
46. *Serm.* 25A.1.
47. *Serm.* 25A.1.
48. *Serm.* 25A.1. Sarah Stewart-Kroeker's article focuses on one of Augustine's homilies dedicated to this psalm (*Enarrat. Ps.* 36.1), with a particular interest in how Augustine encourages the right ordering of emotion. Sarah Stewart-Kroeker, "World-Weariness and Augustine's Eschatological Ordering of Emotions in *enarratio in Psalmum 36*," *Augustinian Studies* 47, no. 2 (2016): 201–26. For her discussion of this particular verse, see p. 216.
49. *Serm.* 25A.1.

"feet were shaken" by the prosperity of the undeserving.[50] The shaken feet of the psalmist, Augustine explains, reflects the psalmist's "doubt" and inclination to "find fault with God."[51] All Christians can be susceptible to such temptation; indeed, as Augustine acknowledges in one sermon, even monastics wrestle with this question.[52] This issue is exacerbated when people become Christians in order to gain temporal prosperity and happiness—a misguided belief that Augustine is at pains to correct.[53]

Envy sets its sights on the wrong sort of happiness. Sarah Stewart-Kroeker, discussing the role of the emotions in Augustine's thought, explains: "A misperception of felicity will result in correspondingly misdirected will and attendant emotions."[54] Envy is one such misguided emotion that arises when we are not oriented toward the true happiness found in God. Thus, as Stewart-Kroeker later explains: "When one covets the goods of those who may be forfeiting eternal happiness for temporal prosperity, one implicitly mistakes the *source* of happiness. This is a serious misperception, which derails the order that guides the whole aim of moral and affective formation."[55] Later in *Sermon* 359A, Augustine cautions the congregation against such a mistake, with reference to Psalm 144.[56] In his reading of the psalm, the iniquitous (Ps. 144:11) are described as materially prosperous: "*Their cellars are full, bursting out from this one to that. Their oxen are fat, their sheep fertile, multiplying in their lambing*" (vv. 13–14).[57] "What marvelous temporal happiness he has described!" Augustine remarks of the psalmist.[58] "So where's the iniquity, where's the vanity? Listen to what follows: *Blessed they called*

---

50. *Serm.* 301.7.
51. *Serm.* 301.7. For further discussion of Augustine's teaching on the doubt and questioning of God's justice prompted by the prosperity of the unjust, see Stewart-Kroeker, "World-Weariness and Augustine's Eschatological Ordering of Emotions," 214–19.
52. *Serm.* 350A.3 (see Hill's note on the monastics as audience of this sermon: *Sermons (341–400)*, 113n1).
53. See *Serm.* 33A.3; *Serm.* 46.10–11; *Catech.* 16.24–17.27. See also this theme in *Civ.* 3.18; 11.25; 15.7.
54. Stewart-Kroeker, "World-Weariness and Augustine's Eschatological Ordering of Emotions," 209.
55. Stewart-Kroeker, "World-Weariness and Augustine's Eschatological Ordering of Emotions," 218. For Augustine's understanding of "happiness," see Babcock, introduction to *City of God (Books 1–10)*, xlix.
56. *Serm.* 359A.14. In contrast with modern translations, the translation of Psalm 144 that Augustine is using leads him to read it as if the psalmist is associating the prosperity described in verses 12–15a with the iniquitous ones of verse 11. See Hill's comment on Augustine's similar use of Psalm 144 in *Sermon 32: Sermons (20–50) on the Old Testament*, trans. Edmund Hill, ed. John E. Rotelle, vol. 2, *The Works of Saint Augustine, Part 3: Sermons* (Brooklyn, NY: New City Press, 1990), 153n40.
57. *Serm.* 359A.14.
58. *Serm.* 359A.14.

the people which has these things" (v. 15a).⁵⁹ The problem is not that the iniquitous enjoy the fruits of prosperity, but rather that their prosperity has been mistaken for blessing. "They had no eyes for the other blessedness, they didn't seek the other kind, which is the true one," Augustine observes.⁶⁰ Instead, he finds this "true" orientation in the final phrase of the psalm: *"Blessed the people whose God is the Lord"* (v. 15b).⁶¹ We are happy when in faith we set our sights upon God—and yet in our greed and envy, we focus instead on accruing material blessings, and have "no eyes for the other blessedness."⁶² In *Sermon* 113, he explains this teaching (drawing again from Ps. 144) in terms that his listeners could readily identify with:

> Sometimes we are passing along a road, and we see the most lovely, fertile farms, and we say, "Who does that farm belong to?" We are told, "So-and-so," and we say, "Happy man"; we are talking nonsense.... Happy is the man of whom the Lord is his God. Not, you see, happy the one whose farm this is, but whose God that is.⁶³

Rather than being distracted by sights of material prosperity, those who seek the truly happy life must learn to look toward God.

Looking toward Home

Whereas envy is symptomatic of our departure from God, contentment will characterize our reunion with God. This happiness is an eschatological goal, toward which Augustine constantly redirects his congregation. However, while he might paint a fine picture of this blessed life when the congregation gathers for worship, no doubt it would sometimes seem a very distant vision. Meanwhile, his listeners are daily confronted with the wealth and prosperity enjoyed by others: images that, in their immediacy and tangibility, suggest a more compelling picture of happiness.

In response, Augustine typically alerts his listeners to the falseness of this vision of the happy life. First Timothy 6:19 often prompts this teaching for Augustine. When the apostle instructs the rich to *"lay hold of true life,"* Augustine explains in *Sermon* 345 that "it undoubtedly means that this life is a false one."⁶⁴ Although we may think that the affluent are those "who really live," the basis of their purported happiness is not "real" in the truest sense.⁶⁵ Rather, this is "a dream life," Augustine

---

59. *Serm.* 359A.14.
60. *Serm.* 359A.14.
61. *Serm.* 359A.14.
62. *Serm.* 359A.6, 14.
63. *Serm.* 113.6. As noted in Chapter 1, the question of the "happy life" was central to the eudaemonistic ethics of Augustine's time (see Chapter 1 for secondary sources).
64. *Serm.* 345.1.
65. *Serm.* 345.1.

cautions.[66] While the false life is seen and envied, the richness of the true life is often not visible during this present age. In *Sermon 25A*, Augustine reminds listeners of Paul's teaching that *"your life is hidden with Christ in God* (Col 3:3)."[67] Using the illustration of "fruit trees" in winter and summer, Augustine explains that while the riches of their life with Christ may not presently be seen, when Christ returns they will experience an abundance; as Paul promises, *"you too shall appear with him in glory"* (Col. 3:4).[68]

In *Sermon 359A*, Augustine instructs the congregation in how to live patiently in the present, with their hearts oriented toward this future goal.[69] To that end, in the opening sections of this sermon (which precede the sections discussed above), Augustine reminds the congregation of the eschatological nature of the Christian life. Those who set their hope "above" find themselves "strangers in this world," journeying toward their "eternal home country in heaven."[70] It is there that "the region of the blissful life" is found: a destination of happiness that we are "at liberty to long for here below, not at liberty to possess here."[71] This true happiness is one we cannot "possess" in this life in the manner of our acquisitive culture, nor does it comply with our desire for immediate gratification. Instead, patience is required in this life in order to attain the happiness of the life to come.

There would be no need for patience if we thought we could be perfectly happy in this life, Augustine notes.[72] But "any who are on fire with a yearning for eternal life, in whatever country they may be happily living, must of necessity live patiently, because they have reluctantly to tolerate the fact of their being strangers and exiles [*peregrinationem*], until they reach the desired home country after loving it so long."[73] This biblical imagery of journey and exile, frequently employed by Augustine, vividly depicts the present experience of Christians en route to an eschatological destination. Augustine puts it well in *Sermon 346B*, where he

---

66. *Serm.* 345.1. For this motif of dreaming/sleeping, see also *Conf.* 6.6.10; 8.5.12.
67. *Serm.* 25A.1.
68. *Serm.* 25A.1. Augustine provides similar instruction to a monastic community in *Serm.* 350A.3–4.
69. *Serm.* 359A.2, 7.
70. *Serm.* 359A.1, 2.
71. *Serm.* 359A.2.
72. *Serm.* 359A.2.
73. *Serm.* 359A.2 (*RBén* 49:258). Clark explains that although "*peregrinatio*" became associated with the idea of "pilgrimage" in Late Antiquity, in Augustine's writing, the "dominant sense" is "of being away from where one wants to be." Gillian Clark, "Pilgrims and Foreigners: Augustine on Travelling Home," in *Travel, Communication and Geography in Late Antiquity: Sacred and Profane*, ed. Linda Ellis and Frank L. Kidner (Aldershot: Ashgate, 2004), 149. However, Clark later acknowledges (with reference to the *Enarrations on the Psalms*) that "when Augustine is preaching, he does sometimes add to *peregrinari* the encouraging sense of a journey home" (p. 154). See also Babcock, introduction to *City of God (Books 1–10)*, xlvii–xlviii; Brown, *Augustine of Hippo*, 323–4.

reflects on Paul's words, "*As long as we are in the body, we are traveling abroad from the Lord* (2 Cor 5:6)."[74] Augustine observes:

> And because everyone who travels abroad obviously has a home country …, we ought to know which our home country is, toward which we must ever be hastening, while turning our backs on all the attractions and delights of this life.… God, you see, hasn't wished us to find true rest anywhere else but in that home country, because if he also gave us rest here, we would find no pleasure in returning there.[75]

If our heart is oriented toward life with God—if that is our "home country"—then we cannot treat our present temporal location as home. Rather, our present status is that of exiled travelers, and patience is required to sustain us as we await our return.

As Augustine explains in other sermons, understanding ourselves as travelers journeying to a distant home changes the way we see and relate to the goods of this world. We can make "use" of such goods, inasmuch as they can benefit and sustain us on our journey.[76] However, we should not try to make our home among them, forfeiting our destination for the immediate pleasure of worldly prosperity. Thus Augustine instructs: "Let them be for our use as we need them, not for our affections to cling to them. Treat them like a tavern for a traveler, not like a mansion for a landowner. Stop for refreshment, and then go on your way."[77] Moreover, the exilic nature of Christian life calls into question our assumption that the wealthy are advantaged and to be envied. "As we long for the face of God, and sigh for the true home of everlasting happiness," Augustine observes in *Sermon* 359A, "it makes no difference, however much worldly happiness we may be flooded with, however full to overflowing we may be with abundance of this world's goods."[78] As exiles, our greatest longing is to arrive home, and affluence cannot hasten, nor poverty hinder, our arrival at this goal.

---

74. *Serm.* 346B.1.
75. *Serm.* 346B.1.
76. *Serm.* 177.2. For the distinction Augustine makes between "use" and "enjoyment" of material goods (e.g., *Doctr. chr.* 1.3.3–4.4), see Burnaby, *Amor Dei*, 104–10; MacQueen, "St. Augustine's Concept of Property Ownership," 209–12; Markus, *Saeculum: History and Society in the Theology of St Augustine*, 67–8. See also O'Donovan, "*Usus* and *Fruitio* in Augustine, *De Doctrina Christiana* I," 361–97. Markus characterizes "enjoyment" as "the attitude we entertain towards things we value for themselves," and "use" as "the attitude we entertain towards things we value for the sake of something else." Markus, *Saeculum: History and Society in the Theology of St Augustine*, 67. He observes that "nothing but God can ultimately serve as a resting-place in which all human longings are satisfied; to seek to 'enjoy' anything else is to be retarded in one's journey or diverted from its true destination" (p. 67). For the question of how Augustine locates the neighbor within this scheme, see footnote (and references) in "Loving Our Neighbor" section of Chapter 1.
77. *Serm.* 177.2.
78. *Serm.* 359A.5.

Redefining Happiness

Responding to those who look enviously toward those who "are called fortunate," Augustine insists that those focused on worldly prosperity can never be happy.[79] However, his definition of happiness may differ from that of his listeners, he explains: "Am I saying, 'Happiness is being healthy, being rich, being loaded with honors, living safe and sound with all one's family?' No; what I'm saying is, 'Happiness is not lacking anything.'"[80] In contrast to those who equate happiness with wealth, power, and prosperity, Augustine characterizes happiness as an absence of need. He then anticipates the response of his listeners, who might conclude: "So the rich are happy, because they don't lack anything."[81] Augustine dismisses this suggestion: "How can they lack nothing if they are not satisfied with what they have, and long to have more? You can see that when they've made their pile, it's nothing but firewood to feed the flames, not to satisfy them."[82] Augustine often emphasizes the insatiability of desire for wealth. "Even with people who already have much one can still talk about desire, not for the thing they possess, but for the one they want to possess," he observes in *Sermon* 177.[83] "He owns this farm, he desires to get possession of another which he doesn't own. But when he's also got that one, he will start desiring another."[84] The vision of happiness promised by material prosperity turns out to be a mirage, beckoning us closer, but always beyond our reach.

However, unlike the invariable disappointment of attempts to find happiness in material prosperity, Augustine seeks to reassure his listeners that their desire for God will be satisfied.[85] Discussing the virtues of faith, hope and charity (1 Cor. 13:13) in *Sermon* 359A, Augustine notes how each will find their fulfillment in the life to come. Faith is required in this present life because we cannot see our

---

79. *Serm.* 359A.6.
80. *Serm.* 359A.6.
81. *Serm.* 359A.6.
82. *Serm.* 359A.6.
83. *Serm.* 177.6.
84. *Serm.* 177.6. To modern readers, Augustine's descriptions may seem remarkably contemporary, capturing well the nature of consumer culture. For theological reflection on modern consumerism, see Cavanaugh, *Being Consumed*. Cavanaugh explains that "consumerism represents a constant dissatisfaction with particular material things themselves, a restlessness that constantly seeks to move beyond what is at hand" (p. 48). Christian faith also speaks of a certain sort of "restlessness," Cavanaugh observes, but he notes that "for Augustine ... the solution to our dissatisfaction is not the continuous search for new things but a turn toward the only One who can truly satisfy our desires" (p. 49).
85. For discussion of Augustine's preaching on the nature of our heavenly life (in comparison with his teaching on this topic in *The City of God*), see J. Kevin Coyle, "Adapted Discourse: Heaven in Augustine's *City of God* and in His Contemporary Preaching," in *History, Apocalypse, and the Secular Imagination: New Essays on Augustine's City of God*, ed. Mark Vessey, Karla Pollmann, and Allan D. Fitzgerald (Bowling Green, OH: Philosophy Documentation Centre, 1999), 205–19.

destination; when we arrive, however, "faith turns into sight."[86] Hope is needed, for otherwise we would abandon the journey; yet upon our arrival, "hope turns into the real thing."[87] And charity, during this life, is expressed as desire for our destination.[88] However, "*the greatest of these is charity* (1 Cor 13:13)," Augustine explains, for unlike faith and hope, charity does not come to conclusion in God's company.[89] Instead, it "grows," "increases," and "is perfected" in the enjoyment of God.[90]

Love for God will be satisfied. In other sermons, Augustine quotes the fourth beatitude to illustrate this future fulfillment of our present desire: "*Blessed are those who are hungry and thirsty for justice, since they will be satisfied* (Mt 5:6)."[91] For Augustine, satisfaction characterizes our anticipated life with God. There, our hunger and longing will be fulfilled—though not by provision of material goods, but through the provision of God's own self. Augustine explains this to his listeners in *Sermon* 255:

> So we shall not be in need of anything; and that's why we shall be blessed. We shall be full, you see, but of our God; and all these things that we desire here as being so important, that's what he will be for us. Here you look for food as something very important; there God will be your food.... Here you seek riches; how will you be lacking anything, when you have the one who made everything?[92]

This statement concludes a passage in *Sermon* 255 in which Augustine has been challenging materialistic conceptions of the life to come. For he is aware that many of his listeners have become so attached to material goods and worldly pleasures that they find it hard to conceive of a happy life without them.[93] Augustine imagines their objections: "What will there be in it for me, where I shall not eat, I shall not drink, where I shall not sleep with my wife? What sort of joy will I have of that?"[94]

In response to these questions, Augustine explains that such "fleshly desires" pertain only to our mortal life.[95] We should not project the needs of this life onto our vision of the next, nor should we assume that the lifestyle of

---

86. *Serm.* 359A.3-4. The theme of sight is significant in Augustine's thought, and features frequently throughout the *Sermons*, e.g., *Serm.* 88.4; 127.11, 13; 135.1; 360B(D25/M61).14-17. For discussion of this aspect of Augustine's thought, see Anatolios, *Retrieving Nicaea*, 241-80; Burnaby, *Amor Dei*, 60-78; Coyle, "Adapted Discourse," 214-15.
87. *Serm.* 359A.4.
88. *Serm.* 359A.2, 4.
89. *Serm.* 359A.4.
90. *Serm.* 359A.4.
91. *Serm.* 77.14.
92. *Serm.* 255.7.
93. *Serm.* 255.7.
94. *Serm.* 255.7.
95. *Serm.* 255.7. See also Chapter 2 for Augustine's caution against thinking of God in materialistic terms.

the rich reflects the true richness of life with God. Augustine entertainingly demonstrates the fallacy of such thinking by contrasting the life of the rich with that of the angels:

> When a rich man is being praised, you will hear, "What a great one he is, he's a lord, he's rich, he's powerful. What a great thing to go where he likes; the transport's there, the money for expenses is there, the slaves are there, the services are there." These are all the things a rich man has…. As for an angel, wherever he likes, that's where he will be. And he doesn't say "Harness the horses"; he doesn't say "Make up the beds"; which rich people say with such pride, and they are ready to swell up like turkey cocks, because they have people to whom they can say, "Harness the horses," and "Make up the beds." Unhappy people, these are words indicating weaknesses, not resources.[96]

Augustine's playful illustration demonstrates the contrast between popular pictures of happiness, and the vision of the happiness that Christians await. Looking at the lives of the rich and famous, our attention is drawn to their wealth, their vehicles, the people at their disposal; all this appears to be evidence of their happiness. However, when happiness is understood as not being in need, these ones turn out to be "Unhappy people," their emblems of wealth revealed as signs of neediness.

The satisfaction of the life to come arises from God's very presence. Teaching on the resurrection life in *Sermon* 362, Augustine explains that when we finally see God "*face to face*," we will praise God "with a kind of never satisfied satisfaction."[97] Augustine then clarifies this oxymoronic statement: "Because there will be nothing lacking, you see, that's why complete satisfaction; but because what is not lacking will always be giving delight, that's why, if one can so put it, it will be an unsatisfied satisfaction."[98] In God's company, we will be continually satisfied, enjoying the "food of truth" that "nourishes, and is not diminished."[99]

Moreover, this hope is not of a merely individual or private satisfaction. As the members of the congregation tend to the needs of the hungry and homeless in this present age, they can anticipate a future when such needs will be no more. In *Sermon* 305A, Augustine observes that the tasks of feeding, housing, and clothing those in need (Isa. 58:7) are "works of necessity"; that is, works that are occasioned by the human needs (such as for food and shelter) that characterize our present temporal existence.[100] However, as there will be no need in God's company, the very categories used to describe societal need will become obsolete. Augustine explains:

---

96. *Serm.* 255.7.
97. *Serm.* 362.29; see Coyle, "Adapted Discourse," 209.
98. *Serm.* 362.29.
99. *Serm.* 362.30.
100. *Serm.* 305A.7. See Ramsey, "Almsgiving in the Latin Church," 238–9.

You don't find a beggar there to break your bread to, or a strange visitor to take into your house. You don't find anyone thirsty, whom you can offer a drink, or naked, whom you can clothe.... All are taking their fill there of the food of justice and the drink of wisdom, all have been attired in immortality, all are living in their eternal home country. The health of them all is that same eternity, eternal health, eternal concord.[101]

The very same "health" that we anticipate will be enjoyed together with our neighbor, in a spirit of "concord."

Needing Less

Teaching the congregation how to live in the present, in the hope of future satisfaction, in *Sermon* 359A Augustine commends the practice of patience. This patient desire for satisfaction in God shapes our current life in tangible ways.[102] Augustine explains that "when you hope, you don't yet have what you are hoping for, but by believing it you resemble someone who does possess it."[103] When we set our hope upon the satisfaction of life with God, our life begins to reflect this true end. Notably, this future hope has a bearing on how we regard material resources in the present, whether we have much or little. Patience helps us to "endure even earthly happiness," Augustine remarks.[104] That is to say, those who are materially

---

101. *Serm.* 305A.8. In his description of heavenly life that concludes *The City of God*, Augustine allows that we will enjoy different "grades of honor and glory," but clarifies that "no inferior will envy any superior" (*Civ.* 22.30).

102. Stewart-Kroeker notes that Augustine's teaching on the eschatological orientation of human love and emotions has drawn much critique, and she provides an account of concerns voiced by Thomas Dixon and Martha Nussbaum. Stewart-Kroeker, "World-Weariness and Augustine's Eschatological Ordering of Emotions," 209–13. These include the criticisms that this aspect of Augustine's instruction "undermines the relationship to the earthly neighbor by funnelling all emotion toward God" (p. 210), and that it also detracts from "this-worldly ethics and politics" (p. 211), instead encouraging "passivity in the present" (p. 212). However, following a sympathetic engagement with these (and other) concerns, Stewart-Kroeker's reading of *Enarrat. Ps.* 36 and related texts leads her to conclude that Augustine's eschatological emphasis helps, and not hinders, the practical work of love in this life: "The heavenly-rooted riches of charity open one's heart to those in earthly need. In this way, Augustine's world-weary vision of earthly life that drives the gaze heavenward complements his exhortations to work in the world to love and serve others" (p. 225). See also Williams's response to the critiques of Nussbaum: Williams, *On Augustine*, 202–5.

103. *Serm.* 359A.3. See also *Serm.* 198(D26/M62).2.

104. *Serm.* 359A.7. See Hill's note about textual issues with this sentence: *Sermons (341–400)*, 221n12.

wealthy also need to exercise a patient love for God, lest they mistakenly think they have already found happiness in their present prosperity. "Whether we have never had it so good or never had it so bad," Augustine teaches in *Sermon* 38, "we must wait for the Lord."[105] The practices of fasting and simplicity (discussed here) encourage this posture of patience, attending to our insatiable desire to have more, and orienting us toward the fulfillment of our hunger in the life to come.

Augustine particularly encourages the congregation to fast during the season of Lent, and a number of his Lenten sermons are devoted to this theme.[106] Those fasting waited until the day's end for their meal, and abstained from meat and wine throughout this season.[107] As Augustine explains in *Sermon* 400, fasting helps us to "*hunger and thirst for justice*" (Mt. 5:6), and sets us apart from those "who think the only good is to enjoy earthly delights."[108] And yet, fasting will not be necessary when we live in God's company, he notes, where "there is total plenty and eternal satiety."[109] Therefore, fasting is a practice of those who "occupy the middle ground."[110] Augustine explains further:

> This is not, as I have already said, an angelic practice; nor on the other hand is it a practice of those people who are slaves to their bellies. It's the business of us in the middle, where our lives are quite distinct from those of the unbelievers, and we are eagerly panting to be joined to the angels. We haven't yet arrived, but we are already on the way; we aren't yet enjoying things there, but we are already sighing for them here.[111]

Fasting marks our departure from a life focused on having and consuming, and anticipates our destination where "complete sufficiency is found in God."[112]

Augustine typically promotes fasting within the triadic context of "prayer, fasting, and almsgiving."[113] One should not be conceived in isolation from the

---

105. *Serm.* 38.1.
106. See especially *Serm.* 205–10. For Augustine's teaching on fasting, see Zumkeller, *Augustine's Ideal of the Religious Life*, 79. See also p. 223. Van der Meer vividly depicts fasting in Augustine's context: Van der Meer, *Augustine the Bishop*, 177–9. For the place of these Lenten sermons in catechetical formation, see Harmless, *Augustine and the Catechumenate*, 300–7. For guidance to monastics regarding fasting, see *Reg. 3:* 3.1. See also *Serm.* 205.2.
107. *Serm.* 198(D26/M62).6; 207.2. Augustine clarifies that, in fasting from these foods, Christians do not regard the foods themselves as "impure"; this would be a "sacrilegious mistake," as food is part of God's good creation (*Serm.* 208.1). Rather, Christians abstain from these foods during Lent in order to "curb our appetites" (*Serm.* 209.3; see also *Conf.* 10.31.46).
108. *Serm.* 400.1, 2.
109. *Serm.* 400.1.
110. *Serm.* 400.2.
111. *Serm.* 400.2.
112. *Serm.* 400.1.
113. *Serm.* 206.1.

others. Thus Augustine cautions those who dedicate themselves to fasting while ignoring the practical needs of their neighbor. "What could be more iniquitous than that what self-denial avoids spending should be hoarded by unabated avarice, or eaten up by spend-thrift luxury?" he asks in one sermon.[114] That which we forgo by fasting should be given to those who need it. As Augustine teaches on another occasion, "Let the hungry Christ receive what the fasting Christian receives less of."[115] Practiced in this way, fasting can help us both to overcome our neediness for more and to respond to the needs of those who have less.

Learning to live with less is another fitting practice for those who look to God for satisfaction. Augustine's monastic community presents us with the clearest illustration of his ideal of simplicity.[116] In the *Rule*, Augustine seeks to ensure that members of the community are provided with the basic essentials of daily life. "Poverty and simplicity were the rule, but a goodly sufficiency was also assured," Zumkeller observes.[117] When distributing common resources, the leader of the monastic community is to provide all with their basic needs of "*Food and clothing* (1 Tm 6:8)."[118] If a member is in need of "clothes and shoes," Augustine instructs, "those who have charge of them should not delay to give them as required."[119] And when members are sick, "they should be given whatever is necessary," Augustine advises—even if prior to joining the monastery, they could not have afforded these extra provisions.[120] Nonetheless, the *Rule* did not provide members with what was unnecessary. Possidius reports that Augustine's "clothing and shoes, and even his bedding, were simple and appropriate," and that the meals in his monastic household "were frugal and economical."[121] If an additional item was gifted to a member of the monastery, Augustine instructs that it should be "put into the *common stock* so that it may be offered *to anyone who needs it* (Acts 4:32, 35)."[122]

---

114. *Serm.* 208.2. In other Lenten sermons, Augustine rebukes those who fast from meat and wine as an excuse to consume more exotic foods and drinks instead: see *Serm.* 205.2; 207.2; 210.10–11.

115. *Serm.* 210.12. Augustine acknowledges that not all are physically able to fast; in this case, he encourages them to "be even more generous" in almsgiving during the Lenten season (*Serm.* 209.2).

116. Note that in *Sermon* 350A, directed to monastics, Augustine integrates his teaching on Psalm 37:1–2, Colossians 3:4, and 1 Timothy 6:17–19 (discussed above) with the monastic commitment "to have nothing superfluous" (*Serm.* 350A.4).

117. Zumkeller, *Augustine's Ideal of the Religious Life*, 39.

118. *Reg.* 3: 1.3. This also included access to a common library, and wine at weekend meals: *Reg.* 3: 5.9; *Reg.* 2: 7.

119. *Reg.* 3: 5.11.

120. *Reg.* 3: 1.5; 3.5.

121. Possidius, *Life of Saint Augustine*, 22.1, 2. See also Zumkeller, *Augustine's Ideal of the Religious Life*, 43.

122. *Reg.* 3: 5.3.

These guidelines helped the monastic community follow the apostolic example, with resources held in common and distributed "according to need."[123] However, this does not necessarily mean equal distribution. Augustine instructs that "*Food and clothing* (1 Tm 6:8)" should be distributed "not equally to all because you are not all equally strong, but to each one according to need."[124] Although those who join the monastery share a common life, they have previously come from dramatically different backgrounds. "The majority came from the lower classes," Zumkeller notes, including those who had been "slaves and freedmen, peasants, and manual laborers."[125] However, they were joined by "men from wealthy and distinguished families, and even senators and substantial landowners."[126] Augustine anticipates that when those who were formerly rich join the monastery, they may need to receive more, because they are unaccustomed to living with less.[127] Elsewhere, Augustine often reminds listeners of the equality and humanity that rich and poor share,[128] yet that does not lead him to insist on equal distribution of resources. For Augustine, it is better that rich and poor are drawn together in a common love for God and neighbor, than divided by a rigid rule of economic distribution.

This is a notable feature of Augustine's *Rule*. Although his monastic instruction clearly has an ascetic dimension, Zumkeller observes that Augustine "was emphatic in requiring that all ascetic effort, especially in monasteries, show consideration for one's fellow-men, and be subordinated to the main object of 'one heart in God' and integrated with it."[129] Within his relatively austere program for monastic life, Augustine displays a willingness to accommodate the needs of the formerly rich,

---

123. *Reg. 3*: 1.3.

124. *Reg. 3*: 1.3. Verheijen's translation may be even more jarring to those inclined to project a modern ideal of "equality" onto Augustine: "Your brother prior should distribute to each of you what is necessary for nourishment and clothing, not according to an egalitarian principle, because your states of health are unequal, but rather to each one according to his needs." Verheijen, *Saint Augustine's Monasticism*, 4.

125. Zumkeller, *Augustine's Ideal of the Religious Life*, 37.

126. Zumkeller, *Augustine's Ideal of the Religious Life*, 37.

127. *Reg. 3*: 3.3–4. See also *Op. mon.* 21.25 for similar instruction regarding the sharing of work in the monastery. A number of commentators observe here Augustine's attentiveness to the particular needs of individuals within the common life of the monastery. For instance, noting this mindfulness of "individual need" in the *Rule*, Martin describes it as "a document which does not erase the individual, reducing the single members of the monastic community to one common and perhaps bland denominator." Martin, "Augustine and the Politics of Monasticism," 179. See also Zumkeller, *Augustine's Ideal of the Religious Life*, 125–6.

128. E.g., *Serm.* 61.8; 113A.3.

129. Zumkeller, *Augustine's Ideal of the Religious Life*, 229. See also Van Bavel, "Evangelical Inspiration of the Rule," 94. For Christian asceticism in this period, and its relationship to monasticism, see Markus, *End of Ancient Christianity*, 63–83. Markus also notes the initial influence of asceticism on Augustine: see pp. 47–9.

in order that they might be able to participate in the community and, over time, overcome their greater neediness.

However, as noted above, when one member of the Christian community possesses more than others, this can give rise to envy, even in the monastery. In the *Rule*, Augustine responds to this issue by reminding members not to view this unequal distribution through worldly eyes. When "special treatment in the way of diet" is provided to those not yet accustomed to the simple fare of the monastery, those "who are stronger" should not "think the former luckier in getting something that they themselves do not get," Augustine advises.[130] "Rather, they should be thankful that they are strong enough to do what others cannot."[131] Similarly, in the next directive, he notes: "All should not desire to receive the extra things which they see given to a few; such things are a concession, not an honor."[132] In marked contrast to the surrounding world, which honors those who have more, in the alternative economy of the monastery, receiving more than other members is not a badge of status, but an indicator of one's neediness. As Augustine succinctly states, "It is better to need less than to have more."[133]

In such a community, therefore, it is of no advantage to be wealthy. It is those who have joined the community from a background of poverty who are considered to be stronger members, for their previous circumstances already required them to live simply.[134] By contrast, those who were formerly rich find themselves to be weaker members, because of their need to have more.[135] Such statements should not be read in a competitive sense, however. In identifying the weaknesses that formerly rich members struggle with, Augustine is encouraging the sympathy of stronger members, not their superiority. Thus he invites them to "consider [*cogitare*] how far the former [those previously rich] have come down from their previous way of life in the world even though they cannot reach the simplicity of living which is possible for those who are stronger in body."[136] Agatha Mary emphasizes

---

130. *Reg. 3*: 3.3.
131. *Reg. 3*: 3.3. Mary offers the crucial insight that the thankfulness Augustine speaks of here is a thankfulness to God. Mary, *The Rule of Saint Augustine*, 125-6. "Not having and not needing the things on which others have to depend is itself a gift of God which is continually given to us," she comments (p. 125). See Chapter 7 for discussion of Augustine's teaching on gratitude.
132. *Reg. 3*: 3.4.
133. *Reg. 3*: 3.5. Lawless notes that this statement is drawn from Seneca, but comments that "Augustine brings this Stoic maxim into the orbit of Luke-Acts 4, 35." Lawless, "Mirror of Perfection," 465. Commenting on this aspect of the *Rule*, Van Bavel observes that it does not reflect a "dualistic" devaluation of the world or human life, but rather is oriented toward "the development of the human personality." Van Bavel, "Evangelical Inspiration of the Rule," 85-6.
134. *Reg. 3*: 3.3-3.5.
135. *Reg. 3*: 3.3-3.5.
136. *Reg. 3*: 3.4 (GL:86).

the "thoughtful consideration" Augustine calls for here: "*Cogitare* implies deep reflection that results in clear understanding.... The troubled monk, Augustine says, must consider his brothers against their former background, against the present conditions and against their future goal."[137] Through his reframing of strength and weakness in these sections of the *Rule*, Augustine enables members to exchange their envy for sympathy, and to exercise compassion toward those members who need more.

The monastic dictum, "It is better to need less than to have more," corresponds with Augustine's teaching to the wider congregation (noted above) that "happiness is not lacking anything."[138] The former statement is focused on practice, while the latter points toward a broader theological context. Both statements, however, attend to concerns that arise from seeing those who have more, and in both cases Augustine responds by reframing perceptions of what is "better" or desirable. As previously discussed, Augustine's teaching that "happiness is not lacking anything" enables him to challenge the assumption that the rich are happy.[139] For paradoxically, he explains, the more one has, the more one lacks; as a result, the rich turn out to be in greater need than the poor: "So if their greed burns more fiercely the more they have, I'm not just saying they are needy; but that they are needier than those beggars there. The beggar's greed, after all, is satisfied with a few coins, while the whole world is not enough for the greed of the wealthy hoarder."[140] Having more does not satisfy our needs, but amplifies them. At times, Augustine's homiletic illustrations of the neediness of the rich can border on satirical, but he nonetheless displays pastoral sensitivity toward the challenges that the rich must overcome. As he later concludes in Sermon 359A, "The heart that is fighting against being corrupted by prosperity is engaged in a severer struggle than the one that is fighting against being broken by adversity."[141] Thus Augustine is committed to helping the rich overcome the neediness of their "prosperity," as well as assisting the needs of the poor in their "adversity."

As discussed in Chapter 3, Augustine does not expect the wider congregation to renounce wealth in the same manner as those joining the monastic community, nor does he require the same commitment to simplicity of life. However, thematic continuity again can be seen between this aspect of his teaching in the *Rule*, and his instruction in the *Sermons*. For example, 1 Timothy 6:8, which Augustine briefly quotes in the *Rule* when describing the provision of goods, similarly defines the material necessities of daily life in his *Sermons*.[142] In *Sermon* 299D, describing what is "necessary for well-being," Augustine quotes 1 Timothy 6:8: "*Having food and clothing, with these let us be content.*"[143] In *Sermon* 58, he draws

---

137. Mary, *The Rule of Saint Augustine*, 128–9.
138. *Reg.* 3: 3.5; *Serm.* 359A.6.
139. *Serm.* 359A.6.
140. *Serm.* 359A.6.
141. *Serm.* 359A.17.
142. *Reg.* 3: 1.3
143. *Serm.* 299D.3.

on these words to illumine the petition of the Lord's Prayer, "*Give us today our daily bread* (Mt 6:11)."[144] This petition can be understood as a "prayer for our daily sustenance," Augustine explains, and anticipating 1 Timothy 6:8, he teaches that "our sustenance consists of food and drink, our shelter of clothing and roof."[145] "People should desire nothing else," he adds, and then reminds them of the apostle's instruction.[146] Passages such as these indicate that Augustine considers this definition of what is needed for daily life to be normative for all, and not just for the monastics.

Of course, not all have even these basic resources with which to find contentment. It is noteworthy that in *Sermon* 61, Augustine draws on 1 Timothy 6:8 to both advocate for those who lack these essentials and also challenge those who have more than is needed. Having instructed the rich according to 1 Timothy 6:17–19, drawing their attention to Paul's call to the rich to share their wealth (v. 18), Augustine continues:

> So give to the poor, my brothers. *If we have food and clothing, let us be content with that* (1 Tm 6:8). The rich man gets nothing more with his riches than what the poor man is pleading for from him, food and clothing. What more do you get from all the things you have? You've got your food, you've got your necessary clothing; necessary, I say, not vain, not superfluous. What else can you get from your riches? Tell me. For sure, it will all be your superfluities. Well, let your superfluities provide the poor with their necessities.[147]

Augustine considers the material "necessities" of daily life to be the same for all, whether rich or poor. After the basic needs of "food and clothing" have been provided for, any additional material resources are "superfluities." That does not mean Augustine expects his wealthier listeners to renounce these non-essentials. However, in this passage, he helps these listeners to at least recognize these additional resources as superfluous, so that they might be used to provide others with their basic needs.

Similar to his instruction in the *Rule* (as described above), this sermon indicates Augustine's awareness that the pampered lifestyle of the rich makes them more needy than their poor sisters and brothers. Although the rich eat more extravagantly than the poor, their basic physical needs are the same, he argues, implying that the rich should share the same simple fare of the poor.[148] Augustine then anticipates the objection of wealthier listeners:

---

144. *Serm.* 58.5.
145. *Serm.* 58.5.
146. *Serm.* 58.5. See also *Serm.* 177.7, where Augustine engages poorer listeners with the teaching of 1 Timothy 6:8–9.
147. *Serm.* 61.12. For Augustine's understanding of "superfluities" (as discussed in Chapter 3) see MacQueen, "St. Augustine's Concept of Property Ownership," 213, 218.
148. *Serm.* 61.12.

"But my expensive dishes," you say, "taste nicer." You're so nice, so persnickety, you can scarcely eat your fill. You don't know what food tastes like when real hunger drives you on. But I haven't been speaking like this in order to force the rich to eat the meals and food of the poor. Let the rich keep to the habits their delicacy requires, but let them be sad that they cannot do otherwise. They would do better, surely, if they could do otherwise.... Go on making use of your special, expensive foods, because you have got into the habit of them, because you cannot do otherwise, because if you change your habits you get sick. Go on making use of your superfluities, but give the poor their necessities.[149]

Here, Augustine is addressing the wider congregation, where the disparity in diet between rich and poor members would be much greater than the variance of provisions in the monastery. However, Augustine's underlying message is the same. It would be "better" if the rich adopt the simple meals of the poor, yet Augustine acknowledges that in practice, this is difficult for those who have become accustomed to more sophisticated diets.[150] Therefore he does not insist on equality of diet, but nonetheless urges that the rich share what they have with the poor, so that neither go hungry.[151]

There is nothing uniquely Christian about the instruction in 1 Timothy 6:8 to find contentment in basic needs; "many people have said that," Augustine notes in *Sermon* 177.[152] However, he goes on to observe, what does make a Christian response to avarice distinctive is "that it is for God's sake that we do whatever we do."[153] For Augustine, the practice of contentment with basic necessities, like that of fasting, finds meaning in its orientation toward God. As we travel toward God, we discover that having more is not a benefit, but a "burden."[154] Learning to need less thus aids us in our journey, but the contentment we may find here is not itself the destination. Augustine makes this clear in *Sermon* 359A, when he anticipates the question of whether the person who is not pursuing "anything more than what they have" can be considered happy.[155] He responds: "I'll praise them if I find them, warmly congratulate them.... It shows great strength of character,

---

149. *Serm.* 61.12.
150. *Serm.* 61.12.
151. *Serm.* 61.12 (though note that in one Lenten sermon, Augustine teaches that during this season of fasting, "everyone should be imitating the fare of the poor" (*Serm.* 210.11)). Brown also notes the thematic link between *Sermon* 61 and the *Rule*, though he offers a different interpretation: Brown, *Through the Eye of a Needle*, 351–2.
152. *Serm.* 177.2.
153. *Serm.* 177.2. Zumkeller distinguishes Augustine's teaching on monastic poverty from Stoicism, noting that his instructions "directed men toward more than a merely natural contentment." Zumkeller, *Augustine's Ideal of the Religious Life*, 145. For Augustine, he explains, "poverty was, not an end in itself ... but a means to something higher, which set us free from the many hindrances on our way toward our eternal goal" (p. 146).
154. *Serm.* 177.3.
155. *Serm.* 359A.6.

great mental control, to be able to fix a limit, to break in the greedy appetite, to restrain covetousness, to set bounds to the fires of lust. That's real virtue, I admit, real virtue."[156] And yet, as he continues, Augustine explains that even this person cannot be truly happy. In this life, those who virtuously restrain their greed for more may still fear losing what they have, and even those who suffer loss yet live righteously (such as Job) experience "trial and temptation."[157] Therefore, Augustine finds wanting any claim to a happy life on the basis of this life alone.[158] In our present life we are "exiles," a situation that demands our patience, until we arrive home.[159] Thus it can be considered "better to need less than to have more," not because having less in itself gains us happiness, but because it enables us to pursue unencumbered the happiness we anticipate in God's company.[160]

Exercising Love

Unlike those who have "used up all their desire on earthly well-being and happiness," Augustine encourages his listeners to seek "well-being and happiness up above."[161] However, as noted, to look toward this future satisfaction does not mean to live dormant in the present. Our love for God, which one day will be "satisfied by sight," in this life is to be "expressed in desire."[162] And in the second half of *Sermon* 359A, Augustine instructs his listeners to express this love in active, practical terms. In an evocative phrase, he tells them "you are exercising the muscles of your desire."[163] The particular exercise he has in mind in the latter part of this sermon is sharing resources with the needy. For although we may be animated by the hope of a future where none are in need, this present time is one of great neediness. In *Sermon* 217, Augustine notes the connection between these two situations: "If you want to live in the good place where nobody goes hungry, in this world *break your bread to the hungry* (Is 58:7)."[164]

---

156. *Serm.* 359A.6. Augustine's portrayal suggests he has the ideals of the Stoic life in view here. Harrison provides helpful comment on Augustine's interaction with Stoicism in his early thought. Harrison, *Christian Truth and Fractured Humanity*, 79–84. Initially, Augustine had suggested that the happiness of "possessing God" could be gained through virtue (p. 81). However, Harrison notes, Augustine later departs from this view: "Although it [virtue] is essential in leading man to happiness it is not its end; rather it serves to lead man to God, the transcendent source and object of happiness" (p. 84; Harrison notes that she is drawing on the work of M. Colish here). See also *Trin.* 13.7.10–8.11.
157. *Serm.* 359A.6.
158. *Serm.* 359A.6.
159. *Serm.* 359A.2.
160. *Reg. 3:* 3.5.
161. *Serm.* 359A.14, 17.
162. *Serm.* 359A.2.
163. *Serm.* 359A.17.
164. *Serm.* 217.5.

In *Sermon* 359A, the parable of Luke 16:1–9 guides Augustine's exhortation to respond to the needs of others.[165] Here Jesus tells of a servant who, discovering that he is about to lose his job, deviously discounts the bills of his master's borrowers, so that when he is unemployed, they might provide for him. Jesus did not tell this parable to commend fraudulent dealing, Augustine is quick to clarify.[166] Rather, he explains, Jesus invites us to consider the example of the servant "because he exercised foresight for the future."[167] In this respect, Augustine's discussion of the parable continues the eschatological theme of his sermon, for it illustrates how our knowledge of the future should elicit action now. If concern for an immediate (temporal) future could stir a corrupt servant into action, how much more should a vision of an eternal future prompt the faithful into action?[168]

"So what are we to do?" Augustine asks.[169] His teaching on this parable focuses on Jesus's closing instruction: "What did the Lord command? *Make yourselves friends with the mammon of iniquity, so that they too, when you begin to fail, may receive you into eternal shelters* (Lk 16:9)."[170] In response to this instruction, Augustine particularly commends his listeners to give to the needy.[171]

By drawing on Jesus's call to "*Make yourselves friends*" (Lk. 16:9), Augustine casts the act of giving in relational terms.[172] The imagery of the parable, as deployed by Augustine, directs attention to the recipients, and the future dependence of the giver upon the relationship established with these recipients in the present. In using our mammon to befriend the neighbor, we hope that they will also befriend us, welcoming us "*into eternal shelters* (Lk 16:9)."[173] In this life, the poor may be unable to extend hospitality to the rich; commenting elsewhere on this verse, Augustine notes that "there are poor people who have no dwellings where they themselves can receive you."[174] And yet, in the life to come, they will dwell in God's company, "where you will wish in vain to be received, like that rich man, if you don't now receive them into your dwellings."[175] Our expressions of friendship and hospitality toward the poor in this life are

---

165. *Serm.* 359A.9.
166. *Serm.* 359A.10.
167. *Serm.* 359A.10.
168. *Serm.* 359A.10.
169. *Serm.* 359A.11.
170. *Serm.* 359A.11.
171. Augustine's teaching on almsgiving was discussed in Chapter 3 (see the relevant notes in Chapter 3 for the secondary sources that informed this discussion).
172. *Serm.* 359A.11.
173. *Serm.* 359A.11.
174. *Serm.* 41.6.
175. *Serm.* 41.6. Augustine's comment about "that rich man" refers to the parable of Luke 16:19–31.

intrinsically linked to our participation in the friendship and hospitality of the life to come.

This teaching, as discussed in Chapter 3, is theologically undergirded by Christ's presence in these needy ones.[176] Commenting on verse 9, Augustine explains: "It's easy, of course, to understand that we must give alms, that a helping hand must be given to the needy, because it is Christ who receives it in them. It's what he said himself: *When you did it for one of the least of mine, you did it for me* (Mt 25:40)."[177] Although Augustine's quotation of Matthew 25:40 follows immediately after his introduction of Luke 16:9 in this sermon, he does not unpack the connection between the two verses. However, the inference is clear: when we share this mammon, we are not only befriending the needy; we are also making friends with Christ. Although Christ is not needy "in himself," he presents himself to us in the needy neighbor, Augustine explains in *Sermon* 236: "He's in want in his people, he's replete in himself. But being in want in his people, replete in himself, he brings those who are in want to himself."[178] For our benefit, Christ enters into this present world of need, becoming needy in his humanity, so that we might be united with him in his divinity. Yet those who desire to be "replete" with Christ in the life to come must befriend him "in want" during this present life.

Who are the needy friends that we are to give to? Augustine is remarkably undiscriminating in this regard: "We mustn't really pick and choose about whom we give them [alms] to, because we are unable to sift through people's hearts. When you give alms to all and sundry, then you will reach a few who deserve them."[179] Augustine is well aware that some may request material aid under false pretenses or motives.[180] But he is also aware that we lack the ability to accurately judge the heart of another; like the wheat and chaff in the church, the good and bad coexist, but we cannot tell one from the other until the end.[181] But even if it was possible for us to distinguish the good recipient from the bad, Augustine observes, God still instructs us to feed our enemy (Rom. 12:20; Prov. 25:21).[182] Thus, he concludes, "If you are obliged to do good even to your enemy, how much more to someone

---

176. As noted in Chapter 3, Canning demonstrates the importance of interpreting Augustine's teaching on almsgiving in light of Augustine's theology of the *totus Christus* (particularly as expressed in Mt. 25:31–46). Canning, *Unity of Love for God and Neighbour*, 331–420.
177. *Serm.* 359A.11.
178. *Serm.* 236.3.
179. *Serm.* 359A.11.
180. E.g. *Serm.* 41.7.
181. *Serm.* 73A.1.
182. *Serm.* 359A.11.

unknown to you, because even if he's a bad man, still he isn't an enemy."[183] Our generosity, then, should be extended to all.[184]

By "*mammon of iniquity*," Augustine understands Jesus to be distinguishing "false riches" from "true riches."[185] The former refers to worldly wealth, which we desire "as a kind of remedy for our infirmity."[186] By contrast, "True riches are what the angels have, seeing they lack nothing."[187] If we are fixated upon worldly wealth, we will be incapable of using this wealth rightly; as Augustine notes elsewhere: "For you will only be able to make just use of a supply of earthly resources, and make friends with it *who may receive you into eternal lodgings* (Lk 16:9), if you do not regard it as mammon for yourselves."[188] Discovering that our true wealth is found in God helps us to perceive the falseness of worldly wealth, and to use it justly, rather than seeking it for ourselves.

Augustine provides some practical instruction on this just use of resources in *Sermon* 359A. For example, he considers whether Jesus's instruction on the mammon of iniquity gives license to source money by iniquitous means, in order to give to the poor.[189] Augustine describes those who do this: "They grab a lot of money by such means, and give some of it in alms, and think they are getting their sins forgiven as by a corrupt judge."[190] God, however, is not a "corrupt judge" who can be bought. Rather, Augustine notes, God is judiciously attentive to the needs of all: "The one you give something to rejoices, but the one you grab it from laments. God has his ears between them in the middle; *With him there is no respect of persons* (Rom 2:4)."[191] For Augustine, then, just use of wealth does not simply mean giving to the poor; it also requires one to consider whether this wealth has been justly gained in the first place.[192] He does, however, add a caveat to this

---

183. *Serm.* 359A.11. Note that Augustine also includes acts of hospitality in this instruction: "You are hospitable, you keep your house ready for strangers; let in the unworthy, in case the worthy should be excluded" (.11). Although in the *Sermons*, Augustine typically speaks in general terms of giving to the needy, on occasion, he gives particular emphasis to acts of hospitality, e.g., *Serm.* 41.6-7; 81.9; 111.4; 239.4, 7. This too is a way to welcome Christ (see *Serm.* 239.2, 4, 6-7). Note also Augustine's own practice of providing hospitality to guests in the "bishops' residence" (*Serm.* 355.2).

184. For this teaching see also *Serm.* 164A. On the question of who one should share alms with see also Canning, *Unity of Love for God and Neighbour*, 377–94; Ramsey, "Almsgiving in the Latin Church," 230–3. Finn lists those that the church in this period tended to prioritize when distributing alms: Finn, *Almsgiving in the Later Roman Empire*, 76.

185. *Serm.* 359A.13.
186. *Serm.* 359A.13.
187. *Serm.* 359A.13.
188. *Serm.* 50.8.
189. *Serm.* 359A.13.
190. *Serm.* 359A.13.
191. *Serm.* 359A.13.
192. Augustine considers this issue in more depth in *Sermon* 178. See also Ramsey, "Almsgiving in the Latin Church," 250–1.

teaching later in the sermon. Here, Augustine considers the hypothetical situation of someone who inherits money from their father, who had gained this wealth "by usury."[193] Augustine's instruction is: "Don't be the heir to his iniquity, just be the heir to the money from iniquity."[194] The heir should not follow the example of their father "by being a money lender at extortionate rates," but rather should put this money to just purpose by distributing it in alms.[195] While Augustine shows a pastoral leniency here, he nonetheless calls for a departure from the family's previous practice: "If your father had learned how to rob, you must learn how to pay out."[196]

When distributing resources, how much should be given? The servant in the parable discounts the amount owed by one debtor from "*A hundred barrels of oil*" to "*fifty*," and the debt of another is reduced from "*A hundred bushels of wheat*" to "*eighty*" (Lk. 16:6–7).[197] Augustine cannot resist the opportunity to elucidate the significance of these numbers. "By fifty from a hundred he wished to signify a half," Augustine observes, and he associates this with the example of Zacchaeus, who gifted half of his wealth to the needy (Lk. 19:8).[198] Augustine often turns to the example of Zacchaeus, whose bold redistribution of wealth provides a model of generosity to which the rich can aspire.[199] Regarding the second debt, Augustine explains that "by making eighty from a hundred he wished to signify two tenths."[200] A tenth, he reminds the congregation, is what "the Pharisees and scribes" customarily gave, and yet Jesus calls for a justice that "*abounds more than that of the Pharisees and scribes*" (Mt. 5:20).[201] If Zacchaeus provides Augustine with an example of maximal generosity, then the tithe of the Pharisees constitutes what is minimal.[202] He sometimes employs this example to put the gifts of reluctant givers into perspective, as in *Sermon 9*: "So, they [the scribes and Pharisees] give tithes, that is, ten percent; you, if you give one percent, you boast about having done something terrific."[203] Yet, while noting these two examples of giving,

---

193. *Serm.* 359A.15.
194. *Serm.* 359A.15.
195. *Serm.* 359A.15.
196. *Serm.* 359A.15.
197. *Serm.* 359A.9.
198. *Serm.* 359A.16.
199. E.g., *Serm.* 359A.12; 105A.1. See also *Sermon 113*, where Augustine discusses Zacchaeus and his unjustly gained wealth (*Serm.* 113.3).
200. *Serm.* 359A.16.
201. *Serm.* 359A.16.
202. Ramsey appears to interpret Augustine differently on this point, suggesting that Augustine's commendation of tithing allows "the rich" to maintain "a life of pleasant abundance." Ramsey, "Wealth," 879.
203. *Serm.* 9.19; see also *Serm.* 85.5. In respect of Augustine's teaching on tithing, Finn clarifies that "this is not a tithe to the church in the sense that the laity were later required to give tithes"; rather Augustine is encouraging his listeners to give a tithe of their resources to the poor. Finn, *Almsgiving in the Later Roman Empire*, 51.

Augustine does not prescribe a set amount to give. In *Sermon* 85, Augustine urges his listeners to exercise discernment: "The scribes and Pharisees used to give a tenth. So what then? Question yourselves. See what you do, how much you do it from, what you give, what you keep for yourselves, what you spend in charity, what you reserve for luxury."[204]

Discernment must be exercised in giving, because it is not adherence to a prescribed formula or standard (such as a tithe) that determines the goodness of the donor's gift, but rather the intention of their heart.[205] For this reason, Augustine reassures all members of the congregation, whether rich or poor, that they all have something to contribute.[206] He gives the example of a person who is unable to offer even "*a cup of cold water* (Mt 10:42)," yet seeing someone thirsty, feels compassion: "God sees what you have inside you; he doesn't have eyes for the capacity of your hand, what he does have eyes for is the will of your heart."[207] Such a person has no mammon to offer, but the currency Augustine is primarily concerned with is love. Through this parable, he encourages his listeners to reorient their hearts: from an envious desire to accrue more goods for oneself, to a holy longing for the fulfillment found in God. During this present time of neediness, responding with love to the needs of others is a way of expressing and exerting our love and longing for God. As Augustine explains to the congregation in his conclusion of this sermon: "You are making friends, you are reaching out in hope, you are exercising the muscles of your desire."[208]

Conclusion

Augustine's pastoral instruction on envy remains pertinent in our own time. Perhaps more than ever, we are exposed to images of the prosperity of others, through a ceaseless stream of images in print, television, film, and social media. Advertisements present carefully curated scenes of the happy life, suggesting that if we could simply have more, happiness is within our reach. Such advertisements can take on perverse scale in the majority world, when they feature on massive billboards erected over the "slum" housing of the urban poor. And yet, even in such incongruous settings, such portrayals of happiness can convince, prompting rich and poor alike to envy those who have attained the happy life, so defined.

Augustine's teaching helps us understand our predicament: our envy of the material prosperity of others indicates that we have set our sights on the wrong sort of happiness. Instead of orienting our love toward God, we have

---

204. *Serm.* 85.5. See Ramsey, "Almsgiving in the Latin Church," 234.
205. See discussion in Chapter 3, and MacQueen, "St. Augustine's Concept of Property Ownership," 201–2.
206. *Serm.* 359A.12.
207. *Serm.* 359A.12.
208. *Serm.* 359A.17.

sought happiness in material goods, and envy of those with more than us is an inescapable consequence. We also struggle to love our neighbor when envy dominates us, viewing them through the lens of competition, not communion. Even in communities without great disparities in wealth, this divisiveness can be found. It is striking that in the radical economic equality of Augustine's monastic community, the smallest differences of circumstance could prompt members to "be aggrieved or think it unfair," threatening the harmony of the community.[209] In the Christian community, when we lose sight of the God who gathers us, and instead become preoccupied with material differences, division is unavoidable. We begin to deplore our richer neighbors, and ignore those who are poorer.

Because the machinations of envy are often internal, perhaps even invisible to ourselves, one simple yet effective pastoral response is to bring them to light, by naming the dynamics of envy, and talking openly about them. As some of Augustine's sermons considered in this chapter demonstrate, this can even take comedic form, helping us to laugh at the tangles of covetousness that we get ourselves into. Such teaching can be remarkably freeing: it helps us recognize the conflict of our misguided desires within, and also reassures us that others understand and share this struggle.

As this chapter has demonstrated, in his *Sermons*, Augustine also seeks to help his congregation by directing them toward God, and the satisfaction that they will find in God's company. Yet turning our sights away from alluring portrayals of prosperity is not easily done, especially in a modern culture saturated by visual media. We are bombarded with images of the good life: an existence full of culinary delight, glamorous company, and stylish living. Given the amount of time that we typically devote to these images on the digital screen, we should not be surprised if society's picture of the good life has a greater hold on us than the biblical vision of our life with God. What is needed, therefore, is a greater awareness of the influences that shape our picture of the good life. We need to grapple with our visual diet, to be aware of what we are ingesting, and its effect on our spiritual nutrition. How can we adjust this diet so that fictitious portrayals of the good life do not unduly weigh us down, and so that our Christian hope can enliven and encourage us?

Augustine's teaching also challenges our belief that happiness comes from having more. For Augustine, happiness in God is not marked by material prosperity, but by absence of need: "Happiness is not lacking anything."[210] While this happiness is eschatological, setting our sights upon this future hope transforms our understanding of happiness in this life, encouraging us to find contentment in the meeting of our basic needs, rather than looking for satisfaction in the never-ending search for more. For the Christian community, the practice of simplicity is one outworking of this transformation; that is to say, as our desires are redirected toward contentment in God, the adoption of a simpler lifestyle becomes possible. When such a practice is shared by a community, it offers an alternative portrayal

---

209. *Reg. 3*: 3.3.
210. *Serm.* 359A.6.

of a satisfied life: a prophetic challenge to wider society, and also a sign of good news for those looking for a different way. Of course, attempts at shared simplicity are not always good news stories; they can often become prescriptive and legalistic. However, Augustine's monastic instruction on this theme invites us to consider a generous simplicity, animated by love for God and neighbor. In its adaptability to diverse needs, it helps us conceive of a community where members can learn to live with less, while also showing grace toward other members who currently need to live with more.

Chapter 5

PRIDE AND THE COMMON LIFE

> On the other hand, those who were regarded in the world as persons of consequence should not look down on their brothers who have entered the religious community from humble circumstances.... They should not boast if they have contributed anything to the common life from their own means, nor should they take more pride in their riches because they are sharing them in the monastery than they would if they were enjoying them in the world. For every other vice prompts people to do evil deeds; but pride lies in ambush even for good deeds in order to destroy them.
>
> —*Reg. 3:* 1.7.

When addressing wealth and poverty in his *Sermons*, Augustine often alerts his listeners to the danger of pride, and directs them toward the humility of Christ. For those considering the challenge of economic inequality in purely material terms, such instruction may seem a moralizing distraction. For example, we might assume that it is the provision of material necessities that is important, not the attitude of the provider.

However, Augustine's teaching on pride and humility provides an important reminder that while the very real material needs of the poor cannot be ignored, they are symptomatic of a deeper malaise, in which proud self-love has displaced love of God and neighbor.

Pride can be a pitfall for both rich and poor. It prompts us to rely upon ourselves rather than God, and to look down upon our neighbor, rather than stand alongside them. None are immune to this temptation. Even those who boldly renounce their wealth and share it with the poor can be compromised by pride, as Augustine cautions his monastic community.[1] Although Augustine clearly expects his congregation to share or even (in the case of the monastics) to give away their possessions, the goal of loving God and neighbor is not simply attained by a change in material status. Pride undermines the common life of the Christian community, separating us from God and neighbor, rather than drawing us together.

Hence, in 418, when a Carthage congregation sings the psalm, "*To you has the poor man abandoned himself, you will be a guardian for the orphan* (Ps 10:14)," Augustine invites them to consider what sort of poverty is being commended to them by the

---

1. *Reg. 3:* 1.7.

psalmist.² "Let's look for the poor man, let's look for the orphan. Don't be surprised at my suggesting we should look for what we see and experience so much of. Isn't the whole place full of poor people? Isn't the whole place full of orphans? And yet in the whole place I am looking for the orphan."³ Although his listeners may have thought the psalmist was endorsing a life of material poverty, Augustine directs them toward a deeper reading, in which both poor and rich are called toward the poverty and humility of Christ, "who for our sake *became poor, though he was rich* (2 Cor 8:9)."⁴ Christ, in his humble poverty, challenges earthly presumptions of status and wealth, and calls us toward a life of loving dependence upon God.

Using *Sermon* 14 as a guide, in this chapter I examine how Augustine's teaching on pride and humility in the *Sermons* addresses rich and poor members of the church community. In particular, I demonstrate that pride divides rich and poor from each other, and that Christ comes to teach us humility, so that we might be formed together into his body, and share life in common.

Abandoning Ourselves to God

In *Sermon* 14, the poor man of Psalm 10:14 captures Augustine's attention because he has "*abandoned himself*" to God.⁵ This posture of dependence upon God, of seeking refuge in God's company, reflects Augustine's vision of the Christian life (an orientation that he more frequently identifies in Ps. 73:28: "*But for me it is good to cling to God*"⁶). Therefore Augustine's purpose in *Sermon* 14 is to call listeners toward this state of reliance upon God that the psalmist invites: "So learn to be poor and abandon yourselves to God," he instructs.⁷

While acknowledging the "poor [*pauperes*]" to whom alms are owed, Augustine clarifies that on this occasion, the "poor man [*pauper*]" of the psalm "has to be understood in a more profound way than that."⁸ The poverty Augustine has in mind is that described in the first Beatitude: "*Blessed are the poor in spirit, for theirs is the kingdom of heaven* (Mt 5:3)."⁹ He does not elaborate on this verse in *Sermon* 14. However, in other sermons, Augustine characterizes the one who is "*poor in spirit*" as "humble," not "puffed up and proud," "following God's will," and not striving after

---

2. *Serm.* 14.1. Details of the date and location of this sermon are provided by Hill: *Sermons (1–19)*, 321n1. For Latin text see *PL* 38:111–16. Boyd-MacMillan comments on rhetorical and pastoral aspects of this sermon: Boyd-MacMillan, "The Transforming Sermon," 158–60.
3. *Serm.* 14.1.
4. *Serm.* 14.9.
5. *Serm.* 14.1.
6. *Serm.* 177.9. This vision of life in God's company (with reference to Ps. 73:28) is described in Chapter 1.
7. *Serm.* 14.2.
8. *Serm.* 14.1 (*PL* 38:112).
9. *Serm.* 14.1.

or placing their hope in worldly wealth.[10] Therefore, in asking the congregation to "look for the poor man," Augustine is not proposing to examine poverty in its material and/or spiritual dimensions.[11] Rather, prompted by Psalm 10:14, Augustine is inviting them to consider what a life abandoned to God looks like.

Through much of this sermon, Augustine approaches this question inversely, depicting the life that has *not* been abandoned to God. For Augustine, this is the life of pride. In Augustine's thought, pride is not simply a character trait; rather, pride denotes a state of self-elevation, a hubristic setting apart of the self from God and neighbor.[12] In *Sermon* 198(D26/M62), Augustine juxtaposes two forms of life: one clings to God, while the other "by culpable ill-will turns its back on the life that enlightens it."[13] This life that turns away "is thereby darkened and becomes proud ... ; it refuses, you see, to cling to God, but with a kind of self-absorbed disdain it wishes to be regarded as God," Augustine explains.[14] Although this account could suggest that pride *results* from this willful turn away from God, Augustine generally associates pride and this self-interested departure so closely that they are effectively synonymous; that is, pride *is* our willful turning away from God toward self. As he states in *Sermon* 159B(D21/M54): "It was pride, you see, that made man apostatize from God."[15] This proud act of apostasy contradicts Augustine's vision of life with God at its most basic level. When overcome by pride, we no longer seek refuge in God, but rather in ourselves, displaying an insistent attitude of self-reliance.

Augustine explains that pride prompted the very first acts of apostasy from God: the fall of the angels, and of the first humans.[16] Thus, in Augustine's account of sin, pride is the beginning, and the cause of all subsequent disordered desire. All human sinning can in some sense be traced back to this primeval act of pride.[17]

---

10. *Serm.* 53A.2; 114B(D5/M12).11. Augustine also describes as "poor in spirit" the exemplary ascetics that Ponticianus encountered (*Conf.* 8.6.15).

11. *Serm.* 14.1. For the connection between poverty and humility in Augustine's instruction, see Van Bavel, "Evangelical Inspiration of the Rule," 94.

12. See Chapter 1 for discussion. MacQueen provides an expansive survey of pride in Augustine's thought, including its social dimensions: MacQueen, "Contemptus Dei," 227–93. Cavadini provides a succinct summary: Cavadini, "Pride," 679–84. See also Torchia's comments on pride within Augustine's early work: Torchia, "The Commune/Proprium Distinction," 360–2.

13. *Serm.* 198(D26/M62).26.

14. *Serm.* 198(D26/M62).26.

15. *Serm.* 159B(D21/M54).11 (Augustine is commenting here on Sir. 10:12–13).

16. E.g., *Serm.* 340A.1. See also *Civ.* 11.13, 15; 12.1, 6; 14.11–14. In Chapter 1 I discussed further this fundamental departure from God, the pride that marks this act of apostasy, and the near-synonymous association in Augustine's thought between pride and self-interested love.

17. Note, however, that Couenhoven has challenged the view that Augustine consistently considers pride as operative in all human sinning: Couenhoven, "Not Every Wrong Is Done with Pride," 32–50.

However, as J. F. Procopé notes, Augustine understood pride "as 'the origin of all sin' in more senses than one."[18] Procopé explains that "if our susceptibility to lusts of the flesh is the continuing consequence of Adam's pride, there are other sins which are directly generated from 'the desire for perverse excellence.'"[19] It is "the aggressive, competitive sins" that Procopé has in view here, such as the love of praise, avarice for greater wealth, envy, and the desire to dominate others.[20] These particular sins arise from a desire to assert oneself over others, whether by claiming their praise, or demanding their submission. It is Augustine's teaching on pride in this more specific sense that concerns this chapter, especially as this desire to elevate oneself over others manifests itself in relationships between rich and poor.[21]

The proud desire to be praised by others is, in effect, the desire to be "regarded as God."[22] In *Sermon* 340A, cautioning listeners against an "appetite for superiority," Augustine reminds them that the devil appealed to this idolatrous desire when tempting Adam and Eve: "How did he persuade him? *If you eat*, he said, *you shall be like gods* (Gn 3:5). He had been made a man, he wished to be a god."[23] In another sermon, Augustine describes this proud desire to be God-like as "robbery," "the act of a usurper."[24] Here, he notes the tragic dimension of this desire: it is God's intention to make us "gods" (Ps. 82:6), "equal to the angels of God"—and yet we reject this gift of "grace" in a deluded attempt to secure God-like status apart from God.[25]

On other occasions, Augustine describes pride as an usurpation of God's order of creation.[26] The Genesis narrative indicates that God has granted human beings

---

18. Procopé, "*Initium omnis peccati superbia*," 319.
19. Procopé, "*Initium omnis peccati superbia*," 319.
20. Procopé, "*Initium omnis peccati superbia*," 319.
21. Of course, the specific attitudes and actions of pride discussed in this chapter cannot be understood apart from Adam and Eve's original proud departure from God (and the preceding fall of the angels), so this chapter necessarily incorporates discussion of pride in its original form.
22. *Serm.* 198(D26/M62).26. See also MacQueen, "Contemptus Dei," 243–5.
23. *Serm.* 340A.1. I focus particularly on this sermon in Chapter 6.
24. *Serm.* 229G.3(4). See Hill's explanatory note regarding the numbering for this sermon: *Sermons (184–229Z)*, 279n1.
25. *Serm.* 229G.3(4). See also *Civ.* 14.13. Note also Augustine's teaching in *Sermon* 198(D26/M62), where he instructs the congregation not to worship the martyrs themselves (*Serm.* 198(D26/M62).12). For unlike "proud human beings" and "proud angels," who "prefer themselves rather than God to be worshiped," "holy human beings" and "holy angels," Augustine explains, "would rather God were worshiped than they themselves" (.46).
26. Markus notes that "pride as a breach of the right rational order" features in Augustine's early writing, and that this emphasis continues to some degree through his subsequent thought: Markus, "Pride and the Common Good," 247–8. However, Markus argues for a development in Augustine's thought, with sin increasingly portrayed as a "retreat of the self from community into privacy" (p. 251). Markus summarizes: "For the hierarchical paradigm of pride Augustine has substituted a social one" (p. 251). (Though note that these two emphases are not mutually exclusive.)

a privileged place in creation, Augustine teaches his listeners in *Sermon* 159B; we have been created "according to the image of God," and the rest of the created world has been placed "under" us.[27] Yet the "commandment" that God gave to humankind in "paradise" reveals that we too are called to serve one who is "above" us.[28] As Augustine explains, "it was man's duty to attend to the things that were under him in such a way that he paid more attention to the one who was over him."[29] Pride, however, rejects this order. Instead of honoring our Creator, we attempt to be our "own independent authority."[30] Yet this grasp for autonomy leads not to freedom and mastery, but travail and servitude.[31]

Pride's usurpation of our place in the order of creation not only rejects our created relationship with God; it also rejects the equality with our neighbor that God intends for us.[32] In his *Homilies on the First Epistle of John*, Augustine explains to his listeners that, while they were created with God "above" them, and the animals "below" them, human beings were created "equal" with one another.[33] For this reason, "a Christian must live in such a way as not to exalt himself over other people."[34] Recognizing God's ordering of creation, and our place within it, enables us to respect the created equality our neighbor shares with us. However, Augustine observes, it is the tendency of "avaricious" pride "to go beyond" what God has provided for us, a tendency that plays out in our relationship with others: "That is how man exceeded the measure: he wanted to be more avaricious, so that he who was made above the beasts would be above men, and that is pride."[35] Although God has created us equal with one another, in our pride we seek to elevate ourselves above others.

With these dynamics of pride in view, we can better understand Augustine's plea to his listeners in *Sermon* 14: "abandon yourselves to God."[36] In this sermon, Augustine gives particular attention to the proud attitudes that members of the

---

27. *Serm.* 159B(D21/M54).5. See Chapter 1 for discussion of this theme.
28. *Serm.* 159B(D21/M54).5. Procopé notes the Neoplatonic schema that informs this "hierarchy," and emphasizes the role of "obedience" within it. Procopé, "*Initium omnis peccati superbia*," 317.
29. *Serm.* 159B(D21/M54).5.
30. *Serm.* 159B(D21/M54).7.
31. *Serm.* 159B(D21/M54).7.
32. In *Sermon* 112, Augustine draws together these two aspects of pride when he describes the temptation of landowners "to lord it over" others, and associates this with "the first man ... not being willing to have a Lord" (*Serm.* 112.2).
33. *Tract. ep. Jo.* 8.7–8.
34. *Tract. ep. Jo.* 8.8.
35. *Tract. ep. Jo.* 8.6, 8. See also *Doctr. chr.* 1.23.23. Cavadini describes the fundamental tendency of pride to "reorder" creation with a "hierarchy of utility" that has one's own interests in view. Cavadini, "Pride," 680. See also Canning, *Unity of Love for God and Neighbour*, 126.
36. *Serm.* 14.2.

congregation may hold toward each another. And yet, these prejudices toward their neighbor also reflect a prideful departure from God. Overcoming the divisiveness of pride within the community, therefore, requires nothing less than the abandonment to God that Augustine invites.

The Pride of the Rich

Paul's injunction to "*Order the rich of this world not to be haughty in mind* (1 Tm 6:17)" regularly prompts Augustine to warn the rich against pride.[37] Though the rich are not the only ones who need to hear this caution, their wealth makes them particularly susceptible to "the disease of pride," which is "the worm in the apple of riches."[38] As Augustine describes in *Sermon* 14, "the riches they have are whispering persuasively to them to be proud, the riches they have make it very hard for them to be humble."[39]

How does wealth foster this disposition in the affluent? When following 1 Timothy 6:17, Augustine sometimes looks to the second half of the verse for explanation, where the rich are also told not to "*set their hopes on the uncertainty of riches.*"[40] Augustine thus concludes, "That's why the rich man grows proud, you see, because he sets his hopes on the uncertainty of riches."[41] Setting our hopes on riches is problematic, not only because material wealth cannot deliver the security it promises,[42] but more fundamentally because it leads us to place our trust in ourselves, rather than in "*the living God*" (1 Tim. 6:17).[43] Unlike the humble rich person who, despite their resources, is "dependent solely on God," Augustine likens the situation of those who are "rich and proud" to that of the devil,[44] whose prideful self-reliance separated him from God.[45] This proud refusal to depend on God comes more readily to those whose resources suggest they have the ability to sustain themselves.

Riches can also nurture pride in the form of exaggerated self-estimation. Material wealth, MacQueen observes, represents "the most prestigious and therefore enviable expression of the power at which the opulent often aim"; it is

---

37. *Serm.* 14.2. Brown contrasts Augustine's instruction on the danger of pride to the wealthy with Pelagian teaching that condemned wealth itself: Brown, *Through the Eye of a Needle*, 349. Note that my reading of Augustine's teaching on the pride of the rich differs somewhat from that of Brown (see pp. 349–50).
38. *Serm.* 14.2; 39.4.
39. *Serm.* 14.2.
40. *Serm.* 36.5.
41. *Serm.* 36.5.
42. *Serm.* 61.11.
43. *Serm.* 85.4, 3.
44. *Serm.* 53A.4.
45. *Serm.* 198(D26/M62).26.

sought "to enhance the 'excellence' of proud men."[46] The more wealth we accrue, the more powerful and important we think we have become. Augustine likens the falsity of this situation to the inflation of a wineskin with air (rather than wine), and instructs the rich not to "be puffed up or become high and mighty."[47]

When wealth heightens our sense of importance, we look down upon those who have less. In *Sermon* 32, Augustine considers what happens when "a man of the world" receives "wealth": "He uses it to oppress the poor man. Mortal man himself, he proudly looks down on his fellow man and equal, he seeks empty honors from men."[48] Inflated with a self-importance derived from their prosperity, this wealthy person no longer recognizes his neighbor as a "fellow man and equal"; instead he dismisses or even exploits the neighbor in pursuit of his own glory. "No sooner have you begun to possess wealth," Augustine comments in *Sermon* 311, "than you have started despising the poor."[49] Augustine highlights the contempt that characterizes attitudes of rich toward the poor.[50] Even in the monastery, where worldly status has supposedly been left behind, Augustine needs to address such prejudice, instructing that "those who were regarded in the world as persons of consequence should not look down on their brothers who have entered the religious community from humble circumstances."[51] "So long as a monk finds himself thinking in the terms of his former life," Mary observes, "he will inevitably look at all his brothers in terms of their previous experience."[52]

Material prosperity can lead the rich to think that they are superior to others. Augustine exposes the falseness of such evaluations, by illustrating their superficial basis. For example, in *Sermon* 61 Augustine highlights how even a fixation on clothing among the wealthy can prompt prejudice toward the poor. In a passage emphasizing the goodness of created things (including riches), he notes in an aside how possession of these riches can make the wealthy proud, "so that they don't recognize other people as their equals," and that they become "more in love with

---

46. MacQueen, "Contemptus Dei," 250, 251. Brown makes the important observation that, in contrast to our "modern" context, "wealth" in Late Antiquity was closely bound up with one's status and the "honors" derived from one's place within Roman society. Brown, *Through the Eye of a Needle*, 4–5.

47. *Serm.* 36.2, 5.

48. *Serm.* 32.20.

49. *Serm.* 311.13. Note also that education can prompt this disdain, as in Augustine's experience: see *Conf.* 6.6.9.

50. Augustine especially describes the attitude of the rich man toward Lazarus (Lk. 16:19–31) in this way, e.g., *Serm.* 14.3; 15A.5.

51. *Reg. 3:* 1.7. Though note that Mary suggests that this caution in the *Rule* is not specifically concerned with "evil and destroying aspects of wealth and high social position." Mary, *The Rule of Saint Augustine*, 77. Rather, she suggests it is directed to members who are sincere in intention, but who have previously been accustomed to having "authority" and "control" and other such benefits of status (p. 77).

52. Mary, *The Rule of Saint Augustine*, 72.

their splendid clothes than aware of their common skin."[53] Later in the sermon, Augustine returns to this theme when he imagines a rich person responding to the suggestion that a poor beggar is their "equal": "'I'm not like him,' he says; 'heaven preserve me from being like him!' Some puffed-up poodle swathed in silk speaks like that about the fellow in rags."[54] Disparity of dress prevents the rich person from recognizing the common equality they share with beggars.[55] But Augustine directs his listeners to look beyond such attire, and consider the humanity we share in common beneath it all: "I'm not asking what you are like in your clothes, but what you were like when you were born."[56] "Come on, then, rich man, call to mind your beginnings; see whether you brought anything here," Augustine continues.[57] Again, Augustine is taking a lead from Paul's instruction on wealth in 1 Timothy 6: "*We brought nothing into this world*, when we were born, of course, *but neither can we take anything out* (1 Tm 6:7), of course, when we leave the world. You brought nothing, you will take nothing away from here, why preen yourself against the poor?"[58] While clothing and appearance may prompt a sense of superiority among the rich, Augustine alerts his listeners to the shallowness of such a view, instead directing them to the fundamental humanity that rich and poor share in common. He offers a vivid rendering of this teaching in *Sermon* 177, when cautioning the rich against pride: "They [the rich] should acknowledge that the poor are their peers; poor people are also people; different clothes, but the same skin; and if a rich person on dying is buried in perfumes and spices, it doesn't mean he won't rot, but only that it will happen later."[59] At birth and at death, the human frailty and mortality that rich and poor alike share can be plainly observed.

Another common trait that all share is dependence upon God. Prosperous listeners may pride themselves upon their economic independence, causing

53. *Serm.* 61.2. Regarding clothing and social status in this period, see Brown, *Through the Eye of a Needle*, 27–30. Note that Augustine's monastic community shared a common wardrobe: see *Reg. 3:* 5.1. For the challenge of this requirement to formerly wealthy members, see Brown, *Through the Eye of a Needle*, 176–7.
54. *Serm.* 61.8.
55. As noted above, for Augustine, we share with our neighbor an equal place in the order of creation (*Tract. ep. Jo.* 8.6–8). Burnaby comments that "if the principle of equality governs Augustine's whole treatment of the love of neighbour, it is simply because he takes seriously the command to love our neighbour 'as ourself.'" Burnaby, *Amor Dei*, 115. On the relationship between this command and the equality of the neighbor, see O'Donovan, *Problem of Self-Love*, 113–14; Canning, *Unity of Love for God and Neighbour*, 161–3.
56. *Serm.* 61.8. For a specific appeal to "common humanity" (in relation to the rich man and Lazarus of Lk. 16:19–31), see *Serm.* 113A.3.
57. *Serm.* 61.9.
58. *Serm.* 61.9.
59. *Serm.* 177.7. In *Sermon* 114B(D5/M12), Augustine strikingly makes this case for equality regarding relationships between masters and slaves (*Serm.* 114B(D5/M12).12). Regarding Augustine's attitude toward slavery, and the nature of his pastoral response, see Van der Meer, *Augustine the Bishop*, 135–6; Lepelley, "Facing Wealth and Poverty," 7.

them to scorn those who rely upon the aid of others. To address these dismissive attitudes toward the poor, Augustine often reminds his listeners that, before God, we are all beggars. Augustine poses this challenge well in *Sermon 123*:

> Just think, I mean, whoever of you are rich: however much you may have, you are God's beggar. The time comes for prayer, and that's when I'll show you up as such. You beg. How can you help being poor, if you beg? I'll tell you something more: you beg for bread. Or are you not going to say *Give us our daily bread* (Mt 6:11)?[60]

The wealthy are no less reliant upon God than the poor for material resources and well-being. Additionally, we all depend upon God's mercy and compassion for our salvation. As those in need, we all come knocking at God's door (Mt. 7:7), and in our longing for God's justice, we all thirst and hunger (Mt. 5:6).[61] In *Sermon 53A*, Augustine notes the implications: "So you are standing as a beggar at God's door; and there's another beggar standing at your door. The way you treat your beggar is the way God treats his."[62] "Even a small gift to the destitute mirrored the mercy of God to a human race that was as totally dependent on him for its survival as beggars were dependent on the rich for alms," Brown observes.[63]

Acknowledging our fundamental impoverishment before God challenges proud or dismissive attitudes we may have held toward the materially poor. Finn provides insight on this aspect of Augustine's preaching: "The analogous relationships between rich and poor, God and man, force the rich to find themselves in the same place as the poor, all too easily on the receiving end of that very contempt which they would visit on the destitute."[64] Later assessing the use of "*mendicus*" (beggar) in the *Enarrations on the Psalms*, where Augustine often employs this image to describe the Christian life, Finn observes: "A word which would in other circumstances measure the social gulf within the Christian community instead sets that entire community over and against God. Social distance within the community is as nothing compared with this."[65] Therefore, Augustine's teaching on our shared status as beggars before God helps overcome this breach of relationship between rich and poor, and reminds listeners of their common identity.

A number of these teachings come together when Augustine draws on the parable of Lazarus and the rich man (Lk. 16:19–31). In one sermon, Augustine observes that "their common humanity" should have prompted the rich man

---

60. *Serm.* 123.5.
61. *Serm.* 61.4, 6; 53A.10.
62. *Serm.* 53A.10.
63. Peter Brown, "Bridge to God: Remembering the Poor, Remembering the Dead," *Christian Century*, April 15, 2015, 22.
64. Finn, "Portraying the Poor," 134.
65. Finn, "Portraying the Poor," 137. Finn also notes that Augustine (and other preachers) avoids using terms for the poor that might fuel the contempt of the rich (pp. 133-4); see Chapter 3 for discussion and references.

to feed Lazarus.[66] In another, he attributes the rich man's failure to act to his "disdainful pride."[67] In *Sermon 36*, Augustine emphasizes how the rich man's love of wealth and extravagant clothing nurtured this prideful disdain of Lazarus:

> The falsity of this life took in that fellow in purple and fine linen, who disdained the poor man lying at his gate covered with sores.... That rich man, for his part, with such a sense of his own importance in his purple and fine linen, died and was buried. And what did he find? Everlasting thirst, never-ending flames. Purple and fine linen were followed by fire. He was burning in the shirt he had been unable to strip himself of.[68]

As he somewhat terrifyingly traces the fate of the rich man's finery, Augustine demonstrates just how ill-founded the rich man's pride was. His "sense of his own importance," and his dismissal of the barely clothed Lazarus, was based upon superficial distinctions of appearance and wealth. The eschatological conclusion of the parable radically upends these distinctions. While Lazarus enjoys the true riches of heaven, the rich man finds himself in the position of beggar, experiencing "a longing for a drop from the poor man's finger, just as *he* had done for crumbs from the rich man's table."[69] Having proudly set himself apart from the poor Lazarus in this earthly life, the rich man discovers that his pride has set himself apart from God (and Lazarus) in the life to come.

The Pride of the Poor

Although he clearly demonstrates how wealth nurtures the growth of pride, Augustine is careful not to equate wealth with pride.[70] It is possible for the rich to demonstrate humility, and conversely, for the poor to be proud.[71] Material poverty does not necessarily result in a humble love for God and neighbor. Augustine gives particular attention to this concern in *Sermon 14*.

---

66. *Serm.* 113A.3.
67. *Serm.* 15A.5.
68. *Serm.* 36.6.
69. *Serm.* 36.6.
70. *Serm.* 299E.5.
71. *Serm.* 53A.2. As noted in Chapter 3, one striking aspect of Augustine's teaching is his recognition that the poor are also moral agents, and his concern to attend to the disordered desires that they wrestle with. Ramsey suggests that Augustine may have in view "the glorification of the poor" featured in some literature of the period, and comments that Augustine "was too profound a student of human nature" to subscribe to simplistic portrayals of the virtuous poor. Ramsey, "Wealth," 878–9. However, unfortunately Augustine's account of pride and humility among rich and poor is not always balanced. For example, in *Sermon 14*, he suggests that pride is all the more insufferable in a poor person, whereas humility is considered more praiseworthy in the wealthy (*Serm.* 14.2).

On this occasion, Augustine clearly thinks his listeners are already familiar with his preaching on the parable of the rich man and Lazarus, and the challenge it presents to the rich. For in *Sermon* 14, following his initial cautionary words to the rich about pride, Augustine imaginatively describes a beggar reciting this message back to him, claiming: "It's me the kingdom of heaven is owed to. I'm like that Lazarus fellow, who lay in front of the rich man's house covered with sores, whose sores the dogs used to lick, and he tried to fill himself with the crumbs that fell from the rich man's table."[72] Identifying himself with Lazarus, the fictional interlocutor argues that "it's our sort to whom the kingdom of heaven properly belongs, not the sort of people who wear purple and fine linen and feast sumptuously every day."[73] The beggar continues to recount the parable (in the manner that Augustine would typically preach it), emphasizing the fate of the rich man. Augustine then describes the beggar's concluding challenge: "'So let us set apart,' he [the beggar] says, 'the poor and the rich. Why urge me to perceive other meanings? It's obvious who are poor, it's obvious who are rich.'"[74]

Perhaps Augustine's pastoral experience would have alerted him to this attitude among poorer members, prompting him to anticipate their objections: Why has Augustine invited the congregation to "look for the poor man" in the form of humility, when there are plenty of materially poor among them?[75] In the parable of Lazarus and the rich man, does not Jesus speak plainly about the welcome extended to the poor, and the demise of the rich? Surely, then, Augustine can "set apart" "the poor and the rich"?[76]

And yet this is precisely what Augustine is trying to avoid. His intention is not to separate the rich from the poor, but rather to draw them together. Pride separated the rich man from Lazarus in his earthly life, resulting in their division in the life to come. Augustine, however, wants all his listeners to enjoy together the unity of heaven, which requires them to overcome the divisiveness of pride on earth. Therefore, while his *Sermons* give greater attention to the pride of the rich, he also attends to pride among the poor, for this too is an obstacle to unity within the Christian community.

Accordingly, Augustine cautions his imaginary interlocutor: "When you identify yourself with that holy sore-infested man, I fear that pride may stop you being what you say you are."[77] As with the rich, Augustine alerts the poor to the way pride arises from undue regard for material wealth. Augustine's interlocutor can only read the parable in material terms; he associates himself with Lazarus, not on the basis of character, but economic status. Similarly, the rich man is condemned, not for any moral failing, but simply because the parable describes him as rich. Like the proud rich (discussed above), this poor interlocutor focuses

---

72. *Serm.* 14.3
73. *Serm.* 14.3.
74. *Serm.* 14.3.
75. *Serm.* 14.1.
76. *Serm.* 14.3.
77. *Serm.* 14.4.

on the external differences of clothing. The kingdom of God does not belong to "the sort of people who wear purple and fine linen," he insists.[78] In another sermon, Augustine provides a similar account of a beggar who is confident that, unlike the rich, he will enter into God's kingdom: "These rags will assure me of that," the beggar insists.[79] Again, sartorial and soteriological criteria are confused.

In *Sermon* 14, the interlocutor's reading of this Lukan parable results in contempt for the rich man, which Augustine opposes: "Don't despise rich people who are compassionate, rich people who are humble."[80] Augustine is compelled to caution his congregation against the interlocutor's interpretation, not only because it places too much weight on material attributes, but especially because it leads to a proud and judgmental attitude, in which the poor look down upon the rich members of the church.[81] This is a tragic outcome in Augustine's eyes. For as he warns his poor listeners, this proud over-identification with Lazarus will actually "stop you being what you say you are."[82] When they look down upon their wealthier neighbor with haughty superiority, they also distance themselves from God; their future will not be that of Lazarus, as they claim, but rather that of the rich man whose attitude of contempt they share.

Instead, Augustine invites his listeners to look more carefully at the parable, and consider how it commends humility to them.[83] Although Augustine sometimes presents Lazarus as an example of humility,[84] the key to Augustine's reading of the parable is Abraham, who welcomes Lazarus to his "bosom" (Lk. 16:22–23).[85] This refutes the view that only the materially poor will enter the kingdom of God, for Abraham, Augustine notes, "was one of the richest people on earth, in gold, silver, household, flocks, possessions."[86] However, he observes, "This rich man was poor because he was humble."[87] For Augustine, the humility of Abraham is evidenced

---

78. *Serm.* 14.3.
79. *Serm.* 114B(D5/M12).11.
80. *Serm.* 14.4.
81. *Serm.* 14.4–6. Commenting on Ambrose's preaching, Brown notes that the rich could feel uncomfortable in church, where they "were exposed to the gaze of a crowd of hundreds drawn from all classes, many of whom might have had good reason to resent them." Brown, *Through the Eye of a Needle*, 142. See also p. 341. In *The Work of Monks*, Augustine acknowledges that sometimes people from humble backgrounds join a monastic community seeking "the opportunity to dominate over those by whom they were formerly despised and ill-treated" (*Op. mon.* 22.25).
82. *Serm.* 14.4.
83. *Serm.* 14.4.
84. E.g., *Serm.* 113B.3 (see Hill's explanation: *Sermons (94A-147A)*, 187n4). See also *Serm.* 20A.9.
85. *Serm.* 14.4. For "Abraham's bosom," see also *Serm.* 113B.3; and L. J. van der Lof, "Abraham's Bosom in the Writings of Irenaeus, Tertullian and Augustine," *Augustinian Studies* 26, no. 2 (1995): 109–23.
86. *Serm.* 14.4.
87. *Serm.* 14.4.

in his dependence on God, even to the point of obediently offering his son to God.[88]

It is this form of poverty that gains both Lazarus and Abraham access into "eternal rest," rather than material poverty, which they do not share in common.[89] Augustine articulates this point clearly in another sermon:

> If his [Lazarus's] merit lay precisely in his poverty, then Abraham would not have preceded him into eternal rest, to welcome him when he followed. But because the same thing was found in the poor man Lazarus as in the rich man Abraham, namely humility, neither riches were a hindrance to the one nor poverty to the other, but the merit of both was their piety.[90]

Although their material circumstances were dramatically different, Lazarus and Abraham find themselves enjoying this rest together, because both had humbly depended on God.

It is important to recall that Augustine foregrounds the humility of Abraham in response to his (fictitious) poor interlocutor—that is, for the benefit of poor members of the congregation who share the interlocutor's views. Augustine is not trying to soften the parable for the reassurance of the rich; indeed, on other occasions, he will ensure wealthy listeners receive the full brunt of the parable's critique.[91] Rather, Augustine notes Abraham's place in the parable as caution to the poor, lest they harbor proud attitudes toward wealthier sisters and brothers. Augustine makes this point in startlingly direct fashion when he turns to address specific members of the Carthage congregation:

> So you see why, although there are plenty of poor people, we are right to look for the poor person. We look in the crowds and we can scarcely find one. A poor man confronts me and I go on looking for a poor man. Meanwhile *you*, mind you stretch out your hand to the poor man whom you do find; it is in your heart that you are looking for the one you are looking for. And *you*, you're saying "I'm poor like Lazarus." This humble rich man of mine isn't saying "I'm rich like Abraham." So you are exalting yourself, he is humbling himself.[92]

Such a proud and overconfident assumption among the poor not only prevents them from abandoning themselves to God; it also distances them from their

---

88. *Serm.* 14.4.
89. *Serm.* 15A.5.
90. *Serm.* 15A.5.
91. E.g. *Serm.* 113B.
92. *Serm.* 14.5. Italics original. Hill suggests that, at the points italicized, Augustine pointed to specific members of the congregation: either a rich person followed by a poor person, or perhaps others, such as "presbyters or deacons" sitting nearby Augustine, who could represent the characters being discussed (possibly to comic effect). *Sermons (1–19)*, 322nn11–12.

wealthier brothers and sisters. By employing members of the congregation in this illustration, Augustine highlights the dissonance introduced among them when rich members are trying to live humbly and generously, while the poor exalt themselves over them.

In his discussion of this Lukan parable in *Sermon 20A*, Augustine comments: "The rich man went ahead and prepared hospitality and a home for the poor man. That's just what you have in the psalm, *all together, rich and poor* (Ps 49:2)."[93] The companionship that the wealthy Abraham and the poor Lazarus enjoy together invites listeners to imagine a future in the company of those they have previously scorned. With the psalmist, Augustine anticipates a future life that is "*all together, rich and poor* (Ps 49:2)."[94] But if the life we await is characterized by such unity, then we need to learn to live together now. And that not only requires the rich to overcome their "disdainful pride" of the poor, but also for the poor to set aside proud and judgmental attitudes toward the rich.[95]

The Pride of the Rich Who Have Become Poor

In commending Abraham to the congregation in *Sermon 14*, Augustine notes that Abraham "was a man of good works."[96] And yet Augustine draws attention not to the works themselves, but to Abraham's humility: "He wasn't puffed up by what might have seemed his very own good works, because this rich man was poor."[97]

The perversity of pride is such that it deprives even good works of their goodness. What appears an act of love toward God and neighbor may turn out to be an attempt to elevate oneself. Augustine's warning to the monastic community about this danger is particularly insightful: "For every other vice prompts people to do evil deeds; but pride lies in ambush even for good deeds in order to destroy them. What advantage is it *to scatter abroad and give to the poor* (Ps111(112):9; 2 Cor 9:9) and become poor oneself, if the wretched soul becomes prouder in despising riches than it was in possessing them?"[98] This caution is particularly directed toward members who were rich before joining the monastery. Augustine warns them that even the seemingly selfless act of renouncing property could be cause for pride, for it could lead them to "boast" about what they have donated "to the common life" (and therefore to consider themselves better than members who had little to contribute financially), or to be proud that their wealth is being used in the monastery (perhaps prompting them to scorn the rich who have

---

93. *Serm.* 20A.9.
94. *Serm.* 20A.9.
95. *Serm.* 15A.5.
96. *Serm.* 14.4.
97. *Serm.* 14.4.
98. *Reg. 3:* 1.7. For the danger of "elitism" in Christian asceticism, and Augustine's attempts to overcome this, see Brown, *Augustine of Hippo*, 244–5, 508–10; Markus, *End of Ancient Christianity*, 63–83, 159.

not embraced the monastic life).[99] Discussing the involvement of the wealthy in Christian asceticism (including the Pelagian movement), Lepelley explains that "members of the high Roman senatorial aristocracy called themselves *melior pars humani generis*, the elite of mankind, and those who were converted to asceticism transposed that pride into their new behavior."[100] Pride may be the "disease of riches," but it is not necessarily eradicated by renouncing riches and embracing poverty, for this renunciation can also become an act of pride.[101]

Pride presents a formidable obstacle in Christian formation, because it is difficult to detect outwardly, and is often indiscernible even to ourselves. Any act of Christian devotion or discipleship can be co-opted by pride. In the *Homilies on the First Epistle of John*, Augustine alerts his listeners to this danger: "Charity feeds the hungry man; pride also feeds him. Charity does it so that God may be praised, pride so that itself may be praised. Charity clothes the naked man; pride also clothes him.... Pride, directing its horses, as it were, carries out in contrary fashion all the good works that charity wants to do and does do."[102] We may outwardly display the works of charity, but this does not mean that charity performs them. For even if they appear to be directed toward God or neighbor, any of these actions can instead be motivated by a prideful desire for our own exaltation.

Why is pride a problem, if it still enables the hungry to be fed and the naked clothed? Pride may be a lesser concern if meeting material need is the only goal; however, if loving our neighbor is our intent, then pride presents a barrier. Earlier in this homily, Augustine describes how we can "desire to extol" ourselves over the person we are supposedly serving: "He was needy, you bestowed something. You seem greater, because you made the offering, than him to whom the offering was made."[103] Pride turns an expression of generosity into a display of superiority. Our action may appear to span the distance with our neighbor, as we respond to their need. And yet, while it may meet the neighbor's immediate demand, an action driven by pride ultimately reinforces our distance, reasserting the belief that we are better than our neighbor. Pride thus sabotages acts of charity, so that they no longer unite us to our neighbor in love.

While good works can also be an expression of love for God, pride can undermine this relationship too. Rather than acknowledging God as the source of our goodness, we claim credit for our actions, as if this goodness was our own.[104] Accordingly, we become "puffed up with pride in the very sacrifices of humility."[105] With this inflated sense of our own importance, we no longer rely

---

99. *Reg.* 3: 1.7.
100. Lepelley, "Facing Wealth and Poverty," 15.
101. *Serm.* 36.2. See also *Sermon* 354, where Augustine cautions those who have committed themselves to chastity against the danger of pride (*Serm.* 354.4–9).
102. *Tract. ep. Jo.* 8.9.
103. *Tract. ep. Jo.* 8.5. For the social "honour" that was often associated with generous acts of almsgiving, see Finn, *Almsgiving in the Later Roman Empire*, 205–14.
104. *Serm.* 198(D26/M62).56.
105. *Serm.* 198(D26/M62).56.

upon God. In *Sermon* 14, Augustine commends Abraham because he was not overtaken by pride in this way.[106] Here, Augustine has in view Abraham's response to God's instruction to sacrifice Isaac, for Abraham "did not hesitate to offer what he had received to the one from whom he had received it."[107] On other occasions, Augustine points to Abraham as one who knew how to "possess wealth" without being "possessed by it."[108] In this respect, although rich, Abraham is regarded as a model of renunciation. However, Abraham's humility consists not only in his willingness to relinquish God's gifts, but also in his unwillingness to take pride in such an act. "He never boasted in himself but in the Lord," Augustine explains.[109] Abraham thus exemplifies the form of poverty that Augustine has been looking for during *Sermon* 14, because though rich in wealth and good works, he did not rely upon himself, instead depending upon God.

The Remedy of Christ's Humility

The quest for the "poor man" of Psalm 10:14 that Augustine and the congregation embark on in *Sermon* 14 eventually comes to fruition.[110] Having addressed various expressions of pride that prevent us from depending on God, Augustine declares: "We have found the genuine poor man, we have found him to be kind and humble, not trusting in himself, truly poor, a member of the poor man who became poor for our sake, though he was rich."[111] While material wealth or material poverty is not without bearing on our pride or humility (as has been illustrated), what distinguishes the "poor man" is that, regardless of his material status, he is "not trusting in himself."[112] Such a poverty realizes the folly of relying upon oneself or asserting oneself over against God or neighbor; it is of this humble poverty that it can be said, "*To you has the poor man abandoned himself*" (Ps. 10:14).[113]

For Augustine, Christ reveals to us the nature and importance of humility.[114] "Humility," like "pride," is a word commonly understood outside of any theological context, and often with unhelpful consequences. Therefore it is crucial to appreciate the distinctly theological nature of Augustine's understanding of humility. Burnaby offers helpful clarification: "Augustinian humility is not a purely moral

---

106. *Serm.* 14.4.
107. *Serm.* 14.4.
108. *Serm.* 299E.5. See Chapter 3 for this attitude to wealth.
109. *Serm.* 14.4.
110. *Serm.* 14.1.
111. *Serm.* 14.9.
112. *Serm.* 14.9.
113. *Serm.* 14.1.
114. Regarding the humility of Christ in Augustine's thought, I have found the following accounts helpful: Burnaby, *Amor Dei*, 171–2; Cavadini, "Pride," 682–3; Daley, "A Humble Mediator," 100–117; MacQueen, "Contemptus Dei," 279–87; Williams, *On Augustine*, esp. 131–4, 141–53; Zumkeller, *Augustine's Ideal of the Religious Life*, 147, 232–40.

characteristic which may belong to any man without regard to his religion. It has nothing to do with self-deprecation. It is the humility of the believer as such, the manward aspect of faith in God as the source of all good, the necessary implication of acceptance of the doctrine of grace."[115] Similarly, Margaret Atkins observes that "the basis of humility is a clear-sighted grasp of the truth about oneself in relation to God."[116] Augustine's teaching on humility does not demean listeners, depriving their humanity, but rather helps them appreciate how to be truly human (and thus addressing pride's pretensions to be more than human). The reason "God became man," Augustine teaches on one occasion, is "that in him we human beings might acknowledge our humanity."[117] The person who "*enters by the gate*" (Jn 10:2) of Christ's humility, Augustine explains in another sermon, is the person "who understands Christ's humility, and understands that while God has become man for us, he himself as a human being is not God, but just a man."[118] The lesson of Christ's humility, in the first instance, is how to live according to our created nature as human beings. Williams explains: "We have to grow, says Augustine, if we are to feed on truth. And the heart of that growth is humility, facing our essential incompleteness at every level, metaphysical, spiritual, cognitive, moral."[119]

Exhortations to contemplate the humility of Christ are frequent in the *Sermons*, for if pride is the "root cause" of humanity's ill health, the humility of Christ is the necessary "remedy."[120] Indeed, Augustine's meditations on the profound nature of Christ's humility alert him to how malignant pride is, and how fundamental a problem. His use of medical metaphor to illustrate this condition and cure for his congregation is frequent and expansive. In *Sermon* 159B(D21/M54), for example, he likens Christ to a skillful doctor who encounters a patient "ailing from a variety of disorders," yet who is concerned to attend to the underlying cause.[121] Augustine explains that as Christ "could see that pride was the root cause of all our disorders, he cured us with his own humility."[122] In other sermons, Augustine helps his listeners appreciate how Christ's humility attends to our pride by likening it to the

---

115. Burnaby, *Amor Dei*, 73. I have not attempted to respond to modern critiques of the role of humility within Christian thought. However, Stephen Pardue's article brings Augustine into conversation with these contemporary debates: Stephen Pardue, "Kenosis and Its Discontents: Towards an Augustinian Account of Divine Humility," *Scottish Journal of Theology* 65, no. 3 (2012): 271–88.
116. Margaret Atkins, "'Heal My Soul': The Significance of an Augustinian Image," *Studies in Christian Ethics* 23, no. 4 (2010): 356. See also Zumkeller, *Augustine's Ideal of the Religious Life*, 235.
117. *Serm.* 77.11.
118. *Serm.* 137.4.
119. Williams, *On Augustine*, 132. Williams adds that God himself "accepts the limits of mortal life so that he can speak directly to us using our own language" (p. 132).
120. *Serm.* 360B(D25/M61).17.
121. *Serm.* 159B(D21/M54).11.
122. *Serm.* 159B(D21/M54).11.

medical practice of applying "contraries" (such as using something cold to aid a patient with a hot fever).[123] "So if we see the art of medicine curing a patient by the application of contraries," Augustine suggests, "it's not surprising if we who were sick with human pride are cured by the humility of God."[124] In this way, Augustine helps his listeners appreciate the gravity of our pride-induced infirmity by drawing attention to the radical nature of the cure required.

Augustine's casting of humility as cure indicates his belief that it was for our sake that Christ became humble. It is not for Christ's own "benefit" that he comes in humility, but "totally for ours."[125] Augustine implies this, again in medical terms, in *Sermon* 360B(D25/M61):

> Accept the doctor's orders. Whatever he imposes on you to be endured, he first underwent himself. And in him, indeed, there was nothing to be cured, because he was in no way ill, but in carrying out his duty of healing, he endured what he was proposing to the patient. He was giving a special bitter potion to a patient swollen and blown up with pride; he himself came in humility, and suffered every conceivable humiliation from proud individuals.[126]

Christ himself suffered no pride that would require him to become humble; unlike the proud desire of Adam and Eve to "*be like gods* (Gn 3:5)," for Christ, "equality with God" was not "robbery" but his very "nature" (Phil. 2:6).[127] However, because we have proudly separated ourselves from God, and exalted ourselves above others, Christ has come in humility, so that we might learn and receive from him our restorative cure.

Although the congregation in *Sermon* 14 may have been instructed to "look for the poor man,"[128] Augustine typically presents Christ as the one who comes looking for us, enabling us to return to God.[129] Indeed, if pride is marked by our attempt to construct a life independent of God, humility requires our acceptance of the necessity of God's grace.[130] As Procopé explains, Augustine discovered that "you cannot presume to subdue the lusts of the flesh *de spiritu tuo*, through your own strength of mind; if you try, the story will be one of pride resisted, not of grace granted to the humble."[131] When teaching on humility in the *Sermons*, Augustine

---

123. *Serm.* 341(D22/M55).4.
124. *Serm.* 341(D22/M55).4.
125. *Serm.* 185.1.
126. *Serm.* 360B(D25/M61).16.
127. *Serm.* 264.3.
128. *Serm.* 14.1.
129. E.g. *Conf.* 7.18.24.
130. Procopé, "*Initium omnis peccati superbia*," 320.
131. Procopé, "*Initium omnis peccati superbia*," 320. And of course, our determined efforts to resist pride can in turn become further cause for pride: see *Conf.* 10.38.63. For discussion of the necessity of grace for humility, see Cavadini, "Pride," 683; MacQueen, "Contemptus Dei," 283–6.

consistently emphasizes God's movement toward us in Christ. Alongside the image of Christ as a doctor, coming to heal the sick (noted above), Augustine also presents Christ as a teacher, enabling us to learn what we could not teach ourselves. This depiction especially arises from Christ's words of invitation: "Take my yoke upon you, and learn from me; for I am gentle and humble in heart, and you will find rest for your souls" (Mt. 11:29, NRSV). Augustine often presents this invitation in dramatic form, so that the congregation can hear Christ addressing them directly: "The master of the angels cries out, the Word of God cries out on which all rational minds are nourished unfailingly, the food that restores and remains entire cries out, and says, *Learn from me*."[132] As Augustine goes on to explain here in *Sermon* 142, although the one who addresses us is the Word through whom all things were made, it is through his humanity that Christ teaches us: "What you must learn from me is what I became because of you," Augustine describes Christ saying.[133] Christ does not come to teach us how to be God, but rather how to be properly human, by learning from his humility.

"Listen to the one who says, *Come to me, all you who labor and are overburdened*" Augustine urges the congregation in *Sermon* 68.[134] On this occasion, Augustine contrasts Christ's lesson of humility with the pride modeled by the rich:

> You must learn what he says: *Learn of me, because I am meek and humble of heart*. You're looking at that rich neighbor of yours, a man of property and of pride. By looking at him and trying to compete with him, you will grow proud too. You won't become humble unless you look at the one who became humble for your sake. Learn from Christ what you won't learn from man; in him is to be found the standard of humility.[135]

Augustine is mindful that many in his congregation will find themselves drawn to the lifestyle of the rich. These powerful role models are also instructive, teaching a proud self-sufficiency, and a disregard for neighbor. For this reason, Augustine is eager to direct his listeners to "look" toward Christ instead, for only in Christ will they discover "the standard of humility."

One aspect of the humility displayed in Christ's human life is his dependence upon God. This Christological theme is not frequently foregrounded in the *Sermons*, but Augustine alludes to it on at least one occasion. When discussing the mediating role of Christ in *Sermon* 198(D26/M62), Augustine notes not only his humble embrace of the "whole range of creation" in his humanity, but also his inseparable dependence upon God:

> The reason this mediator has the whole [range of creation], the reason this mediator took the whole to himself, is that only a mediating creature like this

---

132. *Serm.* 142.11.
133. *Serm.* 142.11.
134. *Serm.* 68.10.
135. *Serm.* 68.11.

can purify from iniquities and liberate from death, a creature which does not presume to be of any avail in itself, but cleaves personally to God the Word, and is coupled and mingled with it in an inexpressible manner, so that it is possible to say, *the Word became flesh* (Jn 1:14). To this end was his lowliness despised and exalted, that people should not in humility despair of themselves, nor presumptuously rely on themselves in pride.[136]

Regarding humility, Augustine's primary emphasis in this passage may be on the "lowliness" of Christ's human form. However, the description of Christ's dependence upon "God the Word" is particularly striking: Christ in his humanity, cleaving to God "in an inexpressible manner" through his union with the Word.[137] Also noteworthy is the contrast of Christ as "a creature which does not presume to be of any avail in itself" with the tendency of humans to "presumptuously rely on themselves in pride." In this way, Christ demonstrates what a human life of humility toward God looks like.[138]

While Christ's example of human humility challenges presumptuous self-reliance, it should not prompt "despair."[139] For it is God's very purpose in the Incarnation to enable us to be humbly united to God. As Williams explains, "The natural and eternal self-surrender of the Son is enacted in the circumstances of weak flesh, both displaying and creating the possibility of obedience to the Father in all circumstances."[140] Christ not only models humility toward God; he enables this humility within us also, so that we come to share in his life of union with God. Brian Daley highlights another related insight of Augustine's teaching, explaining that Augustine came to see that even Jesus's "singular union with God" was not something that he (as human) accomplished, but itself was enabled by "grace."[141] Daley describes the significance of this teaching for our own life with God: "It is this unmerited elevation of a human being to union with God that reveals the reality of grace, the mystery of predestination for glory, in each of us; what we see in the Incarnation is the pattern of what we hope for, in a limited way, for ourselves."[142] In the discovery of this humble union of humanity with God imaged in the Incarnation, therefore, we find hope that we too can share in this life united to God.

However, in the *Sermons*, when directing the congregation toward the lesson of Christ's humility, it is typically his movement from the wealth of his divine life to

---

136. *Serm.* 198(D26/M62).44.

137. Williams discusses Augustine's teaching on the union of Christ's humanity with the divine Word: see Williams, *On Augustine*, 141–53.

138. For the example of "perfect obedience" revealed by Christ's humility, see MacQueen, "Contemptus Dei," 282–3.

139. *Serm.* 198(D26/M62).44.

140. Williams, *On Augustine*, 151.

141. Daley, "A Humble Mediator," 109. Daley suggests that this emphasis comes more to the fore in Augustine's later thought, when he is responding to "the Pelagian view of human self-sufficiency" (p. 109).

142. Daley, "A Humble Mediator," 109–10.

his embrace of human impoverishment that Augustine has in view—a movement that challenges the upward grasping of human pride. Thus, in *Sermon* 14, he instructs his listeners: "Look at this rich man of ours, who for our sake *became poor, though he was rich* (2 Cor 8:9)."[143] As God, Christ's riches are inestimable; Augustine reminds the congregation that any image of wealth they can conceive of is surpassed by Christ, through whom all things were created (Jn 1:3).[144] And yet, in becoming flesh (Jn 1:14), Christ becomes poor: "the Lord of heaven and earth, creator of angels, maker and founder of all things visible and invisible, sucks, cries, is reared, grows, puts up with being his age, conceals his ageless majesty, later on is arrested, scorned, scourged, mocked, spat at, slapped, crowned with thorns, hung on a tree, pierced with a lance."[145] From the unfathomable heights of divine riches, Christ descends to the darkest depths of human poverty, becoming himself the subject of human contempt.

In his humble humanity, Christ undermines the worldly claims of status we use to elevate ourselves over others. For example, Augustine notes that Christ chose "to be born of a woman who was betrothed to a carpenter, so that nobody might boast of the rank of his parents as against the justice of someone poor and base-born, and so become incurably conceited."[146] Locating himself in a simple Nazareth household, Christ challenges attitudes of pedigree or privilege that look down upon—or overlook—the poor. And yet, Christ does not embrace human poverty in order to reject the rich and powerful, but rather to "heal them."[147] Augustine makes this observation when reflecting on Christ's selection of uneducated fishermen as his disciples (in light of 1 Cor. 1:27–28):

> So he chose the weak, the poor, the unlearned, the low-born, not because he abandoned the strong, the rich, the wise, the well-born, but if he were to choose them first, they would imagine they were chosen by right of their honors, by right of their wealth, by right of their family connections, and puffed up in this way about these things, they would not have received the healthy condition of humility, without which no one can return to that life which we would never have fallen from had it not been for pride.[148]

The humble poverty of Christ and his disciples challenges the wealthy of this world, but in order to heal rather than abandon them. And if the rich have become distanced from God through pride, it is by encountering Christ in humble form that they are enabled to return.

Reflecting on Matthew 11:28–29 in *Sermon* 142, Augustine concludes that to learn from Christ's humility is to learn the lesson of love for one another:

---

143. *Serm.* 14.9.
144. *Serm.* 14.9.
145. *Serm.* 14.9.
146. *Serm.* 198(D26/M62).60.
147. *Serm.* 341(D22/M55).4.
148. *Serm.* 341(D22/M55).4.

"He is suggesting love, and the most genuine sort of love for one's fellows, love without mixed motives, without conceit, without arrogance, without deceit."[149] Because "conceit" and "arrogance" sets us apart from others, we need to learn humility in order to truly love one another. In his discussion of the *Rule*, Van Bavel stresses the necessity of humility for community life; humility, he observes, is "the indispensable condition for loving another, since only humility can make a person open to others and prevent him from turning back upon himself."[150] This insightful statement takes on additional depth in light of the preceding discussion of Augustine's conception of humility. It is not simply a humble attitude that makes Christian community possible; rather it is the humility of Christ, attending to our self-oriented pride, and turning us toward others in love.

Members of the Poor Man

While Augustine often calls his hearers to follow or imitate Christ's humility,[151] in *Sermon* 14 he describes the relationship of Christians to their humble Lord in more participatory and ecclesiological terms. Having recounted the humble nature of Christ's human life, he exclaims: "What poverty! There is the head of the poor people I am looking for, the poor man of whom we find the genuinely poor person to be a member."[152] Those who are "genuinely poor" do not simply imitate Christ in humility, but are incorporated into his body, as members of "the poor man," with Christ himself as our "head."

Earlier in this sermon, Augustine exhorted the congregation: "So learn to be poor and abandon yourselves to God, O my fellow poor [*compauperes*]!"[153] It is a wonderfully paradoxical instruction, which could be interpreted in a number of ways. Addressing his listeners as "my fellow poor," Augustine could be suggesting that those who (like him) are materially poor can still learn from the poverty of Christ; or he could be provocatively challenging wealthier members, reminding them that they are poor before God, and need to learn this humble poverty. Or perhaps this instruction is akin to Augustine's memorable statement in *Sermon* 272, "Be what you can see, and receive what you are"[154]: inasmuch as they are in

---

149. *Serm.* 142.12. Love and humility are closely linked for Augustine; "where there is humility there is charity," he states (*Tract. ep. Jo.* prologue). MacQueen notes the nuanced relationship between humility and love in Augustine's thought, explaining that while humility is "a first sign of love," it "cannot be equated with love in its fully actualized and perfected state." MacQueen, "Contemptus Dei," 285. See also *Serm.* 68.10–13.
150. Van Bavel, "Evangelical Inspiration of the Rule," 88.
151. E.g., *Serm.* 23A.3.
152. *Serm.* 14.9.
153. *Serm.* 14.2 (*PL* 38:112). Regarding Augustine's use of *compauperes*, see Finn, *Almsgiving in the Later Roman Empire*, 81.
154. *Serm.* 272.

Christ, they *are* poor, but this truth remains to be realized in their lives. In any case, in *Sermon* 14, Augustine draws a clear connection between the poverty of Christ, and the poverty of those who are members of his body.[155] This teaching suggests that humility is a precondition for participation in the body of Christ; it is by being "genuinely poor" that we share in the life of Christ, "the poor man."[156]

Conversely, Augustine's teaching on other occasions indicates that it is through a life shared with the members of Christ's body that we learn humility. Leaving behind a life of self-centered existence, we find ourselves in the company of others who are different from us, including those of greater or lesser means. Reflecting on Christ's decision to choose fishermen as his first disciples, Augustine observes that "those who were being called to lowliness and humility would have to be called by lowly and humble people."[157] Similarly, we too are trained in humility by sharing the journey of discipleship with those whom we might once have overlooked. Such learning can be difficult or uncomfortable, as was likely the case in Augustine's monastery: Brown observes that the *Rule* "assumed that each brother … would suffer from innumerable little slights that came from the fact that not all their colleagues were of the same class as themselves."[158] However, Augustine's cautionary remarks on pride in the *Rule* also indicate the benefit of learning to live alongside others from different backgrounds. Those formerly poor are advised not to become proud of their new friendship with those previously of high social status, for Augustine warns that "monasteries will become profitable to the rich and not to the poor, if the rich become humble there and the poor become puffed up."[159] As this statement suggests, the profit gained from the common life of the monastery is the lesson of humility received through companionship with others. As for those members who were previously "regarded in the world as persons of consequence," Augustine directs them to "take pains to glory in the companionship of their poor brothers rather than in the rank of wealthy relatives."[160] They may have once taken pride in association with wealth and status; now, friendship with those of little social standing is to be celebrated. Offering valuable reflection on the challenge involved in this instruction, Mary observes: "Trying to understand and get alongside a person who is very different from oneself is only possible if it is entirely devoid of self-seeking."[161] Mary later explains: "I shall not discover their gifts until

---

155. In a recent article, Joseph Cong Quy Lam suggests that, for Augustine, the humility of Christ is defining for the life of the church. Joseph Cong Quy Lam, "*Humilitas Iesu Christi* as Model of a Poor Church: Augustine's Idea of a Humble Church for the Poor," *The Australasian Catholic Record* 93, no. 2 (2016): 180–97.

156. *Serm.* 14.9.

157. *Serm.* 360B(D25/M61).24. Augustine himself experienced something of Christ's call through the humble when he learned from Ponticianus of "uneducated people" living a monastic life (*Conf.* 8.6.14–15; 8.8.19).

158. Brown, *Through the Eye of a Needle*, 176.

159. *Reg. 3*: 1.6.

160. *Reg. 3*: 1.7.

161. Mary, *The Rule of Saint Augustine*, 81.

I have looked for them and ceased from looking at my own. What I shall then find in my companions will be really something to boast of, to glory in. And what we experience together as they share what they have with me is companionship (*societas*)."[162] This is no easy task, and the presence of these instructions in the *Rule* indicates that, even for the most devout, overcoming pride remains an ongoing challenge. The lesson of Christ's humility is an exercise in life-long learning.

Augustine also encourages the wider congregation to learn from the companionship of others in this way. *Sermon* 36 provides a good example. Here, Augustine notes that the rich are not excluded from the body of Christ: "They too were won by the poverty of him who, *though he was rich, became poor for us* (2 Cor 8:9)," he observes.[163] "They too have become members of that poor man."[164] Thus, Christ has incorporated these wealthy members into his humble body. Yet, it remains for them to learn from Christ's humility, for their wealth may lead them to proudly trust in their own resources.[165] Therefore, for the rich man, Augustine's instruction is:

> Let him be humble. Let him be more glad that he's a Christian than that he's rich. Don't let him be puffed up or become high and mighty. Let him take notice of the poor man his brother, and not refuse to be called the poor man's brother. After all, however rich he may be, Christ is richer, and he wanted all for whom he shed his blood to be his brethren.[166]

Notable in this passage is the way that the companionship of the poor helps the rich overcome pride. In order to overcome the temptation of becoming "high and mighty," Augustine directs the rich man toward his fraternal bond with "the poor man," a relationship which runs against the grain of his proud pretensions.[167] Although the rich might typically be inclined to ignore or "refuse" the poor, Christ has died for both rich and poor, making those previously estranged from each other into "his brethren."[168] By paying attention to and willingly associating with the poor, the rich have opportunity not only to learn humility, but also to appreciate more fully their identity as "members of that poor man," Christ.[169]

---

162. Mary, *The Rule of Saint Augustine*, 81.
163. *Serm.* 36.5.
164. *Serm.* 36.5.
165. *Serm.* 36.5.
166. *Serm.* 36.5.
167. As noted, prior to this statement in *Sermon* 36, Augustine has been speaking of Christ as the "poor man," so when he here urges the rich man to "take notice of the poor man his brother," it is possible that he is directing the rich man toward the humble Christ (*Serm.* 36.5). However, I take Augustine's comment as primarily referring to the materially poor in the congregation.
168. *Serm.* 36.5.
169. *Serm.* 36.5.

Van Bavel highlights a passage in *Sermon* 399 where Augustine notes the lesson learnt in the presence of our neighbor: "But concerning the neighbor a rule has been fashioned for you, since you yourself have been created equal to your neighbor," Augustine states.[170] Van Bavel describes the challenge of equality found in this encounter: "If I existed completely alone, there would be no one with whom I could be compared; everything would be up to myself, and I would be ruled by nothing and by no one. But now the other people 'appear' alongside me; I can be compared to them and I am their equal as a fellow creature, not superior to them."[171] Throughout the *Sermons*, Augustine reminds his listeners of their equality with their neighbor by noting what they share in common. As previously discussed, whether rich or poor, all share a common humanity, and a common human experience, whether in birth or in death.[172] Furthermore, Christ has died for all; whether rich or poor, they have been "purchased" at the same "price."[173] Choosing to acknowledge this common life that we share with our needy neighbor helps us to draw near to them in loving humility, rather than looking down upon them in pride.

Sermon 259 provides an excellent example of this pastoral teaching. Reminding the congregation that our present task is to "do good" through "works of mercy," Augustine warns them not to ignore their needy neighbor, with whom they share a common humanity: "Show pity to a man, man, and God will show pity to you. You a man, the other a man, two pitiful creatures."[174] Awareness of shared adversity can prompt a compassionate response, as Augustine explains with an illustration:

> Anyone who is cruel and unfeeling toward someone who has been shipwrecked, for example, will go on being cruel and unfeeling until he's shipwrecked himself. If that has happened to him, though, he is reminded, when he sees a shipwrecked sailor, of his own past life.... And while he couldn't be induced to show pity by their companionship in humanity, he is induced to do so by their partnership in calamity.... So a common experience of misery tends to soften the hardest of human hearts.[175]

Following this teaching, Augustine calls the congregation to show mercy to others by forgiving and giving (Lk. 6:37–38).[176]

What makes *Sermon* 259 especially noteworthy, however, is the practical instruction that emerges toward the sermon's conclusion, as Augustine turns to

---

170. *Serm.* 399.3, quoted in Van Bavel, "Augustine on Christian Teaching and Life," 95. I have quoted Van Bavel's translation here. Note that Van Bavel refers to this sermon by its title "*De disciplina christiana*"; in Hill's translation it features as *Sermon* 399.
171. Van Bavel, "Augustine on Christian Teaching and Life," 95.
172. E.g., *Serm.* 61.8–9.
173. *Tract. ep. Jo.* 5.12.
174. *Serm.* 259.3.
175. *Serm.* 259.3.
176. *Serm.* 259.4.

address the "*agapes*" that the Hippo congregation customarily provided.[177] Of this meal, Hill explains: "The *agape* was the formal meal—laid on at this period, it would seem, for the poor—which sometimes followed the eucharist. Such agapes would be provided by the devout wealthy Christians."[178] On this occasion, Augustine calls the congregation to go beyond simply providing food for these meals: "You should know that you perform a double work of mercy if you give something to the poor in such a way that you give it yourself. What's called for, you see, is not only the kindness of lavishing assistance, but also the humility of lending a helping hand."[179] Hill suggests that this comment was directed particularly toward wealthy benefactors in the congregation, who preferred sponsoring these meals, rather than serving them.[180] Their philanthropic assistance was no doubt beneficial for the recipients of the *agape* meals, but it would not benefit the rich givers, if it reinforced their proud distance from the poor. For this reason, Augustine commends to them "the humility of lending a helping hand."[181] To those accustomed to being served *by* the lower classes, the instruction to play the role of servant *to* the poor would be humbling indeed, if not offensive. And yet, it is exactly this sort of exercise in humility that would assist the healing of pride in the rich giver.

Such an act of humble service would also bring the rich into direct contact with the poor, making a genuine relationship of love possible, as Augustine goes on explain in moving terms:

> I don't know how it is, my brothers and sisters, but the spirit of the person who actually hands something to a poor man experiences a kind of sympathy with common humanity and infirmity, when the hand of the one who has is actually placed in the hand of the one who is in need. Although the one is giving, the other receiving, the one being attended to and the one attending are being joined in a real relationship. You see, it isn't calamity that really unites us but humanity.[182]

It is notable that the expression of service that Augustine has in mind involves the rich making physical contact with the poor—he is remarkably specific about this—for elsewhere he notes the physical aversion his rich listeners have to the poor

---

177. *Serm.* 259.5.
178. Hill, in *Sermons (230-272B) on the Liturgical Seasons*, trans. Edmund Hill, ed. John E. Rotelle, vol. 7, *The Works of Saint Augustine, Part 3: Sermons* (New Rochelle, NY: New City Press, 1993), 184n27. Finn also discusses *agape* meals, and the social tensions these could produce: Finn, *Almsgiving in the Later Roman Empire*, 103–5.
179. *Serm.* 259.5.
180. Hill, in *Sermons (230-272B)*, 184n23. Describing the practice of almsgiving by individuals in Late Antiquity (and with reference to John Chrysostom's preaching), Finn notes the preference of "the well-to-do" to distribute their alms via servants, and suggests this was "on account of the shame or social stigma involved in direct contact with the very poor." Finn, *Almsgiving in the Later Roman Empire*, 101.
181. *Serm.* 259.5.
182. *Serm.* 259.5.

("you turn your faces away, you hold your noses"[183]). However, humility enables us to overcome the prejudices of pride, and to draw near to others, even when this requires us to overcome fears or contravene social norms. Augustine's closing words in this statement also appear to qualify his earlier comments (quoted above) about the "pity" prompted by "calamity."[184] While it may be true that "a common experience of misery" may prompt us to respond generously to others, as Augustine provides instruction on the *agape* meal, he seems to envisage a closer bond still: not just a sympathetic concern for others, but a willingness to be united with them, in a "common humanity."[185] In the physical interaction Augustine commends for the *agape* meal, he suggests something of this bond can be experienced. Within this common bond, rich and poor can transcend the categories of giver and receiver, and instead find that they "are being joined in a real relationship."[186] Christ's lesson of humility brings together those previously divided, enabling them to discover the life they have been gifted in common, and to respond with love.

Conclusion

Amidst contemporary settings of economic inequality, if the church's social task was solely a matter of redistributing material resources, then Augustine's pastoral instruction on pride would appear as redundant moralizing. When handing out emergency food parcels, for example, the question of our attitude and character may seem irrelevant to this task—surely the important thing is getting the job done? However, Augustine's teaching indicates how pride can divide us, even in the act of giving. Thus, if we share Augustine's concern for the growth of charity, and the nurture of a common life oriented toward God, then his teaching on this subject remains indispensable for us.

Pride results in social division, as noted in this chapter. The proud person cannot recognize their neighbor as their equal, instead trying to assert their unique superiority, and regarding others below them with disdain. Those with wealth are particularly susceptible to pride; their resources and status can lead them to look down upon the poor, as if from a great height. However, Augustine's teaching also alerts us to the possibility of pride among the poor, where contemptuous attitudes distance them from the rich. Furthermore, Augustine reminds us that pride can even co-opt our efforts to serve our neighbor. His teaching on this theme remains remarkably salient today, where church projects to "serve the poor" can demonstrate a blind spot regarding the dynamics of pride. For in the act of serving, our unexamined assumptions of superiority can be reinforced. Because we have provided a meal or resources to another, we may assume that we have more to

---

183. *Serm.* 102.4.
184. *Serm.* 259.3.
185. *Serm.* 259.3, 5.
186. *Serm.* 259.5.

offer than they do; that somehow our life experience counts more than theirs does; that there is little that we can receive from them. Those we serve become simply the objects of our ministry, rather than neighbors that we regard as equals. At a broader level, where churches struggle with numerical decline and diminishing status, there can be great appeal in service projects that enable us to "make a difference"—yet is it genuine regard for the neighbor that prompts our service, or a desire to reassure ourselves of the church's importance? Pride can turn actions supposedly intended to benefit our neighbor into occasions that instead enhance our own status and sense of self-importance. As Augustine cautions his monastic community, "pride lies in ambush even for good deeds in order to destroy them."[187]

How can we escape this pitfall? Augustine's teaching reminds us that this proud distancing from our neighbor is inextricably bound up with our proud departure from God. Overcoming pride, therefore, is not simply a matter of changing our attitude, or adopting a different methodology. Instead, we must heed Augustine's instruction: "Learn to be poor and abandon yourselves to God."[188] This lesson is not self-taught. Rather, we receive this learning from Christ, who has come in humble poverty to cure our pride. Accepting Christ as teacher and healer is itself an act of humility, in which we acknowledge ourselves as students in need of instruction, as patients in need of healing. The humble Christ attends to our pride in a variety of ways. His human life of faithful dependence upon God challenges our attempts to assert a life independent of God. Christ's willing acceptance of a life of poverty undermines assumptions of superiority derived from status indicators of wealth, employment, or education. And Christ instructs us in humility through everyday interactions with other members of his body, the church, where we become companions with those of different social backgrounds. As in Augustine's monastic community, humility is the profit we gain when we are drawn together, rich and poor, into a common life.[189]

However, as earlier noted, humility is not an end itself, but rather a means of healing, directed toward the restoration of our love for God and neighbor. As our proud self-exaltation is overcome, we rediscover how to live before God with a rightly ordered love. As we relinquish the quest for God-like status, we rediscover the common humanity we share with our neighbor. Whereas we once may have regarded our neighbor with disdain, or had seen them simply as the beneficiary of our ministry, love enables us to recognize and value our neighbors as equals. And as Augustine's teaching in *Sermon* 14 suggests, as we "learn to be poor," we become members of Christ, "the poor man."[190] Here, the pursuit of a self-centered existence is abandoned, as we discover a new corporate identity shared with other members, who may be richer or poorer than us, but with whom we are being bound together by a common love.

187. *Reg.* 3: 1.7.
188. *Serm.* 14.2.
189. *Reg.* 3: 1.6.
190. *Serm.* 14.2, 9.

Chapter 6

SHEPHERDING THE COMMUNITY

All the same, he [the superior] should consider himself lucky not in having power over you but in being able to care for you with love. Before you he has to be at your head in honor; before God, he should be prostrate at your feet in fear. He should show himself to all around as a model of good works.

—*Reg. 3:* 7.3.

When preaching at a bishop's ordination in Fussala in 411, Augustine draws attention to the self-giving love of Christ, who "*laid down his life for us*" (1 Jn 3:16).[1] The ministry of Christ, characterized by love and servanthood, is a fitting emphasis for the occasion, reminding the new bishop, along with the congregation, of the distinctive pattern that defines pastoral ministry and leadership within the church.

However, as this sermon indicates, Augustine is aware that church leaders do not always follow the servant example of Christ, instead using their office for personal gain.[2] In their public role, church leaders are exposed to many temptations, including the allure of status, the love of praise, and the use of power for one's own benefit. Instead of shepherding their congregation toward love of God and neighbor, such leaders provide their flock (and the wider public) with visible

---

1. *Serm.* 340A.3. Hill provides the date and location for this sermon in *Sermons (306–340A) on the Saints*, trans. Edmund Hill, ed. John E. Rotelle, vol. 9, *The Works of Saint Augustine, Part 3: Sermons* (Hyde Park, NY: New City Press, 1994), 295, 307n1. For Latin text, see Augustine, *Sermones Post Maurinos Reperti*, ed. Germani Morin, vol. 1, *Miscellanea Agostiniana* (Rome: Typis Polyglottis Vaticanis, 1930), 563–75. For a description of Fussala, see Lancel, *Saint Augustine*, 252–3. Van der Meer describes Augustine's approach to ordination sermons (including comment on this sermon): Van der Meer, *Augustine the Bishop*, 256–8.

2. *Serm.* 340A.4. Unfortunately the bishop being ordained on this occasion may have taken a similar path, which lends poignancy to Augustine's sermon. Although scholarship is not unanimous on this sermon's provenance, it is generally agreed that it was delivered at the ordination of Antoninus as bishop of Fussala; see Hill's note (including mention of Lambot's differing view): *Sermons (306-340A)*, 307n1. For detailed discussion of Antoninus's controversial ministry, see Lancel, *Saint Augustine*, 252–7. See also McLynn, "Administrator: Augustine in His Diocese," 318–21.

examples of a church compromised by worldly self-interest. Such issues persist today, where amidst the economic inequalities of our time, pastors can experience the pull toward success and upward mobility no less than their parishioners.

In this chapter I discuss particular manifestations of private self-interest that Augustine associates with pastoral ministry. Addressing such temptations, Augustine teaches listeners that the call to pastoral leadership is not an opportunity for seeking one's *"own advantage"* (Phil. 2:21); rather, it is an invitation to serve others, just as Christ served us.[3] Furthermore, this call questions our desire for contemplative seclusion, reminding us of the needs of others, and the messiness of life in the Christian community.[4] Meditation on Christ's commission to Peter reminds us that our love for Christ is displayed in our love for his sheep (Jn 21:15–17)—a paradigmatic text for pastoral ministry that again directs us to the needs of others.[5] Thus, although the church is often drawn toward power and prosperity, Christ calls us to a different path, marked by service, generosity, and above all, love. In this respect, pastors too are called toward a love that *"does not seek its own* (1 Cor 13:5)."[6] I consider these themes in this chapter, and with particular reference to *Sermon* 340A, trace the formational movement from private self-interest to love of God and neighbor in Augustine's teaching on pastoral ministry.

Self-Serving Shepherds

Preceding Augustine's sermon, the congregation have heard Paul's instruction to Timothy on the qualities needed for bishops (1 Tim. 3:1–7).[7] Augustine notes that this passage includes cautionary words on the danger of pride to bishops: a bishop should be *"Not a new convert, in case being lifted up in pride he should fall into the judgment of the devil* (1 Tm 3:6)."[8] He reminds listeners that "pride is a great vice," and describes the role of pride in the fall of the devil and of Adam and Eve.[9] Therefore, those appointing someone for "a position of eminence" within the church need to exercise careful discernment, lest the new bishop succumb to pride, and share the devil's fate.[10]

Within the context of this ordination sermon, the particular manifestation of pride that concerns Augustine is the desire to attain episcopal office for one's own benefit—accruing status and privileges for oneself—rather than for the benefit of others.[11] In Augustine's context, this position of pastoral responsibility may have

---

3. *Serm.* 340A.4, 1.
4. *Serm.* 78.6.
5. *Serm.* 340A.3.
6. *Reg. 3:* 5.2.
7. *Serm.* 340A.2.
8. *Serm.* 340A.2.
9. *Serm.* 340A.1. See Chapter 5 for further discussion of this section of this sermon.
10. *Serm.* 340A.2.
11. *Serm.* 340A.4–5.

held much allure. Describing Augustine as the "spiritual governor of the town," Van der Meer observes that Augustine "could have had an easy life, if he had wanted it, and even a pleasant one."[12] Van der Meer also notes Augustine's interactions with high-ranking officials, and comments that "the great men of Africa were for the most part known to him personally."[13] However, the social status of this episcopal office must be understood against the backdrop of the complex and changing relationship between church leaders and wider society in this period. In *Through the Eye of a Needle,* Brown extensively documents this change. In 313, Constantine had included clergy in a provision that exempted them "from many forms of public service" and "certain forms of personal taxation."[14] While Brown observes that "these privileges contributed greatly to the social status of the clergy," he also notes that "they did not place Christian bishops and clergymen anywhere near the top of Roman society."[15] Furthermore, in granting this exemption, Constantine's expectation was that clergy would be focused on the needs of the poor, and indeed, would come from the lower classes themselves.[16] Within the social fabric of Roman society, Brown notes, church leaders were expected to be "unobtrusive," "'social paupers' compared with the real leaders of society."[17] However, by the early fifth century, Brown explains, "the social and cultural gap between the civic upper classes of the cities and the personnel of the Christian church had shrunk."[18] Additionally, while bishops (unlike clergy) were now being recruited from upper classes,[19] in Africa, the numerous rural episcopates allowed those of lower class background to become bishops, and thus enabling rapid social advancement—as was notably the case for Antoninus in Fussala.[20]

---

12. Van der Meer, *Augustine the Bishop*, 255. See also Brown, *Augustine of Hippo*, 189–90.
13. Van der Meer, *Augustine the Bishop*, 245.
14. Brown, *Through the Eye of a Needle*, 35. Brown notes that this ruling freed clergy from the time-consuming burden of civic duties, granting them "the precious commodity of leisure" (p. 35). For a more detailed account of this law, its implications for clergy, and subsequent developments, see Angelo Di Berardino, "The Poor Must Be Supported by the Wealth of the Churches (*Codex Theodosianus* 16.2.6)," in *Prayer and Spirituality in the Early Church, Volume 5: Poverty and Riches*, ed. Geoffrey D. Dunn, David Luckensmeyer, and Lawrence Cross (Strathfield, NSW: St Pauls Publications, 2009), 249–68. Di Berardino observes that "the exemption immediately encouraged more requests from Christians to be received into the clergy for the privileges that could be obtained" (p. 257).
15. Brown, *Through the Eye of a Needle*, 36.
16. Brown, *Through the Eye of a Needle*, 43–4; Di Berardino, "The Poor Must Be Supported by the Wealth of the Churches," 259–60.
17. Brown, *Through the Eye of a Needle*, 44. Thus, as Brown later indicates, despite the perceived status of bishops, their influence in society remained limited (pp. 380–4). See also Lancel, *Saint Augustine*, 260–1.
18. Brown, *Through the Eye of a Needle*, 356–7.
19. Brown, *Through the Eye of a Needle*, 357, 343–4.
20. Brown, *Through the Eye of a Needle*, 337–8, 343–4.

Yet to seek out the office of bishop for the status or benefits it offers contradicts the nature of this role. Indeed, the very title of this office indicates that it involves care and concern for others, as Augustine sometimes notes. "'Bishop' is a word coming from the Greek *episkopos*," he explains in one sermon, noting that it "can be translated 'superintendent' or 'overseer.'"[21] Augustine appears to assume this understanding in *Sermon* 340A when he observes that some who hold the office of bishop act in contradiction of their title; he likens this situation to a beggar whose name is "Felix" ("Lucky"), yet whose circumstances are "unlucky [*infelix*]."[22] So also the case of a person who is a bishop in name only: "What does the honor of the name confer on him, but an aggravation of his crime?" Augustine asks.[23] Exploring further this inconsistency between title and reality, Augustine explains to the congregation that the person who is addressed as "bishop" yet "isn't one really" is "the one who enjoys his status more than the welfare and salvation of God's flock, who at this pinnacle of the ministry *seeks his own advantage, not that of Jesus Christ* (Phil 2:21)."[24] Here Augustine identifies another instance of the self-interest that draws us away from God and neighbor, in pursuit of our own benefit.[25] In the case of church leaders, however, this self-interest is more clearly revealed, not only because of the public nature of their office, but also because self-serving behavior directly contradicts the commission they have received to tend to "the welfare and salvation of God's flock."[26] Such a bishop has abandoned their calling, and no longer serves Christ and his body, the church.

In *Sermon* 46, Augustine addresses the problem of shepherds who "feed themselves, and not the sheep."[27] This reflection is prompted by Ezekiel 34, where

---

21. *Serm.* 162C(D10/M27).2. For description of Augustine's episcopal responsibilities see Bonner, *St Augustine of Hippo*, 121–7; Harrison, *Christian Truth and Fractured Humanity*, 122–6. Bonner explains that in Augustine's context, "the bishop habitually discharged duties which are today regarded as being those of the parish priest." Bonner, *St Augustine of Hippo*, 121–2. Regarding Augustine's use of paternal language for the role of bishop (including in *Sermon* 340A.7), see Maria Kilby, "Augustine of Hippo on the Bishop as Spiritual Father," in *Studia Patristica 52*, ed. A. Brent and M. Vinzent (Leuven: Peeters, 2012), 235–45.
22. *Serm.* 340A.4 (MA 1:566).
23. *Serm.* 340A.4.
24. *Serm.* 340A.4. For this tendency among bishops see Brown, *Augustine of Hippo*, 192. On the related question of whether this desire for status among bishops also informed their care for the poor, see Brown, *Poverty and Leadership in the Later Roman Empire*, 1, 8–9; Clark, *Christianity and Roman Society*, 109–10. Finn offers a nuanced evaluation of the status of church leaders, their role in almsgiving, and the question of "patronage": Finn, *Almsgiving in the Later Roman Empire*, 203–14.
25. *Serm.* 340A.4. As noted in Chapter 1, O'Donovan argues that Augustine's use of Philippians 2:21 (and also 1 Cor. 13:5) does not contribute "to the concept of perverse *amor sui*." O'Donovan, *Problem of Self-Love*, 106. See Chapter 1 for discussion of this interpretation.
26. *Serm.* 340A.4.
27. *Serm.* 46.2.

God confronts the *"shepherds of Israel"* (v. 2): *"Behold, you consume the milk, and clothe yourselves with the wool, and what is fat you kill, and my sheep you do not feed"* (v.3).[28] Augustine uses the first three phrases of this verse to illustrate the negligence of these shepherds, who seek their own interest, rather than feeding those in their care.

Firstly, Augustine explains to his listeners that the "milk" in Ezekiel 34:3 refers to resources that the congregation provides for the "temporal support and sustenance" of its leader.[29] Receiving such support is legitimate, Augustine acknowledges; those serving the church should be allowed to "receive the supply of their needs from the people."[30] However, ministry should be motivated by love for the sheep, rather than for the material benefits they provide. "Bad shepherds," Augustine observes, focus on "taking the milk" while "neglecting the sheep."[31]

The "wool" signifies the "honor" given to the shepherd.[32] Honor is like a woolen garment that clothes the pastor; beneath this garment, the leader is "just a man," sharing the same human constraints as those he serves.[33] Again, Augustine notes that it is not inappropriate for a congregation to honor their leader.[34] However, leaders who seek out "the privilege of being honored and praised" are like shepherds who "feed themselves and not the sheep."[35] In order to gather "bigger crowds," and to preserve their popularity, such leaders will tell their congregation to "live how you like," and will avoid challenging listeners for fear of losing their approval.[36] Thus, such leaders gladly adorn themselves with the wool their flock gives them, but in so doing, fail to tend to the flock itself.[37]

---

28. *Serm.* 46.2, 3.

29. *Serm.* 46.3. Here, Augustine is reading Ezekiel 34:3 in light of 1 Corinthians 9:7.

30. *Serm.* 46.5. Note Augustine's use of the word "needs" here, which denotes the basic necessities of life, not extravagant excesses (see Chapter 4 for this distinction). Regarding the material support that Augustine received see Possidius, *Life of Saint Augustine*, 23.1–2. For the financial support of clergy and bishops see also Brown, *Poverty and Leadership in the Later Roman Empire*, 20.

31. *Serm.* 46.5. In *The Work of Monks*, Augustine addresses the issue of monastic members who refuse to perform manual labor because they believe they are eligible to live off resources provided by others. In his response, Augustine indicates that preachers are "entitled" to financial support (*Op. mon.* 21.24), but warns that "he who preaches the Gospel for his own needs is convicted of serving mammon, not God" (*Op. mon.* 26.34).

32. *Serm.* 46.6.

33. *Serm.* 46.6.

34. *Serm.* 46.7.

35. *Serm.* 46.6. Augustine himself was particularly sensitive to this temptation in pastoral ministry; see, for example, *Serm.* 340.1. See also *Conf.* 10.36.59, and Lancel, *Saint Augustine*, 224.

36. *Serm.* 46.8.

37. *Serm.* 46.6–8.

The "fat" sheep are the strong and "healthy" members of the flock.[38] While these members may be more resilient than others, having "grown sturdy on the food of truth," they are "killed" by the "bad example" of self-serving shepherds.[39] Augustine explains that when an otherwise healthy member of the congregation sees their leader living badly, the question arises: "If my pastor lives like that, who am I not to behave as he does?"[40] Therefore, even if some sheep survive the neglect of their self-serving shepherd, they are soon killed off by the poor example of the shepherd's life.

In *Sermon* 137, Augustine provides a similar critique of self-interested church leaders. Here, he describes this sort of leader as a "hired hand," according to the typology of John 10:1–16.[41] Unlike shepherds, hired hands "preach the gospel from ulterior motives, seeking from people their own convenience, whether in terms of money, or honors, or human praise."[42] When confronted by a wolf, hired hands abandon their sheep to preserve their own life (Jn 10:12); similarly, self-interested leaders will turn a blind eye to another's wrongdoing if the person is "a personage of some influence in the Church."[43] In fact, Augustine later explains, some church leaders will even willingly collude in the corrupt practices of others. "From their place of eminence in the pulpit," he notes, they preach according to the Scriptures.[44] However, Augustine continues, "They live in such a way that the bishop will be consulted about grabbing someone else's country place, and his advice will be sought about how best to do it."[45] Augustine reveals that he himself has been approached in this way, but insists that "no such person has ever tempted me," explaining that "we are shepherds, not hired hands."[46] Noting this sermon, Brown comments that "the average Christian bishop could have been coopted readily into the little oligarchies of great landowners."[47] Bishops were often asked to mediate legal disputes, and rich and influential leaders in the community would expect bishops to support their interests, in compliance with the conventions of society.[48] And yet Augustine is clear: he is not one of the "hired hands."[49] God has called him to be a shepherd, and therefore Augustine will not be drawn into this culture of self-interest, for he has sheep to feed.

---

38. *Serm.* 46.9.
39. *Serm.* 46.9.
40. *Serm.* 46.9.
41. *Serm.* 137.5.
42. *Serm.* 137.5.
43. *Serm.* 137.12.
44. *Serm.* 137.14.
45. *Serm.* 137.14.
46. *Serm.* 137.14.
47. Brown, *Augustine of Hippo*, 192.
48. Brown, *Augustine of Hippo*, 190, 192. See notes in Chapter 2 for discussion of this episcopal responsibility and for secondary sources.
49. *Serm.* 137.14; see also *Conf.* 11.2.3.

Leaders as Servants

Becoming a bishop for one's own advantage is just as incongruous as becoming a disciple of Jesus in pursuit of status. In *Sermon* 340A, Augustine reminds the congregation of the disciples' quarrel for greatness, and the "appetite for superiority" it revealed (Lk. 9:46).[50] He notes how Jesus, recognizing the disciples' prideful desire for their "own power," instructs them in humility, by directing them toward the example of the children among them (Mt. 18:3).[51] Furthermore, Jesus teaches the disciples, they should not seek to become lords, but servants: "*Whoever wishes to be the greater among you will be your servant* (Mk 10:44)."[52]

In the Christian community, the vocation of leadership is not a call to power and prestige, but an invitation to service. Although a bishop "presides over the people," they are "the servant of many masters," Augustine explains.[53] Perhaps church leaders in the audience would be reluctant to embrace such a definition. However, Augustine teaches, leaders are to serve those in their care, not only because Christ instructs us to, but because Christ has served us.[54] Therefore, a bishop should not "disdain to be the servant of many people, because the Lord of lords did not disdain to serve us."[55] Christ's servant example radically reconfigures our understanding of Christian leadership. In calling bishops to become servants, Augustine is not inviting the rest of the congregation to become masters. "We are your servants," he acknowledges, "but all of us here have one Lord and master."[56] The bishop is thus a servant amongst "fellow servants," a subject of the just lordship of Christ, not the tyranny of human masters.[57]

---

50. *Serm.* 340A.1.
51. *Serm.* 340A.1. Noting that Augustine interweaves all three synoptic gospels in his recounting of this story, Hill suggests that (at least on this occasion) he is preaching from "a harmony of the gospels." *Sermons (306–340A)*, 307n2.
52. *Serm.* 340A.2. Pellegrino surveys this theme of servanthood in Augustine's teaching on pastoral ministry: Michele Pellegrino, *The True Priest: The Priesthood as Preached and Practised by St Augustine*, trans. Arthur Gibson (Langley, UK: St Paul Publications, 1968), 57–88. In relation to this emphasis, Pellegrino notes that Augustine focuses on the "social function" of pastoral ministry (i.e., the relationship of the priest/bishop to the rest of the church community)(pp. 23–4, 57–8). Augustine also uses the phrase "servants of God" to refer to Christians living an ascetic or monastic life (e.g., *Serm.* 355.2). For Augustine's varied use of this phrase see Van der Lof, "Threefold Meaning of Servi Dei," 43–59; Lawless, *Augustine of Hippo and His Monastic Rule*, 55.
53. *Serm.* 340A.1; see also *Conf.* 10.4.6.
54. *Serm.* 340A.3.
55. *Serm.* 340A.1.
56. *Serm.* 340A.3.
57. *Serm.* 340A.3. Beaver notes that in his letters, Augustine describes himself as "*servus servorum Christi.*" Beaver, "Servus Servorum Christi," 188.

Augustine explores further the servanthood of Christ, who "*did not come to be served, but to serve*" (Mk 10:45).[58] "Let's inquire what service he performed," Augustine invites the congregation.[59] He notes that day-to-day tasks (such as meal arrangements) were often attended to by the disciples, rather than Jesus, so "the service he performed" was not simply the undertaking of servant-like tasks.[60] Instead, Augustine looks to the second part of Mark 10:45, where Christ indicates that he came "*to give his life as a redemption for many.*"[61] Christ served us by giving his life for us, and it is this deeper expression of servanthood that guides our own. First John 3:16 underscores this teaching for Augustine: "*Christ laid down his life for us: in the same way we too ought to lay down our lives for the brethren.*"[62]

In laying his life down for us, Christ teaches us humility (see Chapter 5), a lesson that church leaders need to learn also. In *Sermon* 340A, Augustine invites the one who is "called a bishop" to join him in this "school," where together they can receive instruction from Christ.[63] He recalls the request of the mother of James and John, who asks Jesus to grant her sons positions of status in his kingdom (Mt. 20:20–23).[64] In response, Jesus addresses the two disciples: "*You do not know what you are asking for. And he added, Can you drink the cup which I am going to drink?*" (v. 22).[65] This interaction prompts Augustine to reflect further on the lesson learned from Christ, who is "a teacher of humility both by word and deed."[66] On this occasion, he emphasizes that while Christ "hadn't lost his power," he chose the path of humility in order to benefit us.[67] Augustine then returns to the image of the cup that Jesus spoke of to the disciples (Mt. 20:22): "This then is what we should pay attention to in the Lord; let us mark his humility, let us drink the cup of his humiliation, let us constrict ourselves to his limits, let us meditate on him."[68] To "drink the cup" of Christ is to imbibe his humility, no longer grasping for God-like power and status, but rather accepting the constrictions of humanity, as Christ did for us. For those in pastoral leadership, Augustine clearly spells out the implications of sharing in this cup: "It's easy enough to think about grandeur, easy enough to enjoy honors, easy enough to give our ears to yes-men and flatterers. To put up with abuse, to listen patiently to reproaches, to pray for the insolent, that is the Lord's cup, that is sharing the Lord's table."[69] Sharing Christ's cup entails not

---

58. *Serm.* 340A.3.
59. *Serm.* 340A.3.
60. *Serm.* 340A.3.
61. *Serm.* 340A.3.
62. *Serm.* 340A.3. See also Augustine's discussion of 1 John 3:16 and laying down one's life in *Tract. ep. Jo.* 5.11, 12; 6.1.
63. *Serm.* 340A.4.
64. *Serm.* 340A.5.
65. *Serm.* 340A.5.
66. *Serm.* 340A.5.
67. *Serm.* 340A.5.
68. *Serm.* 340A.5. Earlier in this section Augustine identifies this cup with the cup of Jesus's Gethsemane prayer (Mt. 26:39).
69. *Serm.* 340A.5.

self-exaltation, but rather "humiliation"; it brings not the expansion of one's power, but its limitation.[70] It results not in popular approval, but opposition and insult. Sharing this cup is costly. Yet Christ has drunk this cup for us, and we are called to respond in kind.[71]

The Burden of Love

The office of pastoral leadership, rightly conceived, is for the benefit of others, not one's own. In *Sermon 46*, Augustine is insistent on this point, noting that while he and other bishops benefit from becoming Christians, they do not gain personally from becoming bishops: "Being Christians is for our sake; being in charge is for yours. It is to our advantage that we are Christians, only to yours that we are in charge."[72] People are not appointed to pastoral leadership for "their own advantage," he reiterates, but rather for the benefit of those whom they have been called to serve.[73] Pastoral leaders may have unique roles and responsibilities, but the love that forms the Christian community—the love that "*does not seek its own*"—must form the leaders also, even in the very exercise of their duties.[74]

In the *Rule*, Augustine is clear that "love," and not "power," should guide leaders within the monastic community.[75] The superior "should consider himself lucky not in having power over you but in being able to care for you with love."[76] As Mary notes, if there is "privilege" in the superior's role, it is found "in having boundless opportunities for service."[77] Augustine also explains to members of the monastery that although the superior may appear to have an honored place among them,

---

70. *Serm.* 340A.5. McLynn's article highlights limitations of Augustine's role and influence. McLynn, "Administrator: Augustine in His Diocese," 310–22.

71. Augustine emphasizes this with quotation of Proverbs 23:1–2 (LXX), which fittingly uses the language of hospitality to invite our response: "*Have you been invited by a greater personage? Consider that you are obliged to prepare the same kind of thing*" (*Serm.* 340A.5). See also Augustine's reflections on this proverb in *Serm.* 28A(D9/M24).4–8; 304.1.

72. *Serm.* 46.2.

73. *Serm.* 46.2. Pellegrino notes the rhetorical phrase Augustine sometimes employs to make this point: "We are at your head, but only if we are at your side (*praesumus, sed si prosumus*)" (citing *Serm.* 340A.3). Pellegrino, *True Priest*, 59.

74. *Reg.* 3: 5.2.

75. *Reg.* 3: 7.3. Markus contrasts Augustine's conception of monastic leadership and obedience with that of other expressions of monasticism from this period: Markus, *End of Ancient Christianity*, 162–4. He observes that Augustine conceives of leadership in relation to (and in service of) the wider community, with a corresponding emphasis regarding the obedience of members (p. 163). For Augustine's teaching on monastic leadership and obedience, see also Zumkeller, *Augustine's Ideal of the Religious Life*, 159–65.

76. *Reg.* 3: 7.3.

77. Mary, *The Rule of Saint Augustine*, 302.

"before God, he should be prostrate at your feet in fear."[78] "The person having responsibility stands not at the top of the religious community but at its basis," Van Bavel observes.[79] A right understanding of their role in relation to God enables the superior to serve other members with love and humility.

The mention of the superior's "fear" reflects Augustine's belief that church leaders are accountable to God for those in their care.[80] Later in this same precept, Augustine tells members that the superior "should seek rather your love than your fear, always bearing in mind the account he will have to render to God for you."[81] Awareness of this responsibility that the superior bears on their behalf should elicit the cooperation and support of the other members, Augustine instructs in the next rule: "This is why, by being the more obedient, you show compassion not only to yourselves but also to him, for the higher the position held among you the greater the peril to him who holds it."[82] As the superior's leadership is defined by love, so too the response of the members; Van Bavel explains that "for Augustine, being obedient is primarily an act of love for another."[83] Or, as Augustine himself puts it, "obedience is the daughter of charity."[84] Similar emphases arise in the *Sermons* as Augustine clarifies the nature of his pastoral role. "His [the Lord's] mercy knows, under whose eyes I tremble like this, that I am led on by the duty of love to say these things to you," Augustine concludes in *Sermon* 114B(D5/M12), "and that I am driven by the dread I feel, knowing that I am going to have to give an account to the Lord himself for you all."[85] As with the *Rule*, although Augustine may appear to have an honored position as he preaches, he is motivated by love and a weighty sense of responsibility for those in his care.[86] Again, like the *Rule*, he invites the cooperation of the congregation. "Please give me your help by both your prayers and your obedience," he requests in *Sermon* 340.[87] By supporting each other in prayer "with the perfect love of charity," together pastor and pastored will come to enjoy life in God's company.[88]

In the *Sermons*, Augustine often describes the office of pastoral leadership as a "burden."[89] Preaching on the occasion of his ordination anniversary, Augustine begins: "This particular day, brothers and sisters, is a serious warning to me to think

---

78. *Reg. 3*: 7.3.
79. Van Bavel, "Evangelical Inspiration of the Rule," 97.
80. *Reg. 3*: 7.3.
81. *Reg. 3*: 7.3.
82. *Reg. 3*: 7.4. Van Bavel similarly notes the agreement between Augustine's teaching in the *Sermons* and the *Rule* on this theme: Van Bavel, "Evangelical Inspiration of the Rule," 98. See also Augustine's teaching on Hebrews 13:17 in *Serm.* 82.15.
83. Van Bavel, "Evangelical Inspiration of the Rule," 98.
84. *Serm.* 359B(D2/M5).12.
85. *Serm.* 114B(D5/M12).16.
86. *Reg. 3*: 7.3.
87. *Serm.* 340.3.
88. *Serm.* 340.4.
89. *Serm.* 339.1. For discussion of this theme, and the various aspects of this pastoral "burden," see George Lawless, "Augustine's Burden of Ministry," *Angelicum* 60 (1984): 295–306. Beaver notes practical measures taken later in Augustine's ministry to reduce this load: Beaver, "Servus Servorum Christi," 204–6.

very carefully about the burden I carry."[90] This "burden" lies in the "account" he will need to offer to God for those in his care.[91] On this occasion, Augustine associates this responsibility with the "*lookout*" of Ezekiel 33:2-7, who is charged with the task of warning God's people of impending danger.[92] According to this Ezekiel passage, Augustine observes, if he delivers the necessary warning, he can say, "I have done my part."[93] But even if he himself has been "reassured," concern remains for those in his care: "I have no wish for my glory to be accompanied by your punishment. Yes indeed, I have been given my reassurance, but charity makes me anxious."[94] The burden Augustine experiences, then, is less to do with the performance of duties, as the weight of charity for others, and concern for their reconciliation with God. As Augustine comments in another ordination anniversary sermon, "This burden of mine, you see, about which I am now speaking, what else is it, after all, but you?"[95] Shouldering the task of pastoral leadership therefore involves bearing others and their burdens with love, taking upon oneself a genuine concern for their well-being and their standing before God.

Descending the Mountain

Power and status are not the only temptations that can lure church leaders away from the needs of those in their care. The desire for a life of contemplative seclusion can also be a distraction if it distances us from others and their needs. Augustine hints at this concern in *Sermon* 340A when he states that Christ's "professorial chair [*cathedra*] is in heaven, precisely because his cross was first of all on earth."[96] Here, Augustine is reminding the congregation that, as students together under Christ, they are learning from a teacher who is unlike the self-interested bishops previously described. For Christ teaches them "the way of humility; coming down from heaven to go up again later; visiting those who were laid low in the depths, and raising up those who were willing to join him."[97] Christ has gained his position, not by setting himself apart from a needy world, but by dwelling amongst it, standing alongside the lost and the lowly, even laying down his life for them.

Augustine explores this theme more directly when preaching on the transfiguration (Mt. 17:1-8) in *Sermon* 78. Jesus has led Peter, James, and John

---

90. *Serm.* 339.1.
91. *Serm.* 339.1. Brown comments on this aspect of Augustine's preaching: Brown, *Augustine of Hippo*, 191.
92. *Serm.* 339.2.
93. *Serm.* 339.2.
94. *Serm.* 339.2. See also *Serm.* 17.2.
95. *Serm.* 340.1.
96. *Serm.* 340A.4 (MA 1:566). Clark notes that a "*cathedra*" was used by "emperor," "bishop," and "professor" alike. Clark, *Christianity and Roman Society*, 7.
97. *Serm.* 340A.4.

away from the crowds, and up a mountain (v. 1), where the disciples gain a glorious vision of Christ transfigured, and in the company of Moses and Elijah (vv. 2–3).[98] In response, Peter exclaims, "*Lord, it is good for us to be here*," and offers to build shelters for Jesus, Moses, and Elijah (v. 4).[99] Augustine explains the motivation for Peter's response: "He was finding the crowds a dreadful bore, he had discovered the solitude of the mountain, where he could have Christ to himself as the bread of the spirit. Why go down from there to toil and trouble, while he was experiencing there for God such sacred affection, and hence such virtuous dispositions?"[100] By offering to construct shelters, Peter expresses his desire to remain upon the mountaintop, exchanging toil among the crowds for a life of solitude, with "Christ to himself."

Although Jesus does not reply to Peter's request, Augustine addresses the disciple himself, in a stirring passage:

> Come down, Peter. You were eager to go on resting on the mountain; come down, *preach the word, press on in season, out of season, censure, exhort, rebuke in all long-suffering and teaching* (2 Tm 4:2). Toil away, sweat it out, suffer some tortures, so that by means of the brightness and beauty of right and good activity, you may come to possess in charity what is to be understood by the Lord's white garments. We heard the praises of charity, you see, when the apostle was being read: *It does not seek its own advantage* (1 Cor 13:5). It does not seek its own advantage, because it gives away what it possesses.[101]

While Peter's request may be pious, Augustine nonetheless reprimands him, for he has his own interests in view. Withdrawing from the crowds to a life of solitude may have been edifying for Peter, but it would not benefit others. This is not the way of charity, Augustine reminds the congregation, for charity "*does not seek its own advantage* (1 Cor 13:5)." Zumkeller notes the consonance between Augustine's use of 1 Corinthians 13:5 in the *Rule* and in this sermon; whereas in the former, this verse informs Augustine's efforts to encourage loving service of one another within the monastic community, the latter calls for "service of love" to the wider church.[102]

In this gospel passage, Jesus himself does not remain on the mountain, but instead returns to minister to those in need (Mt. 17:14–18), and to continue his path to the cross (vv. 22–23). Later in this sermon, Augustine reminds the congregation of the downward movement of Christ, who willingly descended into the demands of human existence: "Life came down, to be killed; bread came down, to go hungry; the way came down, to grow weary on a journey; the fountain came

---

98. *Serm.* 78.1–3.
99. *Serm.* 78.3.
100. *Serm.* 78.3.
101. *Serm.* 78.6.
102. Zumkeller, *Augustine's Ideal of the Religious Life*, 199. As Zumkeller explains, an important way in which the monastics served the wider church was through pastoral ministry (pp. 198–9). Commenting on the "lack of education" among clergy in this context, Harrison notes the role of Augustine's monastic community in educating clergy who would then serve the wider church. Harrison, *Christian Truth and Fractured Humanity*, 129.

down, to experience thirst; and are you refusing to endure toil?"[103] In this passage, the humility of Christ challenges not our desire for power or status, but our desire to set ourselves apart from the needs of others, to leave behind the "toil" of the crowds in order to enjoy a quiet life of solitude.

It is this self-serving element of Peter's request that concerns Augustine. The desire to enjoy a life of restful contemplation in God's presence is not wrong in itself. Indeed, Augustine often characterizes the life to come in these terms (see Chapter 4). But in that life, we will not need to absent ourselves from the concerns of others to contemplate God, for none will experience need, and all will enjoy this gift of rest together (again, as noted in Chapter 4). "He was keeping that for you, Peter, after death," Augustine explains.[104] In this life, however, we find ourselves surrounded by others in need, and our present business is to attend to them.

Of course, Augustine's moving address to Peter, inviting him to descend from the mountaintop, suggests something of Augustine's own experience. Contemplative retreat, removed from the busyness of the world, was a well-established ideal among philosophers, and had been very attractive to Augustine.[105] In Milan, Augustine and his friends had "expressed detestation for the storms and troubles of human life," and began plans for "withdrawing from the crowds and living a life of contemplation [*otiose*]."[106] Although these plans were not realized, after his conversion, Augustine continued to seek opportunities for retreat and reflection, first at Cassiciacum, where he retired with friends, then at Thagaste, where he established a Christian community.[107] "A total intention to 'be at leisure and see that you are God' (Ps. 45: 11) was born in me," Augustine recalls, discussing his Cassiciacum retreat.[108] However, these aspirations were unexpectedly upended in 391 when the Hippo congregation compelled Augustine to become their priest.[109] Some commentators indicate the decisiveness of this event: "His ordination meant the abandonment of an ideal."[110] "The life of contemplation was over."[111]

103. *Serm.* 78.6.
104. *Serm.* 78.6.
105. Harrison, *Christian Truth and Fractured Humanity*, 6–7, 177–8. Harrison explains that "the philosopher, like the ascetic, traditionally led a life of self-denial, of withdrawal from society, in order to purify himself morally and intellectually for the task he had undertaken—the pursuit of wisdom" (p. 6). See also Clark, *Christianity and Roman Society*, 62–4, 74–7.
106. *Conf.* 6.14.24 (JO 1:70). For the concept of "*otium*," see Brown, *Through the Eye of a Needle*, 164; Lawless, *Augustine of Hippo and His Monastic Rule*, 51–2.
107. See description of these communities in Brown, *Through the Eye of a Needle*, 163–70; Zumkeller, *Augustine's Ideal of the Religious Life*, 7–13, 24–32. Scholars have debated whether these two communities established after Augustine's conversion (at Cassiciacum and Thagaste) should be considered a continuation of his previous aspirations for a philosophical retreat, or whether Augustine's monastic vision can already be observed here, as Harrison explains: Harrison, *Christian Truth and Fractured Humanity*, 178–82.
108. *Conf.* 9.2.4.
109. Bonner, *St Augustine of Hippo*, 111–12. For Augustine's account, see *Serm.* 355.2.
110. Burnaby, *Amor Dei*, 50.
111. Van der Meer, *Augustine the Bishop*, 5. See also Lancel, *Saint Augustine*, 151; Pellegrino, *True Priest*, 22–5.

This change should not be overemphasized. For example, Lawless observes that while Augustine held pastoral ministry in highest regard, he himself continued to feel drawn toward the contemplative life.[112] Thus Lawless finds here an ongoing "tension" in Augustine's life as priest and bishop.[113] And of course, Augustine managed to produce a staggering amount of theological writing during the course of his pastoral ministry.[114] However, alongside the consequential event of his ordination, Augustine was coming to a new understanding of the Christian life, and the place of contemplation within it. For example, Burnaby notes Augustine's growing appreciation of the Incarnation, and the lesson of humility that Christ teaches.[115] The significance of this lesson for Augustine's pastoral vocation is suggested in a passage concluding Book Ten of the *Confessions* (also quoted by Burnaby), which follows a meditation on the Incarnation: "Terrified by my sins and the pile of my misery, I had racked my heart and had meditated taking flight to live in solitude. But you forbade me and comforted me saying: 'That is why Christ died for all, so that those who live should not live for themselves, but for him who died for them' (2 Cor. 5:15)."[116] Whether Augustine is indeed referring to his ordination here is unclear,[117] but certainly this example of the humble Christ who "died for all" came to shape his understanding of pastoral ministry (as noted already in this chapter). Similarly, in his narration of Augustine's transition

---

112. Lawless, "Augustine's Burden of Ministry," 296-7; Lawless, *Augustine of Hippo and His Monastic Rule*, 41. Additionally, Lawless argues that the "*otium*" Augustine sought at Thagaste was of "decidedly Christian character," and contrasts with "the leisure of the philosophers." Lawless, *Augustine of Hippo and His Monastic Rule*, 51. This leads Lawless to conclude: "We possess here the seeds of the future bishop's mature thoughts on contemplation" (p. 51). See also Zumkeller, *Augustine's Ideal of the Religious Life*, 10-13, 28-30.

113. Lawless, "Augustine's Burden of Ministry," 296-7. See also Pellegrino, *True Priest*, 35.

114. Lancel describes Augustine's practice of turning to theological reflection in the evening, after completion of episcopal duties: Lancel, *Saint Augustine*, 214-15. Pellegrino notes that Augustine's writing came to be devoted toward the service of the church: Pellegrino, *True Priest*, 45.

115. Burnaby, *Amor Dei*, 70-2. Noting Augustine's earlier "fascination with Neoplatonism," Williams writes the challenge that "the presence of God in a mortal life" poses to our "strength," including "the sense of intellectual or spiritual strength that comes from a visionary metaphysic of the sort Augustine has been exploring." Williams, *On Augustine*, 10-11. As Williams explains, Christ "does indeed communicate wisdom, *sapientia*, but he does so through enabling participation in the pattern of his own entry into time" (p. 11). See also pp. 142-3. For the influence of the Incarnation on Augustine's thought, see also Harrison, *Christian Truth and Fractured Humanity*, 30-3.

116. *Conf.* 10.43.70; Burnaby, *Amor Dei*, 72-3. Regarding the temptations Augustine associated with a return to a "public" role, see Brown, *Augustine of Hippo*, 200-1.

117. Lancel, *Saint Augustine*, 503n22. Burnaby's comments, however, seem to imply that this passage is associated with Augustine's ordination: Burnaby, *Amor Dei*, 73.

to the responsibilities of priesthood, Van der Meer notes his movement from "the schools of philosophy and the eternal Ideas" to "the actualities of ordinary life."[118] This required, amongst other things, a willingness to adapt his teaching to the ordinary needs and abilities of the Hippo congregation, most of whom had received little formal education.[119] Lancel captures well the challenge this presented to Augustine: "someone who knew how to speak before the high and mighty of this world ... now had to envisage speaking before the lowly of Hippo, before fishermen (*piscatores*) who were also sinners (*peccatores*), for whom Christ had come more than for philosophers and the erudite, and whom he had to reach with their own words."[120] This call to humbly serve the church community also came to bear on Augustine's conception of monastic life, as Zumkeller observes: "More and more he recognized that service to the Church was a task pleasing to the will of God, to which the comfortable tranquillity of monastic communities must always give place."[121]

Augustine's understanding of the nature of contemplation in the Christian life also developed significantly.[122] Whereas earlier in life, Augustine had believed that contemplation of God could be enjoyed in this life, if only by some, he soon departed from this view.[123] "His ordination to the priesthood in 391 forced a reorientation upon his thought," Burnaby explains, "and he came by degrees to regard the Two Lives as to be lived by all Christians successively rather than by different Christians simultaneously."[124] That is, Augustine now understood the contemplative life as an eschatological goal, no longer the preserve of an elite in

---

118. Van der Meer, *Augustine the Bishop*, 5.

119. Van der Meer, *Augustine the Bishop*, 5–6, 132, 258; Harrison, *Christian Truth and Fractured Humanity*, 22. This challenge was not completely new, for as Brown notes, the diverse company Augustine had gathered at Cassiciacum included some "who were entirely uneducated." Brown, *Through the Eye of a Needle*, 164. See Introduction for the question of the level of education in Augustine's congregation.

120. Lancel, *Saint Augustine*, 151. See also Van der Meer, *Augustine the Bishop*, 6. Augustine's guidelines in *Instructing Beginners in Faith* provide an apposite example of how the Incarnation informed this aspect of his pastoral ministry. See *Catech.* 10.15, and Harrison's discussion: Harrison, *Christian Truth and Fractured Humanity*, 66–7.

121. Zumkeller, *Augustine's Ideal of the Religious Life*, 35. See also Markus's discussion of Augustine's monasticism in relation to other forms of asceticism and monasticism in this period: Markus, *End of Ancient Christianity*, 66–83, 160–2. He uses the images of "the Desert" and "the City" to illustrate the contrast between those who emphasized withdrawal and "spatial separation," and Augustine's monasticism, which could be lived out "within the city" (pp. 160–2).

122. Burnaby traces this development: Burnaby, *Amor Dei*, 60–73. See also Zumkeller's discussion of this development in relation to Augustine's teaching on monastic life: Zumkeller, *Augustine's Ideal of the Religious Life*, 123–4.

123. Zumkeller, *Augustine's Ideal of the Religious Life*, 123; Burnaby, *Amor Dei*, 49–53, 60–73.

124. Burnaby, *Amor Dei*, 63.

this life, but rather the hope of all Christians for the life to come.[125] As *Sermon* 78 illustrates, we should not attempt to attain this contemplative vision now by escaping the needs of the present ("He was keeping that for you, Peter, after death").[126] This teaching is more commonly illustrated in the *Sermons* by the story of Martha and Mary in Luke 10:38–42. Although Martha labors hard with the work of hospitality, it is Mary that Christ commends, for she has chosen to sit and listen to his teaching.[127] In *Sermon* 104, Augustine questions whether, in praising Mary, Christ is also admonishing Martha:

> If that's really the case, let people all give up ministering to the needy; let them all choose the better part, which shall not be taken away from them. Let them devote their time to the word, let them pant for the sweetness of doctrine, let them busy themselves with theology, the science of salvation; don't let them bother at all about what stranger there may be in the neighborhood, who may be in need of bread or who of clothing, who needs to be visited, who to be redeemed, who to be buried. Let the works of mercy be laid aside, everything be concentrated on the one science.[128]

If a life of contemplative repose is our primary purpose in this life, then we could gladly dissociate ourselves from the needs of others. Yet, Augustine teaches his congregation, that is not the nature of this life: "In Martha was to be found the image of things present, in Mary that of things to come. The kind Martha was leading, that's where we are; the kind Mary was leading, that's what we are hoping for; let us lead this one well, in order to have that one to the full."[129] We may desire and anticipate the contemplative life that Mary models, sitting at the feet of Jesus, but the way in which we attain to that life is by following Martha's example, welcoming and serving others in need.

---

125. Burnaby, *Amor Dei*, 50–3, 64–5.
126. *Serm.* 78.6. See also Canning's comments on this theme: Canning, *Unity of Love for God and Neighbour*, 375–7. Augustine's instruction to monastics reflects a similar emphasis, as Zumkeller indicates: Zumkeller, *Augustine's Ideal of the Religious Life*, 124. Zumkeller later acknowledges that Augustine's conception of monastic life features a contemplative dimension (p. 195). He also observes, however, that as Paul's conception of the church as "the Mystical Body of Christ" came to shape Augustine's monastic vision, he increasingly understood monastics to be at the service of this body, of which they too were members (p. 197). Notably, Zumkeller interprets the passage from *Sermon* 78 quoted above in this light: an exhortation, applicable "to Augustine and to his clerics," to loving service of the wider body of Christ (pp. 198–9).
127. E.g., *Serm.* 103.3; 104.1
128. *Serm.* 104.2.
129. *Serm.* 104.4. cf. *Trin.* 1.10.20, and see especially Edmund Hill's comments on Augustine's teaching on Martha and Mary: *The Trinity*, trans. Edmund Hill, ed. John E. Rotelle, 2nd ed., vol. 5, *The Works of Saint Augustine, Part 1: Books* (Hyde Park, NY: New City Press, 2015), 83n56.

Although Augustine does not mention specific leadership roles in these passages from *Sermon* 78 and *Sermon* 104, his mention of preaching, visiting those in need, and burying the dead suggest that his critique has pastoral ministry in view.[130] The call to pastoral ministry is not an invitation to withdraw from the needs of the world, but rather to immerse oneself in them, feeding the hungry with bread for the stomach and nourishment for the soul. Augustine's language—"toil away, sweat it out"—emphasizes that this is arduous and costly work.[131] This includes preaching, which for Augustine is not a private exercise in theological speculation, but rather a weighty task that is borne on behalf of others. He explains this to the congregation on another occasion: "There's nothing better, nothing more pleasant than to search through the divine treasure chest with nobody making a commotion; it's pleasant, it's good. But to preach, to refute, to rebuke, to build up, to manage for everybody, that's a great burden, a great weight, a great labor."[132] Augustine finds great enjoyment in pondering the Scriptures for personal edification; "nobody could outdo me in enjoying such anxiety-free leisure," he claims.[133] But preaching the Scriptures is something altogether different. It requires us to descend from the mountaintop of contemplative solitude to share the wealth of "the divine treasure chest" with others. As Augustine reminds Peter, charity "does not seek its own advantage, because it gives away what it possesses."[134]

Loving the Sheep and the Shepherd

For Augustine, Christ's instruction to Peter to "*Feed my sheep* (Jn 21:15–17)" provides a paradigmatic text for pastoral ministry.[135] In contrast to the hired hands who use church leadership roles to seek their own gain, true pastors are those whose concern is for the sheep, loving them and the God to whom they belong.

---

130. *Serm.* 78.6; 104.2.
131. *Serm.* 78.6.
132. *Serm.* 339.4.
133. *Serm.* 339.4.
134. *Serm.* 78.6.
135. *Serm.* 340A.3. Augustine does not limit this text's application to clergy, however. In *Sermon* 229N, he makes clear that Christ's question, "*Peter, do you love me?*" is addressed to all Christians (*Serm.* 229N.2). See also Canning, *Unity of Love for God and Neighbour*, 281. By locating both sheep and shepherd within the body of Christ (as noted below), Augustine offers an account of pastoral ministry in which the lives of clergy and congregation are mutually bound up in the life of Christ. Commenting on this sermon, Hill observes that Augustine "is certainly no patron of clericalism, of the monopoly of authority in the Church by the clergy." *Sermons (184–229Z)*, 307n4. Canning considers Augustine's teaching on this "Feed my sheep" theme in relation to love of God and neighbor: Canning, *Unity of Love for God and Neighbour*, 277–81.

"*Peter, do you love me?*" Christ asks the disciple.[136] When Peter affirms his love, Christ instructs him, "*Feed my sheep*" (vv. 15–17).[137] By feeding his sheep, we express our love for Christ. We cannot "bestow" any "benefit" upon God, Augustine notes in *Sermon* 340A, for anything that we might offer has already been provided by God.[138] Nor does God, who needs nothing, require our assistance to "become greater."[139] However, Christ's sheep do experience need, and by tending to them with love, we can also offer our love to God.[140] As Canning observes, "'Feed my sheep' indicates the field where a person's love for God can be practised such that something of value can be offered to God."[141]

This rich gospel passage prompts a variety of interrelated teachings in the *Sermons*. In *Sermon* 137, for example, Christ's question to Peter probes the nature of the disciple's love. Here, Augustine has been lamenting those pastors who seek this office "from ulterior motives" rather than from love of God.[142] By contrast, Augustine explains, "the ones who feed the sheep" are "those who preach God because they love God."[143] Accordingly, in Christ's enquiry, "*Do you love me?*" Augustine hears the question, "Are you seeking my interests in the Church and not your own?"[144] Thus, Christ's question asks of the love that motivates the pastor. It is when our love is for Christ, rather than for our own interests, that we are truly able to feed his sheep.

In a sermon preached during the Easter season, Augustine reflects on this instruction to feed Christ's sheep in light of the unity between Christ and his body.[145] He draws on 1 John 4:20 to remind his listeners that their love for God should be evident in love for their neighbor: "We are commanded to love Christ the Lord, whom we can't see; and we all shout and say, 'I love Christ.' *If you do not love the brother whom you can see, how can you love the God whom you cannot see?* (1 Jn 4:20)."[146] He then applies this in pastoral terms: "By loving the sheep, show the love you have for the shepherd; because the very sheep themselves are members of the shepherd."[147] The shepherding metaphor can barely contain the deeper truth Augustine is trying to convey. Love for the sheep expresses our love for God because the sheep and the shepherd are one. Indeed, Christ as shepherd became a

---

136. *Serm.* 340A.3.
137. *Serm.* 340A.3.
138. *Serm.* 340A.3.
139. *Serm.* 296.13.
140. *Serm.* 296.13.
141. Canning, *Unity of Love for God and Neighbour*, 278.
142. *Serm.* 137.9.
143. *Serm.* 137.10.
144. *Serm.* 137.10.
145. *Serm.* 229N.1. See also Canning's comments on Augustine's teaching on this theme in relation to the "*totus Christus*": Canning, *Unity of Love for God and Neighbour*, 279–81.
146. *Serm.* 229N.1. See Chapter 1 for Augustine's use of this verse to discuss love for God and neighbor.
147. *Serm.* 229N.1.

sheep, suffering for the sheep, so that they "might be his members."[148] As a result, to feed Christ's sheep is to feed Christ; to love the sheep is to love the shepherd.

Just as the lives of the sheep are bound up with that of the shepherd, the identity of shepherds (pastors) must also be understood in this way. Augustine explains this effectively in *Sermon* 285 by first considering Peter's threefold denial of Christ (Lk. 22:54–62) that preceded his threefold declaration of love (Jn 21:15–17). Peter had promised Jesus, "*I will lay down my life for you* (Jn 13:37)."[149] However, Peter failed to fulfil this commitment which he had so confidently made, instead denying his Lord. Augustine ascribes this denial to Peter's "self-reliance."[150] In later calling Peter to feed his sheep, Christ invites him to serve in a different manner. "And so when he rises again," Augustine explains, "the Lord entrusts his sheep to Peter, to that one who denied him; but he denied him because he relied on himself; later he would feed his flock as a pastor, because he loved him."[151] The contrast of this statement is between Peter's earlier dependence on self (a form of self-love), and his later love for (and dependence upon) Christ. But in this sermon, the especially striking characteristic that Augustine identifies in Peter's pastoral ministry is his participation in the life of Christ as shepherd. This observation arises from the identification of Christ as "shepherd" in John 10:16, prompting Augustine to clarify how Peter and other "pastors" can also be considered "shepherds."[152] If Christ has instructed Peter, "*Feed my sheep*," then Peter must be a shepherd, Augustine infers, but because Christ describes the sheep as his own, he must be "the real shepherd."[153] Augustine then resolves this question ecclesiologically: "So Peter is a shepherd, not in himself but in the body of the shepherd."[154] In contrast with his earlier attempt to serve Christ by relying his own efforts, Peter now serves in union with his Lord; indeed, from within the very body of Christ. Van Bavel's comment summarizes Augustine's pastoral rendering of the *totus Christus*: "The shepherds themselves are part of the flock and belong also to the sheep, because every Christian is a member of Christ who is the One Shepherd of all."[155]

Preaching on this text in *Sermon* 340A, Augustine again brings the self-giving aspect of pastoral ministry to the fore. Here, he interprets Christ's commission to "*Feed my sheep*" in light of the revelation of Peter's death that immediately follows (Jn 21:18–19): "He prophesied his cross to him, he foretold to him his passion. So it was pointing in that direction that the Lord said, *Feed my sheep*: suffer for

---

148. *Serm.* 229N.1.
149. *Serm.* 285.3.
150. *Serm.* 285.3.
151. *Serm.* 285.3.
152. *Serm.* 285.5.
153. *Serm.* 285.5.
154. *Serm.* 285.5. See also *Serm.* 229N.3.
155. Van Bavel, "The 'Christus Totus' Idea: A Forgotten Aspect of Augustine's Spirituality," 91. While pastoral leadership is a "special" responsibility, Van Bavel adds, "it is Christ himself who works and acts, through and in the leaders of the flock" (p. 91).

my sheep."¹⁵⁶ Feeding the sheep and suffering for the sheep are equated. For it is only by loving the sheep that the sheep are nourished, and this love requires us to lay down our lives. Indeed, this is Augustine's prayer for his own ministry, as he expresses in another sermon: "May the Lord grant us the strength so to love you that we are capable also of dying for you, either in fact or in fellow feeling."¹⁵⁷

Good Examples, Bad Examples

Providing a good example of the Christian life is another way in which church leaders feed the sheep in their care. Augustine's instruction on the servant nature of Christian ministry in *Sermon* 340A (discussed above) reflects this belief. The call to lay down one's life for others is counter-intuitive in a society where pursuit of upward mobility and personal advantage prevails. Accordingly, the church needs visible examples of Christian servanthood to learn from and follow, and as Augustine makes clear in this sermon, Christian leaders are expected to provide such examples.

The responsibility of leadership in the Christian community does not exempt us from the basic responsibilities of the Christian life, nor does it justify a privileged existence (in the manner that some worldly leadership positions might). Augustine is careful to clarify that leaders are subject to the same guidelines as those in their care. In the monastic community, the superior must follow the same rules that guide other members; "he himself should keep these instructions gladly," Augustine states.¹⁵⁸ He provides a practical illustration of this in *Sermon* 356 when discussing the giving of gifts to members of the monastic community. The *Rule* requires that any gifts, even if intended for a specific member, should be "put into the *common stock* so that it may be offered *to anyone who needs it* (Acts 4:32, 35)."¹⁵⁹ Augustine reminds his listeners that he too is subject to this rule, so they should not try to honor him with extravagant gifts: "I don't want your graces to offer me such things as I alone could, as it were, with propriety make use of. I'm offered, for example, a very expensive cloak.... That's not right; I should have the sort of clothes that I can give to my brother, if he hasn't got some."¹⁶⁰ Although many might think bishops are entitled to such privileges, Augustine does not believe that his leadership role elevates him above the rule of life that guides the rest of his community.

For Augustine, such a belief arises not out of an ethical rigorism (as if the credibility of the community depends on the consistency of the leader's example), but rather from the theological conviction that all Christians are equally addressed

---

156. *Serm.* 340A.3.
157. *Serm.* 296.5.
158. *Reg. 3:* 7.3. Similarly, in *Sermon* 340A, Augustine is clear that his instruction on the role of bishop applies to himself also (e.g., *Serm.* 340A.2).
159. *Reg. 3:* 5.3.
160. *Serm.* 356.13. See commentary in Van der Meer, *Augustine the Bishop*, 205-6.

by the same Lord. "Just because we address you from this higher place," Augustine explains to his listeners in another sermon, "it doesn't mean that we are your masters. That one, I mean, is the master of us all, whose chair is above all the heavens; under him we all forgather into one school, both you and we are all fellow pupils."[161] Accordingly, Augustine instructs listeners on another occasion, "I'm not saying listen to me, but with me."[162] Because in preaching Christ addresses the preacher no less than the congregation, they are expected to respond just as faithfully.

Augustine exhorts all mature members of the Christian community (and not just leaders) to provide a positive example to those newer in the faith.[163] However, he nonetheless maintains the expectation that church leaders in particular should be role models of faith. In the *Rule*, Augustine indicates that the superior of the monastery "should show himself to all around as a model of good works."[164] Similarly, when considering leadership in the church community, Augustine recalls Paul's instruction to Titus: "*Offering yourself in all company as an example of good works* (Tit 2:7)."[165] It is not only by preaching that church leaders feed those in their care, but also by their own example. In *Teaching Christianity*, Augustine even goes so far as to say that "whatever the grandeur of the speaker's utterances, his manner of life carries more weight."[166] A faithful life can speak more powerfully than elegant rhetoric.

When discussing the example of church leaders, Augustine sometimes quotes 1 Corinthians 4:16: "*be imitators of me, as I in my turn am of Christ.*"[167] This verse appropriately locates (and qualifies) the example of the leader by placing it in relationship to Christ. Church leaders can nourish their congregation through the example of their own life, but only inasmuch as their example directs the congregation toward Christ. Thus Augustine states on another occasion (speaking of those who might question his own example): "Let them be our imitators, if we are Christ's; but if we are not Christ's, let them be imitators of Christ."[168]

This is an important theological qualification of the role of church leaders as exemplars. For despite his exhortations to leaders to be good role models, Augustine is all too aware that many church leaders neglect those in their care through their bad example. Indeed, the second half of *Sermon* 340A attends to

---

161. *Serm.* 301A.2. For Augustine's homiletical notion of Christ as the "inner teacher," see Introduction, and *Tract. ep. Jo.* 3.13.
162. *Serm.* 261.2.
163. E.g. *Serm.* 228.1.
164. *Reg.* 3: 7.3.
165. *Serm.* 46.9.
166. *Doctr. chr.* 4.27.59; see also *Doctr. chr.* 4.29.61. Possidius notes the beneficial example of Augustine's own "manner of life": Possidius, *Life of Saint Augustine*, 31.8, 9.
167. *Serm.* 179.10.
168. *Serm.* 47.12.

this concern.[169] In one sense, there is no such thing as "bad bishops," Augustine insists, for "if they are bad, they aren't bishops."[170] Yet he concedes this language, and turns to advise the congregation how to live faithfully if they have a bad bishop. Augustine wants to ensure that, regardless of the character of their bishop, the congregation are "without anxiety," and that their "hope should not waver in uncertainty."[171] Reassurance, he teaches, is found in Christ: "The Lord, and bishop of bishops, has given you security, so that your hope should not rest in man."[172] Although the congregation may benefit from the positive example of their leader, their attention should not be on their leader, but on Christ, in whose name their leader serves.[173] It is the food provided for them (Christ) that is important, not the plate the food is served on (the preacher or church leader), be it "a golden vessel," or "an earthenware vessel."[174] "He's the one you must fix your attention on.... He himself is the bread," Augustine explains, with reference to John 6:51.[175] Whether a church leader is good or bad, the congregation should look to Christ for nourishment, and not to the leader.

Augustine offers this theological insight to reassure the congregation that their lives are not jeopardized by bad leaders. Christ himself offered this "reassurance," Augustine suggests, when he instructed his listeners how to respond to their own religious leaders: "*The scribes*, he said, *and the Pharisees*, representing those in authority, *have taken their seat on the chair of Moses; whatever they say, do; but*

---

169. McLynn suggests that in this sermon, Augustine "seems already to expect the worst" regarding Antoninus (the bishop being ordained): McLynn, "Administrator: Augustine in His Diocese," 319. However, while Augustine does draw his cautionary remarks together in a particularly effective manner in this sermon, it remains consistent with his general teaching on pastoral ministry.

170. *Serm.* 340A.6.

171. *Serm.* 340A.8.

172. *Serm.* 340A.8.

173. *Serm.* 340A.8-9; see Émilien Lamirande, "The Priesthood at the Service of the People of God According to Saint Augustine," *The Furrow* 15, no. 8 (1964): 503-4. Pellegrino offers a broader survey of this theme: Pellegrino, *True Priest*, 129-49. He notes the interplay of "divine initiative" and human cooperation in Augustine's account of pastoral ministry (p. 141).

174. *Serm.* 340A.9. The tableware imagery is drawn from 2 Timothy 2:20, which Augustine quotes immediately before this passage. See also *Conf.* 5.6.10. Lamirande notes Augustine's use of the expressions, "dispenser of the Word and the Sacrament" and "minister of the Word and the Sacrament," and highlights the close association between ministry and service. Lamirande, "The Priesthood at the Service of the People of God," 504-5. He explains that "'*dispensator*' usually indicates someone who administers the goods of the Church, one who dispenses, distributes, or confers the gifts of God and thus contains the idea of subordination or of instrumentality" (p. 504).

175. *Serm.* 340A.9.

what they do, do not do; for they say, and do not do (Mt 23:3)."[176] Like the teachers Jesus refers to, some church leaders may not live in accordance with their message; the congregation should not follow their bad example. However, Augustine explains, despite the bad example of the leaders Jesus speaks of, listeners could still be nourished by their words, inasmuch as the leaders were teaching from "the chair of Moses," and not speaking "from what is their own."[177] If a bad bishop is preaching Christ, then, the congregation can still be fed—though Augustine likens the careful discernment required to the delicate task of fetching grapes from a vine growing amidst a thorn bush.[178] Augustine's caution against those who preach "from what is their own" arises from John 8:44: "*The one who speaks a lie is speaking from what is his own.*"[179] By contrast, when preaching is sourced "from the Lord's pantry," it conveys the truth that nourishes the congregation, even if the preacher's own example is lacking.[180]

In his teaching on bad bishops in *Sermon* 340A, Augustine is responding not only to the pastoral concerns of the congregation, but also to the doctrinal concerns prompted by the Donatists, as becomes clear toward the end of the sermon.[181] The Donatists have set themselves apart because they believe the wider church was compromised by "bad bishops" (and in particular, Caecilian).[182] However, even if the leaders the Donatists singled out were bad, Augustine argues that the Donatists should pay heed to Christ's instruction in Matthew 23:3 (as outlined above).[183] A bad bishop should not be imitated, Augustine advises, but "you should listen through him" to Christ.[184] Moreover, Augustine reminds the congregation, their

---

176. *Serm.* 340A.9.
177. *Serm.* 340A.10.
178. *Serm.* 340A.10.
179. *Serm.* 340A.10, 9. Here again, Augustine's theological anthropology is implicit, as his teaching on truth in *Sermon* 28A(D9/M24) makes clear: see *Serm.* 28A(D9/M24).2. "When you pull away, after all, from God's truth, you will remain in your own falsehood," Augustine cautions, with reference to John 8:44 (.2). On Augustine's use of this text, see O'Donovan, *Problem of Self-Love*, 104–5.
180. *Serm.* 340A.9.
181. For comments on Donatism in Fussala, and associated tensions, see McLynn, "Administrator: Augustine in His Diocese," 319–20.
182. *Serm.* 340A.11–12. Regarding Caecilian (Caecilianus), see Lancel, *Saint Augustine*, 164–6. Bonner explains that the Donatists "held that deadly sin on the part of the minister invalidated the sacraments administered by him." Bonner, *St Augustine of Hippo*, 137. For the contrast between the Donatist view of priestly ministry, and that held by Augustine, see Pellegrino, *True Priest*, 142–44.
183. *Serm.* 340A.11. As Hill notes, Augustine does not himself agree with these Donatist accusations: *Sermons (306–340A)*, 307n14.
184. *Serm.* 340A.11.

hope should not be founded upon human leaders.[185] This would not only result in the mistake of the Donatists, where preoccupation with human righteousness or error overshadows the saving, unifying work of Christ.[186] Undue focus on human leaders would also contribute to the unhealthy form of leadership Augustine cautioned against earlier in this sermon, where bishops themselves become objects of honor and devotion, rather than the one who speaks through them.

Augustine thus navigates a careful course as he teaches the congregation about the example of their leaders. On the one hand, church leaders are called to feed the sheep through their good example, demonstrating the servant love of Christ for those in their care. On the other hand, the congregation should not become so focused on the example of their leader (whether good or bad), that their attention becomes diverted from Christ, who alone can truly nourish them.

Conclusion

In our own time, the economic extravagances of celebrity church leaders could be seen as evidence of the church's complicity in the culture of economic inequality, inviting comparison between the humble life of Jesus, and the lavish lifestyles of those who minister in his name. And within the church, instead of helping nurture Christian community amidst economic division, such examples provide a tacit excuse to accept the economic status quo.

The teaching of Augustine traced in this chapter attends to many aspects of pastoral ministry, and is not specific to issues of economic inequality. However, it does clearly illustrate the temptation that private self-interest poses to church leaders. When pastoral ministry is sought with a view to one's own benefit (Phil. 2:21)—be it financial reward, social status, or political power—we set ourselves apart from the Christian community, and indeed, from God. Pastors thus become caught up in the same divisive pattern of sin from which economic inequality derives.

On the face of it, pastoral work may appear a wholly selfless task. Yet, as with any vocation, it can become distracted by self-interested desire. Pastoral roles may not offer exorbitant salaries, yet material advantage can shape our decisions in other ways. Consider, for example, a pastor who receives job offers from two different congregations: one is a vibrant, well-resourced church, offering a full-time role, with support staff and a church vehicle; the other congregation is dwindling, in an under-resourced neighborhood, and only able to offer a part-time position. Augustine acknowledges that it is acceptable for pastors to receive material assistance from their congregation.[187] However, his teaching also alerts us to the possibility that material comfort and security can sometimes be a distraction

---

185. *Serm.* 340A.12.
186. *Serm.* 340A.11–12. See also *Serm.* 198(D26/M62).52–3.
187. *Serm.* 46.3–5.

from the call of Christ. Congregations in both wealthy and poor neighborhoods need people who can preach God's word and gather people around Christ's table. The danger, however, is that pastors become attracted to only one sort of congregation—resulting in another instance of unequal distribution of resources.

Another temptation in ministry to which Augustine's teaching draws attention is that of withdrawal: our desire to escape the commotion of the "crowds," and instead enjoy "the solitude of the mountain."[188] For the contemporary pastor, this can take different forms. For example, in a larger church with a team of staff, we might be inclined to delegate the pastoral work of visiting the sick and needy to others. We withdraw to the executive's desk, from which we formulate strategic plans and vision statements, our schedule clear of the time-consuming task of listening to others. Alternatively, we may see pastoral ministry as a call to contemplation, and spend our time in scholarly reflection in order to evade the crowds. We withdraw to the study, our profound meditations uninterrupted by the complications of parishioners' lives. Of course, both delegation and contemplation have their place in pastoral work; the issue here is the self-interested behavior that they can mask, as we distance ourselves from the needs of our neighbors.

As preceding chapters have noted, sharing in the community that God gathers involves transformation, as our attitudes and desires are challenged and reshaped. Leadership is no exception here. For pastors too are called toward love of God and neighbor, and in Augustine's teaching on pastoral ministry, this teaching is distinctively rendered. Pastors should not preach from their own resources, seeking praise for their own private insight or abilities; rather, they are to supply the community from the common store of "the Lord's pantry," from which they too are nourished.[189] Like shepherds, leaders are to care for Christ's sheep, showing their love for both the sheep, and Christ himself. And like servants, they are to humbly attend to the needs of those in their care, as an expression of gratitude for the one who gave himself for us (1 Jn 3:16). Leaders, and indeed all Christians, are called to this sort of love, because this is the sort of love God displays to us in Christ, and it is on him that our attention should rest.

---

188. *Serm.* 78.3.
189. *Serm.* 340A.9.

Chapter 7

OBSERVING THIS INSTRUCTION WITH LOVE

> May the Lord grant that you observe all these things with love, as lovers of *spiritual beauty*, spreading by your good life *the sweet odor of Christ* (2 Cor 2:15), not like *slaves under the law but as free persons established in grace* (Rom 6:14).
>
> —*Reg. 3:* 8.1.

> When you find that you are doing the things that are written give thanks to the Lord, the giver of all good things.
>
> —*Reg. 3:* 8.2.

At the conclusion of the *Rule*, Augustine invites the monastic community to reflect on their lives in light of the instruction he has provided.[1] This exercise might prompt them to consider whether they have been united in heart and soul, or divided by private concerns.[2] They might ponder their sharing of resources, and the resentment this may have stirred within them.[3] Has their life together been formed by that love which "*does not seek its own* (1 Cor 13:5)," or have they put "personal advantage before the common good"?[4] Where they have succeeded in observing the *Rule*, Augustine instructs them to "give thanks to the Lord, the giver of all good things."[5] And when they have "failed," they should seek God's forgiveness and his assistance for the future.[6]

In this concluding chapter, I explore the question of how the Christian community understands its efforts to live with love in an economically unequal society. If, for example, we can observe economic divisions being overcome within our community, how do we acknowledge and attribute such success? If invited to tell the story of this work to others (e.g., at a conference, or in a newsletter), what story do we tell? If we can only see signs of failure, the absence of any discernible change, how do we respond to this struggle?

---

1. *Reg. 3:* 8.2.
2. *Reg. 3:* 1.2; 5.2.
3. *Reg. 3:* 1.3–4; 3.3–5.
4. *Reg. 3:* 5.2.
5. *Reg. 3:* 8.2.
6. *Reg. 3:* 8.2.

Here again, Augustine's caution against self-reliance and call toward love of God and neighbor is pertinent. For even our pursuit of a life of Christian virtue can become an occasion to assert ourselves, rather than depend upon God. Yet, as I demonstrate in this chapter, a life that claims its own goodness independent of God is not a life of love. Instead, we must acknowledge our reliance upon God for our goodness: a dependence that the church expresses in its practices of prayer. Moreover, we cannot manufacture love, for it comes to us as God's gift (Rom. 5:5). A life inhabited by this love lives in gratitude for the work of God's goodness within.

In his *Sermons* Augustine explores these themes more expansively than in the *Rule*, and in this chapter, I give particular attention to *Sermon* 348A(D30).[7] Augustine preached this sermon in Hippo in 416, as news of debates with Pelagius was beginning to reach his congregation.[8] In this sermon, Augustine alerts listeners to his concerns about Pelagius's teaching, and reminds them of their dependence upon God's grace. In this chapter, however, I do not attempt to cover Augustine's debate with Pelagius and his followers, nor do I enter into the labyrinthine discussions of free will, predestination, and the like.[9] Rather, I focus here on the question of how we retrospectively understand and acknowledge

---

7. A portion of this sermon was published as *Sermon* 348A in *Sermons (341–400)*. The expanded version of this sermon, discovered by Dolbeau, was later published in *Sermons Discovered since 1990*. For details, see Hill's comments in *Sermons Discovered since 1990*, 319n1. The Latin text of the full sermon is provided in: François Dolbeau, "Le Sermon 348A de Saint Augustin contre Pélage. Édition du texte intégral," *Recherches Augustiniennes et Patristiques* 28 (1995): 37–63.

8. Hill provides details of the date, location, and context of this sermon: *Sermons Discovered since 1990*, 319n1.

9. There is a copious amount of secondary literature on these aspects of Augustine's thought. For a general survey of the debate with Pelagius and his followers, and the theological issues at stake, see Bonner, *St Augustine of Hippo*, 312–93. For additional surveys of Augustine's teaching on these themes, see Burnaby, *Amor Dei*, 219–34; Burns, "Grace," 391–8; Stephen J. Duffy, *The Dynamics of Grace: Perspectives in Theological Anthropology* (Collegeville, MN: The Liturgical Press, 1993), 74–119. Augustine's thinking on questions of divine grace and human will undergoes a degree of development during his career; Harrison's survey traces this development, and notes the broader philosophical context of this discussion: Harrison, *Christian Truth and Fractured Humanity*, 25–9, 79–114. Brown and Markus each draw attention to shifts in Augustine's thinking in the early years of his pastoral ministry (when he was also writing the *Confessions*): Brown, *Augustine of Hippo*, 139–50; Markus, *End of Ancient Christianity*, 50–62. "Salvation was now no longer an ordered progression towards a distant goal, but a sustained miracle of divine initiative," Markus writes (p. 50). See also Lancel's account: Lancel, *Saint Augustine*, 189–92. Note, however, that Bonner cautions against uncritically accepting an "arbitrary division of Augustine's thought into earlier and later periods," as if his later views were a complete departure from his earlier thought: Bonner, *St Augustine of Hippo*, 313–14.

God's work among us (in the manner of the *Rule*),[10] and explore how the formational movement explored in this book—the movement from private self-interest toward common love of God and neighbor—features even in this aspect of Augustine's thought.

God's Charity

Augustine begins *Sermon* 348A(D30) with a meditation on the Incarnation, in which God's love, grace, and mercy toward us is revealed. "The reason for the coming and the incarnation of our Lord Jesus Christ—that he found all, when he came, to be sinners," Augustine explains, making reference to 1 Timothy 1:15.[11] It was in response to our need that Christ came among us. Augustine depicts this relationship in medical terms: "The doctor would not have come down, except to the sick."[12] Christ came for this very purpose of healing. Elsewhere in the *Sermons*, Augustine likens the Incarnation to a doctor who comes to a bed-ridden patient,[13] or who bends down "to the level of the sick person's bed."[14] Augustine utilizes the imagery of doctor and patient extensively in the *Sermons*, though on occasion the truth he is trying to convey exceeds the limitations of this vivid metaphor. This is evident in *Sermon* 348A(D30): "If doctors, after all, can cure what they haven't created, with these medicines and herbal remedies they haven't created—so if a human doctor can cure what comes from God with what comes from God, how much more will God cure what is his own with what is his own?"[15] God is not only our healer, but also our Creator. Furthermore, Christ's death on our behalf reveals that God's commitment to our healing transcends conventional medical practice.

---

10. In his commentary on the *Rule*, Bonner observes the notable absence of emphasis on sin in this text; "it is possible to regard the *Rule* as being, under divine grace, an optimistic document," he remarks. Bonner, commentary to *Monastic Rules*, 96. This may be in part due to the specific purpose and audience of the *Rule*, and/or to the relatively early date of the *Rule* (although Augustine was already arriving at some of his most significant ideas regarding human sin and divine grace around this time, as Harrison outlines: Harrison, *Christian Truth and Fractured Humanity*, 85–8). In any case, although I discuss a breadth of sermons in this chapter, I acknowledge that my interest in Augustine's monastic instruction on these themes may prompt a more positive reading of these texts.

11. *Serm.* 348A(D30).1.

12. *Serm.* 348A(D30).1. For discussion of Augustine's use of medical imagery, see Atkins, "'Heal My Soul': The Significance of an Augustinian Image," 349–64; Brown, *Augustine of Hippo*, 169–71; Susan Blackburn Griffith, "Medical Imagery in the 'New' Sermons of Augustine," in *Studia Patristica 43*, ed. F. Young, M. Edwards, and P. Parvis (Leuven: Peeters, 2006), 107–12.

13. *Serm.* 88.7

14. *Serm.* 87.13.

15. *Serm.* 348A(D30).4.

Augustine comments: "Great indeed, brothers and sisters, is the mercy of our doctor, that he wished to provide a remedy for us not from his medicine chest, but in his blood."[16] The cross dramatically presents to us the "mercy" revealed in the Incarnation: Christ giving his very self in order to heal our infirmity, and restore us to health.

In this sermon, Augustine is adamant that no alternative purpose can be construed for Christ's coming: "So there was no other reason to fetch the Son of God, true God and eternal God and coeternal and equal to the Father, to fetch him down from heaven to earth in order to take flesh and to die for us, than the fact that there was no life in us."[17] This observation draws attention to the prodigality of God's love for us. God's sole intent in the Incarnation is our healing and restoration; this healing is not secondary to some other purpose. Similarly, Christ's death finds no other explanation. Commenting on Romans 5:8 Augustine observes, "*Christ died for us*—you heard the apostle—not for himself but 'for us,' because he personally had no cause to die, in whom there was no sin."[18] Additionally, he notes, "In order, though, to die for us, he took flesh in which to die, because when he was God the Word with God the Father, he didn't have the wherewithal to die."[19] As "God the Word," it was not possible for Christ to die, and even when he accepted the mortality of human existence, he himself was not subject to death (as "the punishment of sin"), but accepted this death on our behalf.[20] The incarnate life and death of Christ, then, demonstrates God acting specifically for our benefit; for God, these events could not be self-seeking, for within the "self" of the Godhead, they were not necessary or even possible.[21]

Thus, although the Incarnation reveals to us our ailing state as sinners, it also displays the richness of God's love for us. Romans 5:8, which Augustine cites at the beginning of this sermon, expresses this intent: "*So God, he says, commends his charity among us, in that while we were still sinners Christ died for us.*"[22] Through Christ's life and death, God's charity is demonstrated.[23] As Augustine teaches catechumens on another occasion, our enmity toward God makes this demonstration of divine charity all the more remarkable, displaying the unmerited

---

16. *Serm.* 348A(D30).4.
17. *Serm.* 348A(D30).1.
18. *Serm.* 348A(D30).2.
19. *Serm.* 348A(D30).3.
20. *Serm.* 348A(D30).3, 2.
21. Reflecting on Augustine's theology of creation, Williams observes that creation does not exist "to serve a divine need." Williams, *On Augustine*, 72. As Williams explains, this insight is important for it reminds us that God's love for us is not motivated by self-interest, but rather "is wholly selfless," and has our own good in view (pp. 72–3). See also Burnaby, *Amor Dei*, 163–7.
22. *Serm.* 348A(D30).1.
23. Williams writes: "God's love brings the eternal Word into the human world, and that same love allows us to face our creatureliness and our sin in honesty, knowing that God's will is for our good." Williams, *On Augustine*, 143.

nature of God's love for us.[24] Commenting on Romans 5:8–9 in *Sermon* 348A(D30), Augustine explains that "this is *the grace of God through Jesus Christ our Lord* (Rom 7:25), which first of all the prophets, then he himself by his own mouth, next the apostles after he was no longer present in the flesh, and finally the whole Church holds, acknowledges, preaches and commends, cultivates, and reveres."[25] God has revealed his gracious love for us throughout the history of his people, and this message now lies at the heart of the church's proclamation.

Our Justice, or God's?

Following this meditation on God's gracious love displayed in Christ Augustine cautions listeners against attempting to do themselves what God has already done for them. "Hence the first thing your graces should know ... is that no human being can be delivered from evil and sin by their own merits and powers."[26] Here, Augustine anticipates the teaching of Pelagius and his followers that he will address directly later in the sermon (see below). It is not possible to provide an adequate account of "Pelagian" theology in this chapter, but two aspects pertinent to our discussion should be noted.[27] Firstly, one "evil" from which Pelagians sought to deliver themselves was that of an unjust society. Pelagianism "was born in an age of active cruelty, passive selfishness, and unbridled lust and avarice," Bonner explains, proceeding to describe not only the economic inequalities of the period, but also the increasingly diluted nature of Christian witness.[28] The Pelagian movement objected to this situation.[29] Pelagius sought to raise the bar, insisting that all Christians (and not just ascetics) were called to a life of perfection, and had the capacity to do so.[30] His belief was that Christians, through their holy living, should be visibly distinguishable amidst a morally compromised society, Markus explains.[31] Secondly, the theology of Pelagius and his followers was marked by

---

24. *Serm.* 215.5.
25. *Serm.* 348A(D30).1. See also *Civ.* 10.29.
26. *Serm.* 348A(D30).2.
27. Bonner provides a helpful summary of the Pelagian movement in his article, "Pelagianism and Augustine," republished in Gerald Bonner, *Church and Faith in the Patristic Tradition: Augustine, Pelagianism, and Early Christian Northumbria* (Aldershot: Variorum, 1996), VI: 33–51. See also Bonner, *St Augustine of Hippo*, 312–51; Brown, *Augustine of Hippo*, 340–410; Harrison, *Christian Truth and Fractured Humanity*, 101–14; Markus, *End of Ancient Christianity*, 40–65.
28. Bonner, *St Augustine of Hippo*, 353–5.
29. Bonner, *St Augustine of Hippo*, 355.
30. Markus, *End of Ancient Christianity*, 40–3.
31. Markus, *End of Ancient Christianity*, 43. Bonner observes: "The Pelagians were not monks; but their program, if it had been carried through uncompromisingly, would have turned the entire Christian Church into a monastery." Bonner, *Church and Faith in the Patristic Tradition*, VI: 39.

"a sense of self-sufficiency."[32] Brown notes that this message was well received by Pelagius's aristocratic adherents, for it corresponded with their own "high sense of autonomy."[33] Augustine, by contrast, vehemently opposed the notion that, independent of God, we are able to pursue a just life. As his introductory comments on the Incarnation in *Sermon* 348A(D30) indicated, such a belief reveals that we have appreciated neither the abundance of God's gift to us in Christ, nor the feebleness of our own condition.[34]

"Man was adept enough at wounding himself, but not at healing himself."[35] To understand this aspect of Augustine's teaching—our inability to heal ourselves—we must understand the nature of our wound. "The reason we fell was because we dispensed with God's assistance [*adiutorium*]," Augustine explains.[36] As discussed in previous chapters, sin, for Augustine, is essentially the misguided decision to turn away from God and toward oneself, the insistence on a life independent of God.[37] In this situation of sin, the question is whether we will persist in this assertion of independence from God, or whether we are willing to accept and return to God's loving care. Thus, discussions of the relative abilities of divine and human agents acting independently of one another to effect salvation are somewhat misplaced,[38] for it is our very attempt to conceive of our life independent of God that is the problem.

---

32. Bonner, *St Augustine of Hippo*, 355. Harrison notes the emphasis on human "self-sufficiency in acquiring the good" in Stoic and Neoplatonic thought: Harrison, *Christian Truth and Fractured Humanity*, 80–1. She later notes that while Augustine's teaching on the fall and its debilitating consequences for humanity marked a significant departure from such philosophical views, "Pelagius's thought was firmly rooted in the classical tradition of reflection upon man's moral and intellectual autonomy, and of his perfectibility in this life" (p. 100).

33. Brown, *Through the Eye of a Needle*, 306. Brown explains that such elites believed that nobility was "rooted in their nature" (pp. 306–7).

34. For the importance of both for Christian formation, see *Trin.* 4.1.2.

35. *Serm.* 348A(D30).2. Atkins illustrates the significance of Augustine's healing metaphor by contrasting it with education: Atkins, "'Heal My Soul': The Significance of an Augustinian Image," 353. She observes that whereas we can progress in education through our own initiative, in the case of illness, "we cannot just make ourselves better by our own efforts" (p. 353).

36. *Serm.* 348A(D30).2 (RA 28:53). Bonner explains that in Eden, Adam was given "an aid, an *adiutorium*, without which, having the gift of free will, he could not avoid falling into sin but which, having free will, he could if he chose abandon." Bonner, *St Augustine of Hippo*, 358–9.

37. Markus, *End of Ancient Christianity*, 51; Markus, "Pride and the Common Good," 250–2; Wetzel, "Sin," 800–2. See Chapter 1 for discussion and further references.

38. As Burnaby observes, "The 'help' of grace means no division of labour: it does not mean that part of the work is ours, and part God's." Burnaby, *Amor Dei*, 239.

Augustine illustrates our situation: "You can easily be rid of the very life of our flesh by killing yourself; can you then revive yourself?"[39] God is the giver of life, the source of all goodness.[40] In God's company, we are enlivened by his goodness; distanced from God who is good, we ourselves diminish, and cannot be restored apart from returning to God. Because all goodness comes from God, we should not attribute this ability to ourselves; as Burnaby observes, here lies "the sin of Pelagianism."[41] O'Donovan notes the dynamics of negative "self-love" in this tendency of Pelagian teaching; he explains that "'Self-love' in this context is an admiration of oneself for being what in fact one is not, the source of one's own value and potency."[42] We, as creatures, are not generative of creation's goodness; that attribute belongs to the Creator alone. Accordingly, Augustine urges the congregation, "in order to rise from the wreck of ourselves let us beg for his assistance, so that we may not remain in our sins."[43] He later cautions: "Why, being dead, do you rely on yourself? You were able to die of your own accord, you cannot come back to life of your own accord."[44]

Life is the gift of our Creator, and God's work of creating and recreating continues to unfold among us.[45] In *Sermon* 26, Augustine urges the congregation to look to the Creator for their recreation. Following the psalmist, he directs them to seek out this God in prayer and worship: "*Come, let us worship him and prostrate ourselves before him, and weep before the Lord who made us* (Ps 95:6). As ones who have been ruined by ourselves, may we be remade by the one who made us."[46] In encouraging listeners to look to God for their healing, Augustine is not negating human worth or ability, but rather helping them recognize that their remaking is necessarily the task of "the one who made us." Daley's comments are illuminating in this regard:

> Augustine's position ... is that human perfection, whenever we attain to it, is realized only by our becoming a new creation in Christ. It is reached not simply

---

39. *Serm.* 348A(D30).2.
40. E.g., *Serm.* 29.1. Duffy's comment provides context for this aspect of Augustine's theology: "In the classical culture providing the intellectual climate that was Augustine's heritage, the world was considered a hierarchical unity. All beings interconnected. Augustine, sharing the horizon of earlier Christian writers, saw all things proceeding from and radically depending on God, their first principle, in diverse degrees of participation. Within this horizon, while human agents were considered free and responsible, autonomy did not receive the emphasis it knows in the modern era." Duffy, "Anthropology," 25. See also Burns's comments on the Neoplatonic conception of the world that informed Augustine's thinking on grace: Burns, "Grace," 391–2.
41. Burnaby, *Amor Dei*, 166. See also pp. 147–53.
42. O'Donovan, *Problem of Self-Love*, 99.
43. *Serm.* 348A(D30).2.
44. *Serm.* 348A(D30).4.
45. Burnaby, *Amor Dei*, 170–1.
46. *Serm.* 26.3.

by our human response to God's law, through the use of our natural gifts; rather, God must continue to be involved, through the person of Christ and the gift of the Holy Spirit, in enabling us to grasp the Law fully and to choose freely to do it.[47]

If our healing entails nothing less than "a new creation," then only our Creator can help us. Understanding our transformation in this way also helps us view our encounter with grace in a different light, as Daley indicates in a later comment: "The interaction of sinful humanity and divine grace, then, is not simply an anthropological issue—not simply a question of what we humans can and cannot do on our own—but an encounter of the human race with the divine economy in its most fundamental terms."[48]

In *Sermon* 348A(D30) Augustine cautions his congregation against the teaching of Pelagius and his disciples, which he describes as "a new heresy" that is "secretly spreading its tentacles far and wide."[49] What troubles Augustine, he explains in this sermon, is that this "heresy" is essentially a rejection of the gracious love of God displayed in Christ.[50] As Lancel notes, Augustine saw this teaching as "a moralism which tended to sap the very foundations of Christianity, the incarnation and redemption."[51] Having reminded the congregation of "*the grace of God through Jesus Christ our Lord* (Rom 7:25)," whereby God seeks out those who have departed from him, Augustine finds in Pelagianism a refusal to accept this gift, a persistent desire to navigate life on one's own: "They say that human nature is capable of so much, we by the free decision of our will are capable of so much, that just as we became sinners by ourselves, so too we can be justified by ourselves."[52] This contrasts, of course, with Augustine's earlier illustration of the person who has the ability to take their own life, but who (once dead) cannot "revive" it.[53] Whereas

---

47. Brian Daley, "The Law, the Whole Christ, and the Spirit of Love: Grace as a Trinitarian Gift in Augustine's Theology," *Augustinian Studies* 41, no. 1 (2010): 129.

48. Daley, "The Law, the Whole Christ, and the Spirit of Love," 131.

49. *Serm.* 348A(D30).5. In sections (.5) to (.7), Augustine provides a fascinating account of his previous interactions with Pelagian teaching. For news of the debate with Pelagius arriving in Hippo at this time, see Bonner, *St Augustine of Hippo*, 339. See also Lancel, *Saint Augustine*, 336–7.

50. *Serm.* 348A(D30).8.

51. Lancel, *Saint Augustine*, 343.

52. *Serm.* 348A(D30).1, 8. For discussion of the contrasting conceptions of the human will held by the Pelagians and by Augustine, see Bonner, *St Augustine of Hippo*, 355–8; Burnaby, *Amor Dei*, 220–34; Duffy, *The Dynamics of Grace*, 84–100. Babcock traces Augustine's wrestling with the question of the freedom of the human will to make moral decisions: Babcock, "Augustine on Sin and Moral Agency," 28–55. See especially pp. 30–41.

53. *Serm.* 348A(D30).2. Describing Augustine's view, Duffy explains that while we possess "free will," "in bondage to sin we do not have the capacity to use our free will rightly, to order our loves by the love of God above all and in all. Hence without grace we cannot avoid sin and accomplish the good." Duffy, *The Dynamics of Grace*, 94.

Augustine understands God to be the source of life, goodness, and justice, the Pelagian teaching (as Augustine describes it) appears to envisage justice as obtainable on independent terms. "They say that God made man," Augustine explains, "but that man himself makes himself just."[54]

Augustine addresses this issue in *Sermon* 13, when discussing Psalm 2:11: "*Serve the Lord in fear and rejoice in him with trembling.*"[55] He cautions that "if you think that while indeed you get your being human from him, you get your being just from yourself, then you are not serving the Lord in fear nor rejoicing in him with trembling, but in yourself with presumption."[56] It is the one who made us that makes us just; this is not a work that we should claim for ourselves. Augustine is careful to clarify, however, that this does not mean that we ourselves are uninvolved in this work; to explain this, he turns to Philippians 2:12–13. Augustine explains that although Paul teaches that "*it is God who works in you*" (v. 13), we are instructed to "*Work out your own salvation with fear and trembling*" (v. 12) "because he works in us in such a way that we too are enabled to work ourselves."[57] Here Augustine specifically addresses the belief that we can become just if we set our mind to it. He imagines someone thus voicing: "But it is my will that is good."[58] Augustine responds: "I grant you it's yours. But who was it who gave you even that, who stirred it up in you? Don't just listen to me; ask the apostle: *For it is God*, he says, *who works in you both to will*—works in you both to will—*and to work with a good will* (Phil 2:13)."[59] If we can discern a good will within us, enabling us to pursue the work of justice, that is undoubtedly a good thing. Augustine's concern is that we know how to rightly attribute these good things; for even the very desire for justice within us is a sign of God's presence, enabling us to will that which is good.

In *Sermon* 169, Augustine cautions against attempts to claim a justice of our own, independent of God, and appeals to the example of Saul/Paul. Discussing Philippians 3:3–16, Augustine notes that while Paul had previously observed "*the justice which is in the law,*" and "*was without reproach*" (v. 6), he now regarded this of little worth, instead desiring to "*gain Christ, and be found in him, not having my justice, which is from the law*" (vv. 8–9).[60] Augustine draws attention to this last phrase: "If he said *mine*, why did he add *from the law*? I mean, if it's from the law, how is it yours?"[61] In his ensuing discussion, Augustine explains that although the law comes from God, some may think the law can be fulfilled by their "own powers."[62] Such a person could be considered "without

---

54. *Serm.* 348A(D30).8.
55. *Serm.* 13.2.
56. *Serm.* 13.2.
57. *Serm.* 13.3.
58. *Serm.* 13.3.
59. *Serm.* 13.3.
60. *Serm.* 169.6–7.
61. *Serm.* 169.7.
62. *Serm.* 169.8.

reproach" if they managed to observe the precepts of the law, but their efforts would be characterized by "fear of punishment" rather than "love of justice."[63] Implicit in Augustine's phrase "love of justice" is both our love of God's very self (since God is justice), and our dependence upon God for that love (for it is by the Holy Spirit that we can love God (Rom. 5:5)).[64] To observe the law from "fear of punishment," however is neither to love God (for our covetousness, lust etc. has only been curbed, not converted), nor does it involve reliance upon God.[65] As Duffy observes, "Obedience to the commandments and good works motivated not by love of God but by fear of hell or hope of a reward is rooted in self-love, hence contrary to the basic precept of loving God in and above all else."[66] When our pursuit of justice is neither directed toward, nor aided by, God, we are pursuing a justice of our own. Thus it became conceivable that Saul, who religiously obeyed the law God gave, could persecute the church in which God was present: "It came about because he was establishing his own justice, not seeking God's justice."[67] Saul's persecution of the body of Christ (Acts 9:4) presents a graphic image of how the pursuit of one's "own justice" constitutes a rejection of the grace of Christ.[68] "Love was lacking," Augustine observes, "the love of justice, the love of Christ's charity."[69] Saul's efforts ran contrary to love because he attempted to assert a justice of his own, rather than loving and embracing the justice of God. Accordingly, Augustine exhorts the congregation: "Remove yourself, remove, I repeat, yourself from yourself; you just get in your own way."[70] "Let there be justice in you," he later adds, "but let it be from grace, let it come to you from God; don't let it be your own."[71]

Markus comments that "in the Pelagian programme he [Augustine] saw a sanction for that insidious pride which ruptures community."[72] This is true both of our communion with God and of communion with our neighbor. Our misguided attempts to establish our own justice can distance us from others. In *Sermon* 115, Augustine draws on the parable of the Pharisee and the tax collector (Lk. 18:9–14) to depict this pitfall. He notes the Pharisee's prayer (*"Thank you, God, for my not being like other people"*) and his disdain for the nearby tax collector.[73] Augustine

63. *Serm.* 169.8.
64. *Serm.* 169.8; 159.3; 130A(D19/M51).11.
65. *Serm.* 169.8; 130A(D19/M51).11.
66. Duffy, *The Dynamics of Grace*, 116.
67. *Serm.* 169.9.
68. *Serm.* 169.9.
69. *Serm.* 169.9.
70. *Serm.* 169.11.
71. *Serm.* 169.11.
72. Markus, *End of Ancient Christianity*, 55. Markus discusses here the contrast between the "tolerance" of Augustine and the "perfectionism" of Pelagius (pp. 54–5). Harrison notes that the teaching of Pelagius was attractive to "those who desired to 'set themselves apart' from the ordinary run of Christian devotion and practice." Harrison, *Christian Truth and Fractured Humanity*, 103.
73. *Serm.* 115.2.

then imaginatively restates the Pharisee's prayer: "'I,' he [the Pharisee] says, 'am in a class by myself; this fellow belongs to the rest. I am not,' he says, 'in the least like this man, by reason of my just deeds, which ensure that I am not unjust.'"[74] This self-righteous attitude distances the Pharisee from the tax collector. Notably, it is his treatment of wealth and temporal goods that prompts the Pharisee's pride (v. 12). By contrast, the tax collector's profession was generally associated with ill-gained wealth and corruption. Yet Augustine cautions his congregation against adopting the Pharisee's deceit, lest celebration of their works of justice leads them to look upon others with scorn.

As these examples illustrate, by drawing on a rich variety of images and biblical narratives, Augustine cautions the congregation against attempting to establish a life of virtue on their own merits, instead urging them to willingly receive the healing "medicine" God offers.[75] Williams's statement expresses well this aspect of Augustine's thought: "God asks not for heroes but for lovers; not for moral athletes but for men and women aware of their need for acceptance, ready to find their selfhood in the longing for communion with an eternal 'other.'"[76] The church is a community undergoing rehabilitation, as Augustine's interpretation of the parable of the Good Samaritan (Lk. 10:25–37) reminds us. For Augustine, the Samaritan is Christ, who has found us wounded on the road, and who has brought us to the inn—the church—for the slow process of healing.[77] We are not treated in isolation; it is in the church community—in the company of God and neighbor—that our healing takes place. For Augustine, almost every aspect of this ecclesial life has a restorative function. In various sermons he will remind the congregation of the healing they receive through the reading of Scripture, preaching, baptism, Eucharist, prayer, and acts of charity.[78] These ecclesial practices are not magic

---

74. *Serm.* 115.2.
75. *Serm.* 348A(D30).4. Another notable example is found in *Sermon* 32, where Augustine contrasts the self-reliance of Goliath with the humble dependence of David (*Serm.* 32.9–10, 12).
76. Williams, *Wound of Knowledge*, 96–7.
77. *Serm.* 131.6; 179A.7–8; 198(D26/M62).43. See also *Serm.* 299D.2. For discussion of Augustine's interpretation of this parable, see Roland Teske, "The Good Samaritan (Lk 10:29–37) in Augustine's Exegesis," in *Augustine: Biblical Exegete*, ed. Frederick Van Fleteren and Joseph C. Schnaubelt (New York: Peter Lang, 2004), 347–67.
78. For descriptions of the healing function of these practices see *Serm.* 32.1 (reading of Scripture, preaching); *Serm.* 131.6 (baptism); *Serm.* 228B.1 (Eucharist); *Serm.* 278.6 (prayer); and *Serm.* 259.3 (acts of charity). Harrison notes the different views that Pelagius and Augustine held on baptism. Harrison, *Christian Truth and Fractured Humanity*, 110. She explains that whereas Pelagius taught that in baptism our "natural capacity and knowledge of the good" were "completely restored," Augustine believed that after baptism we continue to suffer the "effects" of sin, and thus we are "still convalescing," and in need of God's gracious assistance (p. 110). See also Brown, *Augustine of Hippo*, 367.

remedies, however; we are not healed by applying them to ourselves. Rather, they are curative because of the doctor who administers them and who is at work in them. Thus Augustine encourages his congregation: "Let us gladly accept being cured at the inn."[79]

Turning to God through Prayer

As he responds to the teaching of Pelagianism in *Sermon* 348A(D30), Augustine reminds the congregation of their Christian practices of prayer.[80] Here he finds a concrete example of the dependence upon God he seeks to encourage. Earlier in this sermon, he had exhorted listeners not to "cling" to themselves, but to God: "Let our hope be in nothing but in God. Let us send up our sighs to him."[81] In prayer, we give voice to this desire to cling to God, and to trust in God for our transformation. By reflecting on these practices of prayer, Augustine clearly illustrates where the Pelagian teaching diverges from that of the church. For as he explains, "these people act in such a way, argue in such a way that there seems to be no point in our praying."[82] Whereas Christ has "taught us how to pray," Augustine fears that the Pelagian teaching contradicts the dependence upon God that Christ models and invites.[83]

Augustine directs the congregation to the petitions of the Lord's Prayer (Mt. 6:9–13), noting how it commends the grace of God (Rom. 7:25) to us.[84] He begins with the opening petition (v. 9): "*Hallowed be*—well, what?—*thy name.*"[85] In the *Sermons*, Augustine typically interprets this as a request that God's name would be made holy in our lives, as he does here: "Is God's name not holy, then? How can it be hallowed, except in us?"[86] Our voicing of this petition indicates our dependence upon God for this hallowing work within us; for as Augustine observes, "if it's from your free will, if it's from the powers of your own nature that you can hallow

---

79. *Serm.* 131.6.
80. I discuss aspects of prayer in Augustine's monastic instruction below, but see also his guidelines for prayer in *Reg. 2*: 2 and *Reg. 3*: 2.1–3. For Augustine's teaching on prayer in relation to his monasticism, see Zumkeller, *Augustine's Ideal of the Religious Life*, 181–7.
81. *Serm.* 348A(D30).4.
82. *Serm.* 348A(D30).9.
83. *Serm.* 348A(D30).9. Dupont surveys Augustine's use of this prayer motif in the *Sermons*, in comparison with Augustine's anti-Pelagian works: Anthony Dupont, "The Prayer Theme in Augustine's *Sermones ad Populum* at the Time of the Pelagian Controversy: A Pastoral Treatment of a Focal Point of His Doctrine of Grace," *Zeitschrift für antikes Christentum* 14, no. 2 (2010): 379–408. For a summary of this theme in *Serm.* 348A(D30) see pp. 399–403.
84. *Serm.* 348A(D30).11.
85. *Serm.* 348A(D30).11.
86. *Serm.* 348A(D30).11. See also, for example, *Serm.* 56.5. *Sermons* 56–9 all exegete the Lord's Prayer.

God's name in yourself, what are you praying for, why are you begging from the supreme majesty what you have in your own power?"[87]

Augustine finds a similar example in verses 12–13, "*Forgive us our debts, as we too forgive our debtors*, and *Do not bring us into temptation*."[88] These petitions similarly give voice to our dependence upon God. By prayerfully confessing our sin, we acknowledge before God the reality of our situation. "*Forgive us our debts* (Mt 6:12), we say, and so we should, because we are saying the truth," Augustine teaches in *Sermon* 58.[89] "Does anybody live in the flesh, and not have debts? Is there anybody living, for whom this prayer is not necessary?"[90] Augustine likens our praying of this petition to the prayer of the tax collector in the temple (Lk. 18:9–14): "It's good to imitate the tax collector, and not to be self-satisfied like the Pharisee, who went up to the temple, and boasted of his merits, and covered up his wounds. But the other knew very well why he was going up, and he said, *Lord, be gracious to me, a sinner*."[91] The prayer of the tax collector exemplifies humble dependence on God, whereas the Pharisee's self-justifying declaration is barely a prayer at all, as Augustine notes on another occasion.[92] If we become convinced of our own justness, like the Pharisee, we will not sense the need for this prayer of confession.[93] The petition, "*Forgive us our debts*" thus appears redundant.[94]

In *Sermon* 348A(D30), Augustine considers this Lord's Prayer petition alongside the next, "*Do not bring us into temptation*."[95] He explains to listeners that Pelagius and his followers interpret the petition "*Do not bring us into temptation*" as a request for protection from misfortune (such as injury or loss), rather than from the temptation of sin, which they believe they do not need God's assistance to overcome.[96] Augustine considers this a misreading of the Lord's Prayer, which he demonstrates by appealing to other gospel passages.[97] In Mark 14:38, he notes, Jesus instructs us to "*Watch and pray, lest you should enter into temptation*."[98] And in Luke 22:32, we learn that Jesus has voiced such

---

87. *Serm.* 348A(D30).11.
88. *Serm.* 348A(D30).11. Dupont discusses Augustine's use of Matthew 6:12 in the *Sermons*: Dupont, "Prayer Theme in Augustine's *Sermones ad Populum*," 394–405.
89. *Serm.* 58.6.
90. *Serm.* 58.6.
91. *Serm.* 58.6. Dupont surveys Augustine's use of this parable in the *Sermons*, with particular interest in Augustine's discussion of prayer in response to Pelagian teaching: Anthony Dupont, "Prayer in Augustine's Anti-Pelagian *Sermones ad Populum*: Luke 18,9-14 as Case Study," *Annali di storia dell'esegesi* 27, no. 2 (2010): 157–82.
92. *Serm.* 115.2.
93. *Serm.* 115.3.
94. *Serm.* 58.6; 115.3.
95. *Serm.* 348A(D30).11.
96. *Serm.* 348A(D30).11. Duffy explains that in Pelagian teaching, grace became "an external framework" of divine assistance; "no room is given to the internal action of God upon the person." Duffy, *The Dynamics of Grace*, 86.
97. *Serm.* 348A(D30).12.
98. *Serm.* 348A(D30).12.

a prayer on Peter's behalf: "*I have prayed for you, that your faith may not fail.*"[99] Augustine observes that Pelagian teaching implies that "we have it entirely under our own control that our faith should not fail."[100] By contrast, these petitions of the Lord's Prayer, alongside the other examples Augustine cites, remind the Christian community to be prayerfully dependent upon God for the ability to endure temptation.

From the congregation's practices of prayer, Augustine takes one further example, inviting them to recall the words of blessing that would typically conclude the sermon: "You have heard me ... when I say, 'Turning to the Lord, let us bless his name; may he grant us to persevere in his commandments, to walk in the right way of his instruction, to please him with every good work,' and other such."[101] Again, Augustine notes, if we consider that by ourselves we can fulfil these commandments and good works, then such a prayer is unnecessary.[102] With this concern in view, Augustine turns to the apostle Paul for guidance: "Let us see if he wished for his people the sort of things we pray for over you."[103] In 2 Corinthians 13:7, Augustine finds evidence that Paul also prays for the church in this manner: "*We pray to God that you may do nothing evil.*"[104] He elucidates the significance of Paul's choice of verb:

> "We teach you," he could have said, "not to do anything evil, we order you, we command you." And to be sure, if he had said that, he would have said something perfectly in order, because our wills do also contribute something; it's not the case, after all, that our wills do nothing, but only that they are not sufficient by themselves. However, he preferred to say, *We pray*, in order to emphasize the role of grace, so that those correspondents of his might understand that when they did not do anything evil, they were not shunning evil solely by their own will, but were fulfilling with help from God what had been ordered.[105]

As Augustine's careful explanation indicates, praying for God's assistance is not an abdication of our own role. Rather, prayer is the acknowledgment that on our own we are unable to fulfil what God commands. Therefore, as we seek to faithfully obey God's commands, we must seek God's help.

---

99. *Serm.* 348A(D30).12.
100. *Serm.* 348A(D30).12.
101. *Serm.* 348A(D30).13. Hill provides a translation of Dolbeau's discussion of this prayer, its role within the liturgy, and the question of whether it was accompanied by a physical movement: *Sermons Discovered since 1990*, 128n35.
102. *Serm.* 348A(D30).13.
103. *Serm.* 348A(D30).13.
104. *Serm.* 348A(D30).13.
105. *Serm.* 348A(D30).13.

For Augustine, there is no contradiction between obeying God's commands, and asking God to help us obey them, for he finds both approaches modeled in Scripture; "what is commanded is also prayed for," he explains.[106] He demonstrates this principle with a series of biblical examples, identifying passages that command us to display understanding, wisdom and self-control, and then in each case, illustrating how Scripture elsewhere directs us to pray for these same things.[107] Therefore, because he finds both command and prayer in Scripture, Augustine advises the congregation: "When a command is given, acknowledge the will's freedom of choice; when prayer is made about what has been commanded, acknowledge the favor of grace."[108] To pray for "what has been commanded" does not excuse human responsibility. With good humor, Augustine makes this very clear:

> Whatever we are enjoined to do, we have to pray that we may be able to fulfill it, but not in such a way that we let ourselves go, and like sick people lie flat on our backs and say, "May God rain down food on our faces," and we ourselves wish to do absolutely nothing about it; and when food has been rained down into our mouths, we say, "May God also swallow it for us." We too have got to do something.[109]

Augustine instructs his congregation to obey God's commands; to think that prayer absolves us of the need to act is a misunderstanding. But rather than attempting to fabricate a goodness or justice of our own, in prayer we acknowledge that it is ultimately God, and not ourselves, who is the source of our goodness and justice.

---

106. *Serm.* 348A(D30).14; see also *Serm.* 165.1. This teaching also invites comparison with Augustine's prayer, "Grant what you command, and command what you will" (*Conf.* 10.29.40). Regarding this prayer see Bonner, *St Augustine of Hippo*, 317–18.

107. *Serm.* 348A(D30).14.

108. *Serm.* 348A(D30).14. Bonner also observes that pastoral context has a bearing on whether divine grace or human responsibility needs emphasizing. Bonner, *St Augustine of Hippo*, 315.

109. *Serm.* 348A(D30).14; see also *Serm.* 156.11; 169.13. Duffy describes our human response in terms of receptivity: "For him [Augustine], persons responding to divine overtures are receptive, not passive. Conversion requires knowledgeable consent and comes about as fulfillment of both human and divine intention and action." Duffy, "Anthropology," 30. Discussing the development of Augustine's thinking on this question, Burnaby notes the importance Augustine placed on human "consent" to the work of grace within us: Burnaby, *Amor Dei*, 228–30. Without such "consent," Burnaby writes, "there is an end of any understanding of grace as a loving relation between persons" (p. 230). For further comment on our consent as a meaningful response to divine grace, see Eugene TeSelle, "Exploring the Inner Conflict: Augustine's Sermons on Romans 7 and 8," in *Augustine: Biblical Exegete*, ed. Frederick Van Fleteren and Joseph C. Schnaubelt (New York: Peter Lang, 2004), 328–9.

Giving Thanks

Nearing the end of *Sermon* 348A(D30), Augustine instructs the congregation: "We've got to be keen, we've got to try hard, and to give thanks insofar as we have been successful, to pray insofar as we have not."[110] Augustine's instruction to his congregation in this sentence resonates with that provided to the monastic community:

> When you find that you are doing the things that are written give thanks to the Lord, the giver of all good things. But when any one of you sees that he has failed in some way, he should be sorry for the past and be on his guard for the future, praying that his *sin may be forgiven* and that he may not be *led into temptation* (Mt 6:12–13; Lk. 11:4).[111]

It is noteworthy that this precept features at the close of the *Rule*. In the preceding directives of the *Rule*, Augustine provides extensive instruction to the monastic community about the life they are called to. This concluding exhortation to prayer does not suggest that, rather than obeying these instructions, they should instead ask God to enact them on their behalf. Instead, this prayer has a retrospective function. "When you find that you are doing the things that are written," the *Rule* states.[112] The community is to pursue God's commands actively and wholeheartedly, but as they then reflect on what they "are doing," prayer enables them to rightly attribute their successes and failures.

Augustine encourages this practice of reflective self-examination.[113] For the monastic community, this evaluative exercise arises out of regular reading of the *Rule*: "And so that you may be able to look at yourselves in this little book *as in a mirror* it should be read to you once a week, lest you neglect anything through forgetfulness."[114] It is attentiveness to these "things that are written" in the *Rule* that enables members of the community to reflect on their life and work, prompting prayers of thankfulness or confession.[115] In this respect, Augustine's likening of the *Rule* to a mirror is apt, for it has a reflective quality, enabling members to see themselves more clearly, and to recognize both the beauty of God's handiwork in their lives and the marks of sin that remain. Martin comments that "it is obvious that what he [Augustine] has in mind is no ordinary mirror, since in it we see not only what we are now, but also what we can and ought to be through God's call and

---

110. *Serm.* 348A(D30).14.
111. *Reg. 3:* 8.2.
112. *Reg. 3:* 8.2.
113. E.g., *Tract. ep. Jo.* 5.10; 6.2–3. See Chapter 1 for discussion of the nature of this self-reflection.
114. *Reg. 3:* 8.2. Note that this sentence precedes that quoted above ("When you find that you are doing ... ") in *Reg. 3:* 8.2.
115. *Reg. 3:* 8.2.

grace."[116] This metaphor of a mirror also features in the *Sermons*. On one occasion, Augustine indicates that his "sermons" serve as "a mirror."[117] In another sermon, as Augustine instructs catechumens to memorize "the creed," he explains the mirroring function it will provide: "Call your faith to mind, look at yourself; treat your creed as your own personal mirror. Observe yourself there, if you believe all the things you confess to believing, and rejoice every day in your faith."[118] As with the *Rule*, Augustine encourages regular use of this "mirror," and highlights the way it enables reflective self-examination.

On other occasions, Augustine identifies Scripture as a mirror. *Sermon* 301A provides a particularly apt example. Commending "the gospel and the living word of God" to the congregation, Augustine remarks: "Here it is, presented to us as a kind of mirror in which we can all take a look at ourselves, and if our inspection reveals any dirt on our faces we can carefully and methodically wipe them clean, so that we don't have to blush the next time we look in the mirror."[119] After these opening remarks, Augustine later returns to this theme, inviting the congregation to "listen to what he [Christ] said, and as I said, take a look at ourselves, and anything we find defective in ourselves let us work at putting right with all diligence, according to the standard of beauty which pleases his eyes."[120] The Scripture-reading Augustine here turns to is Luke 14:28–33, which includes Christ's call to renunciation.[121] In the mirror of this gospel passage, the congregation are invited to see themselves, and to consider what it reveals about their attachment to possessions.[122] In this way, the gospel enables listeners to identify and attend to the "dirt" of disordered love for wealth, so that Christ's "standard of beauty" might be seen in them.[123]

As noted above, following such an exercise of self-reflection, if the monastic community discover that they "are doing the things that are written," Augustine advises them to "give thanks to the Lord, the giver of all good things."[124] The call to acknowledge God as giver, the one who grants us the ability to do good, is widespread in the *Sermons*. Consider, for example, Augustine's concluding remarks in *Sermon* 159: "So let us all, human as we are, examine ourselves, and whatever good we find in ourselves that concerns our justification, let us give thanks for it to the one who gave it us; and in giving thanks to the one who gave it us, let us also ask him for what he has not yet given us."[125] As with the *Rule*, in this sermon a process of self-examination leads to twofold prayer: where "good" is discovered

---

116. Martin, "Augustine and the Politics of Monasticism," 170.
117. *Serm.* 82.15.
118. *Serm.* 58.13.
119. *Serm.* 301A.1; Pellegrino, general introduction to *Sermons (1–19)*, 37.
120. *Serm.* 301A.2.
121. *Serm.* 301A.2.
122. *Serm.* 301A.5.
123. *Serm.* 301A.1, 2.
124. *Reg. 3:* 8.2.
125. *Serm.* 159.9.

within, listeners are encouraged to "give thanks"; where it is lacking, they should pray for God's provision.

Augustine frequently draws on 1 Corinthians 4:7 to remind listeners that God is the giver of our goodness, such as in *Sermon* 333: "Whenever you receive the capacity for such good works, you should so receive it that you know who gives it, so that you won't be ungrateful to the giver.... Preserve what you have received. *For what do you have that you have not received?* (1 Cor 4:7)."[126] All good things, including our ability to do good, come as gifts from God. As Augustine explains earlier in this sermon, we can still, in a sense, regard them as "ours."[127] His concern, however, is that we rightly acknowledge where this goodness comes from. Because, like all created beings, our goodness comes from somewhere.[128] Augustine explains this teaching to the congregation in *Sermon* 29, when preaching on Psalm 118:1: "*Confess to the Lord since he is good.*"[129] To help his congregation appreciate that their goodness comes from their Creator, Augustine directs them to the Genesis narrative: "If we examine all good things on what they get their being good from, we should call to mind, *And God made all things, and behold they were very good* (Gn 1:31). So nothing would be good unless it had been made by the good. And by what sort of good? By one that nobody made."[130] After considering the goodness displayed in various aspects of creation, Augustine concludes, "They are all good, but made good. And it's from God that they get their goodness, not from themselves. The one who made these things is good beyond all of them, because no one made him good, but he is good of himself."[131] Goodness is intrinsic to God; unlike created beings, "he is good of himself." As Creator, God makes good; as creation, we are "made good."

"So, *Confess to the Lord since he is good*," Augustine exhorts his listeners.[132] At this point in the sermon, it is a "confession" of praise that he has in view here (Mt. 11:25).[133] Recognition that God is good, and the source of our goodness, prompts our worship.[134] However, in this sermon, Augustine has also noted the second meaning of "confession," the acknowledgment of our sin before God.[135] Thus, again like the monastic rule, Augustine encourages a twofold response, where God's enabling presence in our good works is acknowledged, and God's assistance amidst our failings sought: "The praise of your Lord is put to you very briefly—*he is good*. If you

---

126. *Serm.* 333.6.
127. *Serm.* 333.1. See Burnaby, *Amor Dei*, 239.
128. *Serm.* 29.1; see discussion and references earlier in this chapter.
129. *Serm.* 29.1.
130. *Serm.* 29.1.
131. *Serm.* 29.1.
132. *Serm.* 29.1.
133. *Serm.* 29.2.
134. *Serm.* 29.4.
135. *Serm.* 29.3. Augustine also uses "confession" in both senses in the *Confessions*, e.g. *Conf.* 10.2.2. See also Bonner's discussion of Augustine's use of this term: Bonner, *St Augustine of Hippo*, 48–50.

too are good, praise what makes you good; if you are bad, praise what can make you good."[136]

In these various forms of twofold response, Augustine not only provides a guide for how to acknowledge our successes, but also for how to respond to our failures. As he puts it in *Sermon* 348A(D30), we are not only "to give thanks insofar as we have been successful," but also "to pray insofar as we have not."[137] Augustine elaborates further: "When you give thanks, you are taking care not to be condemned as ungrateful, while when you ask for what you do not yet have, you are taking care not to be left empty-handed, because blocked by your own incapacity."[138] Failure is a reality of Christian life that Augustine anticipates, and one in which pastoral guidance is also needed. Earlier in this sermon, Augustine reminds listeners of "the conflict we have with the flesh" described by Paul in Romans 7:22–25 ("*I see another law in my members …* ").[139] The Pelagians, he notes, would advise those experiencing such struggle to take confidence in "your own strength and virtue."[140] Paul, by contrast, "confessed his weakness in order to obtain health and strength"; amidst his struggles, he looked to Christ for deliverance (Rom. 7:25).[141] Prayer is the necessary response to failure: not only because we need to seek God's forgiveness for our previous failings, but also because our future efforts will also fail if we attempt to pursue the good on our own. Augustine's direction in the *Rule* speaks to both aspects: "But when any one of you sees that he has failed in some way, he should be sorry for the past and be on his guard for the future, praying that his *sin may be forgiven* and that he may not be *led into temptation* (Mt 6:12–13; Lk 11:4)."[142] Following the petitions of the Lord's Prayer, the monastic is guided to pray for forgiveness for past mistakes, and to seek God's assistance in overcoming future temptations.

It is noteworthy that Augustine includes this provision in his instruction to the monastic community. The monastics may be revered and considered worthy of imitation, but sinners they remain,[143] and Augustine anticipates that they will often struggle to observe the preceding instructions of the *Rule*. Commenting on Augustine's thought, Markus observes: "Perfection is the distant goal, imperfection the inescapable condition—for monk and lay person alike."[144] As Augustine consistently

---

136. *Serm.* 29.4; cf. *Reg. 3*: 8.2. See also *Conf.* 2.7.15.
137. *Serm.* 348A(D30).14.
138. *Serm.* 348A(D30).14.
139. *Serm.* 348A(D30).10. See also *Conf.* 8.5.12. For Augustine's understanding of the "struggle" of the "Christian life" as outlined in Romans 7, see TeSelle, "Exploring the Inner Conflict," 313–45.
140. *Serm.* 348A(D30).10.
141. *Serm.* 348A(D30).10.
142. *Reg. 3*: 8.2.
143. See Zumkeller's account of "backsliders" in the monasteries: Zumkeller, *Augustine's Ideal of the Religious Life*, 72–6.
144. Markus, *End of Ancient Christianity*, 65. For the perfectionist aspirations of Pelagian theology, and Augustine's response, see pp. 42–3, 51–5, 63–5. As Markus notes, Augustine's emphasis on grace was unsettling for some monastics (pp. 63–5). For these concerns, and Augustine's response, see Brown, *Augustine of Hippo*, 400–6; Lancel, *Saint Augustine*, 426–30.

reminds listeners in the *Sermons*, our healing will be completed in the life to come; in this life, although we are being cured, our infirmity remains.[145] Acknowledging his own weakness, Augustine explains to listeners: "We are all imperfect, you see, and will only be made perfect where all things are perfect."[146] Praying to God amidst our failures frees us from our deluded projects of private perfectionism, and enables us to wait upon the one from whom we all depend for healing.

To confess our thanks to God for enabling us to pursue the good, or to confess to God our sinful deviation from the good, Augustine notes, essentially amounts to the same thing; "it all redounds to the praise of the creator."[147] Either way, we are rightly orienting ourselves toward God as the source of our goodness, rather than claiming that prerogative as our own. This right attribution of our good works is important not only for our own Christian formation, but also for the benefit of our neighbor. Augustine teaches on this theme in *Sermon 54*, as he considers Jesus's instruction to "*let your light shine before men, that they may see your good works, and glorify your Father in heaven*" (Mt. 5:16), reconciling it with the subsequent command, "*Take care not to perform your justice before men, to be seen by them*" (Mt. 6:1).[148] Read together, these commands rebuke those who perform justice in pursuit of their "*own interests*" (Phil. 2:21), seeking praise for themselves.[149] Instead, we should be motivated to seek justice "for the praise of God and the advantage of those who get to know about it."[150] In this case, it is God and neighbor we have in view, not ourselves. "People of this sort do not even count the justice they perform as their own," Augustine adds, "but as his by faith in whom they live."[151] Such a person is a shining "light," he explains, "because it is the brightness of charity that he radiates, not the smoke of pride that he belches out."[152] When we acknowledge God as the "author" of our works of justice, love is displayed (rather than self-congratulatory pride): not only love for God, from whom we gratefully receive this ability, but also love for our neighbor.[153] Because instead of trying to attract the neighbor's praise for ourselves (a self-serving action that cannot benefit the neighbor), we are directing them toward the one who is truly good, and thus loving them in the fullest sense possible (see Chapter 1).[154]

---

145. E.g., *Serm.* 278.5. Markus notes that in responding to both Donatism and Pelagianism, Augustine emphasized that our perfection takes place eschatologically: Markus, *End of Ancient Christianity*, 52–3.
146. *Serm.* 142.14.
147. *Serm.* 68.2. See also *Serm.* 67.4.
148. *Serm.* 54.1. See also *Serm.* 149.12.
149. *Serm.* 54.3.
150. *Serm.* 54.3.
151. *Serm.* 54.4.
152. *Serm.* 54.4.
153. *Serm.* 54.4.
154. Lancel suggests that Augustine wrote the *Confessions* with a view to the benefit of others: Lancel, *Saint Augustine*, 210. For Lancel's overall account of the context and purpose of the *Confessions*, see pp. 205–13.

Observing with Love

"May the Lord grant that you observe all these things with love," Augustine writes toward the end of the *Rule*.[155] This is Augustine's prayer for the monastic community. His concluding emphasis on love recapitulates the theme with which both the *Regulations for a Monastery* and the *Rule* begin: love for God and one another as the priority and purpose of the community.[156]

Augustine contrasts loving enactment of the *Rule* with legalistic observance. Members are exhorted to be "lovers of *spiritual beauty*," living not as "*slaves under the law*," but rather "*as free persons established in grace* (Rom 6:14)."[157] This distinction between the enslavement of the law and the freedom of love features frequently in the *Sermons*. Consider, for example, *Sermon* 212, a short sermon on the creed. At the conclusion of this brief account of Christian faith, Augustine directs catechumens to learn the creed "by heart," and (recalling Jer. 31:33) offers the encouragement that God will inscribe it "on your hearts," in order "that you may love what you believe, and faith may work in you through love."[158] He adds: "In this way may you please the Lord God, the giver of all good things, not out of fear of punishment like slaves, but out of a love of justice like free people."[159] Augustine thus instructs the catechumens not to see the creed as an external written code to which they must comply, but rather to internalize it, allowing it to shape their hearts, in order that what is believed is also loved. As Jeremiah foretold, it is God who does this work within our hearts, setting us free from enslavement to the law, and stirring a love of justice within us.[160]

In his contrast between "fear of punishment" and "love of justice," Augustine acknowledges the question of motivation.[161] God's commandments—whether articulated in a creed, or the Scriptures, or a monastic rule—may be observed for different reasons. Augustine alerts listeners to the important distinction between

---

155. *Reg. 3:* 8.1.
156. *Reg. 2:* 1; *Reg. 3:* 1.2. See Chapter 1, and also Zumkeller's summary of the theme of love in Augustine's monastic instruction: Zumkeller, *Augustine's Ideal of the Religious Life*, 260–1.
157. *Reg. 3:* 8.1. Van Bavel observes that "the whole Rule really witnesses to this freedom, since one notices straightaway how few concrete prescriptions and laws about details are given." Van Bavel, "Evangelical Inspiration of the Rule," 85.
158. *Serm.* 212.2.
159. *Serm.* 212.2.
160. For some, Augustine's insistence on the primacy of divine grace may appear to inhibit human freedom. Yet freedom, as Augustine conceives it, is only possible by God's grace, as Duffy explains: "Freedom is not indifference before alternatives; it is free will put to proper use, fulfilling the innate desire of a restless heart to rest in God. Only that person is truly free who is in love with God and all else for the love of God and hence by conversion is freed from the shackles of sin.... Grace and true freedom are not at war; the former is the condition of possibility for the latter." Duffy, *The Dynamics of Grace*, 99. For further discussion, see pp. 99–100, 116–17.
161. *Serm.* 212.2.

following these commands from fear or from love. In *Sermon* 145, following Paul's example in Romans 7:7, Augustine considers the commandment "*You shall not covet*" (Exod. 20:17; Deut. 5:21).[162] He anticipates a listener who insists that they have followed this command.[163] But Augustine challenges the listener to "take a look inside," for on closer examination, they may find that their observance of this command was motivated by fear, not love; "You were afraid of the punishment, you didn't love justice."[164] By this, Augustine means that the listener does not follow the commandment out of desire for what is good; their covetous desire remains, but is restrained by fear of penalty.[165] By contrast, Augustine invites the listener to consider another scenario: "Supposing God said to you, 'Go ahead and do it; I won't condemn you, I won't sentence you to gehenna; but I will deny you the sight of my face.'"[166] In this case, Augustine advises the listener, they would be observing this command "because you love the giver of the commandment."[167] As previous chapters have noted, it is through such love for God that his commandments are fulfilled, not through rigorous adherence to religious codes or ethical standards. Augustine puts it provocatively in another sermon: "So don't waste time wondering how to do what Christ commands; you cannot not do it, if you love Christ. Love, and you do it."[168] It is only by loving justice—by loving God—that the requirements of justice can be fulfilled.

Yet, as this chapter has indicated, pursuing the Christian life with love means no longer attempting a virtuous life on our own. "Men choose because they love," Brown observes, but explains that Augustine had long realized "that they could not, of themselves, choose to love."[169] "Where do you get this charity from?" Augustine goes on to enquire of his interlocutor in *Sermon* 145.[170] "Have you got charity? 'I have,' you say. Where from? 'From myself.' You are a long way from sweetness, if you've got it from yourself."[171] Reflecting on the unsurpassed greatness of charity (1 Cor. 13:1–3), Augustine asks the listener why they attribute the creation of their physical body to God, yet not the even greater gift of charity.[172] "But if you do really have it [charity], you haven't given it to yourself," Augustine concludes.[173] "God has given it to you; because *the charity of God has been poured out in our hearts—by*

---

162. *Serm.* 145.3.
163. *Serm.* 145.3.
164. *Serm.* 145.3.
165. *Serm.* 145.3; 169.8.
166. *Serm.* 145.3.
167. *Serm.* 145.3.
168. *Serm.* 130A(D19/M51).5.
169. Brown, *Augustine of Hippo*, 375.
170. *Serm.* 145.4.
171. *Serm.* 145.4. Burnaby observes: "That the love of God, our love for God, is God's gift, was his [Augustine's] final reply to the Pelagianism which saw in the Incarnation only the *demand* of God's love that we should love Him in return." Burnaby, *Amor Dei*, 176.
172. *Serm.* 145.4.
173. *Serm.* 145.4.

you, perhaps? perish the thought—*through the Holy Spirit who has been given to us* (Rom 5:5)."[174] Burns explains the transformative nature of this gift: "The presence of the Spirit changes the person's dispositions so that God and the good which God commands are loved for their own sake rather than only on the basis of the self-love which fears punishment and hopes for reward."[175] It is surely no formality, then, that prompts Augustine in the *Rule* to write "May the Lord grant that you observe all these things with love."[176] For a community to be ruled by love, God needs to grant this gift.[177]

Thus, the contrast between legalistic and loving observance of God's commands is more than a matter of disposition. It raises the question of whether our following of these commands is oriented toward self-interest, or toward God. As noted earlier in this chapter, the legalistic pursuit of one's own justice seeks to establish independence from God. Love, by contrast, makes no such claims of its own, instead freely embracing the justice that is God. Moreover, love is more than a matter of dutiful obedience: as Burnaby observes, "the paradox of the command to love is that if it be obeyed because it is commanded, it is not obeyed."[178] Love of justice is enabled by God's gift of love within. "Charity is the indwelling and operation of the Spirit, not a created quality of the person," Duffy writes.[179] Therefore, to "observe all these things with love," is to observe them with God.[180] When we observe God's commands with love, we will gladly embrace the work of God's goodness among us. Following the precepts of the Christian life in this spirit becomes a way of expressing our love for God, of seeking God's goodness among us, and of desiring unity with God.

---

174. *Serm.* 145.4. See Chapter 2 for Augustine's interpretation of this verse and relevant references.
175. Burns, "Grace," 397.
176. *Reg. 3*: 8.1.
177. In other sermons, Augustine introduces the language of "delight" to this teaching; see, for example, *Serm.* 159.2–9; 153.10; 155.14. Noting Augustine's existing use of Romans 5:5, TeSelle explains this development: "Now he [Augustine] understands this verse to refer to God's infusing of delight in the good, overcoming the other delight in temporal things. This new delight 'draws' or 'leads' the will, inviting consent and making it possible." TeSelle, "Exploring the Inner Conflict," 325. See also Burnaby, *Amor Dei*, 220–6, 234. Harrison observes that "the emphasis upon God's grace, and of the Holy Spirit as the source of inward delight in righteousness and love of justice, as opposed to fearful observance of the law, come to increased prominence in Augustine's later anti-Pelagian works." Harrison, *Christian Truth and Fractured Humanity*, 97. Harrison explains that God enables us to delight "in what is good" by making it "attractive" and "pleasing" to us (p. 112). See also Duffy, *The Dynamics of Grace*, 103; Brown, *Augustine of Hippo*, 148.
178. Burnaby, *Amor Dei*, 234.
179. Duffy, *The Dynamics of Grace*, 115.
180. *Reg. 3*: 8.1.

Conclusion

If preceding chapters have considered questions of "what are we to do?" (to put it in basic terms), in this concluding chapter I have addressed the question, "how do we understand what we have done?" It is conceivable that, from Augustine's teaching on themes of poverty, wealth, and community (discussed in preceding chapters), we could extract an ideal "Augustinian" mode of life, purposed to overcome the social ills of economic inequality. We could dedicate ourselves to this ideal, following carefully its principles and practices, and attributing positive changes within our community to our enthusiastic efforts. Noting the apparent failure of some other Christian communities to respond to socioeconomic issues, we might conclude that they have not sufficiently committed themselves to the pursuit of justice, in the manner that we have. Our performance of justice, then, would become the criterion that determines our faithfulness or failure, and that also sets us apart from other Christians.

This scenario may not strike us as problematic if our focus is solely upon material issues of economic inequality. However, if with Augustine, we are concerned about the more fundamental divisiveness that sets us apart from God and neighbor, then we will realize that such an account of the Christian life is wanting. We may have boldly relinquished our claim to private possessions, yet if we continue to assert our own private goodness, apart from God, the basic disorder of sin persists.

One aspect of our modern setting that can prompt this temptation is the perceived need to promote our work to others. It is no longer enough, it would seem, to serve faithfully in one's own context. Rather, we feel legitimated in our work when invited to speak about it at conferences, or when our ministry features in a podcast series, or when our social media account gains followers. The financial assistance of donors can also create this expectation; we feel compelled to provide regular updates on our work, to show appreciation for this support. And so we talk about the programs we have provided, or the lives changed through our ministry. It is entirely fitting, of course, that we share stories with one another, in order to bear witness to what God is doing. Such stories can challenge and inspire, and help others imagine new possibilities. However, this pressure to constantly broadcast our story does endanger us somewhat, as it brings a temptation to place ourselves at the center of the narrative. We can unwittingly give the impression that these success stories can be credited entirely to our innovative thinking, our ministry model, and our sacrificial commitment.

As I have outlined in this chapter, Augustine invites us to a humbler understanding of the Christian life. We are not called to any pretense of perfection, but rather to acknowledge our affliction from sin—the disease that divides us from one another, and from God. Confessing our struggles, we look not to our own curative powers, but to Christ, and the healing that he brings. Indeed, God gathers the church for the purpose of this healing. This restoration requires our effort and obedience; learning to love God and neighbor demands the whole of our life. However, the recovery of communion with God and neighbor is not simply the result of our attempts to do good. Rather, we receive it as a gift of God, our Creator and healer.

As contemporary practitioners, we can learn to see our ministry in this light by approaching it prayerfully. Holding our work before God with open hands, we learn to relinquish our agenda, recalling that it is God's work, and not our own. Instead of becoming fixated upon our own activity, in prayer we grow in attentiveness to God's formative work in our lives. And as good things begin to be glimpsed among us—as social divisions are overcome, and a common life begins to form—then we learn to give thanks to God, from whom this goodness comes.

"May the Lord grant that you observe all these things with love."[181] Whether applied to Augustine's monastic precepts, or his homiletic instruction to the wider Christian community, this concluding statement is critical, because without love, such guidelines are of little value to us. Indeed, the very purpose of Augustine's pastoral and monastic instruction is to cultivate love, as he emphasizes at the beginning of the *Regulations for a Monastery* and the *Rule*.[182] If Augustine's pastoral and monastic instruction has enduring value for us today, it is not because it offers an ethical ideal that we might enact, but because God can continue to use it to grow this love within us: challenging us in our self-absorption, drawing us closer to our neighbor, and restoring us to himself.

---

181. *Reg. 3*: 8.1.
182. *Reg. 2*: 1; *Reg. 3*: 1.2.

CONCLUSION

In the preceding chapters I have traced one aspect of Christian formation that Augustine encourages in his *Sermons* and monastic instruction: namely, the movement from private self-interest toward common love of God and neighbor. I have shown how this theme informs a variety of interrelated pastoral topics and teachings, each pertinent to questions of economic inequality. Furthermore, by reading the *Sermons* alongside Augustine's monastic instruction (principally the *Rule*), I have demonstrated how his vision of a common life extends to the wider congregation.

In these areas, I have sought to make a constructive scholarly contribution, advancing our understanding of Augustine's pastoral theology and ministry. However, as stated in the Introduction, my underlying purpose in exploring these themes in Augustine's teaching is to illustrate their ongoing importance for the church in contemporary contexts of economic inequality. Through most of this book, these contemporary concerns have sat in the background, as I have tried to hear Augustine's teaching on his own terms. However, as I hope is already apparent to the reader, much of his teaching remains remarkably pertinent in our own time, and in this Conclusion, I aim to articulate this more clearly. In the Introduction, I identified two initial questions that ministry amidst economic inequality has prompted for me: What does it mean to be the church amidst contexts of economic division? And how does God seek to form such a church? In this Conclusion, I begin by recapitulating the teaching of Augustine discussed in the preceding chapters to demonstrate how it helps us understand these questions. I then turn to consider characteristics of the common life that arises out of Augustine's vision of Christian formation (again, drawing from previous chapters). With a particular view to the task of pastoral ministry, I consider how we can anticipate and nurture these aspects of the common life that God forms among us.

God's Formational Work among Us

While we might be inclined to focus on the economic or political origins of our contemporary economic divisions, Augustine helps us look deeper still, to our fundamental departure from God. Originally, we enjoyed a life of abundance in God's company. Man "lived in the enjoyment of God, from whose goodness he himself was good," Augustine explains, noting also that "he lived without any lack."[1] However, as narrated throughout this book, humanity chose to seek a life independent of God, asserting its autonomy and independence. The proud human soul "had looked at itself, and been very pleased with itself, and become a lover of its own power."[2] Divided from God, we have also become divided from one another, each seeking our own private interest. Our love becomes bound up with material resources, and we focus upon our "own portion," while "possessing division" with our neighbor.[3] Our present-day evils of economic inequality can be understood as a result of this proud and avaricious self-interest, which continues to be manifest among us.

God, however, has not abandoned us to this incapacitated state. Rather, like a doctor lowering "to the level of the sick person's bed," God has come in Christ to heal us.[4] This healing involves a restoration of our hearts, helping us recognize the disorder of our desire, and redirecting our love toward God and neighbor (Mt. 22:37–40). In the preceding chapters, I have drawn attention to this formational movement away from private self-interest, and toward common love of God and neighbor. The spirit of this formational movement, I have argued, is well expressed by Augustine's teaching in the *Rule* when he speaks of the love that "*does not seek its own* (1 Cor 13:5)."[5] Over the course of this discussion, I have illustrated this theme in Augustine's *Rule* and *Sermons*.

In his preaching, Augustine helps his listeners appreciate how God nurtures this formational movement in their lives. Firstly, Christ seeks us out in that "*far country*" of private self-interest, coming "to join us in our exile," and helping us return to our senses.[6] For Augustine, this aspect of Christ's ministry can be observed in the reading and proclamation of Scripture, through which "he speaks even now."[7] Christ also encounters us in our neighbor, whose needs call into question our preoccupation with ourselves. "That Christ is poor for us here, he tells us himself: *I was hungry, thirsty, naked, a stranger, in prison*," Augustine teaches.[8] The humble Christ calls us homeward, but this return demands a relinquishment of our proud self-interest, and a sharing in his humility, through which "he was showing us the way."[9]

As God draws us back to himself, God also gathers us together with one another. The Holy Spirit "makes those whom he gathers together undivided," overcoming our divisiveness and indwelling us, that we might have "one heart and soul."[10]

---

1. *Civ.* 14.26.
2. *Serm.* 142.3.
3. *Serm.* 359.2.
4. *Serm.* 87.13
5. *Reg.* 3: 5.2.
6. *Serm.* 362.4.
7. *Serm.* 301A.1.
8. *Serm.* 123.4.
9. *Serm.* 123.1.
10. *Serm.* 71.35.

Through this unifying work, we are formed into the one body of Christ, like "many grains" formed into "one loaf."[11] Within this body, the Holy Spirit binds us in love to one another and to God. Augustine observes (in reference to 1 Jn 4:16) that "so entirely is love or charity the gift of God that it is even called God."[12] In the gift of the Holy Spirit, God gives himself to us, and the presence of this loving gift enables us to give ourselves to God and to our neighbor in love.

In this book, I have considered how this formational movement relates to Augustine's pastoral instruction on wealth, poverty, and attitudes toward rich and poor. I have demonstrated that we can better appreciate Augustine's teaching on such economic matters when considered in light of this theological account of Christian formation. On this basis, I have argued that this movement from private self-interest toward common love of God and neighbor remains fundamental to the formation and identity of the church amidst our own contexts of economic division, and should shape our response to these issues. As we grapple with the inequalities in our neighborhoods, a greater appreciation of these dynamics of Christian formation alerts us to the work that God is doing within and through us.

For example, one way this aspect of Augustine's pastoral teaching aids us is by challenging our assumptions about, and responses to, economic division. As we consider the disparity of wealth in our communities, our attention might focus on external causes, such as unfair economic policies or unjust salaries. Scrutiny of such matters is important. However, Augustine's teaching challenges us to also look beneath the surface, and examine the nature of our desires. In particular, it alerts us to the privatizing tendency of sin: our desire to put fences around our lives, our property, our sense of self. We need to acknowledge this divisive self-interest at work within us, and confess our need for healing. As Augustine encourages, we must "gladly accept being cured at the inn."[13]

If Augustine's teaching helps us better appreciate the underlying dynamics of sin amidst our contemporary context of economic inequality, it also helps us to understand the nature of God's redemptive work among us. Christian formation amidst economic division is not simply a matter of finding the right practical responses, such as donating to a food bank, or visiting a homeless shelter (though of course such responses are vital). Instead, God reorders our life from within, renewing our heart, and turning us toward God and neighbor. This interior transformation comes to bear on every aspect of our lives. Just as Augustine's exhortatory comments about the love that "*does not seek its own* (1 Cor 13:5)" in the *Rule* follow his earlier discussion of shared clothing and the practical work of the monastery, we must consider how this love can shape our daily existence, be it the question of where we live, or how to use our time, or which career options to pursue.[14]

---

11. *Serm.* 272.
12. *Serm.* 156.5.
13. *Serm.* 131.6.
14. *Reg. 3:* 5.2, 5.1.

The Church amidst Economic Inequality

In light of this account of Christian formation, we can understand Christian community as the consequence of God's work among us. That is, when Christ meets us in our self-interested private existence, and calls us back to himself—when the Holy Spirit casts out our divisive demons, and unites us with "one heart and soul"[15]—then we find ourselves to be part of the church that God is gathering.

Amidst our economically divided society, it is vital that we understand the existence of the church within this broader salvific narrative. Preoccupied with our own interests, we can find ourselves attending church services if they appeal to our personal tastes, and looking for another church when they do not. We make polite conversation with others, but are careful not to transgress personal boundaries. We share time together in worship services, but the rest of our lives—homes, resources, career, family life—remain private. We have no sense that, in Christ, our lives are now closely bound up with one another.

Thus, these themes from Augustine's pastoral instruction remain valuable for us today. They help us appreciate what God has been and is doing among us, and highlight the centrality of Christian community within God's work. Augustine's insight reminds us that God's formative work will challenge and disrupt our self-interested desires; rather than resisting such intrusions, we can learn to recognize God's grace in them. Similarly, this teaching helps us anticipate that God's work will draw us toward one another, often weaving our lives together with those who appear unlike us, including those from different economic situations. Here too, we can learn to embrace this aspect of God's gracious work among us. "You are both walking along the same road, you are companions together," Augustine instructs.[16] Whether rich or poor, our lives are bound up with one another, for we share the same journey.

Augustine's teaching directs us toward a fundamental aspect of the church's witness in an economically divided society: the gathering together in unity of those once divided. Such activity may not appear especially impressive, and may not attract much attention. Yet when Christians of diverse economic backgrounds are able to share their lives together (even if only in a small and tentative manner), this unity offers a powerful witness to the God who seeks "to gather us together and make us one."[17] For Augustine, the forming of true unity amidst division is a work that only God can bring. This unity, therefore, is central to the church's identity amidst economic division; it is the distinguishing mark of the church as it lives amidst "the earthly city" that "is often divided against itself."[18]

---

15. *Serm.* 71.35.
16. *Serm.* 53A.6.
17. *Serm.* 71.18.
18. *Civ.* 15.4.

Encouraging the Formation of a Common Life

Augustine's consistent emphasis on God's initiative in our formation reminds us that Christian community is not primarily the fruit of human labors. Rather, the love that unites us "*has been poured into our hearts through the Holy Spirit which has been given to us* (Rom 5:5)."[19] In this sense, perhaps the well-worn phrase "intentional community" is misleading, for it can imply that community is restored through our own determined efforts. Community, Augustine's teaching reminds us, is God's intention. If we discover this intention within us to gather together with other Christians and share in each other's lives, then we can give thanks that God has gifted this intention to us, enabling us "*to work with a good will* (Phil 2:13)."[20]

Nonetheless, we too have a role to play in this formation (see Chapter 7), whether in our own lives, or as we support others in their spiritual growth. Indeed, the very existence of the *Sermons* and the *Rule* testify to this. In these texts, we see Augustine actively contributing to the formation of the Christian community. In the *Rule*, Augustine gives particular attention to the daily life shared by members, providing pastoral guidance for the practical challenges they will face. In the *Sermons*, Augustine both reminds listeners of the unity that God is forming among them, and alerts them to obstacles that would inhibit their sharing of this common life. It is these sorts of pastoral contributions that I have in mind in these concluding pages, with church ministers, leaders of Christian communities, and others with pastoral responsibilities in view. As we minister in neighborhoods with varied economic needs, and as we tend to members of our church communities, with their own diverse circumstances, how can we encourage the formative work that leads to a common life in God? What can we learn from Augustine's teaching and example?

Given the rich and profound nature of Augustine's thought, these concluding comments on contemporary applications of Augustine's teaching may well seem trivial by comparison. However, I offer them not as a comprehensive summary of what we might take from Augustine, but rather as examples that are suggestive of the directions in which Augustine's teaching might lead us. And indeed, what is important here is the direction in which we are moving. As noted, Augustine is under no illusion that a perfect Christian community might be seen in this life; for him, our life together will only be perfected eschatologically.[21] But as Augustine explains to the monastics, "the more you are concerned about the common good rather than your own, the more progress you will know that you have made."[22] An increasing awareness and concern for one another, and a willingness to attend to the needs of others, is an indicator of the "progress" that arises from God's

---

19. *Serm.* 71.18.
20. *Serm.* 13.3.
21. Markus, *End of Ancient Christianity*, 79–80. See discussion in Chapter 2.
22. *Reg.* 3: 5.2.

formative work among us.[23] How can those in pastoral ministry encourage growth in this direction? Reflecting on Augustine's pastoral instruction from the preceding chapters, and with a particular focus on concerns of economic division, I identify here five ways in which the formation of a common life might be nurtured.

1 Nurturing a Common Love for God

Imagine a group of dedicated young adults who have decided to establish a community house in the inner city. They are starting from scratch, and seek direction from their pastor. There are many practical questions to be considered, of course, as they consider location and look for suitable participants. But how might their pastor help them, as they explore a shared life together? In light of Augustine's teaching, nurturing a common love for God among these participants would be an important place to begin.

As will be evident from the preceding chapters, Augustine constantly tries to cultivate love for God amongst his listeners. For modern readers, it would be easy to take this as a given; as if to say, "Yes, of course we must love God—but what does Augustine have to say about community?"[24] This, however, would be to miss the point. Augustine does not present Christian community as an end in itself. The Christian life is not directed toward an idealized portrayal of human society, but toward God. However, as we are drawn in love toward God, we are also drawn toward one another. Thus, our common life arises out of our love for God, and will be fully realized when we are reunited with God in that "perfectly ordered and wholly concordant fellowship in the enjoyment of God and of each other in God."[25]

Nurturing this love of God is thus a fundamental responsibility of pastoral ministry. In contexts of economic need, this might seem counter-intuitive. For example, the practical tasks of worship (preparing liturgies, writing sermons, and the like) take time; surely this time and resource would be better spent in practical service in the community? Yet Augustine's teaching reminds us that the church's life of prayer and worship is not unrelated to concerns of socioeconomic division. To the contrary, it is only through loving God that we are free of the worldly loves that divide us. Love for God contrasts with the greed that hoards resources for private benefit, or the envy that jealously eyes up the possessions of others. For as Augustine explains, God "is the God of all people, offering himself to be enjoyed by all in common, totally in all, totally in each."[26] Our love for God does not lead to

---

23. *Reg.* 3: 5.2; Zumkeller, *Augustine's Ideal of the Religious Life*, 154.
24. Charry notes that in Augustine's thought, "the goal of life is knowing and enjoying God," but she explains that this emphasis was later lost in the church. Charry, *By the Renewing of Your Minds*, 128. As a consequence, Charry later observes, "It is virtually impossible for Western Christians to see the social and ethical implications of formation through the enjoyment of God" (p. 129).
25. *Civ.* 19.17.
26. *Serm.* 47.30.

competition or greed, for God remains available to all. Moreover, wealth or status does not privilege one's access to God, nor does poverty disadvantage it. God can be equally enjoyed by unemployed and entrepreneur alike. For Augustine, this unity of heart and soul is found when the common life shared by believers is oriented, like the community in Acts 4, "*toward God.*"[27]

If God is "to be enjoyed by all in common," one important practice is to ensure that worship gatherings are open to all, including the homeless and the well heeled.[28] Perhaps on other occasions in the week (e.g., a food bank), observers might note a distinction between those who provide, and those who receive, but in worship, both come as equals to worship God in common. The discovery of this common life found in mutual love of God should then have a bearing on the rest of the life of the church community. Even when we are not joining together in prayer and worship, this common love should still shape our interactions with one another.

It must be conceded that the church's worship does not always appear to encourage this common life. Sometimes our church services seem to place greater emphasis on entertainment or personal improvement. We look for a worship experience that attends to our needs and desires. Our preoccupation with self is thus reinforced, not challenged; we appear to have little in common with those seated around us. We can learn much, therefore, from Augustine's contrasting portrayal. When he invites his congregation to "Lift up your hearts" in worship, he reminds them of the unity they share in God; when our hearts are directed to heaven, we become "woven from the top," like Christ's undivided garment.[29] This is an important theological dimension of worship: one that is easy to lose sight of in our individualistic culture, yet which we need to recover. How might this aspect of Augustine's teaching guide the practical expression of our worshipping life? It could inform our choice of songs, for example, prompting us to consider which lyrics enable a community to give voice to their common love of God. We might give further thought to which biblical texts encourage this aspect of Christian devotion, and how our preaching could best communicate them. We could also consider whether our worshiping life includes robust liturgical practices that are not readily eroded or co-opted by a culture fixated with self.

Thus, as the church engages with issues of economic division, an important pastoral response is attending to the practices of Christian worship. Not because these practices are tools by which we engineer a common life, but rather because in worship we learn to set our hearts in the right direction—toward the one who unites us with "*one soul and one heart.*"[30]

---

27. *Serm.* 77.4.
28. *Serm.* 47.30.
29. *Serm.* 159B(D21/M54).18. See Chapter 2 for discussion of this metaphor.
30. *Reg.* 3: 1.2.

2 Foregrounding the Neighbor

Another valuable insight we can draw from Augustine's teaching is the important role that our neighbor plays in our Christian formation. In the preceding chapters, I have focused especially on our relationship with those neighbors whose economic circumstances are different to our own, and from whom we are often divided as a result. Those serving pastorally can encourage the formation of a common life by keeping such neighbors in the foreground of our thinking. Whether from the pulpit, or in pastoral conversations, or in the church's decision-making, questions such as "Who is our neighbor?" and "How is Christ calling us to love this neighbor?" need to be asked of us.

This emphasis is necessary for, in our hurried and harried modern life, the neighbor can quickly recede to the back of our mind. While we might have good intentions of supporting those around us, the demands of work and family responsibilities can leave us exhausted and with little time to spare. Or we may be tempted to withdraw, streamlining our daily existence to avoid the problems and interruptions of others (as discussed in Chapter 6). Furthermore, as we become increasingly captivated by a digital lifestyle, opportunities to relate with actual neighbors are reduced. Those we might have met in the supermarket queue, for example, we will not encounter when buying our groceries online.

Therefore, one practical pastoral response is to help the congregation recognize the obstacles that obscure vision of our neighbor. For example, Augustine's teaching on envy aids us in this way. In our greedy and envious desire to have more, we often overlook those who have less, attending instead to our own concerns. Focusing our eyes "on the smattering of rich people ahead," we do not notice "the hordes of the poor trailing behind."[31] We may also struggle to relate with love to those who have more than us. Our preoccupation with their material prosperity can prompt envious resentment and proud contempt. Such prejudices distance us, fostering division rather than unity.

Individualistic accounts of the Christian life can also lead us to overlook our neighbor. When Christian identity is understood as a private relationship between oneself and God, the integral place of the neighbor in Christian formation may not be recognized. However, Augustine observes that it is through encounter with our neighbor, "*whom you can see*" (1 Jn 4:20), that our love for God is expressed.[32] Accordingly, he instructs, "Let us start from our neighbor, in order to arrive at God."[33] This teaching encourages not simply love of neighbor as an abstract principle, but an attentiveness to the particular neighbor before us.

As the *Sermons* demonstrate, pastoral instruction plays an important role in enabling us to understand the role of the neighbor in God's salvific work among us. Augustine invites his listeners to recognize their neighbor, whether rich or poor, as given by God. In *Sermon* 25A, he instructs: "You rich man, the poor man

---

31. *Serm.* 9.19.
32. *Serm.* 90A(D11/M40).5.
33. *Serm.* 90A(D11/M40).5.

has been appointed your comrade in this life."[34] Or in *Sermon* 53A: "You are a member of Christ, and you have something to give; he's a member of Christ, and he is in need in order that you may give it. You are both walking along the same road, you are companions together."[35] There is a certain "givenness" about these neighborly relationships. Whether rich or poor, God has made us companions, with a responsibility to assist each other, sharing in one another's needs. Moreover, God encounters us through the needs of our neighbor, as Augustine's teaching on Matthew 25:31–46 and Acts 9:4 reminds us. Christ is present in the hungry and impoverished, awaiting our response. "Recognize him here needing charity," Augustine urges.[36] Because of Christ's presence in the poor, our practical expressions of love for such neighbors are also expressions of love for God. These examples provide a good demonstration of a theological foregrounding of the neighbor. In our own time, pastors can learn from this approach, by drawing attention to the neighbor, and reminding the community of the important role the neighbor plays in our journey of faith. When responding to the economic need of another, such pastoral instruction can help the community to recognize that such situations are not so much "problems" to be "fixed," as occasions for mutual growth in love.

Augustine advises, "Let us start from our neighbor, in order to arrive at God."[37] This is a valuable teaching for the nurture of a common life. As Martin observes of Augustine's monastic instruction, "In a paradoxical reversal, it seems that the very attention to the personal and individual awakens the possibility of transcending the personal and individual."[38] Rather than entertaining an abstract notion of Christian community, our task begins with the neighbor before us. Perhaps it is here that we discover the extent of our private self-interest, as we instinctively attempt to protect our time or resources from the claim of another. Yet it may also be here that we encounter God's transformative work within, drawing us toward our neighbor in love.

3 Enabling the Sharing of Resources

The sharing of material resources is another important characteristic of a common Christian life that Augustine draws our attention to. He does not expect everyday listeners in his congregation to renounce their resources and hold them in common, in the manner of the monastery. However, as indicated in Chapter 3, he does teach them to share their resources with those in need, in a spirit that reflects some thematic continuity with the *Rule*.

In the *Sermons*, this call to share is typically expressed in exhortations to give alms to the needy. Augustine encourages such acts of giving, and helps listeners appreciate their theological meaning. Yet, as I have argued, if we are interested

---

34. *Serm.* 25A.4.
35. *Serm.* 53A.6.
36. *Serm.* 123.4.
37. *Serm.* 90A(D11/M40).5.
38. Martin, "Augustine and the Politics of Monasticism," 180.

in the significance of Augustine's teaching for issues of economic division, then we should not limit our enquiry to the specific practice of almsgiving. The more important lesson Augustine teaches us regards the desires that guide our use of resources. This is not a superficial concern; rather, Augustine draws our attention to the "root" of our actions, whether greed or charity.[39] Our avaricious desire for material goods prompts us to hoard what we have, securing our resources from the claims of others. In envy, we become preoccupied with the prosperity of others, and distracted from the poverty of our neighbor. Thus redistribution of goods to the needy, although important, does not itself address the underlying issues. What is required, rather, is a transformed heart. Augustine encourages this transformation by challenging our avaricious desire "even for things which are called your own."[40] In our modern setting, this aspect of Augustine's teaching may be unsettling, questioning notions of "private property" that have become regarded as sacrosanct.[41] However, Augustine helps us to see that this greedy desire is problematic for Christians, not for reasons of economic ideology, but because it is contrary to charity, which "*does not seek its own good, but that of others* (1 Cor 13:5; Phil 2:4)."[42]

Teaching on money and property is something that pastors often feel uneasy about, lest they be accused of being too radical (or not radical enough). "Is it our business to be raising such questions?" we might wonder. The example of Augustine's preaching attends to this query. Pastors need to address our love of material goods, because it is closely bound up with our love for God and neighbor, and thus such teaching is inherent to the pastoral task. As the preceding chapters have documented, in the *Sermons*, we find numerous examples of preaching that boldly tackles this issue. Today's preachers can learn much from studying how Augustine gives voice to scriptural teaching on themes of wealth and poverty.

As our love for God and neighbor is renewed, we come to recognize that the material resources we have are not for our benefit alone, but rather gifts from God, to be shared with others.[43] Thus Augustine instructs listeners to "hold onto what you have in such a way that you provide for the needy."[44] Rather than sporadic contributions to occasional needs, this directive suggests a sustained commitment to sharing, a predetermined decision to give, ready in advance to respond to the neighbor. Such an approach recognizes that sharing resources is intrinsic to the identity and formation of Christian community, not incidental. Church communities can assist with this by creating pathways for goods to be shared with those who most need them.

39. *Serm.* 179A.5.
40. *Serm.* 107A.2.
41. As noted in Chapter 3, for the concept of private property in modernity, see Cavanaugh, *Theopolitical Imagination*, 17–19.
42. *Serm.* 107A.1.
43. MacQueen, "St. Augustine's Concept of Property Ownership," 213. See discussion in Chapter 3.
44. *Serm.* 107A.7.

There are many different forms that such giving can take. I do not seek to compare or evaluate them here, but consider one simple practice, prompted by the example of Augustine's monastic community. As noted, when individuals joined the monastery, they gave over their resources for common use, and no longer regarded them as their own.[45] Laudable as this may be, most Christians today would find this requirement impractical and discouraging. However, in a similar spirit to Augustine's community, church congregations could establish a charitable fund for members to contribute to, with resources redistributed to those in need. If members are already in the habit of giving individually, such a fund might seem unnecessary. But one of the pitfalls of private giving is that the donor has a certain ownership of their gift; they determine which cause is worthy of their gift, they may be able to direct the recipient in the gift's use, and they can claim credit as the benefactor. However, if our contributions are made to a common fund, we relinquish this ownership of the gift. It now belongs to the community, to be distributed by the community. This is a basic practice which many congregations may already follow in some shape or form, but I note it here to highlight how it enables a form of sharing that is in keeping with the spirit of Augustine's community.

Augustine presents a clear challenge regarding our use of wealth, and our obligations to those in poverty. Yet as noted in Chapter 4, even in the *Rule*, Augustine does not call for equal distribution of resources, but rather distribution "according to need."[46] This may confound contemporary readers, with our often-unquestioned assumption that economic equality is itself the highest good. However, Augustine approaches these issues differently; he is more concerned with the transformation of our desire and the overcoming of need, than achieving a calculated equality. For as the example of the monastic community suggests, resolving material differences does not necessarily resolve the divisions between us; even small differences in circumstance can prompt envy.[47] The pursuit of an abstract ideal of economic equality, as an end in itself, will not yield a common life.

Instead, we should strive for a loving generosity that enables all to live without need. For those in pastoral ministry, this requires an alertness to the diverse needs in the community, and varied abilities to give. Where is assistance needed, and where are resources available? When is the time to challenge members to give, and when is reassurance and grace needed? These are not questions that can be resolved with a formula or policy. Rather, we need to engage with these questions week by week, ever attentive to the movement of God within and beyond the Christian community.

---

45. *Reg. 3*: 1.3–4.
46. *Reg. 3*: 1.3.
47. E.g., *Reg. 3*: 3.3–4; 5.1.

4 Narrating the Common Life We Share

As noted, for Augustine, the common life we share as members of Christ's body does not automatically mean an economic uniformity. Augustine's pastoral and monastic instruction alerts us to the divisive attitudes that can arise out of differences in economic background.

Material prosperity, for example, can foster unsympathetic or dismissive views of those with less. "No sooner have you begun to possess wealth, than you have started despising the poor," Augustine challenges listeners.[48] In our own context, such a tendency can be observed in attitudes toward those dependent upon welfare payments for their survival. The supposed passivity of these welfare recipients is criticized, while we attribute our prosperity to our meritorious hard labor. Other visible markers confirm our sense of superiority, be it the size of our home, the clothes that we wear, or the subtle differences in speech that reflect our upbringing or education.

While critiquing the pride of the rich, Augustine is not blind to the prejudices of the poor. "Don't despise rich people who are compassionate, rich people who are humble," Augustine urges them.[49] For Augustine, no economic class is immune to the danger of pride and greed. His teaching confronts both rich and poor on such issues, and thus reminds us not overlook the moral agency of the poor. This is an important insight for the nurture of a common life, for irrespective of our economic background, we can all harbor prejudices and resentments against others.

Augustine also reminds us that our supposedly benevolent actions are not always well motivated. As he warns in the *Rule*, "pride lies in ambush even for good deeds in order to destroy them."[50] By sharing our resources with a needy neighbor, we can find ourselves subtly confirming our sense of superiority and self-importance.[51] Thus, in the very action that could draw us together in charity, pride instead reinforces the dividing line between us.

Therefore, in the church's practical ministry, it is crucial that we examine the internal stories that shape our actions and attitudes. Consider, for example, a congregation that hosts a community afternoon tea, providing coffee and fresh baking in a warm, welcoming space. Whereas the host church is a predominantly affluent congregation, most who attend the afternoon tea have very limited financial resources. Each week, the church members work busily in the kitchen, while attendees chat together in the lounge over coffee. Important material needs are met here: the hungry are fed, and the cold are given shelter. Yet are social divisions being overcome, or reinforced? It would be easy for the church members to remain with their team in the kitchen, secure in their serving role. Similarly, the visitors might feel more comfortable interacting with other guests, whose situation may be closer to their own. To encourage more interaction, the leadership might

---

48. *Serm.* 311.13.
49. *Serm.* 14.4.
50. *Reg. 3:* 1.7.
51. *Tract. ep. Jo.* 8.5.

designate some members as "welcomers," to mingle with visitors in the lounge, or invite some visitors to become "helpers" to share in the kitchen duties. Yet at a more subtle level, the "us" and "them" distinction could remain. What is needed is a different story, an awareness of our common humanity that supersedes our preoccupation with material differences.

We can learn from Augustine's efforts here. By inviting listeners to see themselves and others in light of the Christian story, Augustine helps them recognize the common nature of the life they share. Scripture reminds us that irrespective of differences in appearance and circumstance, we share the same basic human needs and creaturely finitude (e.g., 1 Tim. 6:7–8). To the Christian community, the story of our redemption presents an even clearer picture of the equality we share. Here, the defining categories of rich and poor, helper and helped are called into question. For before God, we discover that each of us are "beggars," dependent on God's provision, forgiveness, and healing.[52] Augustine also challenges our notions of privilege, reminding us that in our common task of learning to love God and neighbor, wealth does not advantage us, nor does poverty disadvantage us. We seek the same destination, and by sharing our neighbor's "burden" on our common journey, we can "both arrive."[53]

Churches can foster this learning by finding or creating contexts where people of varied economic backgrounds can spend time together: a neighborhood garden, for example, or a community art space. More important here than the specific form of the project is the opportunity it provides for mutual relationship between those who might otherwise have been divided by differing economic circumstances. In such company, the barriers of pride can be dismantled, as we come to know and value our neighbor. The falsity of our stereotypes is exposed, and our assumptions about what we each can or cannot offer are challenged. Through this process, we can come to a greater recognition of the common humanity we share in Christ.

As noted above, participation in a service project does not inevitably lead to such transformation. Our work needs to be shaped by Christ's story; amidst our activity, we need to hear his story narrated to us. Augustine's *Sermon* 259 is worth recalling here, where he provides practical instruction for the *agape* meal.[54] Perhaps here we have an instance where the church's practice was insufficiently shaped by the Christian story; the existing distinctions of economic class appeared to prevail, with the privileged offering support to the hungry yet maintaining their social position. Augustine calls those hosting the meal to greater humility and to genuinely interact with those they are serving. For in this exchange, givers and receivers "are being joined in a real relationship."[55] This sort of pastoral instruction is needed to guide our practical service in the community, and it should not be

---

52. *Serm.* 61.7–8.
53. *Serm.* 107A.5.
54. *Serm.* 259.5.
55. *Serm.* 259.5.

limited to the pulpit. Project planning meetings, team retreats, individual pastoral conversations: these too provide important opportunities for reflection on how the narrative of Scripture informs our practice of ministry. "Where have we succumbed to the subtle divisions of pride?" we can ask each other, and "Where have we glimpsed Christ drawing us toward a common life?"

5 Recognizing the Participation of All

As we grapple with the economic divisions of our present time, the example of Augustine's monastic community offers an inspiring picture. The practice of a common life is a powerful witness in a society preoccupied with private gain. Clearly, we remain in need of such expressions of Christian community today, and as church leaders consider how to support these efforts, Augustine's teaching offers valuable wisdom about the care and oversight required.

For contemporary practitioners, one important question this teaching raises is how new expressions of Christian community understand their connection to the established church. A striking aspect of Augustine's monasticism is the close relationship of the monastery to the wider Christian community.[56] This contrasts with the impulse, displayed most notably in the Donatist and Pelagian movements, to separate from (what was perceived as) a compromised church in order to establish purer or more dramatic expressions of Christianity.[57] In our own context, Christian communities can display a similar impulse. For example, concerns about economic inequality and skepticism about the wealth and consumerism seen in the church might prompt some to reject the "institutional" church in favor of alternative forms of Christian community. Members may share a common life together, yet it is a life set apart from, even defined in contrast to, the wider church.

Augustine is well aware that, like "weeds among the wheat," in the church "bad Christians" coexist alongside "the good ones," and he often voices frustration at the lack of commitment of nominal Christians.[58] Conceivably, he could have established a monastic community apart from this blemished church. Yet despite the distinctive and demanding nature of the life that his *Rule* outlines, this is a life lived within the unity of the wider church.[59] I suggest that this approach does not dilute the prophetic witness of the monastic community, but rather offers a more radical witness still. For pursuit of our "own justice," a life of ethical virtue apart from the church that God gathers, can indicate that we are still trying to preserve a life on our own terms.[60] By contrast, to share in the common life of the church requires a certain humility of us. Augustine notes the obstacle that a church of "poor, uneducated, low-born fishermen" posed to potential upper-class converts,

---

56. Zumkeller, *Augustine's Ideal of the Religious Life*, 431–2.
57. Markus, *End of Ancient Christianity*, 40–3, 51–5.
58. *Serm.* 73.1, 3.
59. Verheijen, *Saint Augustine's Monasticism*, 65. See discussion in Chapter 2.
60. *Serm.* 169.9.

observing that "those who were being called to lowliness and humility would have to be called by lowly and humble people."[61] Perhaps in an analogous way, through the "lowliness" of the church, God invites humility of those who aspire to a loftier vision of the Christian life. It may be the case, for example, that in establishing a new Christian community, we turn down the assistance of other church members, thinking them unsuited to the rigors of such work—and yet, as God forms this community, those we dismissed turn out to be central participants. By recognizing our unity with the wider church, in all its shortcomings, we undergo a deeper transformation, no longer insisting on a church that conforms to our standards, but receiving the community that God offers.

Of course, dedicated expressions of Christian community have a special and indispensable role to play. For example, while members of Augustine's monastery belong to the wider church, their life is noticeably different from that of other members. However, this difference is not defined over against the church, but rather serves to benefit the church. As Zumkeller observes, Augustine's "ideals for monastic living were influenced by his deep consciousness of their common responsibility for the Church."[62] If their common life comes to reflect that of the early Christian community, this faithful example is not for their own benefit (something from which to derive a smug self-satisfaction), but rather for the edification of the wider church. As Markus puts it, the monastic community provides "a privileged anticipation of the Church's eschatological realisation."[63] Similarly, in our own context, where particular expressions of Christian community appear to be "successful," these should not prompt unhelpful comparison or resentment. Rather, such examples can be a source of encouragement and direction, for they can offer insight of the formational work that God is doing amongst us all.

Pastors can encourage unity between specific Christian communities and the wider church through their teaching. Rather than asserting one form of Christian life over another, they can instead draw attention to their common calling, helping members to recognize the one God who is at work in these varied contexts. Again, Augustine provides an instructive example here. In this book I have argued that although the manner of life Augustine prescribes in the *Rule* was only envisaged for monastics, aspects of this instruction are reflected in Augustine's teaching to the wider community. For example, ordinary members of the congregation might not share daily life together, but the Spirit is forming them also into "one heart and soul."[64] The call to renounce private property may not be practicable for those with responsibilities of employment or family, but they are nonetheless advised to "possess property" without becoming "possessed by it."[65] Whereas an emphatic difference in teaching would have heightened the sense of division between church

---

61. *Serm.* 360B(D25/M61).24.
62. Zumkeller, *Augustine's Ideal of the Religious Life*, 198.
63. Markus, *End of Ancient Christianity*, 80.
64. *Serm.* 71.35.
65. *Serm.* 125.7.

and monastery, these thematic continuities in teaching affirm the common vision that all Christians are called toward.

As noted in Chapter 7, Pelagian teaching, with its lofty ethical goals, struck a chord with upper-class Christians.[66] In our contemporary context, a similar dynamic can sometimes be observed: undertaking bold experiments in Christian community is often easier for middle- or upper-class Christians who have the freedom to do so, and financial or social safety nets to fall back on if the experiment fails. Although such intentional communities may be established in response to economic division, the poor and vulnerable may find it hard to participate in these forms of Christian life. Church leaders can address this issue by weaving such communities into the life of the wider church, and articulating their shared identity. By building these ecclesial relationships, we affirm that the Christian life is not limited to those whose circumstances allow them to make dramatic renunciations and to live an exemplary ethical life. Rather, while not all may choose a monastic form of life, all can share in the common life of the church, each according to their abilities: beneficiaries and benefactors, unemployed and retired, children and elderly.[67] The forming of a common life among Christians takes place not only in inspirational settings of monasteries and community houses; it can also be observed in the everyday gatherings of "ordinary" church life: as solo parents meet for a prayer support group, or as retirees gather for Bible study, or among those of diverse backgrounds who congregate for prayer and worship. By recognizing how God nurtures a common life in these settings too, we recognize and value the place of all members in this formational work.

Conclusion

In this book I have illustrated many aspects of Augustine's pastoral instruction that remain pertinent to the life of the contemporary church as it ministers amidst economic inequality. In these concluding pages, I have also suggested different ways in which this instruction might guide the practical work of pastoral ministry, with a view to the formation of a common life. These various aspects of Augustine's teaching, however, are unified by the central theme of that love which "*does not seek its own* (1 Cor 13:5)."[68] Augustine reminds us that love for God and for neighbor is both foundation and culmination of the Christian life: "These are the chief commandments which have been given us."[69] His additional pastoral instruction—about our use of resources, our responsibilities to our neighbor, or the shape of our common life—is valuable, but only inasmuch as it encourages this love of God and neighbor. Here lies a valuable lesson for our own time: the church

---

66. Brown, *Through the Eye of a Needle*, 287–8, 306–7. See discussion in Chapter 7.
67. See *Serm.* 267.4.
68. *Reg.* 3: 5.2.
69. *Reg.* 2: 1.

offers faithful witness not by demonstrating its ethical superiority, or adherence to an ascetic code, but by learning to love God wholeheartedly amidst a culture divided by self-interest. Augustine helps us to see that the possibility of a genuine common life between those economically divided is found in our mutual love for God: a love that unifies rather than divides.

Emphasizing love does not mean an indifference to the serious societal concerns of economic division. In this book, I have sought to demonstrate in Augustine's teaching the way in which love of God and neighbor finds practical expression in a life shared with others. An increasing concern for "the common good" indicates our "progress" in the Christian life.[70] However, in such endeavor, Augustine encourages humility, for the church is not a picture of perfect community, in which all divisions have been overcome. In this life, we are people in recovery, awaiting the healing work of the Creator in our lives. The formation of love for God and neighbor is thus a lifelong task.

Augustine's teaching reminds us that love comes to us as a gift (Rom. 5:5). It is the sign of God's formational work among us, not the result of our own attempts at self-improvement. To the monastic community, Augustine expresses the hope that "the love that abides for ever will reign in all matters of passing necessity."[71] This is a hope for the whole Christian community: that God, who is love, might increasingly inhabit us, shaping our daily lives, our attitudes, our actions, quelling our pursuit of "personal advantage," and nurturing a love of "the common good."[72] Therefore, when we discover love for God stirring within us, when we notice genuine charity toward our neighbor, when we experience something of a common life with others, let us, with Augustine, "give thanks to the Lord, the giver of all good things."[73]

70. *Reg. 3*: 5.2.
71. *Reg. 3*: 5.2.
72. *Reg. 3*: 5.2.
73. *Reg. 3*: 8.2.

BIBLIOGRAPHY

Adkin, Neil. "Pride or Envy? Some Notes on the Reason the Fathers Give for the Devil's Fall." *Augustiniana* 34 (1984): 349–51.

Alexander, Patrick H., John F. Kutsko, James D. Ernest, Shirley A. Decker-Lucke and David L. Peterson, eds. *The SBL Handbook of Style: For Ancient Near Eastern, Biblical, and Early Christian Studies*. Peabody, MA: Hendrickson, 1999.

Allen, Pauline. "The Horizons of a Bishop's World: The Letters of Augustine of Hippo." In *Prayer and Spirituality in the Early Church, Volume 4: The Spiritual Life*, edited by Wendy Mayer, Pauline Allen and Lawrence Cross, 327–37. Strathfield, NSW: St Pauls Publications, 2006.

Anatolios, Khaled. *Retrieving Nicaea: The Development and Meaning of Trinitarian Doctrine*. Grand Rapids, MI: Baker Academic, 2011.

Atkins, Margaret. "'Heal My Soul': The Significance of an Augustinian Image." *Studies in Christian Ethics* 23, no. 4 (2010): 349–64.

Augustine. *Sermones Post Maurinos Reperti*. Edited by Germani Morin. Vol. 1 of *Miscellanea Agostiniana*. Rome: Typis Polyglottis Vaticanis, 1930.

Augustine. "The Work of Monks." Translated by Mary Sarah Muldowney. In *Saint Augustine: Treatises on Various Subjects*, edited by Roy J. Deferrari, 321–94. Washington, DC: Catholic University of America Press, 1952.

Augustine. *The Rule of Saint Augustine: Masculine and Feminine Versions*. Translated by Raymond Canning. Introduction and commentary by T. J. van Bavel. London: Darton, Longman and Todd, 1984.

Augustine. *Sermons*. Translated by Edmund Hill. Edited by John E. Rotelle. 11 vols. Vol. 1–11 of *The Works of Saint Augustine, Part 3: Sermons*. Hyde Park, NY: New City Press, 1990-7.

Augustine. *Confessions*. Translated by Henry Chadwick. Oxford World's Classics. Oxford: Oxford University Press, 1991.

Augustine. *Confessions*. Edited by James J. O'Donnell. 3 vols. Oxford: Clarendon, 1992.

Augustine. *Teaching Christianity*. Translated by Edmund Hill. Edited by John E. Rotelle. Vol. 11 of *The Works of Saint Augustine, Part 1: Books*. Hyde Park, NY: New City Press, 1996.

Augustine. *The Augustine Catechism: The Enchiridion on Faith Hope and Charity*. Translated by Bruce Harbert. Edited by Boniface Ramsey. The Augustine Series. Hyde Park, NY: New City Press, 1999.

Augustine. *On Genesis*. Translated by Edmund Hill. Edited by John E. Rotelle. Vol. 13 of *The Works of Saint Augustine, Part 1: Books*. Hyde Park, NY: New City Press, 2002.

Augustine. *The Monastic Rules*. Translated by Agatha Mary and Gerald Bonner. Edited by Boniface Ramsey. The Augustine Series. Hyde Park, NY: New City Press, 2004.

Augustine. *Instructing Beginners in Faith*. Translated by Raymond Canning. Edited by Boniface Ramsey. The Augustine Series. Hyde Park, NY: New City Press, 2006.

Augustine. *The Manichean Debate*. Translated by Roland Teske. Edited by Boniface Ramsey. Vol. 19 of *The Works of Saint Augustine, Part 1: Books*. Hyde Park, NY: New City Press, 2006.

Augustine. *Homilies on the First Epistle of John*. Translated by Boniface Ramsey. Edited by Daniel E. Doyle and Thomas Martin. Vol. 14 of *The Works of Saint Augustine, Part 3: Homilies*. Hyde Park, NY: New City Press, 2008.

Augustine. *Vingt-six Sermons au Peuple d'Afrique*. Edited by François Dolbeau. 2nd ed. Vol. 147. *Collection des Études Augustiniennes—Série Antiquité*. Paris: Institut d'Études Augustiniennes, 2009.

Augustine. *The City of God*. Translated by William Babcock. Edited by Boniface Ramsey. 2 vols. Vol. 6–7 of *The Works of Saint Augustine, Part 1: Books*. Hyde Park, NY: New City Press, 2012–13.

Augustine. *The Trinity*. Translated by Edmund Hill. Edited by John E. Rotelle. 2nd ed. Vol. 5 of *The Works of Saint Augustine, Part 1: Books*. Hyde Park, NY: New City Press, 2015.

Ayres, Lewis. "The Fundamental Grammar of Augustine's Trinitarian Theology." In *Augustine and His Critics: Essays in Honour of Gerald Bonner*, edited by Robert Dodaro and George Lawless, 51–76. London: Routledge, 2000.

Ayres, Lewis. "'Remember That You Are Catholic' (*Serm*. 52.2): Augustine on the Unity of the Triune God." *Journal of Early Christian Studies* 8, no. 1 (2000): 39–82.

Ayres, Lewis. *Augustine and the Trinity*. Cambridge: Cambridge University Press, 2010.

Babcock, William S. "Augustine on Sin and Moral Agency." *The Journal of Religious Ethics* 16, no. 1 (1988): 28–55.

Barnes, Michel René. "Augustine in Contemporary Trinitarian Theology." *Theological Studies* 56, no. 2 (1995): 237–50.

Beaver, R. Pierce. "Augustine of Hippo, Servus Servorum Christi." *Church History* 3, no. 3 (1934): 187–206.

Bonner, Gerald. *Church and Faith in the Patristic Tradition: Augustine, Pelagianism, and Early Christian Northumbria*. Aldershot: Variorum, 1996.

Bonner, Gerald. *St Augustine of Hippo: Life and Controversies*. 3rd ed. Norwich: Canterbury Press, 2002. First published 1963 by SCM Press.

Boyd-MacMillan, Ronald R. "The Transforming Sermon: A Study of the Preaching of St. Augustine, with Special Reference to the *Sermones ad Populum*, and the Transformation Theory of James Loder." PhD thesis, University of Aberdeen, 2009.

Breidenthal, Thomas. "Jesus Is My Neighbor: Arendt, Augustine, and the Politics of Incarnation." *Modern Theology* 14, no. 4 (1998): 489–503.

Bright, Pamela. "Wealth as a Test of the Community: Reflections of Clement of Alexandria and Augustine of Hippo on Wealth and Communal Solidarity." In *Prayer and Spirituality in the Early Church, Volume 5: Poverty and Riches*, edited by Geoffrey D. Dunn, David Luckensmeyer and Lawrence Cross, 337–48. Strathfield, NSW: St Pauls Publications, 2009.

Brockwell, Charles W., Jr. "Augustine's Ideal of Monastic Community: A Paradigm for His Doctrine of the Church." *Augustinian Studies* 8 (1977): 91–109.

Brown, Peter. *Augustine of Hippo: A Biography*. New ed. Berkeley: University of California Press, 2000.

Brown, Peter. *Poverty and Leadership in the Later Roman Empire*. Hanover: University Press of New England, 2002.

Brown, Peter. *Through the Eye of a Needle: Wealth, the Fall of Rome, and the Making of Christianity in the West, 350–550 AD*. Princeton: Princeton University Press, 2012.

Brown, Peter. "Bridge to God: Remembering the Poor, Remembering the Dead." *Christian Century*, April 15, 2015, 20–3.

Burnaby, John. *Amor Dei: A Study of the Religion of St. Augustine*. Eugene, OR: Wipf and Stock, 2007. Previously published 1938 by Canterbury Press.

Burnell, Peter J. "Is the Augustinian Heaven Inhuman? The Arguments of Martin Heidegger and Hannah Arendt." In *History, Apocalypse, and the Secular Imagination: New Essays on Augustine's City of God*, edited by Mark Vessey, Karla Pollmann and Allan Fitzgerald, 283-92. Bowling Green, OH: Philosophy Documentation Centre, 1999.

Burns, J. Patout. "Grace." In *Augustine through the Ages*, edited by Allan D. Fitzgerald, 391-8. Grand Rapids, MI: Eerdmans, 1999.

Canning, Raymond. *The Unity of Love for God and Neighbour in St. Augustine*. Heverlee-Leuven: Augustinian Historical Institute, 1993.

Canning, Raymond. "St. Augustine's Vocabulary of the Common Good and the Place of Love for Neighbour." In *Studia Patristica 33*, edited by Elizabeth A. Livingstone, 48-54. Leuven: Peeters, 1997.

Canning, Raymond. "Common Good." In *Augustine through the Ages*, edited by Allan D. Fitzgerald, 219-22. Grand Rapids, MI: Eerdmans, 1999.

Cary, Phillip. "Interiority." In *Augustine through the Ages*, edited by Allan D. Fitzgerald, 454-6. Grand Rapids, MI: Eerdmans, 1999.

Casey, Damien. "In Search of the Preferential Option for 'the Other' in Origen and Augustine." In *Prayer and Spirituality in the Early Church, Volume 5: Poverty and Riches*, edited by Geoffrey D. Dunn, David Luckensmeyer and Lawrence Cross, 349-59. Strathfield, NSW: St Pauls Publications, 2009.

Cavadini, John C. "Pride." In *Augustine through the Ages*, edited by Allan D. Fitzgerald, 679-84. Grand Rapids, MI: Eerdmans, 1999.

Cavanaugh, William T. *Theopolitical Imagination*. London: T&T Clark, 2002.

Cavanaugh, William T. *Being Consumed: Economics and Christian Desire*. Grand Rapids, MI: Eerdmans, 2008.

Cavanaugh, William T. *Migrations of the Holy: God, State, and the Political Meaning of the Church*. Grand Rapids, MI: Eerdmans, 2011.

Charry, Ellen T. *By the Renewing of Your Minds: The Pastoral Function of Christian Doctrine*. New York: Oxford University Press, 1997.

Clair, Joseph. *Discerning the Good in the Letters and Sermons of Augustine*. Oxford: Oxford University Press, 2016.

Clark, Gillian. "Pastoral Care: Town and Country in Late-Antique Preaching." In *Urban Centers and Rural Contexts in Late Antiquity*, edited by Thomas S. Burns and John W. Eadie, 265-84. East Lansing: Michigan State University Press, 2001.

Clark, Gillian. *Christianity and Roman Society*. Cambridge: Cambridge University Press, 2004.

Clark, Gillian. "Pilgrims and Foreigners: Augustine on Travelling Home." In *Travel, Communication and Geography in Late Antiquity: Sacred and Profane*, edited by Linda Ellis and Frank L. Kidner, 149-58. Aldershot: Ashgate, 2004.

Collinge, William J. "Developments in Augustine's Theology of Christian Community Life after A.C. 395." *Augustinian Studies* 16 (1984): 49-63.

Couenhoven, Jesse. "'Not Every Wrong Is Done with Pride': Augustine's Proto-Feminist Anti-Pelagianism." *Scottish Journal of Theology* 61, no. 1 (2008): 32-50.

Coyle, J. Kevin. "Adapted Discourse: Heaven in Augustine's *City of God* and in His Contemporary Preaching." In *History, Apocalypse, and the Secular Imagination: New Essays on Augustine's City of God*, edited by Mark Vessey, Karla Pollmann and Allan D. Fitzgerald, 205-19. Bowling Green, OH: Philosophy Documentation Centre, 1999.

Coyle, J. Kevin. "'Spirituality' in Augustine's *Confessions*." In *Prayer and Spirituality in the Early Church, Volume 4: The Spiritual Life*, edited by Wendy Mayer, Pauline Allen and Lawrence Cross, 281-93. Strathfield, NSW: St Pauls Publications, 2006.

Daley, Brian. "A Humble Mediator: The Distinctive Elements in Saint Augustine's Christology." *Word and Spirit* 9 (1987): 100–17.
Daley, Brian. "The Law, the Whole Christ, and the Spirit of Love: Grace as a Trinitarian Gift in Augustine's Theology." *Augustinian Studies* 41, no. 1 (2010): 123–44.
Demura, Kazuhiko. "*Anima Una et Cor Unum*: St Augustine's Congregations and His Monastic Life." In *Prayer and Spirituality in the Early Church, Volume 4: The Spiritual Life*, edited by Wendy Mayer, Pauline Allen and Lawrence Cross, 257–66. Strathfield, NSW: St Pauls Publications, 2006.
Di Berardino, Angelo. "The Poor Must Be Supported by the Wealth of the Churches (*Codex Theodosianus* 16.2.6)." In *Prayer and Spirituality in the Early Church, Volume 5: Poverty and Riches*, edited by Geoffrey D. Dunn, David Luckensmeyer and Lawrence Cross, 249–68. Strathfield, NSW: St Pauls Publications, 2009.
Djuth, Marianne. "The Royal Way: Augustine's Freedom of the Will and the Monastic Tradition." In *Augustine: Biblical Exegete*, edited by Frederick Van Fleteren and Joseph C. Schnaubelt, 129–43. New York: Peter Lang, 2004.
Dolbeau, François. "Le Sermon 348A de Saint Augustin contre Pélage. Édition du texte intégral." *Recherches Augustiniennes et Patristiques* 28 (1995): 37–63.
Drobner, Hubertus R. "The Chronology of St. Augustine's *Sermones ad Populum*." *Augustinian Studies* 31, no. 2 (2000): 211–18.
Duffy, Stephen J. *The Dynamics of Grace: Perspectives in Theological Anthropology*. Collegeville, MN: The Liturgical Press, 1993.
Duffy, Stephen J. "Anthropology." In *Augustine through the Ages*, edited by Allan D. Fitzgerald, 24–31. Grand Rapids, MI: Eerdmans, 1999.
Dunn, Geoffrey D. "Poverty as a Social Issue in Augustine's Homilies." In *Studia Patristica 49*, edited by J. Baun, A. Cameron, M. Edwards and M. Vinzent, 175–9. Leuven: Peeters, 2010.
Dunn, Geoffrey D. "Augustine's Homily on Almsgiving." *Journal of Early Christian History* 3, no. 1 (2013): 3–16.
Dupont, Anthony. "*Sermo* 90A (Dolbeau 11, Mainz 40). Self-Love as the Beginning of Love for Neighbour and God." *Augustiniana* 57 (2007): 31–48.
Dupont, Anthony. "Prayer in Augustine's Anti-Pelagian *Sermones ad Populum*: Luke 18, 9–14 as Case Study." *Annali di storia dell'esegesi* 27, no. 2 (2010): 157–82.
Dupont, Anthony. "The Prayer Theme in Augustine's *Sermones ad Populum* at the Time of the Pelagian Controversy: A Pastoral Treatment of a Focal Point of His Doctrine of Grace." *Zeitschrift für antikes Christentum* 14, no. 2 (2010): 379–408.
Finn, Richard. *Almsgiving in the Later Roman Empire: Christian Promotion and Practice (313–450)*. Oxford: Oxford University Press, 2006.
Finn, Richard. "Portraying the Poor: Descriptions of Poverty in Christian Texts from the Late Roman Empire." In *Poverty in the Roman World*, edited by Margaret Atkins and Robin Osborne, 130–144. Cambridge: Cambridge University Press, 2006.
Fitzgerald, Allan D., ed. *Augustine through the Ages: An Encyclopedia*. Grand Rapids, MI: Eerdmans, 1999.
Frend, W. H. C. *The Donatist Church: A Movement of Protest in Roman North Africa*. Oxford: Clarendon Press, 1952.
Gerlin, Andrea. "Community and Ascesis: Paul's Directives to the Corinthians Interpreted in the Rule of Augustine." In *Collectanea Augustiniana: Augustine: "Second Founder of the Faith,"* edited by Joseph C. Schnaubelt and Frederick Van Fleteren, 303–13. New York: Peter Lang, 1990.

Grabowski, Stanislaus J. "The Holy Ghost in the Mystical Body of Christ According to St. Augustine." *Theological Studies* 5 (1944): 453–83.

Grabowski, Stanislaus J. "The Holy Ghost in the Mystical Body of Christ According to St. Augustine II." *Theological Studies* 6 (1945): 62–84.

Gregory, Eric. *Politics and the Order of Love: An Augustinian Ethic of Democratic Citizenship*. Chicago, IL: University of Chicago Press, 2008.

Griffith, Susan Blackburn. "Medical Imagery in the 'New' Sermons of Augustine." In *Studia Patristica 43*, edited by F. Young, M. Edwards and P. Parvis, 107–12. Leuven: Peeters, 2006.

Harmless, William. *Augustine and the Catechumenate*. Rev. ed. Collegeville, MN: Liturgical Press, 2014.

Harrison, Carol. *Augustine: Christian Truth and Fractured Humanity*. Oxford: Oxford University Press, 2000.

Hauerwas, Stanley. *After Christendom? How the Church Is to Behave If Freedom, Justice, and a Christian Nation Are Bad Ideas*. Nashville, TN: Abingdon Press, 1991.

Hoskins, John Paul. "*Acts* 4:32 in Augustine's Ecclesiology." In *Studia Patristica 49*, edited by J. Baun, A. Cameron, M. Edwards and M. Vinzent, 73–7. Leuven: Peeters, 2010.

Kamimura, Naoki. "The Emergence of Poverty and the Poor in Augustine's Early Works." In *Prayer and Spirituality in the Early Church, Volume 5: Poverty and Riches*, edited by Geoffrey D. Dunn, David Luckensmeyer and Lawrence Cross, 283–98. Strathfield, NSW: St Pauls Publications, 2009.

Kilby, Maria. "Augustine of Hippo on the Bishop as Spiritual Father." In *Studia Patristica 52*, edited by A. Brent and M. Vinzent, 235–45. Leuven: Peeters, 2012.

Lam, Joseph Cong Quy. "*Humilitas Iesu Christi* as Model of a Poor Church: Augustine's Idea of a Humble Church for the Poor." *The Australasian Catholic Record* 93, no. 2 (2016): 180–97.

Lambot, C. "Nouveaux Sermons de S. Augustin I–III 'De lectione evangelii.'" *Revue Bénédictine* 49 (1937): 233–78.

Lamirande, Émilien. "The Priesthood at the Service of the People of God According to Saint Augustine." *The Furrow* 15, no. 8 (Aug 1964): 501–7.

Lancel, Serge. *Saint Augustine*. Translated by Antonia Nevill. London: SCM Press, 2002.

Lane Fox, Robin. *Augustine: Conversions to Confessions*. New York: Basic Books, 2015.

Lawless, George. "The Rule of Saint Augustine as a Mirror of Perfection." *Angelicum* 58 (1981): 460–74.

Lawless, George. "Augustine's Burden of Ministry." *Angelicum* 60 (1984): 295–315.

Lawless, George. *Augustine of Hippo and His Monastic Rule*. Oxford: Clarendon Press, 1987.

Lepelley, Claude. "Facing Wealth and Poverty: Defining Augustine's Social Doctrine." *Augustinian Studies* 38, no. 1 (2007): 1–17.

Levering, Matthew. "The Holy Spirit in the Trinitarian Communion: 'Love' and 'Gift'?" *International Journal of Systematic Theology* 16, no. 2 (2014): 126–42.

Lunn-Rockliffe, Sophie. "The Diabolical Problem of Satan's First Sin: Self-Moved Pride or a Response to the Goads of Envy?" In *Studia Patristica 63*, edited by M. Vinzent, 121–40. Leuven: Peeters, 2011.

MacMullen, Ramsay. "The Preacher's Audience (AD 350–400)." *The Journal of Theological Studies* 40, no. 2 (1989): 503–11.

MacQueen, D. J. "St. Augustine's Concept of Property Ownership." *Recherches Augustiniennes et Patristiques* 8 (1972): 187–229.

MacQueen, D. J. "Contemptus Dei: St Augustine on the Disorder of Pride in Society, and Its Remedies." *Recherches Augustiniennes et Patristiques* 9 (1973): 227–93.

Markus, R. A. *Saeculum: History and Society in the Theology of St Augustine*. Cambridge: Cambridge University Press, 1970.
Markus, R. A. "De Ciuitate Dei: Pride and the Common Good." In *Collectanea Augustiniana: Augustine: "Second Founder of the Faith,"* edited by Joseph C. Schnaubelt and Frederick Van Fleteren, 245–59. New York: Peter Lang, 1990.
Markus, R. A. *The End of Ancient Christianity*. Cambridge: Cambridge University Press, 1990.
Martin, Thomas F. "Augustine and the Politics of Monasticism." In *Augustine and Politics*, edited by John Doody, Kevin L. Hughes and Kim Paffenroth. Augustine in Conversation: Tradition and Innovation, 165–86. Lanham, MD: Lexington, 2005.
Mary, Agatha. *The Rule of Saint Augustine: An Essay in Understanding*. Villanova, PA: Augustinian Press, 1992.
McLynn, Neil B. "Administrator: Augustine in His Diocese." In *A Companion to Augustine*, edited by Mark Vessey and Shelley Reid, 310–22. Malden, MA: Blackwell, 2012. Wiley Online Library.
Migne, J.-P., ed. *Patrologia Latina*. 217 vols. Paris, 1844–64.
Morin, D. G. "Deux nouveaux Sermons retrouvés de Saint Augustin." *Revue Bénédictine* 36 (1924): 181–99.
O'Donovan, Oliver. *The Problem of Self-Love in St. Augustine*. New Haven, CT: Yale University Press, 1980.
O'Donovan, Oliver. "*Usus* and *Fruitio* in Augustine, *De Doctrina Christiana I*." *The Journal of Theological Studies* 33, no. 2 (1982): 361–97.
Pardue, Stephen. "Kenosis and Its Discontents: Towards an Augustinian Account of Divine Humility." *Scottish Journal of Theology* 65, no. 3 (2012): 271–88.
Pellegrino, Michele. *The True Priest: The Priesthood as Preached and Practised by St Augustine*. Translated by Arthur Gibson. Langley, UK: St Paul Publications, 1968.
Possidius. *The Life of Saint Augustine*. Translated by Michele Pellegrino and Matthew O'Connell. Edited by John E. Rotelle. The Augustinian Series. Villanova, PA: Augustinian Press, 1988.
Procopé, J. F. "*Initium omnis peccati superbia*." In *Studia Patristica 22*, edited by Elizabeth A. Livingstone, 315–20. Leuven: Peeters, 1989.
Ramsey, Boniface. "Almsgiving in the Latin Church: The Late Fourth and Early Fifth Centuries." *Theological Studies* 43, no. 2 (1982): 226–59.
Ramsey, Boniface. "Wealth." In *Augustine through the Ages*, edited by Allan D. Fitzgerald, 876–81. Grand Rapids, MI: Eerdmans, 1999.
Rashbrooke, Max. "Why Inequality Matters." In *Inequality: A New Zealand Crisis*, edited by Max Rashbrooke, 1–17. Wellington: Bridget Williams Books, 2013.
Rebillard, Éric. "*Sermones*." In *Augustine through the Ages*, edited by Allan D. Fitzgerald, 773–92. Grand Rapids: Eerdmans, 1999.
Sanlon, Peter T. *Augustine's Theology of Preaching*. Minneapolis, MN: Fortress, 2014.
Stewart-Kroeker, Sarah. "World-Weariness and Augustine's Eschatological Ordering of Emotions in *enarratio in Psalmum 36*." *Augustinian Studies* 47, no. 2 (2016): 201–26.
TeSelle, Eugene. "Exploring the Inner Conflict: Augustine's Sermons on Romans 7 and 8." In *Augustine: Biblical Exegete*, edited by Frederick Van Fleteren and Joseph C. Schnaubelt, 313–45. New York: Peter Lang, 2004.
Teske, Roland. "The Good Samaritan (Lk 10:29-37) in Augustine's Exegesis." In *Augustine: Biblical Exegete*, edited by Frederick Van Fleteren and Joseph C. Schnaubelt, 347–67. New York: Peter Lang, 2004.
Tilley, Maureen A. "Family and Financial Conflict in the Donatist Controversy: Augustine's Pastoral Problem." *Augustinian Studies* 43, no. 1/2 (2012): 49–64.

Torchia, N. Joseph. "The *Commune/Proprium* Distinction in St. Augustine's Early Moral Theology." In *Studia Patristica 22*, edited by Elizabeth A. Livingstone, 356–63. Leuven: Peeters, 1989.

van Bavel, T. J. "The Evangelical Inspiration of the Rule of St Augustine." *The Downside Review* 93, no. 311 (1975): 83–99.

van Bavel, T. J. "The Double Face of Love in Augustine." *Augustinian Studies* 17 (1986): 169–81.

van Bavel, T. J. "Augustine on Christian Teaching and Life." *Augustinian Heritage* 37, no. 1 (1991): 89–112.

van Bavel, T. J. "The 'Christus Totus' Idea: A Forgotten Aspect of Augustine's Spirituality." In *Studies in Patristic Christology*, edited by Thomas Finan and Vincent Twomey, 84–94. Dublin: Four Courts Press, 1998.

van der Lof, L. J. "The Threefold Meaning of Servi Dei in the Writings of Saint Augustine." *Augustinian Studies* 12 (1981): 43–59.

van der Lof, L. J. "Abraham's Bosom in the Writings of Irenaeus, Tertullian and Augustine." *Augustinian Studies* 26, no. 2 (1995): 109–23.

van der Meer, F. *Augustine the Bishop: The Life and Work of a Father of the Church*. Translated by Brian Battershaw and G.R. Lamb. London: Sheed and Ward, 1961.

Verbraken, P.-P. "Le Sermon LXXI de Saint Augustin sur le blasphème contre le Saint-Esprit." *Revue Bénédictine* 75, no. 1–2 (1965): 54–108.

Verbraken, P.-P. *Études critiques sur les Sermons authentiques de Saint Augustin*. Instrumenta Patristica 12. Steenbrugis: In Abbatia S. Petri, 1976.

Verheijen, Luc. *Saint Augustine's Monasticism in the Light of Acts 4.32-35*. The Saint Augustine Lecture 1975. Villanova University Press, 1979.

Verheijen, Luc. *Nouvelle approche de la Règle de Saint Augustin*. Vol. 2. Louvain: Institut Historique Augustinien, 1988.

Wetzel, James. "Sin." In *Augustine through the Ages*, edited by Allan D. Fitzgerald, 800–2. Grand Rapids, MI: Eerdmans, 1999.

Wilken, Robert L. "Tutoring the Affections: Liturgy and Christian Formation in the Early Church." *Antiphon* 8, no. 3 (2003): 21–7.

Williams, Rowan. *The Wound of Knowledge: Christian Spirituality from the New Testament to St. John of the Cross*. 2nd, rev. ed. Cambridge, MA: Cowley, 1990.

Williams, Rowan. *On Augustine*. London: Bloomsbury, 2016.

Zumkeller, Adolar. *Augustine's Ideal of the Religious Life*. Translated by Edmund Colledge. New York: Fordham University Press, 1986.

INDEX

Adam and Eve 35, 43 n.84, 48 n.105, 150, 150 n.21, 176, 206 n.36
almsgiving 96, 96 n.64, 102–3, 132, 141–3, 141 n.176, 172 n.180, 236
Anatolios, Khaled 49 n.114, 49 n.118, 50 n.123
asceticism/ascetics 4, 9, 19 n.124, 61, 94 n.52, 109–10, 134, 134 n.129, 161, 189 n.121
Atkins, Margaret 163, 206 n.35
Augustine
   The City of God 2, 11 n.61, 41–2, 41 n.66, 47, 47 n.103, 58 n.184, 66 n.38, 112 n.171
   Confessions 8, 51, 188, 218 n.135
   economic context 6, 6 n.19
   education 8–9
   Enchiridion on Faith, Hope, and Charity 44 n.85
   episcopal responsibilities 176–80, 178 n.21
   Homilies on the First Epistle of John 27, 35, 37–8, 56 n.169, 65, 77, 151, 161
   Instructing Beginners in Faith 33
   The Literal Meaning of Genesis 46, 46 n.97, 121
   monasticism/monastic instruction 2–4, 9, 16–21, 23–5, 29, 120, 227, 235, 240
   ordination 16, 175–6, 175 n.2, 184–5, 187–9
   preaching (*see* preaching of Augustine (setting))
   Regulations for a Monastery 33, 34 n.12, 221, 225
   Rule 17–18, 20–6, 20 n.130, 22 n.136, 25 n.154, 26 n.155, 61, 66–7, 79, 87, 90, 107–8, 111, 118, 120, 133–7, 170, 183, 194–5, 201, 216–17, 219, 221, 223, 225, 228–9, 231, 235, 237–8, 241
   Sermons (*see Sermons* of Augustine)
   Teaching Christianity 13 n.77, 33, 35 n.22, 49, 49 n.115, 56 n.170, 195
   The Work of Monks 158 n.81, 179 n.31
avarice (greed) 45–7, 45 n.90, 64–5, 88–92, 107, 109, 115–16, 139, 236. *See also* envy
   entitlement 91–3, 91 n.31, 92 n.34, 98
   harvest economy 93–5
   for inheritance 91–3
   MacQueen on 90
   surplus wealth 95–103
Ayres, Lewis 69 n.55, 80 n.130

Babcock, William S. 42, 208 n.52
baptism 53, 71–3, 73 n.84, 85, 211 n.78
Beaver, R. Pierce 181 n.57, 184 n.89
bishops 10, 17–18, 68 n.49, 91 n.28, 175–8, 175 n.2, 178 n.24, 180–3, 196–8
Bonner, Gerald 7, 80 n.129, 94 n.53, 178 n.21, 197 n.182, 203 n.10, 205 n.27, 205 n.31, 206 n.36, 215 n.108
Boyd-MacMillan, Ronald R. 11, 12 n.70, 148 n.2
Brown, Peter 3 n.8, 6–7, 6 n.22, 8 nn.33–4, 10 n.55, 67, 68 n.49, 89 n.11, 90 n.25, 99 n.84, 110 n.161, 122 n.40, 138 n.151, 152 n.37, 153 n.46, 154 n.53, 158 n.81, 177, 177 n.14, 177 n.17, 189 n.119, 206, 222
   on economic division 8, 106 n.129
   on harvest economy 93
   on the poor 15
   on the *Rule* 17, 17 n.109, 169
   on wealth 119, 122
Burnaby, John 42 n.75, 43 n.84, 44 n.86, 50, 53 n.145, 70 n.59, 83 n.153, 101, 102 nn.101–2, 113 n.178, 154 n.55, 162, 188–9, 206 n.38, 207, 215 n.109, 222 n.171, 223
   on self-love 37 n.35, 42
Burns, J. Patout 52, 207 n.40, 223

Canning, Raymond 22 n.136, 32 n.3, 36 n.32, 50–1, 54 n.154, 55 n.162, 56 n.170, 57 n.180, 58 n.188, 76, 76 n.101, 100, 102, 102 nn.100–2, 113 n.179, 141 n.176, 192
catechumens 12, 33, 73, 204, 217, 221
Cavadini, John C. 45 n.90, 48 n.105, 149 n.12, 151 n.35
Cavanaugh, William T. 74 n.87, 91 n.31, 92 n.34
   on consumerism 128 n.84
charity 54–5, 70–1, 81–2, 88–92, 95–6, 103, 111, 114, 122, 129, 161, 173, 184, 186, 191, 203–5, 211, 220, 222–3, 229, 235–6
Charry, Ellen T. 2, 26 n.156, 232 n.24
Christian formation 19, 23, 49, 59, 78, 85, 145, 161, 199, 208, 212, 220, 227, 229–31, 234, 236–7, 239, 241
   formational movement 20–1, 23, 29, 87–8, 228–9
   observing commands with love 221–3
   perfection 21, 58 n.188, 81–2, 81 n.138, 205, 219–20, 224
   reflective self-examination 216–17
   role of neighbor 56
church 1, 10, 18, 20, 24, 28, 31, 67, 72–3, 75, 81–5, 113 n.185, 116, 148, 173, 176, 179, 186 n.102, 189, 194, 198, 205, 211, 227, 233, 236–43
   church leaders 175, 177–8, 181, 184–5, 194–6, 199, 240, 242
      examples of 194–8
      loving sheep and shepherds 191–4
      self-interested 176–80
      as servants 175, 181–3, 194, 198–9
   contemporary 3, 5, 27, 29, 35, 59, 84, 114–15, 117, 227–43
   early church community 61, 79, 107
Clark, Gillian 6 n.19, 12 n.72, 13 n.75, 13 n.77, 126 n.73, 185 n.96
clergy 17, 18 n.121, 177, 177 n.14, 186 n.102, 191 n.135
common good 21–4, 22 n.136, 22 n.139, 40, 46–7 n.97, 47, 66, 84, 90, 111, 111 nn.166–8, 113, 201, 243
common life 5, 17, 19–24, 61, 72, 107, 112, 134, 147, 174, 225, 231–42
   economic divisions 240–2
   love for neighbors 234–5
   nurturing common love for God 232–3
   sharing of resources 235–40
community 4 n.10, 5, 9 n.46, 19 n.128, 22 n.136, 47, 61, 68, 82, 84, 86–7, 90, 108, 114–16, 135, 145, 153, 155, 157, 168, 176, 180–1, 183, 187 n.107, 195, 198, 201, 211, 214, 224–5, 230, 232–3, 236, 239–42. *See also* church; monastic community
   responsibilities of leadership in 194
   sharing of goods 107–12, 235–7
companionship 72, 76–7, 160, 169–71
Couenhoven, Jesse 45 n.90, 48 n.105, 149 n.17
creation 38, 41, 50, 94, 132 n.107, 150–1, 204 n.21, 207–8, 218
Creator 37–8, 50–1, 97, 151, 203, 207–8, 218, 220, 224, 243. *See also* God; Jesus Christ

Daley, Brian 166, 166 n.141, 207–8
desire 38, 40, 57, 60, 63–4, 88, 90, 129, 139, 144, 222, 229, 234, 236. *See also* love
   avarice (*see* avarice (greed))
   disordered 49, 89
   for material prosperity 39–40, 64, 125, 128, 144
   for prosperity of another 120–5 (*see also* envy)
devil 48 n.105, 63–4, 68–9, 121 n.31, 150, 176
division 62–9, 71–2, 78–9, 81, 84–5. *See also* economic division
Dolbeau, François 3 n.9, 202 n.7
Donatists 62, 64, 66–8, 66 n.42, 75, 83 n.151, 197–8, 197 n.182, 240
   conflict with Catholic church 66–8, 68 n.52
Duffy, Stephen J. 38, 39 n.49, 207 n.40, 210, 213 n.96, 215 n.109, 223
Dunn, Geoffrey D. 12 n.72, 14, 14 n.89, 99 n.85, 103
Dupont, Anthony 32 n.4, 35 n.18, 212, 213 n.91

economic division 1, 4–6, 20, 26, 29, 31, 67, 84, 198, 201, 227, 229–30, 232–3, 236, 240, 242–3. *See also* division

Brown on 8
rich and poor 1, 5–7, 14–17, 20, 32, 54, 57, 62, 65, 67–8, 73, 77, 93–5, 103–6, 106 n.129, 114, 118–19, 122–3, 129, 134–8, 144, 155, 157, 229, 235 (*see also* envy)
terms for the poor 14–15, 113, 122, 148
economic equality 28, 134 n.124, 145, 171, 237
economic inequality 1–3, 19–20, 28, 31, 44 n.85, 84–5, 89, 114, 117–18, 120, 147, 173, 176, 198, 224, 227–30, 240, 242
envy 117–20
Roman tax system 7
envy 117–27, 120 n.25, 136, 144–5, 232, 234, 236. *See also* avarice (greed)
eschatological goal 81–2, 118, 125–7, 131 n.102, 140, 189
Eucharist 11–12, 18, 73–5, 74 n.87, 85, 172, 211

faith 31, 55, 85, 105, 120, 125, 128–9, 163, 195, 214, 217, 220–1, 235. *See also* hope
fasting 73, 132–3, 132 n.107, 138 n.151
financial metaphors 98 n.77, 99–100, 115
Finn, Richard 13 n.75, 13 n.77, 14 n.80, 15 n.90, 16 n.100, 104, 104 n.111, 104 n.113, 142 n.184, 143 n.203, 155, 155 n.65, 178 n.24
freedom (human) 41, 51, 208 n.52, 215, 221 n.160
Frend, W. H. C. 67, 68 n.52

God 2, 38, 53, 84–6, 90, 94–5, 98, 101, 118, 121, 132, 145, 155, 164, 180, 184–5, 187, 199, 207, 223, 229. *See also* Creator; Holy Spirit; Jesus Christ
charity of 203–5
communion with 41, 70–1, 75, 83, 210, 224
dependence upon 148–52, 154, 162, 165–6, 212–14
goodness of 41, 52, 113 n.178, 144, 153, 160–1, 202, 207, 209, 215, 218, 220, 223, 225, 227–9
grace of (*see* grace)
image of 38, 38 n.42, 151
love for 5, 22–4, 26–7, 31, 51, 64, 85, 88, 101–2, 110–13, 116, 129, 139, 160–1, 174–5, 192, 221–2, 222 n.171, 228, 232–3, 236, 242–3
returning to God 43, 48–53, 58
separation from 63, 71
thankfulness to 75, 201, 216–20, 243
Trinity 69–72, 69 n.55, 75, 80 n.128, 83–4
unity of 69–71, 69 n.55, 73, 75, 79–81
good life 40, 57, 119, 145
gospel 26–7, 31, 34, 51, 62–3, 72, 88–9, 92–3, 114, 186, 192, 213, 217
Grabowski, Stanislaus J. 72 n.72, 72 n.74, 78 n.115, 83 n.148
grace 39 n.49, 50, 75, 117, 146, 150, 163–4, 166, 194, 202, 203 n.10, 205, 208, 208 n.53, 210, 212, 213 n.96, 215 n.109, 219 n.144, 221 n.160, 230
greed. *See* avarice (greed)

happy life/happiness 118, 124–32, 125 n.63, 139 n.156, 144–5
with basic necessities 131–9
Harmless, William 11, 20 n.129, 27 n.160, 73 n.84
Harrison, Carol 7, 8 n.40, 11 n.63, 13 n.76, 19 n.124, 29 n.168, 34 n.14, 38 n.47, 61, 68 n.52, 139 n.156, 186 n.102, 187 n.105, 203 n.10, 210 n.72, 211 n.78, 223 n.177
healing 34, 78, 172, 174, 203–4, 206–8, 206 n.35, 211, 211 n.78, 220, 224, 228, 243
Hill, Edmund 13 n.75, 28 n.167, 32 n.4, 59, 79, 110 n.156, 121 n.31, 159 n.92, 172, 172 n.180, 181 n.51, 191 n.135, 214 n.101
Holy Spirit 27, 55, 62–3, 69–72, 72 n.74, 76–9, 78 n.115, 82–5, 210, 228–30
blasphemy against 62–3, 82, 83 n.151
hope 23, 82, 117, 126, 128–31, 145, 152, 190, 196, 212. *See also* faith
hospitality 17, 140–1, 142 n.183, 183 n.71, 190
humanity 34, 36–7, 66, 134, 141, 154–5, 163, 166–7, 171, 174, 182, 206 n.32, 208, 228, 239
humility 19, 53, 147–8, 156–8, 160–2, 168 n.149, 181, 184, 228, 239, 241, 243
Christ's 162–8, 173–4, 182, 187–8

Incarnation 54 n.154, 166, 188, 203–4, 206, 208, 222 n.171
inheritance 36, 43–4, 67 n.45, 89, 91, 93, 95, 113, 113 n.181

Jesus Christ 19, 24, 26, 28, 31–6, 48–51, 48 n.108, 53–5, 63–4, 66, 68, 80, 82, 84, 88–93, 95, 98, 100, 102–3, 102 n.102, 110, 126, 140–3, 157, 174, 176, 181–3, 185–6, 193, 195–9, 203–4, 210–13, 220, 228, 230, 234–5. *See also* Creator; God
   on avarice 88–9, 91
   body of Christ 72–3, 75–8, 106, 169–70, 178, 192, 210, 229, 238
   death of 203–4
   humility of 162–8, 173–4, 182, 187–8
   love for 191–4
   love for the poor 103–4
   as poor man 168–74, 170 n.167, 228
   self-giving love of 175
   servanthood of 53, 175, 181–3, 194
   transfiguration of 185–6
justice 72, 91–2, 143, 155, 167, 205–12, 215, 220–4, 240

Lancel, Serge 7 n.31, 8, 10, 25 n.154, 49 n.114, 83 n.149, 83 n.151, 188 n.114, 189, 208, 220 n.154
Lawless, George 9, 17 n.112, 18, 18 n.118, 20, 20 n.130, 22 n.136, 23, 25 n.154, 79 n.122, 135 n.133, 188, 188 n.112
Lent. *See* fasting
Lepelley, Claude 7, 15 n.97, 68 n.52, 108 n.144, 109, 119, 120 n.18, 161
love 65, 76 n.101, 77, 90, 101–2, 116, 168 n.149, 210, 228–9
   burden of 183–5
   for Christ 191–4
   disordered 38 n.47, 39–40, 47, 51, 96 n.60, 118
   love of God 23, 26–7, 34 n.14, 36, 50–1, 55–6, 59, 77 n.104, 80, 80 n.129, 113, 123, 175–6, 191 n.35, 192, 199, 202–5, 204 n.23, 208, 210, 221 n.160, 222 n.171, 227–9, 232–3, 236, 239, 242–3
   love of God and neighbor 32–6, 32 n.3, 33 n.10, 34 n.14, 39, 46, 48, 55–60, 56 n.170, 85, 88, 101, 110, 113, 116, 134, 146–7, 149, 156, 160, 174–6, 178, 199, 202–3, 211, 220, 224, 227–9, 236, 239, 242–3
   love of justice 210, 221–3
   love of money (*see* avarice (greed); desire)
   love of neighbor 35–6, 49, 55–60, 56 n.170, 121, 123, 154 n.55, 160–1, 174–6, 191 n.135, 199, 202–3, 227–9, 234–6, 239, 242–3
   observing God's commands with 221–3
   sharing of resources with needy 107–12, 114, 116, 139–44, 235–7
Lunn-Rockliffe, Sophie 118 n.4, 119

MacQueen, D. J. 44 n.86, 45 n.90, 46 n.91, 48 n.105, 52 n.136, 90, 92 n.35, 94 n.51, 109 n.149, 149 n.12, 152, 168 n.149
Markus, R. A. 4, 5 n.18, 6 n.22, 19 n.128, 21, 46, 46 n.92, 47 n.98, 61, 66 n.38, 81, 81 n.136, 81 n.138, 134 n.129, 183 n.75, 205, 210, 210 n.72, 219
   on enjoyment 127 n.76
   on pride 150 n.26
Martin, Thomas F. 3, 22 n.136, 77 n.111, 82, 108 n.140, 134 n.127, 216, 235
Mary, Agatha 24 n.148, 135, 135 n.131, 153, 153 n.51, 169, 183
material goods 38 n.46, 39, 57, 66–7, 69, 84, 90, 94, 109, 112, 120, 129, 145, 236
McLynn, Neil B. 183 n.70, 196 n.169
monastic community 3–4, 9, 16–18, 19 n.128, 20, 23–4, 34, 61, 72, 79, 81–2, 87–8, 90 n.25, 107–9, 112, 116, 118, 120, 133–4, 136, 145, 147, 154 n.53, 160, 174, 183, 186, 189, 194, 201, 216–18, 221, 237, 240–1, 243

North Africa
   arrival of refugees in 7, 7 n.31
   preaching of Augustine in 10, 27

obedience 151 n.28, 166, 183 n.75, 184, 210, 223
O'Donovan, Oliver 36 n.27, 37 n.35, 38 n.47, 41 n.60, 42, 50 n.119, 52, 52 n.136, 57, 58 n.183, 178 n.25, 207

patience 117–18, 126–7, 131–2
Pelagius/Pelagianism 7 n.23, 109, 161, 202, 202 n.9, 205, 205 n.27, 207–9, 208 n.49, 211 n.78, 212–14, 213 n.91, 213 n.96, 222 n.171, 240, 242
Pellegrino, Michele 11, 14 n.84, 181 n.52, 183 n.73, 196 n.173
Pentecost 72, 74–5, 77
poor/poverty 5, 8, 10, 14, 37, 65, 88–9, 107, 114, 133, 135, 138 n.153, 147–9, 155–6, 159, 162, 167–8, 174, 229, 233, 236–7. *See also* wealth
    Augustine's preaching on 103–6, 103 n.105, 113 n.185
    beggars 14 n.88, 15, 105, 136, 154–7, 178
    Brown on 10 n.55
    Christ as poor 168–74, 170 n.167, 228
    in Christian preaching 12 n.72, 13
    pride of 156–60
    sharing of resources with 107–12, 114, 116, 139–44, 235–7
    terms for the poor 14–15, 113, 122, 148
Possidius 87, 120 n.18, 133, 195 n.166
prayer 11, 27–8, 51, 137, 184, 194, 216–17, 219–21, 225, 242
    Lord's Prayer 73, 137, 212–14, 218
    practices of 202, 212–15
preaching of Augustine (setting). *See also* Sermons of Augustine
    church setting 10
    congregation 3–4, 6–19, 12 n.72, 13 n.76, 21, 23–4, 27–8, 31–2, 34–5, 37, 40, 42, 50–1, 50 n.119, 53, 56–7, 62–5, 67–8, 71, 73, 75–6, 78, 80–1, 84–5, 87–8, 90–1, 93, 95–103, 105–14, 113 n.185, 117–21, 123, 125–6, 128–30, 134, 137, 137 n.146, 139–40, 144, 147–51, 154–5, 157–61, 163–5, 167–8, 171–2, 176, 179, 181–2, 192, 194–5, 197–9, 202, 205, 207, 210–22, 228, 231–2, 234–6, 238–9
    in North Africa 10, 27
pride 19, 42–3, 45–7, 45 n.90, 48 n.105, 65, 119–21, 147–51, 160–2, 173–4, 176, 239
    of the poor 156–60
    of the rich 152–6

private good 22 n.136, 40, 46, 46 n.97, 48, 90, 224
Procopé, J. F. 45 n.89, 150, 151 n.28, 164
property 80, 99, 100 n.88, 115, 236
    common 109
    of Donatists 67–8, 68 n.51
    ownership 92 n.35, 94, 94 n.51, 107
    private 90 n.25, 92 n.35, 94, 241
    sharing of 24, 87, 90 n.25

Ramsey, Boniface 5, 7 n.23, 94 n.52, 98 n.77, 103, 143 n.202, 156 n.71
Rebillard, Éric 11, 12 n.72, 25 n.152
renunciation 14, 51, 107–11, 108 n.144, 110 n.157, 161–2, 217, 242
Roman society 5, 6 n.19
Roman tax system 7

salvation 83, 155, 178, 202 n.9, 206
Sanlon, Peter T. 49 n.118, 100 n.88
Scripture 11, 11 n.63, 27, 32–4, 45, 49, 66, 71, 100, 180, 191, 211, 215, 217, 221, 239–40
self-interest/self-love 22–4, 34, 37–40, 37 n.35, 41 n.60, 42, 44–6, 46 n.91, 50–2, 50 n.119, 64, 70, 87–8, 93, 118, 147, 176, 178, 207, 210, 223, 228, 243
    private 19, 20 n.129, 29, 176, 198, 203, 227–30, 235
Sermons of Augustine 3–7, 10–15, 10 n.57, 13 n.75, 18, 20–1, 24–9, 52, 52 n.136, 62, 65, 67–8, 83, 89, 115, 217, 227–8, 231, 235
    Lenten 132, 133 n.114, 138 n.151
    Sermon 9 123, 143
    Sermon 13 209
    Sermon 14 14, 148, 151–2, 156–8, 156 n.71, 160–2, 164, 167–9, 174
    Sermon 16A 53
    Sermon 20A 160
    Sermon 21 38 n.47
    Sermon 25A 106, 123, 126, 234
    Sermon 26 207
    Sermon 28A(D9/M24) 197 n.179
    Sermon 29 218
    Sermon 32 153, 211 n.75
    Sermon 36 156, 170
    Sermon 38 132
    Sermon 41 15

Sermon 46 178, 183
Sermon 47 112
Sermon 48 27
Sermon 50 98
Sermon 53A 106, 155, 235
Sermon 54 220
Sermon 58 136, 213
Sermon 61 137, 138 n.151, 153
Sermon 65A 63
Sermon 68 165
Sermon 71 62–4, 68–9, 72, 77–8, 82, 84
Sermon 77 79
Sermon 78 185, 190–1
Sermon 85 14, 144
Sermon 86 64, 97, 100–1
Sermon 90 38, 75 n.92
Sermon 90A(D11/M40) 31–5, 32 n.4, 33 n.10, 37–43, 38 n.47, 42 n.70, 55–6, 58–60
Sermon 96 41–3, 41 n.60
Sermon 104 191
Sermon 107 95
Sermon 107A 88–9, 91, 91 n.31, 95, 97–8, 101–4, 107, 109, 111, 113–15
Sermon 112 151 n.32
Sermon 113 125
Sermon 114B(D5/M12) 154 n.59
Sermon 115 210
Sermon 123 54, 155
Sermon 125 109
Sermon 137 76, 78, 180, 192
Sermon 142 41 n.60, 42, 44, 165
Sermon 145 222
Sermon 159 217
Sermon 159B 151
Sermon 159B(D21/M54) 149, 163
Sermon 169 209
Sermon 177 89 n.11, 96–7, 111, 128, 138, 154
Sermon 178 94
Sermon 179A 41 n.60, 42–3
Sermon 198(D26/M62) 45, 149, 150 n.25, 165
Sermon 212 221
Sermon 217 139
Sermon 229N 191 n.35
Sermon 236 141
Sermon 255 129
Sermon 259 171, 239
Sermon 261 53
Sermon 263A 54
Sermon 272 74, 168
Sermon 278 34
Sermon 285 193
Sermon 299D 136
Sermon 301A 26, 217
Sermon 302 119
Sermon 305A 130
Sermon 311 153
Sermon 330 41 n.60, 42–3, 50–1
Sermon 333 218
Sermon 340 184
Sermon 340A 150, 176, 178, 181–2, 185, 192–4, 194 n.158, 195, 197
Sermon 345 101, 102 n.102, 119, 125
Sermon 346B 53, 58, 126
Sermon 348 48 n.113
Sermon 348A(D30) 202–3, 206, 208, 212–13, 216, 219
Sermon 350A 133 n.116
Sermon 353 122
Sermon 355 16–17, 107, 112
Sermon 356 17 n.107, 18 n.121, 194
Sermon 359 66, 80
Sermon 359A 117–20, 124, 126–8, 131, 136, 138–40, 142
Sermon 360B(D25/M61) 164
Sermon 362 130
Sermon 399 33 n.8, 37, 122, 171
Sermon 400 132
simplicity 64, 132–3, 135–6, 145–6
sin 19, 19 n.128, 29, 34, 46 n.91, 48 n.105, 89, 150, 206, 213, 218–19, 224. *See also* salvation
   Adam and Eve 48 n.105
   Burnaby's description of 44 n.86
   forgiveness of 71–2, 83
   Markus on 46
   and pride 45 n.90
Stewart-Kroeker, Sarah 123 n.48, 124, 131 n.102
Stoicism 138 n.153, 139 n.156

Tilley, Maureen A. 67–8, 68 nn.50–1
Torchia, Joseph 46–7 n.97, 96 n.60, 112 n.175

unity 61–2, 64, 78, 84

van Bavel, T. J. 55, 56 n.169, 56 n.171, 62 n.5, 66, 105 n.124, 135 n.133, 168, 171, 171 n.170, 184, 184 n.82, 193, 193 n.155, 221 n.157
van der Meer, F. 10–11, 10 n.59, 12 nn.71–2, 13 n.76, 67, 68 n.49, 96 n.61, 119, 177, 189
Verheijen, Luc 22 n.136, 62 n.5, 75, 81–2, 134 n.124

wealth 5, 29, 34, 38–40, 44, 65, 88–9, 95, 97, 99–100, 101, 105–8, 109 n.149, 110, 114, 121, 125, 128, 130, 142, 144–5, 147, 149, 152–3, 157, 162, 170, 173, 229, 233–4, 237–8. See also poor/poverty
  Brown on 119, 122
  superfluous 94, 115, 137
  surplus 9–8, 93–5, 116
Williams, Rowan 6 n.22, 38 n.42, 48, 48 n.110, 77 n.104, 80 n.128, 163, 163 n.119, 166, 188 n.115, 204 n.21, 204 n.23, 211

Zumkeller, Adolar 16–18, 17 n.107, 21 n.135, 23, 34 n.12, 109, 133–4, 138 n.153, 186, 186 n.102, 189, 190 n.126, 241

www.ingramcontent.com/pod-product-compliance
Lightning Source LLC
Chambersburg PA
CBHW062128300426
44115CB00012BA/1851